T0272505

"This book is a workers' story of construction: making a flag, making a map, making a university, making love, making a dress, and making history. The men and women— Enrique and Ricardo Flores Magón, Dorothy Healey, Elizabeth Catlett, Paul Shinsei Kōchi, Alexandra Kollontai, and M. N. Roy, to name only a few—are brilliant, brave, and colorful; the ideas are respectful, wise, fresh, tender, and indomitable; the spirit of the writing throughout is as free as the Mexican muralists and as glorious as the hymn that gives this book its title. You can hear in the background the roar of Pacific breakers, the clang of the closing prison gate, the factory whistle, the rhythmic rattle of a continental freight train. The reverberations continue: 'Awaken and arise,' they say!"

PETER LINEBAUGH, author of *Red Round Globe Hot Burning*

"Set against the backdrop of the twentieth century's first revolutionary conflagration, the Mexican Revolution, *Arise!* tells the story of global capitalism's polyglot gravediggers and their struggle to overcome difference and distance to build a better world. We are living through a time when race, ethnicity, and nationality are presented as impermeable and intractable, but Heatherton culls multiple archives to present a different history forged through solidarity and struggle. In gorgeous prose, written with conviction and authority, Heatherton distills how the circuits of capital and empire created tremendous wealth and power for some but also tremendous enemies and powerful struggles that conjoined the oppressed in an international struggle from below."

KEEANGA-YAMAHTTA TAYLOR, author of *Race for Profit: How Banks and the Real Estate Industry Undermined Black Homeownership*

"This lucid and compelling account shows the Mexican Revolution as a beacon for the most important global radical movements of its time. Like the other great revolutions of the modern era, the Mexican Revolution contained multitudes, and *Arise!* introduces them to us, not only as inspiring figures from the past, but also as harbingers of a better future."

ANGELA ZIMMERMAN, author of *Alabama in Africa: Booker T. Washington, the German Empire, and the Globalization of the New South*

Arise!

AMERICAN CROSSROADS

Edited by Earl Lewis, George Lipsitz, George Sánchez, Dana Takagi, Laura Briggs, and Nikhil Pal Singh

Arise!

GLOBAL RADICALISM IN THE ERA OF
THE MEXICAN REVOLUTION

Christina Heatherton

UNIVERSITY OF CALIFORNIA PRESS

University of California Press
Oakland, California

© 2022 by Christina Heatherton

Library of Congress Cataloging-in-Publication Data

Names: Heatherton, Christina, author. Title: Arise! : global radicalism in
the era of the Mexican Revolution / Christina Heatherton. Other titles:
American crossroads ; 66. Description: Oakland, California : University
of California Press, [2022] | Series: American crossroads ; 66 | Includes
bibliographical references and index. Identifiers: LCCN 2022003327
(print) | LCCN 2022003328 (ebook) | ISBN 9780520287877 (cloth) | ISBN
9780520287884 (paperback) | ISBN 9780520962880 (ebook) Subjects: LCSH:
Radicalism—Mexico—History—20th century. | Globalization—Mexico—
History—20th century. | Revolutions—Mexico—History—20th century.
| Socialism—Mexico—History—20th century. | Mexico—Politics and
government—20th century. Classification: LCC HN120.Z9 R34 2022 (print) |
LCC HN120.Z9 (ebook) | DDC 303.48/409720904—dc23/eng/20220210 LC
record available at *https://lccn.loc.gov/2022003327* LC ebook record available at
https://lccn.loc.gov/2022003328

31 30 29 28 27 26 25 24 23 22
10 9 8 7 6 5 4 3 2 1

For Jordan T. Camp

CONTENTS

Introduction: How to Make a Rope   1

1 · How to Make a Flag: Internationalism and the
Pivot of 1848   21

2 · How to Make a Map: Small Shareholders and Global
Radicals in Revolutionary Mexico   47

3 · How to Make a University: Ricardo Flores Magón and
Internationalism in Leavenworth Penitentiary   72

4 · How to Make Love: Alexandra Kollontai and the
Nationalization of Women   97

5 · How to Make a Living: Dorothy Healey and Southern
California Struggles for Relief and Revolution   122

6 · How to Make a Dress: Elizabeth Catlett, Radical
Pedagogy, and Cultural Resistance   145

Conclusion: How to Make History   175

Acknowledgments   185
Notes   193
Bibliography   245
Index   283

How to Make a Rope

"THE IDEAL ROPE," explained the Upson-Walton Company in their 1902 booklet, achieves a tension "so perfect" that if a heavy weight were attached to one end, pulling the rope to its full length, "the weight would not turn." For such a weight, an industrialist of the period might envision loads of grain, barrels of oil, or cases of precious minerals. For a rancher, bales of wool or bundles of leather might stretch the imaginary cables. The shipper might picture cargo drawn high above the ocean, then lowered gently without rotation onto the docks below. Ropes, however, were commonly enlisted into more nefarious service. Coiled, tangled, or laid flat, each length was potent with malice, thirteen simple twists away from becoming a noose. In the Jim Crow era of vigilante violence and sexual warfare, ropes could fasten commodities as easily as they might bind arms, break necks, or strain against the turning weight of a human body. Neither the mining owner, the shipping magnate, nor the commercial rancher would expect to see such grisly functions portrayed in trade brochures. Nor would they need to. As the history of the nineteenth century had already proven, the means of securing capital were often indistinguishable from the mechanisms of organizing racist terror.[1]

In November 1871, the *Chicago Tribune* published an eyewitness account of such terror. Three Black men—Squire Taylor, forty-five, George Johnson, thirty-nine, and Charles Davis, sixty-eight—were kidnapped from a county jail by the Ku Klux Klan and lynched in Charlestown, Indiana. Aware that an "impending mob" was coming that night, the reporter had arranged to sleep in the sheriff's office, ensuring he was "awake at the hour of the contemplated violence." When the Klan did arrive, the sheriff refused to unlock the cell doors. The mob proceeded to bludgeon the bars with axes, sledgehammers, and chisels, "white heat sparks follow[ing] every blow." The reporter observed how the Klansmen's eyes "seemed to glow" through their masks "like those of famished wolves." For nearly four hours, Taylor, Johnson, and Davis were trapped, watching in horror as the locks before them were battered, their executioners pounding and panting without restraint. Around two in the morning, the sheriff tried to halt further structural damage to the jail. He retrieved the keys from their hiding place in the back of the building. Knotted on a piece of string and anchored to a window bar, the keys swung between the jail's outer walls and the bleak expanse of night. The *Tribune*'s article was entitled "Mask and Manilla." The "mask" referred to the Klan's muslin hoods while "manilla" described the "brand new whitish-brown" ropes used to hang the men. Each rope, it noted, had been prepared in advance with a noose, "showing that some one was at work who understood his business."[2]

Manila, a fiber that Filipinos called *abacá*, was a derivative of the plantain plant. The fibrous bark was ideal for rope, making it one of the most valuable "Indigenous products of the Archipelago," according to mid-nineteenth-century trade guides. Spanish galleons sailing between colonial port cities in the Philippines and Mexico had used manila rope for their rigging. Found to be sturdy, less likely to mold or to be eaten by insects than other fibers, manila imports to the United States grew precipitously after 1850, soon replacing Indian jute and Russian hemp. When the abolitionist John Brown was captured in 1859 trying to spark an armed insurrection of enslaved people in Harpers Ferry, Virginia, southern states competed to deliver the rope to hang him: Kentucky's hemp rope ultimately beat out South Carolina's cotton.[3] Manila soon surpassed all these domestically grown fibers. By the turn of the century, manila was the most popular rope-making fiber in the United States, and, as headlines suggested, it was nearly synonymous with rope itself.[4]

The 1902 Upson-Walton booklet observed that a surplus of manila fiber was "brought into our lap" following the 1898 Spanish-American War and the Philippine-American War of 1899–1902. The United States had seized imperial control over the Philippines, obtaining a near monopoly over the country's exports, two-thirds of which consisted of manila.[5] Though demand for the rope-making fiber soared, especially after it was deemed "strategic war material" during World War I, the sustainability of the *abacá* supply was soon cast into doubt. "The user of Manila hemp," reasoned the Waterbury Company in its 1920 catalogue, "is dependent entirely upon our foreign possessions in the far East." This fraught dependence meant that "the procuring of hemp ... for rope-making is attended with some difficulty."[6] Indeed, US reliance on manila was imperiled as Filipino workers and rebels fiercely resisted US imperial policies (just as they had overthrown Spanish colonial rule, from which US governing practices were adapted). Catalogues of US cordage companies in the early twentieth century attest to this industrial and geopolitical crisis. They agree that no solution could be found in a "domestic" market. Rather, for a profitable, plentiful, and stable supply of rope-making fiber, US industrialists had only to look south of their border.[7]

While manila imports declined, US imports of Mexico's rope-making fibers, henequen and sisal, exploded. Primarily used as agricultural twine to bind bushels of grain and bales of hay, both were easily joined with other fibers to make ropes of varying widths and strengths. Derived from the spiny agave cactus, the fibers (often both described as henequen) grew plentifully in the southernmost Mexican state of Yucatán, a product of its hot, dry climate, its flat landscape, and the unrelenting input of its Indigenous labor force. Beginning in the 1870s, landless Maya Indians had been conscripted to work on henequen plantations or haciendas after their commonly held *ejido* lands were expropriated by the state under the regime of President Porfirio Díaz. Consigned to debt peonage, the Maya had little choice but to accept labor contracts that could be sold or traded among local Yucatecan henequen capitalists, or *henequeneros,* though rarely ever paid off. Locked into debt, the workers faced brutal conditions, long hours, and regular lashings with henequen whips. *Henequeneros* justified the beatings with the adage *Los indios no oyen sino por las nalgas* ("The Indians only hear with their asses"). In addition to exhaustion, injury, and disease, many Maya also succumbed to epidemics of suicide. In 1909, British travel writers insisted that henequen labor regimes had cracked the Indigenous workforce on a "wheel of tyranny so brutal that the heart of them is dead."[8]

As demand for henequen fiber boomed, *henequeneros* conspired with Mexican federal officials to capture workers from around the country. In a coordinated plan called *el enganche* ("the hook"), thousands of war deserters, prisoners, "vagrants," and political dissidents, including Huastec Indians from Veracruz and Yaqui Indians from the Northern border, were ensnared. Hunted by the Mexican government as well as US officials, rebellious Yaquis were sent to the Yucatán haciendas in chains, declared by Díaz to be "obstinate enemies of civilization."[9] Two thirds of the Yaqui subsequently died. Barbarous labor conditions meant shortened lives for the workers and high turnover rates for the *henequeneros.* Between 1878 and 1910, labor recruiters added an additional ten thousand contract workers from Cuba, Italy, Spain, the Canary Islands, China, Japan, Java, with nearly three thousand from

Korea. Enclosed by barbed wire, disciplined by overseers, and dependent on *tiendas de raya,* company stores that often had jail cells attached, henequen plantations were effectively transformed into a "vast federal prison" for indentured segments of the global working class and so-called *indios bárbaros* ("hostile Indians"). Through debt and corporal punishment, henequen workers were forced to accept hunger, unsanitary conditions, and insufficient medical care. Records reveal that women were routinely coerced into relationships with *henequeneros,* ensuring that the threat of rape or compulsory sexual arrangements menaced every hacienda. Out of these brutal regimes, a motley international force of the criminalized, the violated, and the expropriated produced the raw material of twentieth-century rope.[10]

No other company benefitted from Yucatecan henequen more than the Chicago-based McCormick Harvesting Machine Company. McCormick sold agricultural machines that harvested grain and bound it into sheaves using henequen binder twine. These reaper-binder machines scaled up commercial production, enabling agribusiness in the Midwestern United States to explode. Such explosions occurred alongside an intensified expropriation of Indigenous land. Laws like the 1887 Dawes Act privatized millions of acres of communally held tribal lands in the region, enabling their settlement and agglomeration for capitalist agriculture. Through new reaper-binder technology and ongoing settler colonial violence, Native territories in the Midwest were further transmogrified into the nation's "bread basket." With J. P. Morgan's financial backing, McCormick absorbed several major competitors, becoming International Harvester (I. H.) in 1902. I. H. investors learned that a blend of Philippine *abacá* and Mexican henequen made ideal binder twine for Midwest grain and quickly invested in the Yucatán. By 1910, I. H. owned 99.8 percent of the entire Yucatecan fiber trade. In Chicago as in the Yucatán, millionaires pressed wealth from the tangles of international misery.[11]

Aware of growing concerns over the Yucatán's labor conditions, I. H. officials addressed the matter in a 1910 issue of their company magazine, writing, "There is nothing in the nature of slavery in Yucatán. Every man is free and receives his pay as regularly as the workman in the American factories."[12] The statement was unwittingly ironic, given that workers had famously protested against labor conditions in McCormick's Chicago factories, where the reaper-binder machinery was made. Demanding an eight-hour day with no cut in pay, McCormick's iron molders had joined thousands of Chicago workers and tens of thousands nationally in a general strike on May 1, 1886, organized by the industrial union the Knights of Labor. On May 3, two striking

McCormick workers were killed by the police. The next day, demonstrators poured into Chicago's Haymarket Square in protest. A bomb went off during the rally and police responded by firing into the crowd. When the dust settled, several men were dead and over a hundred were injured. Eight high-profile activists were arrested and charged with conspiracy to murder. All eight were convicted in a show trial designed to intimidate organized labor. Four organizers—August Spies, Albert Parsons, Adolph Fischer, and George Engel—were executed in a gruesome public hanging. Before he was hung, Spies shouted from the platform, "The time will come when our silence will be more powerful than the voices you strangle today."[13]

If the Knights of Labor had organized under the slogan "an injury to one is the concern of all," Haymarket demonstrated the maxim's global resonance. Around the world, the first of May became known as International Worker's Day, or May Day. In May 1913, the Yucatán-based Casa del Obrero Mundial (House of the World Worker) organized Mexico's first major May Day demonstration, complete with a Haymarket commemoration. Subsequent Mexican legislation declared the holiday a "cause of pride not only for the proletariat of the United States but of the whole world." In 1921, the Irish-born, Chicago-based veteran labor organizer Mary "Mother" Jones was on a labor delegation in Mexico City and bore witness to this solidarity. Jones was shocked to see Mexican workers enter the hall carrying the Mexican flag alongside a banner dedicated to *Los Martiers de Chicago*. Said Jones, the honor that workers gave to Haymarket was "the most remarkable demonstration I had witnessed in all my years in industrial conflict." To this day, May Day in Mexico is celebrated as the "Day of the Martyrs of Chicago." From their harvest in Yucatán to the hanging of the Haymarket organizers and back, ropes interlinked the brutal circuits of capital and empire, as well as the swell of international resistance rising against them.[14]

In the tumultuous first decades of the twentieth century, ropes were often curious composites of coexisting global regimes of accumulation, including manila from the US imperial control over the Philippines, cotton or domestically produced hemp from brutal Jim Crow sharecropping regimes, and henequen produced through the violent exploitation of expropriated Indigenous peasants and an indebted and dispossessed global proletariat. A further understanding of the financing, property regimes, policing, and relations of social reproduction, along with the transport, storage, distribution, consumption, and destruction of this raw material would reveal a vast interlocking universe of exploitation, expropriation, and oppression. Ropes, the ligatures of the global economy, materialize the processes by which the lives of people across disparate spaces are densely interwoven. A social history of ropes demonstrates that when capitalism links spaces it also links the fates of the people compelled into its regimes of accumulation.

As historian Peter Linebaugh writes in his landmark study of crime in eighteenth-century London, the social history of hanging "must also be an economic history of the trades and working conditions of its victims."[15] Accordingly, a full accounting of the forces that set value in motion requires a global geographic analysis of capital and a social history of its antagonists. Ropes, through such a socio-spatial and economic history, can illuminate the movement of capital, commodities, and labor, as well as the bonds shared by Yucatecan peasants, Chicago labor organizers, dispossessed Native people, victims of Jim Crow terror, and others who might otherwise be untraceable within discretely imagined national, racial, ethnic, or labor histories. Unbraiding the strands of the accumulation process exposes obscured histories of solidarity and evinces possible futures of shared struggle. Ropes, in other words, help demonstrate how capital, geography, and histories of opposition converge. They illustrate how people have been concretely conjoined across space and how they have consequently understood their fates as interlinked within a global class struggle.

While ropes are not the subject of this book, they serve to illustrate its stakes and scope. Ropes also illustrate the book's key challenge: to render vivid the relationships between space, imaginaries, the color line, and the global class struggle. The rope, for example, that lynched Mexican rancher Antonio Rodríguez in Rock Springs, Texas, on November 3, 1910, was tied to global regimes of butchery and wider currents of resistance. The rope that bound Rodríguez to a mesquite tree, that prevented his escape as he was covered with dry branches and doused with gasoline, that trussed him as he was burned alive before a gaping mob of thousands, this rope—a tool of the man's trade—became an instrument of despotic power. Rodríguez was accused of killing his boss's wife, Effie Henderson. The charge came from the boss himself, a man with an established record of violence against the woman. Like Squire Taylor, George Johnson, Charles Davis, and many others before him, Rodríguez was kidnapped from his jail cell by a mob of white vigilantes intent on exacting their own justice. Without trial or due process, Rodríguez was set on fire beneath an endless Texas sky.[16]

A flurry of US newspapers vindicated Rodríguez's killers, hailing a common defense of lynching: the protection of white womanhood. Lynchings were not merely forms of racist terror but, as Ida B. Wells argued, they were also bloody rituals of aspirational authority.[17] Lynchings symbolically affirmed an order wherein white men were, by law, the dominant owners, heirs, and sellers of property and capital, whether or not they actually possessed property or capital themselves. This order manifested at regional, national, and international levels. The killing of Rodríguez, a Mexican foreign national, constituted a brazen flouting of international law. Less than one hundred miles from the US–Mexico border, his murder represented a totality of racist terror, state power, and socio-spatial control codified through notions of gender, class, nationality, and race. The rope that killed Antonio Rodríguez was, in other words, a color line.[18]

But the same rope also twined together measures of international outrage. Demonstrators defended Rodríguez across the United States and in Mexico and Cuba. Enraged leaders called for boycotts of US goods. Protestors rallied at the offices of US newspapers and businesses in Mexico, at the US ambassador's home, and in the streets, often under fire from Mexican troops. On November 12, Mexican Revolutionary leader Ricardo Flores Magón described the "explosion of indignation" rocking Mexican cities. In *Regeneración,* his internationally circulating newspaper, he relayed protesters' condemnation of the murder and of the systemic violence perpetrated against Mexicans in the United States. For Flores Magón, this violence was in keeping with the avaricious behavior of US capitalists. It was racism that had killed Rodríguez and, as he described, "capitalism foments racial hatred." On November 20, 1910, the Mexican Revolution officially broke out. During this first major social revolution of the twentieth century, the economic geography of the lynch rope would unravel, and the politics of the color line would throb at the heart of the global class struggle.[19]

THE COLOR LINE

Quemaron vivo á un hombre. ¿Donde? En la nación modelo, en la tierra de la libertad, en el hogar de los bravos, en el pedazo de suelo que todavía no sale de la sombra proyectada por la horca de John Brown. ("They burned a man alive. Where? In that model nation, the land of the free, home of the brave, on the same piece of land that has still not escaped the shadow cast by the hanging of John Brown.")

PRÁXEDIS G. GUERRERO,
"Blancos, Blancos," *Regeneración,* November 19, 1910

The notion of a "color line" colloquially refers to an easily identifiable, observable, and knowable line demarcating racial difference. In its most common usage, the term seems to require no explanation, an idiom seemingly interchangeable with racism—itself a phenomenon that assumes shared definitions even as it is experienced and comprehended with enormous variation. If race was constituted through clearly fixed and shared definitions, it would not require such persistent explanation or such constant and violent redefinition of its boundaries.

The anachronistic terminology of "color" can be misleading for modern-day scholars since it seems to refer to fixed and observable differences in skin. In one of the earliest usages of the term, abolitionist Frederick Douglass, in his 1881 essay "The Color Line," described color itself as being "innocent" but clarified that it was the "things with which it is coupled [that] make it hated." In Douglass's definition, the color line is unstable and uneven, "neither uniform in its operations nor consistent in its principles." While he devoted much of the essay to a discussion of anti-Black racism at the heart of US slavery, he described the color line as expansive, linking slavery to Indigenous land theft and genocide, violence against Asian immigrants, and military aggression against Mexico. He described the logic employed by Scottish settlers in California in their lynching of Chinese workers. When the settlers were asked to account for their actions, Douglass wrote, "their answer is that a Chinaman is so industrious he will do all the work, and can live by wages upon which other people would starve." This expression of economic self-interest as a justification for homicide represented for Douglass the "inconsistencies of the color-line feeling."[20]

The "color line" is more commonly attributed to W. E. B. Du Bois, who popularized the term in his many writings. His definition of the color line—in keeping with Douglass's—also repudiated any fixed meaning. Analyzing the global situation, Du Bois perceived the color line as a set of logics and spatial practices at work, an ascendant way of thinking that naturalized intensely destructive global processes of exploitation, expropriation, and extermination. His prediction that "the problem of the twentieth century" would be "the problem of the color line" became the core of his materialist analysis of emergent US political, economic, military, and cultural power. In this, he was remarkably prescient.[21]

In his early writings, Du Bois located the operation of the US color line in common practices of meaning-making that defined national exteriority. In reviewing the popular foundational myths of the nation, he examined how the practice of "murdering Indians" was depicted as advancing US civilization. He noted how so-called American heroes were celebrated relative to their violent humiliation of Mexicans during the US-Mexican War. He detailed how the enslavement of Africans, a transparent contradiction to US democratic principles of freedom and liberty, was continually resolved by the reassertion of Black inhumanity. More generally, he saw how freedom under the color line was predicated on the idea that "another people should not be free." While enshrined in popular culture and historical mythmaking, Du Bois recognized that these characteristics found "secure foothold" in the policies and philosophies of the state. When the state was defined against that which was deemed external, chaotic, unruly, and violent, its very legitimacy depended upon continual maintenance of a racist order.[22]

While the metaphor of a color line connotes a physical demarcation, a solid boundary across which difference is maintained, Du Bois deftly identified its constant fluctuations. Taking a historical view, he charted the color line's evolution as both a logic and a practice, finding spatial expression in the movement of capital. Through the color line, uneven socio-spatial relations were organized according to purported racial differences and construed as natural. Race did not exist prior to such spatial ordering; it was the outcome rather than the referent of the color line. Racial regimes, which Cedric Robinson describes as constructed social systems wherein race is proposed as a justification for existing power relations, are ceaselessly in need of repair. The violence that accompanies them is directly related to their fragility and utter instability. Rather than a fixed border, the color line names the processes by which racial regimes attain legibility through space.[23]

While continually reasserted through tremendous violence, racial regimes, notes Robinson, are "unrelentingly hostile to their exhibition."[24] This was particularly true of the racial regimes that produced the aspirational identities of whiteness. At the turn of the twentieth century, the shadows of the Klansmens' hoods concealed the identities of perpetrators from the victims of racist terror. They also concealed the unrequited ambitions of the small men who participated in racist vigilante violence. Owning modest means and meager assets, the "middling" men in lynch mobs could briefly associate with the landed interests and social powers they did not possess.[25] Wrought through such violence was an imagined leveling, a fleeting sense of shared purpose, power, and racial identity with men more influential than themselves. Whether hiding behind masks or "at no times disguised," lynchers moved vainly in the incongruous shadows of power.[26] "We looked at him clearly, with world-old eyes," wrote Du Bois, "and saw simply a human thing, weak and pitiable and cruel."[27]

Writing about Mexico in 1914, shortly after the US invasion of Veracruz, Du Bois named the global dimensions of these racist projections. "We have Cuba by the industrial throat and the Philippines on its knees, albeit squirming," he wrote. "Why not Mexico with its millions of brown peons?" Du Bois here impersonated the sneering mentality of US capitalists, imagining the "darker" world as an endless site of investments and its people as the means of accumulation, all for the taking. In doing so, he also emulated the fraudulent swagger of these middling men who believed themselves to be the superiors of Black people, Italians, Chinese, Japanese, and "mongrels" in the United States, all those deemed to be "easy to whip and keep whipped." From the perch of this purported superiority, Du Bois describes an imagined entitlement to the spoils of foreign interventions: the belief that the "comfortable stream of dividends flowing into white pockets" belonged somehow to all men who identified as white, regardless of their class or actual means. Du Bois expanded on these insights within the year with a fascinating article for the *Atlantic* magazine entitled "The African Roots of War." There he extended the damning portrait of these pitiable people, owning little but their illusions of power, believing that their fates were not only tethered to the success of capitalist imperialism but that they were one and the same.[28]

"The African Roots of War" links these subjectivities to broader political-economic transformations. Du Bois narrated how a nascent bourgeoisie had revolted against their exclusions from the wealth of colonial empires in the late eighteenth and early nineteenth centuries. "Slowly," he wrote, "the divine right of the few to determine economic income and distribute the goods and services of the world has been questioned and curtailed." As the global capitalist system massively expanded in the late nineteenth century, he described the emergence of a "democratic despotism." Under this system, Western nations pursuing imperial expansions sought to harmonize the interests of capital and labor. Once the antagonist of industrial capital, the "white workingman" was newly "asked to share the spoil[s]" of imperial gain. Cleverly deploying the day's popular language of finance, Du Bois described how the "'Color Line' began to pay dividends." Aspiring classes were duly convinced they were the direct beneficiaries or "small shareholders" of the New Imperialism. Those deemed "white" in Western Europe and in North America were constructed in the dominant imaginary as racially superior to the "dark" world, and further convinced that they were princelings of this new system. In this seemingly democratized form of imperialism, "captains of industry" emulated kings, aspiring workers fancied themselves global investors, and a new cycle of accumulation emerged in the shell of the old. As subordinate groups in Western nations became convinced that the imperial interests of capitalists were their own, a new mode of global economic leadership began to emerge. The color line thereby named the spatial imaginary of the New Imperialism.[29]

SHADOW HEGEMONY

Du Bois's commentary on Mexico, as well as his essay "The African Roots of War," offered remarkable if underappreciated assessments of space and subjectivity relative to specific phases of capitalist development. His analysis of capitalism and imperialism anticipated the publication of Lenin's analysis by almost two years.[30] His ability to characterize the phase of capitalist accumulation coming into being in the late nineteenth century also foretold analyses of modern-day political economists. "The imperial width of the thing," as he described it, "the heaven-defying audacity—makes its modern newness."[31] The late nineteenth and early twentieth centuries saw the emergence of a distinct form of geoeconomic power, what Du Bois called the "New Imperialism" and what Giovanni Arrighi has described as the "systemic cycle of accumulation" under US hegemony.[32]

This mid-nineteenth- to early twentieth-century period marks a critical overlap between what Arrighi theorizes as the waning of British hegemony (of the late eighteenth through early twentieth centuries) and the emergence of US hegemony (from the late nineteenth century to the present). In this period of transition, the era of the New Imperialism, nation states not only pursued expansion through overt and formalized territorial seizure, but also through the more insidious mechanisms of financial control, debt regimes, and threatened militarism. Rather than simply installing a foreign government or practicing direct administration in countries where states sought land, labor, raw materials, or strategic geopolitical locations, investors exerted dramatic financial control over sites of investment and subsequently insured these investments with the threat or actuality of military intervention. These developments took shape, no doubt, through the accretion and ongoing processes of colonial territorial seizure. While territorialism and capitalism "cross-fertilized" one another throughout the reign of the British Empire, in the emergent US model of hegemony, they were, as Arrighi notes, "indistinguishable."[33] In the reorganization of the expanding global economy, US forces gradually developed the capacities to dictate the terms through which capital was administered, governed, managed, and dispensed on a global scale. US hegemony was refined in Latin America and the Caribbean, with the deepest and most devastating advances initially made in Mexico.[34]

While the Mexican Revolution is often understood as a contained nationalist event, the allied struggle of the Mexican peasantry and working class was largely mobilized against dramatic transformations of property ownership, state power, governance, and social structures wrought by the ascendant influence of foreign capital in the political economy. Within these transformations, the United States occupied an increasingly decisive role. By the outbreak of the Mexican Revolution in 1910, the US capitalist class owned more than 22 percent of Mexico's surface, accounting for nearly a quarter of all US investment and exceeding the total holdings of Mexican entities. Conglomerates like the International Banking Corporation, the first American multinational bank, emerged in Mexico in 1902, facilitating US investments in Mexican government bonds, mining, oil, agriculture, and other industries. These profits further capitalized ventures in China, India, Panama, the Philippines, and the Dominican Republic, a capitalist infrastructure later formalized and fortified by US state policy. The relationship of the United States to Mexico would therefore play a major part in the emergence of US hegemony during the late nineteenth and early twentieth centuries. Because the Mexican Revolution threatened specific material investments as well as the propertied logic of the period, it challenged growing US hegemony within the model of the New Imperialism. It was therefore a prime site within which the shifting logics of capital, labor, property, imperialism, and revolution could be thought anew. Indeed, as this book observes, from the vantage point of the Mexican Revolution, the internationalization of capital in the period helped to produce a decidedly internationalist consciousness.[35]

The period of the New Imperialism marked a critical turning point in global hegemony as world economic leadership began a shift to the United States, albeit under the long shadow of the British Empire. US power grew according to nearly every standard measure: as the world's leading industrial producer, home to the richest multinational corporations on the planet; the leading disseminator of cultural industries—particularly with the advent of film; and, for the first time in its history, as a leading exporter rather than importer of capital.[36] What was new was the formal consolidation of the powers, state capacities, and interests with which the United States would come to officially superintend the global capitalist economy. Following the money, so to speak, traces an alternate path of American globalized power, one that preceded the height of US political hegemony by midcentury.[37] As historian Odd Arne Westad has noted, this unparalleled economic growth in the late nineteenth century made the United States an economic superpower "well before it took on that role militarily and politically."[38] These developments would come to establish the form of US global power in the century to come.

US hegemony is customarily defined as a post-World War II phenomenon, often characterized by Henry Luce's phrase the "American Century." Perhaps the midcentury represented not the emergence of an epoch but a prelude to the apex of US power, a period when the United States as a hegemon exerted its greatest global influence. The Second World War marked a gruesome confluence of military, political, cultural, and geo-economic power when, as film scholars have observed, the dropping of the atomic bomb made humans for the first time into cameras.[39] The unleashing of atomic flashes in the skies of Hiroshima and Nagasaki made the cities into light boxes. As a result, the shadows of Japanese people were permanently burned into the walls and grounds where they stood. The era of the New Imperialism began in the shadow of British hegemony. It materialized in the flickering shadows of Klan hoods and reached its apex in the monstrous dematerialization of people into atomic traces. For purposes of this study, the evolution of US leadership over the global economy can be characterized by this generalized state of striving, a defensive subjectivity of becoming, a longing for power requited through racist terror—an era, in other words, of *shadow hegemony*.[40]

The shadow has multiple valences. It indexes how regimes of accumulation under emergent phases of US hegemony developed in relation to previous modalities of empire. Temporally, this regime emerged in the shadow of the British Empire, under its tutelage, emulating its forms of development and aspiring to its hegemonic position. Spatially and procedurally, it was grounded in the structures, logics, laws, social organization, and administrative infrastructures developed under colonial rule. The system entered into crisis once it began to cast its own hegemonic shadows.[41]

This book is also the story of other shadows. It considers how interpretations of internationalism were conditioned by shifts in the political geographies of global capital accumulation. It contends that overlooked forms of internationalism arose out of and as a response to the particular modalities of geo-economic power emergent in the late nineteenth and early twentieth centuries. In the shadows, it observes, people congregated, commiserated, struggled, and sometimes collectively decided that conditions could be otherwise. In his novel of radical internationalist organizing during the Mexican

Revolution, Paco Ignacio Taibo II describes this as the *Shadow of the Shadow*.[42] As this book seeks to show, *shadow hegemony* often unwittingly provided cover for its own undoing.[43]

Arise! follows the internationalization of US capital in the late nineteenth through the early twentieth centuries and traces the concurrent efforts of global radicals to produce an internationalist consciousness. It draws on Douglass and Du Bois to theorize struggles over the production of space and the territoriality of power in the early twentieth century. It traces the paths of figures from different radical traditions like Mexican revolutionary leader Ricardo Flores Magón, Southern California–based communist organizer Dorothy Healey, radical feminist and Soviet ambassador to Mexico Alexandra Kollontai, and African American artist and organizer Elizabeth Catlett, as well as many lesser-known migrant workers who traveled to Mexico and to the United States, as they converged in unanticipated spaces and struggles. It considers how they theorized, dramatized, and challenged racist and gendered social relations of capital in this era of shadow hegemony and consequently developed new articulations of struggle. It observes how revolutionary thinkers were uniquely positioned to understand how capital crossed national borders and exploited workers and peasants—linking the destinies of those it dispossessed. Following their lead, it foregrounds the influence of the Mexican Revolution, the first major social revolution of the twentieth century.[44]

THE MEXICAN REVOLUTION

The ascendancy of shadow hegemony was coterminous with the rise of Porfirio Díaz as the president of Mexico, first elected in 1876. For seven terms and over thirty-four years he ruled the country until he was overthrown in 1910 at the outset of the Mexican Revolution. The Porfiriato, the period of his reign, marked an era of relative stability after nearly a half century of volatility following Mexico's independence from Spain. President Díaz bridged an era of Liberal reform to the era of New Imperialism. In the period preceding his reign, Liberals, led by Mexican president Benito Juárez, had wrested power from conservative colonial vestiges and French foreign occupiers. Díaz himself had been a military hero against French Intervention. Against the memories of Spanish as well as US, British, and French colonial invasions, he gained legitimacy in developing the modern Mexican state. The Porfiriato, the decisive though contested period of economic, social, and political development, ultimately set the stage for revolution.[45]

Through Díaz's stewardship, Mexico underwent a violent process of modernization and integration into the world market, the benefits of which were unevenly distributed across the country. Modernization expanded the resources of the federal government and created extensive public infrastructure in railroads, roads, and pipelines, just as it had in other Latin American countries. This refashioning facilitated the cultivation, transport, and export of raw materials and induced massive imports of foreign capital. Accordingly, the federal government centralized state and class power, often wresting funds, rights, and control of local state entities to become the major broker between foreign finance, industrial capital, and Mexican land, labor, and industry. Among the resulting socio-spatial transformations were staggering expropriations of commonly held Indigenous *ejido* lands by the state for commercial agriculture. Some Indigenous populations, hitherto existing somewhat beyond the jurisdiction of the Mexican state, found themselves in violent confrontation with *rurales*—rural police forces—opposing their autonomy. While an emerging bourgeoisie attempted to keep pace with these developments and largely supported Díaz, the peasantry, constituting over 75 percent of the population, experienced violent dispossession, criminalization, and persecution. A newly proletarianized workforce further bore the brunt of exploitation in massively expanding industries. A frustrated middle class saw national resources, industries, and state functions expand with foreign investments, processes for which they were taxed but within which they were politically unrepresented. Given stagnant political formations, they were unable to voice their expanding grievances and vote Díaz out. Splits began to emerge among elite factions and their international supporters. To handle the multiple contradictions, the Díaz regime expanded its repressive measures, often by embedding them in new industrial and state infrastructure. Railroads, for example, spread with dramatic promises of travel and expanded trade, all the while ferrying soldiers in greater numbers, at greater speeds, over greater swaths of the land.[46]

Some scholars have disputed whether the simultaneity of regional struggles for autonomy that exploded after 1910 all clearly congealed in one singular Mexican Revolution. Indeed, the landless peasants who followed Emiliano Zapata in uprisings throughout the south-central part of the country were distinct from struggles in the Northwest and Southeast by insurgent Indigenous Yaqui and Maya Indians against the state's colonial violence. These in turn were connected to but often at odds with struggles for land and against local oligarchy united in the North under Pancho Villa. Political struggles for representation emerged in new middle-class oppositional formations and among factions of the elite. Support amassed for wealthy landowners like Francisco Madero, who initially displaced Díaz as president. Former Díaz loyalists split into their own political and military factions. Radical anarchosyndicalists in the Partido Liberal Mexicano (Mexican Liberal Party or PLM) led by Ricardo and Enrique Flores Magón organized across the US–Mexico border in concert with newly proletarianized fractions of the country. The violent repression of PLM-affiliated strikes by mineworkers in Cananea, Sonora, in 1906 and by textile workers in Río Blanco, Veracruz, in 1907 became flashpoints in the lead-up to Revolution. Further, the PLM moved across the border, where Mexican workers struggled with fellow miners in the Southwest United States, and with many worldwide who sympathized with the Revolution.[47] That these and other variegated struggles did not conform to any one political agenda does not negate the seismic rupture of the Mexican Revolution. As this book argues, the Mexican Revolution, the first major revolutionary conflagration of the twentieth century, produced conditions within which internationalist challenges to the New Imperialism arose.[48]

The book moves through the history of the Mexican Revolution into its afterlife (or, as some have argued, its culmination) in the 1940s to demonstrate the influence of the Revolution and the global visions it helped produce. It does not rehearse arguments that the United States played *the* determinate role in fomenting conditions of revolutionary revolt. Historians of the Revolution have situated US investments among many international forces exerting financial, political, and diplomatic pressure.[49] Scholars have also carefully excavated the roles of US capitalists in Mexico and drawn important connections between the expansion of US hegemony and investments and political influence in Mexico.[50] These texts have enlivened discussions of the history of capitalism and social history from the often overlooked vantage point of Latin America.[51] In drawing upon these texts, *Arise!* also seeks to contribute to scholarship uncovering streams of internationalism in the era of the Mexican Revolution.[52]

CONVERGENCE SPACES

The challenge for organizers and theorists has long been to understand the conjoined but distinct forms of oppression under capitalism, and crucially, the ways in which struggles between them have been linked. In other words, the process of uniting people in shared struggle across spaces of difference is certainly not as straightforward as expecting the workers of the world to unite. Relating exploited industrial Western workers to expropriated Indigenous people of the Americas; African people dispossessed of their lands, enslaved within plantocracies, and later subjugated under Jim Crow; colonial subjects concentrated in space and brutally conscripted into extractive economies; and people subjected to military occupation and imperial rule—and the convergences between them—requires some theoretical elaboration. This book offers a framework to broaden the way the revolutionary subjects of history are recognized and also expand the ways capital itself is understood and contested.[53]

In doing so, the book seeks to avoid the narrowing tendencies in the historiography of so-called "American" radicalism, namely, to delink and make discrete different struggles as singularly national, sectoral, ethnic or racially bound. Such particularizing might lend itself to clear exposition, but at the cost of understating the astounding ways class struggles have been understood and collectively fought out by people on the move. Such tendencies circumscribe the nature of struggle and underestimate its extraordinary fluidity, ingenuity, and creativity. This book seeks instead to describe how differently situated people were often thrown together in unexpected ways, and how, in those tumultuous convergences, they fought, made new meaning, and took overt and sometimes subtle inspiration from one another, establishing a more dynamic history of struggle that can enliven our sense of the reach, scope, sites, and stakes of early twentieth-century revolutionary actions and ideas.[54]

These goals set up multiple quandaries: How can mutable and overlapping processes of exploitation, expropriation, and oppression be understood within spatial struggles? How can an overarching struggle be articulated without simplifying, flattening, or rendering equivalent different forms of systemic violence? How can contestations over capital and the territoriality of power be represented without relying on reified notions of states, races, or class struggle in the process? How can the class struggle be represented across geographic space and at different scales while attending to the gendered relations of property and power? The interventions of this book are therefore theoretical and methodological.

Arise! offers a social and spatial history of class struggle. It observes how capital produces its own negations, at a variety of spatial scales, often through unanticipated alliances. It traces various stages throughout the accumulation process to examine how the international movement of capital has produced radical spaces of opposition. The key concept for thinking through various coterminous struggles introduced here is *convergence space*, which refers to contradictory socio-spatial sites wherein people from different backgrounds and different radical traditions have been forced together and have subsequently produced new articulations of struggle. The concept enables broad global movements of capital, repression, opposition, and ideas to be briefly stilled and their dynamics observed. Rather than flattening difference across spaces and struggles, this method seeks to examine the intersections of categories in motion.[55]

This project traces a wide range of characters and convergence spaces. It considers Mexican revolutionaries and global radicals in Mexico alongside workers, cultural figures, and soldiers. It also transcends the physical space of Mexico to consider the imaginaries projected onto revolutionary Mexico that extended beyond the county's borders. It focuses on art centers in Mexico City and New York City, farmworker strikes along the US–Mexico border, the Soviet embassy in Mexico City, mobilizations by the Los Angeles Unemployed Councils, and internationalist movements inside Leavenworth Federal Penitentiary in Kansas. Aligning social history and critical geography, the open-ended concept of convergence spaces captures how organizing work and spatial imaginaries were involved in the making of an internationalist consciousness in the early twentieth century.

This book examines a range of sources: memoirs, oral histories, personal correspondence, radical publications, jailhouse newspapers, prison records, private book collections, and lithographic prints, culled from national and international archives, as well as unofficial collections circulated by social movements. In the traditions of social history, anti-racist geography, and feminist political economy that emphasize people's collective struggles in insurgent place-making, each chapter considers the revolutionary process of the making of a different convergence space.

MAKING INTERNATIONALISM

Internationalism recognizes how people have been unevenly waylaid by the development of capitalism across space and developed forms of revolutionary solidarity in spite of social and spatial divisions, including national borders. It has historically reflected distinct spatial imaginaries of the world system.

Accordingly, its interpretations have been varied. Its most readily accessible history is organizational. Through such a lens, entities such as the First International (1864), Second International (1889), and Third International (1919) can offer concise illustrations of the ambitious webbing through which global labor, anarchist, socialist, and communist movements attempted to forge links over space and across movements. Similarly, institutional studies of liberal internationalism, covering entities like the League of Nations or the Geneva Convention, can offer discrete and observable histories of how humanitarian ideals became codified through international law. *Arise!* argues that while conceptions of internationalism have certainly been informed by these entities and are significantly recovered through their histories, something significant is lost to heuristics when this history is presented as merely reducible to or delimited by these organizations.

This book is concerned with the rich archive that emerges from the excess, the imagination and practice of internationalism by figures often left out of many organizational histories. It argues that their visions, activities, and aspirations offer an important source through which the broader histories of internationalism can and should be assessed. These include workers and radicals from the Global South such as Ricardo Flores Magón, whose insights root the political-economic arguments. It also considers key figures of radical traditions who traversed these institutions but could not be fully situated within them, like W. E. B. Du Bois, whose analysis of the New Imperialism and the color line grounds the study and the political-economic overview of the first chapter. Chapters highlight convergences of figures who made extraordinary experiments of internationalism in the spaces in which they found themselves and with the resources available to them. The second chapter highlights how radicals like M. N. Roy came to internationalism in revolutionary Mexico, while others, like John Reed, confronted the logic of the New Imperialism as a major fetter to its development. Within the walls of Leavenworth Penitentiary, as chapter 3 demonstrates, global radicals like Ricardo Flores Magón and working-class soldiers of empire found creative ways to teach and learn from each other about the meaning of revolution and the practice of internationalism. Chapter 4 considers how feminists radically reimagined gender, sexuality, and the organization of the family in their conceptions of the state and revolution through the lens of Alexandra Kollontai's travels in Mexico City. Chapter 5 examines how Mexican farmworkers and their families in rural California towns were connected to urban organizing efforts, largely led by women like Dorothy Healey, as they struggled against starvation, unemployment, and eviction in cities like Los Angeles. Chapter 6 centers the material realities and dream worlds of Black domestic workers in global Harlem and traces how, through the artist Elizabeth Catlett, their visions aligned with the revolutionary legacy of the Mexican Revolution. As the conclusion argues, these expansive conceptualizations of internationalism still have much to teach us at present.

A final word: In his study of the Guyanese working people, Walter Rodney encouraged readers to consider convergences as spaces of fragmentation. His work is attendant to the ways that "cultural convergence(s)" were inadequate on their own to "contribute decisively to solidarity among the working people." At the same time, he noted that class consciousness could not alone overcome "barriers created by legal distinctions, racial exclusiveness, and the separate trajectories of . . . culture."[56] Following this standpoint of irresolution, this study does not impute an unreasonable faith in convergences that did not congeal. But had they been allowed to develop, this study asks what different times we might be living in.

ONE

How to Make a Flag

INTERNATIONALISM AND THE PIVOT OF 1848

BAGDAD, MEXICO

Where the mouth of the Rio Grande yawns into the Gulf of Mexico, a bustling Mexican port called Bagdad once linked the southernmost tip of Texas to the waterways of the global economy. After the 1848 Treaty of Guadalupe Hidalgo, the river was declared a *zona libre,* a duty free zone, attracting commerce from around the planet. Cocoa, mahogany, anchovies, lace, silk, cigars, sugar, and guns, carried by Dutch, French, Danish, Russian, Spanish, German, and British vessels, all found brisk trade. In 1863–64, Bagdad was one of the busiest international shipping locations. Sailors wrote home that a man could walk for miles atop the bobbing decks of ships, all docked together under the flags of the world. During the US Civil War, Bagdad was home to around thirty thousand residents and a rowdy mix of travelers passing through: Mexican traders, German spies, British sailors, Confederate soldiers, and Yankee capitalists, as well as fugitive slaves, gun-dealers, liquor sellers, and sex workers. When a hurricane swept the town into the sea in 1867, local religious figures interpreted it as righteous condemnation for the town's sin and lawlessness. What remained of Bagdad was erased by later storms, submerging every structure—its docks and warehouses, bars and brothels, weigh stations and record houses—deep into the ocean.[1]

Bagdad's founder, Don Carlos, or as he was known in his home state of Connecticut, Charles Stillman, was the chief landowner, real estate trader, creditor, transporter, industrialist, and arms dealer in the town and its surrounding area. Not coincidentally, Stillman went on to become one of the most influential US global investors. This was due in no small part to his investments in Mexico. With Mexico's independence from Spain in 1821,

21

Stillman, like other US financiers, saw ripe opportunities for investment. US politicians and military officials began a complementary pursuit of Indigenous lands in Mexico's northern territory extending all the way to the Pacific Ocean. US trade interests developed into overt land speculation and aggressive plans for territorial expansion. Like many investors, Stillman acquired land in and around Bagdad through the dubious purchase of Mexican communal land rights. According to historian John Mason Hart, Stillman's land holdings in 1828 represented the first major incursion of American capitalist interests into newly independent Mexico. Stillman continued to expand his properties in alignment with the territorial ambitions of the United States.[2]

During the US-Mexico War, often described in the United States as the Mexican-American War, Stillman was contracted by the US government to supply troops from his properties along the Rio Grande. This "wicked war," as General Ulysses S. Grant described it, raged from 1846–48. Mexican soldiers suffered brutal losses of around twenty-five thousand known casualties while US soldiers endured the highest casualty rate and saw the highest number of desertions of any US war. With the Treaty of Guadalupe Hidalgo at the war's end, the United States annexed over five hundred thousand square miles, nearly half of Mexico's territory, including the present-day states of California, New Mexico, Arizona, Nevada, and Utah, along with parts of Colorado and Texas. Stillman was able to procure land in territories newly claimed by the United States as well as in unceded territories just south of the new Mexican border. Largely Indigenous Mexicans who held competing land claims found that their legal challenges went unrecognized by US law, overlooked by its judges, and dismissed under threat of US guns. In these ways, Stillman was able to secure Bagdad as his own private port.[3]

Bagdad acquired new meaning during the US Civil War as a global port that bordered the Confederacy. The main commodity traded at Bagdad was cotton—Confederate cotton, picked by enslaved African people and their descendants in the Southern United States. During the Civil War, the Union attempted to strangle Confederate trade. Through a blockade of Southern ports, it sought to take the South's major source of value out of circulation. Capital, after all, is value in motion. With the blockade, cotton was rendered immobile and Southern warehouses groaned under its unsold weight. In Bagdad, Charles Stillman was able to put value in motion, turning a profit at each step.[4]

Stillman received a percentage of storage costs from the many warehouse facilities he owned. He took a portion of the overland transportation costs by wagon and stagecoach delivery. When ships approached Bagdad's port, encountering beaches piled high with cotton bales, Stillman stood to earn still more from the offloading and delivery from ships in dock. From his co-ownership of a steamboat company, he earned a percentage of the costs accrued as cotton cargo traversed the Rio Grande. Stillman even received profits from his competitors. As a major real estate holder and lead partner in a banking consortium in the surrounding areas near Brownsville, Texas, and Matamoros, Mexico, he was paid by his rivals in the various forms of rent, loan payments, and interest. Cotton bought for domestic consumption was often processed in textile facilities that Stillman owned in Monterrey, Mexico, one of the first industrial factories in the area. Stillman and his partners were able to facilitate such colossal movements of cotton and capital that, as historian Joseph Contreras has argued, the area of northeastern Mexico became a "virtual appendage of the expanding US economy."[5]

Perhaps Stillman's greatest profit, beyond what he earned in production, storage, transportation, delivery, and processing, came from the procurement of cotton itself. Crucially, Stillman's ships were able to circumvent the Union blockade because he had registered under the name of a Mexican trading partner. Instead of the flag of the Union, the region that Stillman purportedly supported, or the flag of the Confederacy, whose slave economy Stillman was helping to materially support, Stillman's ships sailed under the neutral flag of Mexico. Under Mexico's banner, Stillman was able to smuggle cotton out of Confederate states, convert it into *los algodones*—Mexican cotton—and discharge it for sale on the global market.[6]

Stillman's machinations had broad manifestations. The Union blockade of Confederate ports had contributed to a severe worldwide cotton shortage. European textile industries, especially in British cities like Liverpool and Manchester, were immobilized. Consequently, European traders bought cotton at Bagdad in a frenzy. They purchased cotton with gold and also made payments with guns, armaments, and medical supplies. To guarantee a supply of guns to southern ports, Confederate officials gave Stillman and his partners additional bonuses, paid in cotton. Thus, Stillman's trade not only helped to finance the Confederate South, it also helped to arm its military.[7]

In these ways the cotton picked by enslaved people on the plantations of Louisiana and Arkansas, and others located east of the Mississippi River, was radically deracinated. This cotton was resold along networks throughout European, Mexican, and northern US ports like New York and Boston where its price sometimes quadrupled. Through these circuitous routes, cotton—grown on land violently expropriated from Indigenous people through settler colonial regimes; cultivated and harvested by enslaved African people in the Confederate South; transported by the indebted "mariners, renegades, and castaways" of the world—was imported into northern cities, spun in their industrial textile mills, often by young immigrant working-class women, and even woven into the uniforms of Union soldiers. The further transubstantiation of cotton saw it abstracted into tradable units, exchanged as stock, and bloodlessly rendered onto balance sheets. From these vast entanglements, Stillman emerged from the US Civil War as one of the richest men in the world.[8]

Stillman's attempt to pass off Confederate cotton as *los algodones* enacts a common conceptual conceit in the spatial imaginaries of capital. Here, capital is routinely and defensively disaggregated from the nature of the regimes that produced it. While regimes such as slavery can be uniformly acknowledged as racist, once the capital produced through them takes new form, becoming, for example, industrial capital or finance capital, its link to specific regimes is more often mystified. As the story of Bagdad suggests, there is no stage at which racism enables the process of capital accumulation and then suddenly ceases to exist once that capital changes form. Capital is never scrubbed free of its past crimes. To believe otherwise is to enlist the faith of a money launderer, hoping that by changing form, wealth can be absolved of all its past incriminations. Rather than disappearing through anodyne transformation or merely with the passage of time, such practices are rather authorized through the accumulation process, congealed as capital, and more often reproduced through subsequent social relations, particularly when they remain unexpressed (or regarded with "false innocence").[9] Racism, the "exaggeration" of regional, cultural, religious, as well as other distinctions into "racial" typologies of inferiority and dominance, as Cedric J. Robinson writes, cannot be sequestered into an odd or aberrant feature of the accumulation process.[10] Regardless of the form capital takes, the nature of any specific regime of accumulation, or even the flag flying over its operations, racism has been irrevocably constitutive to the history and development of capitalism in ways its self-presentation more often elides.[11]

Resurrecting the story of Charles Stillman helps situate the development of US interests in Mexico and the broader transformations of accumulation regimes in the late nineteenth century. Mexico, as Gilbert G. González notes, was victim to annexation twice over: first geopolitically and subsequently economically. Indeed, in the aftermath of the United States's vast annexation of Mexico's land in 1848, Mexico's unincorporated spaces became primary sites of intensified investment, especially for US capital. Stillman, along with a host of other financiers, invested new surpluses of capital into the Mexican state, particularly through the purchase of Mexican war bonds. Such investments represented a major shift in US state formation. After decades indebted to foreign capital, largely British finance, US investors became the major creditors of another national economy for the first time in Mexico. These late nineteenth-century investments in Mexico represented a pattern of investment and a form of indirect rule that would come to prefigure key features of US hegemony in the twentieth century.[12]

Like its present-day namesake, the brief history of Bagdad, Mexico, encapsulates the processes whereby militarism, racism, and debt financing have constituted the foundations of the US political economy. Through these processes, the United States gained the capacities to dictate the terms through which capital was administered and dispensed.[13] Charles Stillman invested his fortune—a product of Mexican war bonds and land concessions, cotton picked by enslaved Africans, and land stolen from Indigenous people—into the National City Bank of New York, where his son, James Stillman, became president. This entity, today's Citibank, has played a critical role in the restructuring of other national economies through similar methods of punitive debt financing. Indeed, the brief history of Bagdad illustrates how US interests in Mexico represented a dramatic precursor to the patterns of rule later implemented across US cities and the Global South throughout the twentieth century.[14]

This chapter identifies 1848 as a critical pivot of shifting political geographies and accumulation strategies of global hegemony. It argues that the mid-nineteenth century marked a vast expansion and integration of the global capitalist economy. As observers of the period like Frederick Douglass and Karl Marx as well as contemporary theorists like Giovanni Arrighi have noted, the era also witnessed the fitful emergence of a new spatial logic of capital accumulation. Territorial acquisition was becoming a driver of accumulation rather than an objective of state power. The shift to a nimbler capital-driven logic marked an evolving break with modalities of colonial rule under British hegemony. Mexico occupied a unique and central role in these shifting spatial strategies. When compared with competing interests of other European powers, Charles Stillman's machinations help illustrate these shifting relations. This chapter considers the period from 1848 at the end of the US-Mexico War up until the outbreak of the Mexican Revolution in 1910 as a key turning point in the ascendancy of US hegemony.

Arguing for 1848 as a pivot in the geography of global capital means dislodging a surprisingly fixed conception of capitalist space among geographers of US Empire. Comprehending US expansion as distinct from the territorialist model characteristic of European colonialism often involves a critical appraisal of geographer and politician Halford Mackinder's 1904 article "The Geographic Pivot of History." Mackinder argued that economic expansion as a function of territorial expansion was no longer feasible at the turn of the century. Like Frederick Jackson Turner's infamous "frontier thesis," this conceptualization marked an end of absolute space in the territorial US, against which a new economic geography of capital emerged, a seeming prelude to US Empire. Inheriting the spatial imaginary and settler colonial nationalist mythology conceived by imperialists at the end of the nineteenth century is a regrettable concession. Presuming that the contours of the contiguous United States, as they currently stand, would always be what they ultimately became, also skirts the historical contingency of US state formation. It subsumes forms of ongoing imperialism and commits the most grievous error of reproducing empire's spatial logic. Territorial expansion did not simply reach a natural physical limit. What is forgotten in this formalistic rendering of capital's shifting geographic logic is resistance. The geographic pivot of the late nineteenth century is impossible to understand without an analysis of the global class struggle that drove it.[15]

1848 is, of course, primarily identified with mass proletarian uprisings and the publication of the *Communist Manifesto*. With its call for the "workers of the world" to unite, the *Manifesto* and organizing of the First International has predetermined many definitions of internationalism. By expanding the spatial frame of 1848 to center Mexico, and by considering the shifting geographies of accumulation that this period helped to inaugurate, this chapter argues that the definition of internationalism can accordingly be expanded. It contends that in the late nineteenth century, various forms of internationalism arose alongside the contested political, social, and spatial forces that were reshaping the world. From the vantage point of radicals in the lead-up to the Mexican Revolution, the chapter demonstrates how the internationalization of capital produced a broad internationalist consciousness.[16]

GEOGRAPHIES OF BRUTALITY AND THE
US REPUBLIC

In July 1847, during the US-Mexico War, US reporter and one-time fervent war supporter Anne Royall published "Outrageous in Mexico," an article condemning attacks on Mexican women by US soldiers. Rape, rarely recognized as a crime in the United States when it was committed against nonwhite women, was suddenly denounced by astonished figures like Royall when it was used as a brutal weapon of war against Native people in Mexico. Accustomed to the indiscriminate violence of "Indian Wars" and settler colonial regimes, US soldiers waged war against Mexican people with equal wantonness, disregarding formal rules of engagement to routinely rape, rob, and kill unarmed civilians. US property regimes made all non-white women, who could not own, sell, or inherit property (and, if enslaved, were considered property themselves) extraordinarily vulnerable. In their violations of Indigenous people across borders, US soldiers and civilians carved a widening geography of brutality.[17]

Of the war, Frederick Douglass wrote, "The taste of human blood and the smell of powder seem to have extinguished the senses, seared the conscience, and subverted the reason of the people."[18] The excessive violence and sadism of US soldiers led to thousands of desertions, including several hundred who defected to the Mexican side. Some of these soldiers were new immigrants to the United States who, having escaped tyranny in their home countries, refused to perpetuate it against people in another. The San Patricio Battalion, composed of mostly Irish and some German soldiers, became one of the staunchest defenders of the Mexican cause against the US military. Their deserters' handbill defined liberty against "those who desire to be the lords of the world, robbing properties and territories which do not belong to them." Perhaps they were familiar with abolitionists like Douglass, who had traveled to Ireland during the potato famine and spoken passionately against slavery, British colonialism, and US aggression against Mexican people, connecting common "degradation" and the struggle against it. Either way, these men refused to perpetuate in Mexico what they had escaped under British rule in Ireland, or under despotic conditions in Germany.[19]

Ulysses S. Grant decried the US-Mexico War as "one of the most unjust ever waged by a stronger against a weaker nation." He condemned the US government for "following the bad example of European monarchies" and indulging in a reckless "desire to acquire additional territory."[20] Grant's observation about the United States' tragic if not farcical imitation of an old European regime in 1848 was prescient. The US military conquest of Mexico did represent a regression to a dated strategy. In this, the country was not alone.

After the United States annexed nearly half of Mexico's territory in 1848 with the Treaty of Guadalupe Hidalgo, France set its sights on the remaining land. That same year, Napoleon Bonaparte's nephew, Louis Napoléon III, became head of the French state. By 1851, he had consolidated his power, staged a coup, and, on the anniversary of his uncle's coronation, anointed himself Emperor of France's "Second Empire." The younger Napoléon aspired in vain to his uncle's stature. His rule was a "caricature," or in Karl Marx's more damning description, a "farce." Marx's 1852 book *The Eighteenth Brumaire of Louis Bonaparte* describes the French leader's efforts to recreate the "costumes" of the past, along with its "borrowed language" and "battle slogans," drawing on the legitimacy of the French Revolution, to conjure the "dead of world history." In doing so, he observed how Napoléon III's new bourgeois order tied itself aspirationally to past dynasties, a regime he likened to "shadows that have lost their bodies."[21]

Napoléon III sought to emulate his uncle's vast territorial ambitions. He sent French troops to New Caledonia, Algeria, Senegal, Lebanon, and China and conscripted colonized soldiers into new colonial wars. He sympathized with the ambitions of the slaveholding Confederacy and sought a major foothold in Mexico. During the US Civil War, he sought to take advantage of Mexico's own internal strife. From the southern state of Veracruz, Liberal forces led by Benito Juárez had warred against Conservative forces based in Mexico City. When Liberals took the capital, President Juárez sought to stabilize the country. In 1861, he declared a moratorium on servicing foreign debts. Ostensibly enraged, Napoléon III sent French troops to recover the funds. Compared to other foreign bondholders, France's share of Mexico's debt was relatively small, hardly enough to justify an invasion. Undeterred, Napoléon III launched an invasion. He installed Maximilian of Habsburg, Archduke of Austria, as the new Emperor of Mexico in 1864.[22] As Marx joked, "To be sure! The oddest means ever hit upon for the consolidation of a government consists in the seizure of its territory and the sequestration of its revenue."[23]

To stave off the French invasion, Juárez sought money and arms. After the Civil War, Charles Stillman and other northern financiers who had amassed massive fortunes were eager to move their new surpluses of capital. Juárez successfully convinced Stillman, William Dodge, J. P. Morgan, Henry du Pont, and Charles Schwab, among other US capitalists, to invest their money in Mexican war bonds, thereby aiding in the war effort against the French. With this aid, Mexico emerged victorious. When Emperor Maximilian was executed by Mexican forces in 1867, the robes of the French Second Empire fell, exposing a sad charade of an *ancien régime*.[24]

Marx had written *The Eighteenth Brumaire of Louis Bonaparte* in a flurry. He had attempted to capture Napoléon III's coup as events unfolded. He also used the events to reflect on the missteps of proletarian revolutions and to reassess the power struggle against the bourgeoisie described in the *Communist Manifesto*. Marx and Engels had written the *Manifesto* before uprisings against absolutist regimes and monarchies had swept Europe in 1848. They had noted the swelling of industrial working-class power and its correlation to the exploding size of the global capitalist economy. Their *Manifesto* correctly predicted that an emerging and consolidating working class would assert its power across the continent, opposing the bourgeois struggle for state power through proletarian internationalism. They appraised the revolutionary role of the bourgeoisie in developing the means of production and abolishing monarchies. What they had not anticipated, however, was how formidable the bourgeoisie would become. Under Napoléon III's authoritarian regime, the bourgeoisie supported a brutal counterrevolution, utilizing law, a modern police force, and mechanisms of surveillance to violently suppress working-class dissent. Though bourgeois revolutions had by this point proved "weak," the bourgeois counterrevolutions, in historian Angela Zimmerman's words, were "terribly effective." Marx realized that there would be no simple transition of power for the proletariat. The *Brumaire* revised the *Manifesto*'s theories of the state and history. It distinguished romanticized histories of bourgeois revolutions, which appeared to "storm swiftly from success to success," from those histories of proletarian revolutions, which, by contrast, had to "criticize themselves constantly" to reassess situations as they unfolded in unpredictable ways.[25]

Significantly, Marx's *Eighteenth Brumaire* was not first published in France, where it was set, nor in England, where Marx was living at the time, nor in his native Germany, to whose struggles he remained connected. The first edition was instead published in New York City by Joseph Weydemeyer, a revolutionary German émigré, one of thousands who had fled or been exiled after participating in the 1848 revolutions against autocracy and despotism. These "'48 ers" absorbed the lessons of the *Brumaire,* particularly its assessment of Napoléon III's regime, learning difficult lessons about the ferocity of bourgeois class interests. The *Eighteenth Brumaire* famously describes how people make history, but not under conditions of their own choosing. This was decidedly the case with the '48ers. Roughly 190,000 Germans fought for the Union Army. Many, like Weydemeyer, were exiled revolutionary veterans and socialist internationalists who immigrated to the United States, joined the abolitionist movement, and transposed their own struggle against tyranny onto the US Civil War against slavery.[26]

LIBERAL INTERNATIONALISM

The concept of internationalism is often fixed to the 1848 publication of the *Communist Manifesto,* published during popular uprisings throughout Europe. Poorly received in its time, the *Manifesto* was regarded as the program of a broader global revolutionary movement only in retrospect. The document intended to outline the specific goals and mission of the Communist League, a group that counted Karl Marx and Friedrich Engels as members. Their *Manifesto* describes the class struggle between the growing proletariat and ascendant bourgeoisie under a vastly expanding industrial capitalism. Their aim was to embolden the workers of the world to unite against broadening conditions of capitalist exploitation. Plucked from its context, its concept of internationalism, some have argued, appears limited to Western European male industrial workers. But as the nineteenth century unfolded, it became clear that resistance to capital was as globally interlinked as the geographies of accumulation that capital produced.

While internationalism is commonly attributed to Marx, the term was actually coined by Jeremy Bentham, the English theorist of utilitarianism, in the late eighteenth century. In an era of dramatically shifting political structures and disjointed legal systems, Bentham sought to delineate internal and international jurisprudence and determine which branches could regulate the "mutual transactions between sovereigns." In doing so, he grappled with laws that would enable a nation to act as a sovereign body once it passed from dependence to independence. By this transition, he was not thinking of countries like Haiti, where enslaved people would soon overthrow slavery and establish the first Black republic, or countries like Mexico, where people would soon wage a war of independence against Spain. Bentham's writings were replete with racist colonial assumptions. "Liberty without security," he wrote, "is that which is possessed by Hottentots and Patagonians." Liberty "by security," by contrast, was "the pride of Englishmen."[27] Bentham was building and banking on a new world order, a new liberal international where men with "English-bred minds" would superintend a global economy through territorial expansion, speculation, and commercial enterprise.[28]

By 1825, Bentham was "little known in England" but well known "in the plains of Chili and the mines of Mexico." In correspondence with Latin American independence leaders like José de San Martín and Simón Bolívar, Bentham rejected colonialism, particularly the monopoly character of colonial trade. He foresaw a new order of liberty emerging through the production of new markets. As his own designs in Latin America made clear, this new order would conserve reactionary features of the old. For example, Bentham once schemed with former US vice president and infamous duelist Aaron Burr to invade Spanish territories. Burr had planned to crown himself emperor of Mexico and appoint Bentham legislator, predicting that Mexicans would follow Bentham "like a flock of sheep." But Bentham had his own schemes in the region. He planned to build an interoceanic canal through Latin America, a project that had long been desired by Spanish officials. He foresaw that this project would be funded by British capitalists on land owned by newly independent Mexico. This land, he believed, would soon be ceded to "the Anglo-American United States" since Mexico's largely Indigenous population was, in his estimation, "not as yet of sufficient age to go alone." As later commentators would describe, the liberal internationalism espoused by Bentham was little more than a "fig leaf," professing order while barely concealing empire's enduring barbarism.[29]

Bentham's theory of internationalism described a new world coming into being in the early nineteenth century. By 1818, it appeared that a "war to the death" was being waged "between the old and the new social order."[30] Frustrated aristocrats, ambitious bankers, aspiring merchants, and middle-class representatives were opposing monarchies and absolutist empires. At the same time, rebellions of enslaved people, dispossessed peasants, a growing industrial working class, and colonial insurgents were gathering. Taken together, these struggles were reshaping the nature of states and economies. With the Haitian Revolution, 1791–1804, France lost a ruthless slave economy of sugar. After Mexico's War of Independence, 1810–1821, Spain lost a filched lifeblood of silver and minerals. Britain's loss of the new United States meant the loss of sovereign claims over the tobacco, cotton, and rice cultivated by enslaved people upon stolen Native land. The absolute rule of empires was shaken in this Age of Revolution. In the transforming world, merchant bankers became uniquely capable of moving capital and managing an integrated market, meeting for example "pay-rolls in Flanders out of Mexican dollars coming in payment for calico delivered in Spain." By the early nineteenth century, financiers were gaining power and influence from their abilities to superintend a rapidly integrating global economy.[31]

In the ascendant bourgeois order, liberal figures like Bentham were consolidating power necessary to reshape landscapes, investing in major infrastructure projects like transnational canals. They also adapted preexisting political administrative structures to exert authority over the territories of their investments (encouraging, for example, the United States to seize Mexican land). Where suitable, they often stoked longstanding colonial prejudices to advance their aims, such as determining whether a population was "of sufficient age" for independence. Compared to the limited spoils of colonial trade, this new order, as espoused by liberals like Bentham, offered more freedom and democracy, albeit a freedom reserved for investors rather than the enslaved, dispossessed, exploited, and colonized. In the expansion of the global capitalist economy in the nineteenth century, Bentham's concept of internationalism synthesized advancing forms of bourgeois reterritorialization with colonial social orders and brutal racist hierarchies.[32]

Bentham is perhaps best known for his theory of the panopticon, published in 1791. His concept of internationalism is imbued with related questions of surveillance and oversight. In contrast to the dungeon-like prisons of the French Bastille, Bentham's panopticon proposed to deploy a spatial logic of isolation and control. It imagined a physical separation of people from one another, making them visible only to an unseen central authority. Modeled on the spatial management of plague-ridden French villages, this configuration would expose them to continuous monitoring and curtail disruptive or insurrectionary communication. Bentham reasoned that the threat of insurrection, like the panic of contagion, could be contained if people internalized the mechanisms of surveillance or, in other words, if people were made to believe that they were always being watched. This supervisory "strategy of space" was adaptable to multiple sites such as poorhouses, schools, and, most famously, prisons.[33]

The panopticon was not Jeremy Bentham's idea but an adaptation of his brother Samuel's theory, developed while overseeing shipbuilders on British dockyards. Samuel Bentham's mandate was to prevent the scavenging of wood scraps and timber waste created during ship production. These leftover "chips" were customarily used by workers to warm their homes, cook food, and construct furnishings like narrow stairs or cabinet doors. Shipbuilding was a highly specialized form of labor, and the salvaging of chips had been a customary part of compensation since 1634. Samuel's efforts to surveil workers and stop the scavenging of chips aligned with broader efforts to mechanize and de-skill production, install low wages, and subordinate labor on the dockyards. While workers opposed these measures through strikes and riots, the production process was eventually rationalized. Consequently, the taking of chips was transformed from long-standing custom into criminalized act. The panopticon, a critical component of nineteenth- and twentieth-century carceral logic, was born out of efforts to surveil workers and repress labor. By elevating capital's line of sight while hindering workers' communication and solidarity, Bentham's theory of internationalism shares much in principle with the theory of the panopticon. The implications of this process could be further seen throughout the entire production of British ships.[34]

THE CURSED INTERNATIONAL

The power and reach of the British empire were exemplified by its ships, vessels for the administration of war, commerce, colonialism, and slavery. The interconnected geographies of accumulation could be understood throughout the production of ships, as could the interlinked spaces of resistance they produced. The capital for producing British ships, for example, was largely a product of British colonial relations, particularly in India. In the nineteenth century, colonized Indian workers were conscripted to labor throughout the British empire while Indian soldiers were deployed worldwide to protect existing sites of British investment and open new ones. British colonial administrators deindustrialized the country and reorganized production to vastly expand the growth of strategic commodities such as grain, cotton, and opium. While grain grew plentifully, it was kept in reserve for British trade, even during times of famine. By the 1870s, the skeletal remains of starving Indian people could be found at the steps of grain depots, the grain possessing greater speculative value than their lives.

Indian-grown opium was transported from cities like Bengal to Chinese cities like Canton. As Chinese people were hooked on the drug through an illegal and illicit trade, Britain gained a foothold in the Chinese economy, colonizing Hong Kong in 1842. The "commodities imported from East

India," Marx noted, "were chiefly re-exported to other countries, from which a much greater quantity of bullion was obtained than had been required to pay for them in India." Indeed, the surplus gained from taxes and tribute on colonial goods, particularly from India, was so immense that it enabled Britain to become a lender of capital to other states and municipalities. In this position, Britain became a global creditor and, thereafter, the dominant economic power of the nineteenth century. This capital was subsequently reinvested into its colonial infrastructure, including the construction of British ships.[35]

The British ships that operated illegally as slave ships after the end of the British trade in 1807 were vessels of both trade and war. The grotesque processes that transformed African people into "Atlantic commodities" occurred largely aboard ships, as Stephanie Smallwood describes. The "value" of enslaved people was continually assessed in relation to the space and commodities required to keep them alive, especially as they became sick, distressed, wounded, or insane, or attempted to take their own or their captors' lives. In 1781, a British Solicitor General pronounced that slaves had as much humanity "as wood." He litigated the infamous case of the *Zong,* in which over 150 slaves were thrown overboard, allowing the ship's owners to file an insurance claim for lost "cargo." In refusing to press criminal charges, the Solicitor General had declared, "What is this claim that human people have been thrown overboard? This is a case of chattels." The *Zong* joined the infamous diagram of the slave ship *Brookes* in the abolitionist imagination. Both ships illuminated the cold calculations whereby enslaved people were assessed as abstract mediums of exchange to be traded, sold, stored, or, when deemed financially advantageous, murdered. In 1840, British painter J. M. W. Turner commemorated the *Zong* in "The Slave Ship (Slavers Throwing overboard the Dead and Dying—Typhoon coming on)." Alongside the painting, he displayed a poem condemning this brutal commodity logic, which ends, "Hope, Hope, fallacious Hope! Where is thy market now?"[36]

If Bentham's liberal internationalism was haunted by colonialism's starved skeletons and slavery's restless spirits, it was also hounded by the curses of dispossessed peasants. In Germany's eastern Rhineland, peasants in the early nineteenth century were confounded by a profound shift in property relations as the Black Forest became parceled off to private owners. With the expropriation of forest land, peasants were suddenly punished for foraging, hunting, or engaging in other customary practices of survival. Soon thousands were incarcerated for theft or trespassing, and new "criminals" flooded

German courts. As forests made famous by the Brothers Grimm underwent rapid capitalist development, fairytale monsters were replaced by lurking forest managers, tax collectors, and bailiffs. Peasants fought against dispossession in the ways they could, organizing and also emigrating in huge numbers, an average of forty thousand per year between 1830–40, with a large number of radical '48ers exiled after 1848. When protest and organization did not suffice, peasants enchanted the forests and bewitched the trees so that anyone who cut them down would carry their curses.[37]

The wood from these forests was felled by new timber companies. It was then floated down the Rhine and transported to England, where it often became the masts of British ships. One gains a sense of the world linked in struggle, the basis of internationalism. The ships were built with surplus capital from brutal colonial rule. They carried barrels of grain kept from the mouths of starving people not deemed valuable enough to feed. When they illegally functioned as slave ships, they transported enslaved African people who were treated as if their very lives were commodities. They were further constructed with wood that carried the curses of dispossessed and criminalized peasants. While observing dispossession in the German Rhineland, a young Karl Marx, then a journalist for the *Rheinische Zeitung,* became politicized. He saw how "the organs of the state" could become the "ears, eyes, arms, legs" of property owners. He came to believe that the liberal economic order advocated by figures like Bentham was the cause rather than the cure for this cursed international. With this understanding, Marx would become a revolutionary, perceiving a world linked in struggle before 1848.[38]

THE ABOLITIONIST INTERNATIONAL

As steel rails traversed land and steam engines pushed ships across water—moving goods, people, raw materials, and weapons alike—revolutionary ideas transited the globe. "Steam, skill, and lightning," observed Frederick Douglass, "have brought the ends of the earth together." Douglass linked slavery to questions of Indigenous land theft and genocide and military aggression against Mexico, likening the United States' lust for land, war, and slavery to "hungry sharks in the bloody wake of a Brazilian slaveship." Douglass was one of many abolitionists who traveled the world in what historian Manisha Sinha has described as an "abolitionist international." In speeches to Irish abolitionist societies, religious houses, and workingmen's groups in England, Ireland, and Wales, Douglass described imperialism and the colonial subjugation of Ireland in the same breath as he spoke of India, parts of Africa, and the Caribbean. "The oceans that divided us, have become bridges to connect us," said Douglass in 1848. The "wide 'world has become a whispering gallery.'"[39]

For Douglass, 1848 marked a decade since his own self-emancipation from slavery. It also marked the ten-year anniversary of the emancipation of the West Indies. West India Day, as it was celebrated in August, was a revered holiday and popular recruitment event for abolitionists. From Bussa's uprising in Barbados to the Demerara Rebellion in Guyana, the Baptist War in Jamaica, and unrest throughout the Bahamas and beyond, Douglass recognized that enslaved people themselves were the driving force behind abolition. While Douglass's prior West India Day speeches connected the abolition of West Indian slavery to the struggle to end slavery in the United States, his speech of August 1848 in Rochester, New York, offered a broader global view. Douglass described the radical reshaping of space and time, enabling disparate struggles to be connected by "interests, sympathies and destiny." In a speech entitled "The Revolution of 1848," he demonstrated how struggles against slavery and tyranny were as interwoven as the global circuits of accumulation that united them.[40]

Haiti, as Douglass described, was the "original" and most influential "emancipator of the nineteenth century." The uprising of enslaved African people in the world's most productive colony, the economic engine of the French empire, represented the greatest slave rebellion in world history.[41] Its tremors struck at the foundations of imperial palaces. From the boardrooms of royal chartered companies to the trading floor of London's Stock Exchange, wealth, in all its certitude, began to tremble as "all the Atlantic mountains shook."[42] In the wake of the Haitian Revolution, fever dreams of abolition deliriously swept the colonized world. From Kingston to Caracas, Rio de Janeiro to New Orleans, Douglass observed that "insurrection for freedom kept the planters in a constant state of alarm and trepidation." Enslaved and colonized people marched and organized under pictures of the revolutionary leader Toussaint L'Ouverture. In their collective imaginations and in physical acts of overtaking ships, enslaved people steered themselves toward Haiti's free soil. Slaveholders and colonizers, fearing revolutionary contagion, took extreme measures to sequester the spirit of Haiti. The revolution, however, could not be contained. Haiti radiated hope and promise to the enslaved, expropriated, and exploited, engendering its own internationalism and setting the world aflame.[43]

A "fearful succession" of revolutions and "outbreaks" exploded by the mid-nineteenth century. Douglass described a "general insecurity brood[ing] over the crowned heads of Europe" with ongoing attempts by figures like Bentham to establish liberal bourgeois orders. As the "famine-stricken" Irish seethed against British colonialism, the industrial working class mobilized in "the buzz and din of the factory" and mines, and "oppressed and plundered" peasants resisted their dispossession, Douglass observed the ways the "dormant energies of the oppressed classes all over the continent" had been "stirred" by the French and Haitian Revolutions. He recognized links between these struggles, noting how the French provisional government had heeded the call of the Haitian Revolution and decreed the "unconditional emancipation of every slave" throughout French colonies in 1794. Although Napoléon Bonaparte reversed this decision in 1802, the emancipatory politics set in motion by the Haitian Revolution reverberated internationally. By calling together movements against despotism, colonialism, exploitation, and slavery, Douglass drew a powerful continuum of struggle against "tyrants of the old world, and slaveholders of our own."[44]

When Haiti became free territory, its leaders sought to expand the geography of freedom. While they searched for formal recognition internationally, they also proffered support to others. Iterations of Haiti's constitution offered refuge to fugitive slaves and welcomed enemies of empire to become "children of Haiti." To be Haitian was to be Black, a political choice rather than an inheritable status. Outlined in the 1805 Constitution, a person was determined to be Black if they rejected slavery, renounced French colonialism, and accepted Haitian law. Article 44 of the 1816 Constitution stated that "all Africans and Indians," as well as their descendants who resided in the republic, would "be recognized as Haitians." As Haiti's legacy spread, people confronting slavery, colonialism, and Indigenous caste oppression increasingly sought support and refuge in Haiti. Opponents of slavery and colonialism throughout the Americas also recognized Haiti as a beacon of freedom.[45]

From its inception, the republic drew upon vibrant anti-colonial traditions. As leaders sought to replace French laws, street names, and everything that "revive[d] memories of the cruelties of this barbarous people," they urgently looked to rename the island of Saint-Domingue. Haïti had been the name used by the Indigenous Taino. It was reclaimed by revolutionary leaders as a means to honor the living presence of Taino people and their long-standing resistance to colonialism. For a time, Haitian soldiers called themselves "Las Incas," in honor of the Indigenous-led resistance of the Great

Rebellion against Spanish colonialism in the Southern Andes. In this 1781–84 rebellion, Túpac Amaru and other Andean revolutionaries had fought against colonial dispossession and *mita,* the Spanish system of forced Indigenous labor, later described by Peruvian radical José Carlos Mariátegui as mining in service of the "annihilation of human capital."[46]

Throughout Latin America, the Haitian and French Revolutions found poignant resonance. The Haitian Declaration of Independence was translated into Spanish, among other languages. Spanish ships intercepted copies of the aptly named Haitian newspaper *Le Télégraphe* on its way to Spanish ports. Horrifying Spanish officials, Haitians specifically called for the liberation of their colonies, including Mexico. Despite edicts barring incendiary written materials, officials in Mexico confiscated volumes, pamphlets, and newspapers about the French revolution, as well as playing cards that vividly depicted events of the revolution, including the execution of the French King Louis XVI. At the turn of the century, a message found pasted on a Mexican street corner proclaimed: "The most wise are the French; to follow their suggestions is not absurd. However much the laws may try, they can never stifle the cries that are inspired by nature." Official attempts to squelch anticolonial fervor failed. Mexico would send up its own "cry" in 1810, declaring its independence a few years after Haiti's in 1804.[47]

Wars of independence throughout the Americas were influenced and even incubated by Haiti. In 1795, José Leonardo Chirino, a man of African and Native descent and frequent visitor to Saint-Domingue, had led a slave rebellion in Coro, Venezuela, drawing upon both French and Haitian revolutionary traditions. Revolutionary Venezuelan leader Francisco de Miranda also found refuge in Haiti in 1806. There he wrote his *Proclamation to the Inhabitants of South America* and invented a new flag of independence to oppose Spanish colonial rule. These experiences were not lost on Simón Bolívar, the great liberator of South America. Twice in 1816, Bolívar was granted refuge by the newly independent Haitian government. By 1817, he was sailing Haitian ships manned by Haitian crews after being sheltered by the Haitian leader Alexandre Pétion. Pétion's support was conditional: he requested that Bolívar abolish slavery in every territory he liberated from Spain and refuse to sell any Africans found aboard captured vessels into slavery. In this way abolition, the centerpiece of the Haitian Revolution, became a central part of independence wars against the Spanish Empire.[48]

Abolition infused the Mexican independence movement from its inception. Three months after declaring independence from Spain in 1810, Miguel

Hidalgo issued a decree abolishing slavery. While not yet formal law, New Spain became a haven for fugitive slaves who often had Mexico in their heads as a southern escape route on the underground railroad.[49] This was formalized in 1829 when Black Indigenous Mexican President Vicente Guerrero declared an end to slavery in the country. The second article of the 1857 Mexican Constitution reaffirmed the prohibition of slavery. It added that all enslaved people could recover their liberty merely by setting foot on Mexican soil. Mexico saw itself, in contrast to the United States, as a place where slavery was not only abolished but also "unthinkable."[50]

DEBT, STABILITY, AND THE COLOR LINE

The United States emerged in the shadow of the Haitian Revolution and defined itself largely in relation to the world's first Black republic. For example, the newly independent United States quickly and generously sent its first formal allocation of foreign aid to Haiti. This aid, however, was not sent to assist Haitian rebels but instead to fortify French colonial forces as well as slave owners. Apart from the Adams administration between 1798 and 1801, US officials attempted to define themselves on the world stage alongside other major European powers. In speaking to the French ambassador in 1801, Thomas Jefferson wondered whether the United States, France, and Britain could cooperate to "confine this disease to its island." As long as "we don't allow the blacks to possess a ship," he advised, "we can allow them to exist and even maintain very lucrative commercial contacts with them." Once Haiti gained its independence, the United States joined the European powers in refusing to grant Haiti official diplomatic recognition.[51]

Some of the greatest gains the United States realized in relation to the Haitian Revolution were territorial. US officials pressed for the cession of vast swaths of French territory once it became clear that Napoléon's forces could not retake Saint-Domingue after 1802. Under the 1803 Louisiana Purchase, the United States annexed 827 million acres, doubling the size of the country. The annexation decisively failed to expand the geography of liberty. Settlement, particularly of the agriculturally rich Missouri River Basin, entailed the violent displacement and forced removal of Sioux, Cheyenne, Arapaho, Crow, Pawnee, Osage, and Comanche people, among others. Only after land was "cleared" by settlers and volunteer militias could the expanding cotton economy take root. The Louisiana Purchase intensified a brutal geography of accumulation: land violently wrested from Native people, made alienable, and transformed into private property was put into productive use through the forced labor of humans, themselves diabolically transformed into commodities under chattel slavery, all to reap cotton, the blood-rich raw material of the new republic.[52]

Land was also made productive through relations of debt. Jefferson had promoted a unique theory for seizing lands "which they [Native people] have to spare and we want." He suggested that the United States "push our trading houses" to sink Native people deep in debt. When these debts got "beyond what the individuals can pay," they would "become willing to lop them off by a cession of lands." Jefferson's theory was soon confirmed. Shortly after the Louisiana Purchase, Choctaw and Chickasaw people were cut off from Spanish markets in Pensacola and confined to US traders. In these circumscribed conditions they racked up huge debts. Without money, they were forced to offer what they did have in abundance: land. This coercive debt relationship was replicated throughout the nineteenth century.[53]

Debt was critical to US state formation from its founding. Soon after its independence, debts from as early as the Revolutionary War were bundled and sold to European financiers, largely British capitalists, in the form of bonds. National debts do not represent an absence or lack of capital; rather, they should be understood as capital. Marx, writing in the mid-nineteenth century, described the magical process whereby debt "endows barren money with the power of breeding and thus turns it into capital" without exposing it to the customary risks. Marx noted that "the sum lent is transformed into public bonds, easily negotiable, which go on functioning in their hands just as so much hard cash would." Indeed, the circulation of its bonds did not hinder the United States' economic development. Rather, the sale of those bonds financed the industrialization, urbanization, expansion, militarization, and state-making practices of the country in its formative years. As Marx further remarked, "With the national debt arose an international credit system." Through the sale of its bonds—its debt—the United States was firmly entrenched in this credit system from its inception.[54]

Investment in the emerging American republic, particularly on behalf of financiers from the British Empire, from which the United States had just won its independence, was uncertain. European investors, largely British, were eventually swayed to purchase US debts, seeing them as "stable" relative to other forms of investments. The Louisiana Purchase, for example, was enabled by a bridging loan provided to the US government by the London bank of Baring Brothers. Interest rates on that and other US loans issued by London banks were lower than those issued on Latin American bonds based on the racist assumptions that Anglo-Saxons were better equipped to repay their loans.[55] In an era of profound unrest and revolutionary revolt, market volatility was coterminous with the conflagrations of class struggle. Both the French Revolution and the Haitian Revolution—the first successful slave uprising in history—epitomized such conflagrations. In contrast to formerly popular investment sites, in particular France and Haiti, the United States emerged as a relatively more secure option, particularly for European investors. Insofar as the new government appeared equipped to control the uprisings of its own working class, maintain a system of slavery, manage racial hierarchies in workplaces, and subjugate Indigenous populations through genocidal practices, its economic development represented a more "stable" investment than the other revolutionary countries.[56] Security, therefore, meant racism, and racism meant security. Racist regimes came to be reproduced at intimate scales. As Scott Sandage writes, white men who supported or appeared to support abolition were spied upon by credit rating agencies and routinely denied business and personal loans.[57]

Primarily tutored by its former foe, Britain, the United States developed its own methods for deploying racism to secure different modes of accumulation. These nineteenth-century practices included the establishment of cotton credit chains through the reproduction and maintenance of African slavery; territorial expansion through Indigenous dispossession; the development of railroad capital secured through racial terror against Asian migrant workers; industrialization, which required the exploitation of immigrant workers from throughout Europe; and notably, the military conquest of Mexican land, the subjugation of its people, and the exploitation of its resources and financial infrastructure. Understanding how dominant notions of security continue to be conflated with repressive and genocidal racist orderings requires consideration of these foundational relationships that established the US political economy.[58]

Rather than a mystical force unleashed upon the world, the color line, as W. E. B. Du Bois elaborated it, was constructed and reinforced as a necessary corollary to the expansion of US capital. Its racist practices and logics qualified the country to receive British and other European financing. In turn, these practices and logics produced the dictates that the United States would come to impose on other countries. When the United States assumed the position of financier rather than debtor, its racist logic represented an inimitable synthesis of the formations that had effectively produced its own political economy. The first time that the United States would take on this role, displacing the British as the major financier of a national economy, occurred in Mexico.

Before the US Civil War, Frederick Douglass had toured cotton factories in Northwest England, where unemployment would soon rage. Under the Union blockade of Southern ports, while men like Charles Stillman made fortunes, English looms gathered dust and English workers faced starvation, eviction, disease, and death. As Du Bois noted, masses of people succumbing to hunger or fever and being forced into sex work "were prevalent."[59] Between November 1861 and November 1862, employment in counties like Lancashire fell by three hundred thousand. Marx wrote in the *New York Tribune:* "A great portion of the British working classes directly and severely suffers under the consequences of the Southern blockade."[60] In an effort to restore the economy, the British Chancellor of the Exchequer, William Gladstone, endorsed the recognition of Confederate independence in October 1862. The British Prime Minister mulled intervention on the side of the Confederacy. Abolitionists like Douglass now asked the British people to nevertheless do the unthinkable and support the Union cause. In public meetings, newspaper articles, and books, they pled with British people to disavow the Confederacy and oppose slavery at the expense of their own immediate economic interests. In "The Slave's Appeal to Great Britain," Douglass challenged British people: "Must the world stand still, humanity make no progress, and slavery stand for ever, lest your cotton-mills stop, and your poor cry for bread?"[61]

Astonishingly, many British workers agreed. From mill towns in Manchester to financial and trade centers in London, British workers organized mass public meetings supporting the abolition of slavery and opposing British military support for the Confederacy. These public meetings grew in number and size after emancipation became a Union war aim in January 1863. On March 26, 1863, Karl Marx attended a meeting of the London Trades Council at St. James Hall where workers expressed their solidarity with abolition. John Bright, a Quaker and mill owner, chaired the meeting. He later wrote to US abolitionist politician Charles Sumner describing abolition's "transcendent importance to labour all over the world." It was unusual for a Trades Council meeting to discuss "political issues," with workers declaring their opposition to the Confederacy and support for abolition. Henry Adams, who reported the meeting to the US State Department, described it as "an act almost without precedent in their history." Similar meetings spread across the country, often passing resolutions supporting the Union. In kind, Northern US workers sent shiploads of money and aid across the Atlantic. In the British county of Lancashire, Northern provisions amounted to over £27,000 worth of goods with over £1,000 in cash aid. British dock workers refused payment for unloading the goods. Railway workers transported the aid for free, an act of solidarity that moved many and brought others to join the cause.[62] As Frederick Douglass had observed, new spaces of accumulation had produced new political arrangements, new social organizations, and new sensibilities in a shared global space. Through capital's relative annihilation of space, Douglass believed a common vision of freedom could cohere.

> A change has now come over the affairs of mankind. Walled cities and empire have become unfashionable.... Oceans no longer divide but link nations together.... Space is comparatively annihilated. Thoughts expressed on one side of the Atlantic are distinctly heard on the other.[63]

It was out of these large public meetings of workers opposing slavery that the International Working Men's Association (IWMA) arose in 1864. In his inaugural address, Marx noted that "it was not the wisdom of the ruling classes" but "the heroic resistance" of the working classes that prevented Europe from crusading to propagate "slavery on the other side of the Atlantic." This resistance resonated deeply with abolitionist struggles led by enslaved people themselves. Shortly after its founding, the IWMA had multiple abolitionist celebrations. In 1865, it published an address "To the People of the United States of America" that proclaimed, "No more shall the salesman's hammer barter human flesh and blood in your market places, causing humanity to shudder at its cold barbarity." From its inception, the IWMA imbricated abolition with the class struggle. More than empathy, more than mere acknowledgment of other national struggles, the solidarity of the First International was built upon the powerful understanding that people could recognize one another even if they never saw each other, a possible abolitionist internationalism at the heart of proletarian internationalism.[64]

Streams of internationalism rose up alongside and against the internationalization of capital. This could be poignantly seen in Mexico at the time. In 1867, with its coffers depleted from its war with France, the Mexican state found itself unable to pay back its debts, many of which had been falsely inflated by US investors. In lieu of money, the Juárez government offered these investors what it did have in excess: land. With massive land concessions, US capital began an earnest penetration into Mexican business affairs and into the financing of the new Mexican state. These processes only intensified during the Porfiriato. Indigenous communities lost enormous tracts of their communal land holdings or *ejidos*. Through so-called "vacant lands" decrees (*baldíos*), large landowners could claim that this land was unoccupied and/or underutilized. When peasants brought their land title challenges to court, local magistrates usually ruled in favor of the landowners. By 1906, a full quarter of all of Mexico's territory, some forty-nine million hectares, were further seized for government-initiated "settlement acts." As a result of these processes, big landowners owned 81 percent of all local communities in Mexico by 1910, pushing many peasants off their land and out of their villages.[65]

Díaz had opened Mexico up to foreign capital at precisely the same time that industrial countries were seeking spaces of capitalist investment and Mexico was pulled into the "frenetic" development of world capitalism. To facilitate this process, Mexican banks made a disproportionate amount of credit available to foreign interests. The federal government also eased restrictions on foreign trade and lending. US capital, along with British capital, took advantage of Díaz's concessions and invested much fixed capital in the landscape, especially in the form of railroad lines. Thousands of miles of rail were laid at the end of the nineteenth century. The lines were often extensions of US lines and provided outlets from mines to prominent American centers and ports. During the Porfiriato, more than a quarter of all US investment lay in Mexico.[66]

By the end of the Porfiriato, the main source of export earnings, Mexico's mineral resources, were almost entirely foreign-controlled. By 1897, US investments in Mexico totaled more than $200 million. This figure *quintupled* in the following fourteen years. Trade between the United States and Mexico grew from $7 million in 1860 to $36 million in 1890, and $166 million by 1910. US companies like Rockefeller's Anaconda Mining, the

Guggenheims' American Smelting and Refining Company, and the Phelps Dodge Corporation gained a disproportionate share of the market. As noted in the introduction, by the outbreak of the Revolution in 1910, American investors owned more than 22 percent of Mexico's surface. By the following year, US capital had captured 80 percent of all mining interests.[67]

US capitalists not only determined the movement of capital and the forms of its investment, but in their relations with the emergent bourgeoisie, they began to exert significant local authority in the appointment of judges, control of banks, determination of employment with foreign companies, and dispensing of credit. Thus, the pattern of rule developed in Mexico did not constitute direct control over state power but rather disproportionate influence over political and juridical systems that indirectly determined the dispensing of state funds, assets, land, and the adjudication of legal challenges. The imperialist penetration of US finance into different regions of the country significantly reshaped forms of local governance without ever requiring a declaration of war or a change of flag.[68]

As Mexico's unincorporated spaces became primary sites of intensified investment, observers noted a shift in the spatial logic of capital. Unlike the territorial objectives that had driven US interests in the US-Mexico War, and unlike the farcical imperial fantasies that drove Napoléon III's invasion of Mexico, the objectives of US financiers at the end of the Civil War were related but distinct. By the late nineteenth century, US investors perceived that they could exert dramatic economic and political power without the military mobilization required for direct territorial acquisition. This new modality was irrevocably tied to the old. As Mario Gill describes, one-half of Mexico was lost to annexation in 1848, while "the other half fell via an open door to finance capital." After fighting for independence, first from Spain and later from the United States and France, the Mexican government now faced a different kind of invasion from a force that flew no flag.[69]

YANKEE IMPERIALISM

In the late nineteenth and early twentieth centuries, people across Latin America and the Caribbean raged against what was popularly perceived as "Yankee imperialism." As figures like José Martí, Augusto Sandino, and James Weldon Johnson attested, US power was obscenely evident in multiple forms. It was easy to observe, for example, in the looming or actively violent presence of its military forces. From afar, it was less easy to see more shadowy forms of influence: the crude racialized management techniques employed by mostly white supervisors in US-owned companies; the creeping diffusion of US culture in new tastes, values, and sounds; or the swaggering and predatory attitudes of Yankee fortune hunters in Latin American bars and brothels.[70]

Writing in Mexico in 1906, revolutionary leader and journalist Ricardo Flores Magón observed another, more insidious form of control: *el incremento del capital americano en nuestro país* ("the increase of American capital in our country"). In its courts, public offices, banks, and effectively in all the internal affairs of the country, he saw Mexico becoming increasingly subordinate to American influence. It won't be long, he wrote, until nothing is done in the country without the approval *del Tío Samuel,* "of Uncle Sam." In his many writings, Flores Magón identified US power as operating through more formidable though less easily identifiable methods, securing the political capacities to dictate the terms of domestic capital investment. In doing so, he explained how American financers, rather than national democratic institutions, controlled the production of Mexico's physical and economic infrastructure. This less visible form of control was generative of the other more obvious and visceral forms of American power, a sinister sign of things to come.[71]

In 1914, Flores Magón addressed the workers of the world in his "Mexican Manifesto," writing more bluntly: "Workers of America! Have we Mexicans no message for you? Workers of the World! Is there nothing we can teach you? . . . Do you suppose that we, over whose wealth of mine and field and forest the earth's money-lords have warred, do not comprehend the capitalist system, or that, until we have read Karl Marx, we can be robbed of surplus value without being aware of it?" Here, as in his many other writings, Flores Magón sought to overcome barriers in comprehending who composed the working class and what constituted the class struggle. He commanded the workers of the world to understand the Mexican people as a revolutionary force, not only for the liberation of Mexico but for the global class struggle as a whole. "Master the great lesson," he wrote, "[for it is] written for you in blood beyond the Rio Grande."[72]

TWO

———

How to Make a Map

SMALL SHAREHOLDERS AND GLOBAL RADICALS IN
REVOLUTIONARY MEXICO

IN THE AGE OF THE NEW IMPERIALISM, the world was turned inside out. The dark slumbering core of the earth was flooded with light, wrenched by fiery blasts, then hacked and dragged, bit by craggy bit, to the surface. From the forced mouths of mine shafts, its innards were scavenged. Silver, copper, and zinc were dredged out of Mexico; gold was wrested from the Yukon lands of the Klondike; and diamonds were plucked from the bowels of South Africa. From deposits of unburied iron, a new exoskeleton of rail fused together across the horizon. Railways screamed over continents with the velocity of finance, tearing new pathways of commerce and trade, and bruising the land around it. Coals disgorged from the mines of West Virginia, Colorado, and Manchuria were made radiant with fire and fed, inexhaustibly, to furnaces. Skies blackened with the spew of smokestacks. Ash drifted onto windowsills. Ash was coughed up from throats. Where forests had been felled and burned to make charcoal, this era reached deep beneath tombs, down past the ancient muck and humus to grab the earth's vital forces. Oil that had coursed through subterranean veins was transfused into the life-blood of modern industry. Rubber ran like devil's milk from Congolese vines into waiting Belgian ships, becoming tires, wire insulation, and machine belts, the sinews of industrial production. From the ground, grains were coaxed to even heights over gridded fields, sheathed into uniform bushels, then loaded into gaping containers. Over rails, roads, ship lines, and pounded copper wires, goods were moved, tracked, and transubstantiated into value. This new geometry of motion was animated by global capital, but it was built and shaped by disciplined muscle. Hands, arms, backs, and thighs were lowered and bent, again and again, becoming pulsing metronomes of economic time. From the dark center of the earth at the turn of the century, capital came dripping with dirt and blood from every pore. How, some wondered, could it be otherwise? The world had been turned inside out. Could it also be turned upside down?[1]

SURELY INTERNATIONALISM

Across the windswept expanse of the Sonoran Desert, where the Colorado River snakes through the Mexicali Valley and slips down jagged rocks before it spills into the Sea of Cortez, there, where the US border looms like a mirage, an Okinawan immigrant named Shinsei "Paul" Kōchi found internationalism. Shipwrecked and shoeless, Kōchi walked for miles in a daze. He stepped gingerly on thorny scrub and walked reverently around the discarded canteens and dried bones of those who had come before. It was to them, the "numerous and nameless," that Kōchi dedicated his reflections in *Imin no Aiwa* (*An Immigrant's Sorrowful Tale*). Following the river north, Kōchi searched for food, warmth, and shelter with a small band of survivors from China, Mexico, and Japan in December 1917. Worldwide, millions had fled their countries, compelled by starvation, debt, dispossession, political repression, and the ravages of the First World War. Immigrants who were not allowed to enter countries "with dignity through the front door" routinely risked their lives "breaking in through the back gate." Those who perished were often "buried in the sea" while others "left their bones to dry on the empty desert." As Kōchi observed, the "tragedy" of these journeys came not from heedless risk nor naïve adventurism but "a contradiction born precisely out of modern capitalist society."[2]

For many like Paul Kōchi, the world of 1917 was at once tragic and aflame with possibility.[3] At twenty-eight, he and his "comrade" Seitoku Miyasato had set sail for Mexico, escaping arrest and political persecution at home. The two friends hailed from Nakijin Village in Okinawa, the largest island in a South Sea chain annexed by Japan only decades prior. Despised by mainland Japanese, Okinawans struggled against accusations of being "backwards" southerners in need of centralized political rule, strengthened work ethic, linguistic assimilation, and the abandonment of their "savage" cultural traditions.[4] Kōchi and Miyasato were active in an underground reading group of village teachers opposed to Japanese despotism. Authorities blacklisted members upon discovering their copies of *Daisan Teikoku,* a journal critical of the government. Fearing repression, the pair planned to escape Okinawa, leaving their young families behind. Convinced they would return after a brief sojourn, they boarded a steamer at the port in Naha. Once aboard, Kōchi noted the "inexpressible feeling" that welled up in his fellow passengers as they looked upon the possible "last sight of their homeland" and of their loved ones. As the "unfeeling" ship set sail, Kōchi and Miyasato watched their young wives and children disappear, "looking permanently abandoned," as the harbor receded.[5] The men stood together on the deck, "arm still linked to arm," until their "mountain home sank beneath the horizon."[6]

Internationalism, for Kōchi, began with a sense of identification. In Hawai'i, where the ship refueled, he felt profound kinship with the Indigenous Kanaka Maoli dockworkers loading and unloading cargo. He observed the first-class passengers' delight as they threw coins at young Hawaiians, compelling them to dive into the waves chasing the sinking pocket change. He recognized that Hawai'i, "in its climate, customs, products, as well as its recent history," was like Okinawa: a remote chain of mountainous islands inhabited by people whose language, culture, and sovereignty were all threatened from the mainland. Hawai'i, like Okinawa, was also dominated by sugarcane cultivation, a commonality that would have been apparent to the nearly ten thousand Okinawans who labored in the Hawai'ian sugarcane plantations at the time. Kōchi listened and felt profoundly moved by the musical resonance between the two cultures: "That heart-tugging farewell *Aloha Oe* was, in fact, the farewell song to the fleeing king of Hawaii. (Our famous *Sanyamā* was just such a song for the king of Okinawa.)" Such connections only deepened throughout his journey.[7]

As the ship briefly docked in Southern California's San Pedro harbor, Kōchi, Miyasato, and all the other Asian passengers found themselves trapped aboard. The 1917 Immigration Act and similar diplomatic agreements prevented immigrants from the so-called "barred Asiatic zone" from entering the country. Kōchi railed against these laws and against the nativism fomented during the First World War that kept Asians from ever setting "one foot down" on US soil.[8] A flurry of indignation overtook the passengers. One Japanese man jumped overboard, desperate to reach shore. Passengers looked on in horror as the man drowned in the cold waters of the Pacific. Despondent in his confinement onboard, Kōchi stared at Catalina Island off the California coast. Slowly he began to reappraise his situation. He considered the long, violent history of US settlement and Indigenous dispossession that drove Native people like the Tongva "into the mountain recesses" to starve. He realized that if the same exclusionary nativism that was applied to him had also been "radically applied" to the United States, no settler would be allowed to set foot in the country. Kōchi condemned US immigration laws and observed that the national boundaries they maintained were themselves illegitimate. Considering the intertwined histories of racist immigration laws and rapacious settler colonialism, Kōchi imagined internationalist bonds forged through shared rage: a web of refusal seething within and against national borders.[9]

With five hundred immigrants from Japan, India, and China still aboard, barred from entering the United States, the steamship *Anyōmaru* chugged south, destined for Brazil. While many in the upper decks sailed leisurely toward exotic lands and thrilling business ventures, most passengers had been coerced onboard by the churning transformations of the global economy. Since the late nineteenth century, countries newly pulled into the frenzy of modern finance saw intensified investment in extractive industries and commercialized agriculture. The subsequent evisceration of communal land holdings and subsistence farming practices had uprooted millions of peasants, including those en route from the "barred Asiatic zone." Many of the *Anyōmaru*'s passengers were bound for contract work in the Caribbean and throughout Latin America, often following labor recruiters' promised jobs. Japanese and Okinawan immigrants sought to join compatriots in Brazilian mining communities. Along with Chinese counterparts, they also sought contracts in places like Peru and throughout the Caribbean. The swirling chaos of colonialism and war also produced its own global circuits, dragging colonial soldiers, particularly from India, onto foreign battlefields. As their labors were conscripted into war economies, their ranks expanded in what Priyamvada Gopal describes as a "world-wide belt of insurgencies."[10] Radical Japanese students who called themselves "comrades of the four seas" invited Kōchi and Miyasato to join them in Cuba. The two friends had other plans. A ship's porter had hinted about the possibility of sneaking into the United States through Mexico. This is what the pair resolved to do once the ship docked in Oaxaca.[11]

From the moment their "feet touched down" in Mexico, Kōchi and Miyasato were immediately conscious of being "immigrants owning nothing but our bodies." They were detained and quarantined in harrowing conditions along with other immigrants.[12] The men looked on in horror as a prisoner from India was stripped and then doused with sulfur, his money belt stolen in the process. As they shared with him their meager funds, the man thanked them for being "Buddhas in Hell." A few days later, several dozen

Asian immigrants, including some of their fellow Okinawan villagers, joined their cell. The area was "well-known for its searing winds," which blew through the barred windows day and night, creating "sandstorms" inside the jail.[13] Covered in the same dust, Kōchi understood his fellow prisoners as "convicts banished to Siberia in Tsarist Russia," a timely comparison given that Russian people had recently overthrown that Tsarist regime during the Bolshevik Revolution. The experience was not lost on the men. Given their travels, confinements, and commitments, Kōchi declared retrospectively that he and Miyasato were already "internationalists."[14]

Released from prison and into the heat of the Revolution, Kōchi and Miyasato (along with their Spanish-speaking countrymen) raced toward the US border. The men traversed a convulsive landscape, dancing to guitars in Mazatlán and narrowly escaping bandits as their train hugged the western coast through Culiacán. They launched a small boat out of Guaymas. For a week, they sailed north up the inlet of the Gulf of California. In a disaster, the boat caught fire, forcing all passengers to jump overboard. When they reassembled on shore, they discovered that only thirteen of the original passengers remained. Shipwrecked in the Sonoran Desert on December 2, 1917, the small group had next to no supplies. They collected "snow waters" from the Colorado River in rusty tin cans. They ripped strips of cloth and tore out their trouser pockets in vain attempts to protect their feet from sagebrush, cacti, and the cold. A crumbling biscuit was shared among the men. Tearing down the shore, Kōchi called out for his friend. His cries of "Miyasato! Miyasato!" were swallowed by the sea. The group was forced to press on.

In his travels throughout northern Mexico, Kōchi continually discovered and rediscovered internationalism. His group was saved by an Indigenous Yaqui family, who fed the men, gave them shelter, and offered them homemade leather shoes. The warmth of the family reminded him of home. He encountered a French trader who smuggled him to the border under a pile of hay to avoid the eyes of Mexican guards. This kindness, he said, "was surely internationalism." When Kōchi finally reached the border, it was a group of Chinese immigrant workers who met him. Wrote Kōchi, "It seemed that for them we were all immigrants travelling the same road and they understood our situation from their hearts. This 'class consciousness' cuts across race and nationality and promotes mutual understanding which, if preserved and extended, would make the deserts bloom."[15]

Paul Kōchi's story demonstrates how the uprooted, dispossessed, and despised of the world came to know each other in shadows, in the tangled spaces of expulsion, extraction, transportation, debt, exploitation, and destruction: the garroting circuits of modern capital. Whether crammed in tight ship quarters; knocking together over the rails; sweating and swaying in the relentless tempo of industrial agriculture; inhaling the dank air of mine shafts; hearing each other breathing, coughing, fighting, singing, snoring, and sighing through thin walls; or corralled like livestock in jails and prisons, the contradictions of modern capital were shared in its intimate spaces. Within such sites, people discovered that the circuits of revolution, like the countervailing circuits of capital, were realizable in motion, often through unplanned assemblages. Roaring at their backs were the revolutionary currents of the late nineteenth and early twentieth centuries, currents that howled from the metropolitan hearts of empire and wailed across the peripheries of the global world system. Standing before them, in the middle of its own revolution, was Mexico. From the vantage point of these struggles, the new century did not simply portend the inevitability of urban revolts and insurgencies at the point of production but an epoch of peasant wars, rural uprisings, anti-colonial movements, and, of course, the Mexican Revolution. Mexico, as both a real country and an imagined space of revolution, would become a crucible of internationalism for the world's "rebels" like Paul Kōchi.[16]

Paul Kōchi's *Imin no Aiwa* presents internationalism as nearly an inevitable phenomenon. By narrating his path from Okinawa to the United States through Mexico, Kōchi describes how travel along the contradictory routes newly limned by capital and imperialism enabled him to acquire a radical global consciousness. In describing his encounters with Indigenous people and other immigrants along the way, he offers a sense of how such consciousness could be produced through the contradictory social spaces of ships, trains, boats, in detention, and through covert passage across Mexico toward the US border. Kōchi's story offers an important perspective into the relationship between the political economy of the period and the formation of a revolutionary consciousness. In this, Kōchi was not alone.

The transformation of the global economy certainly set the stage for the development of an internationalist consciousness. But if all that was required for internationalism were the conditions of a hard journey, the world would be full of internationalists. As significant as Kōchi's travels were, there were far more people who lived during the era of the Mexican Revolution, who even came to Mexico at the time, who did not become internationalists. This was particularly true for the fortune hunters who arrived seeking land, fame, or wealth in the country in spite of the many radical possibilities presented by the Revolution. This was also true for many Asian immigrants like Kōchi, particularly Chinese immigrants who suffered extraordinary violence and repression at the hands of state and non-state actors. The paths of those who came, saw, but chose moderate or outright reactionary paths reveal some of the fetters inhibiting the making of internationalism. This chapter explores both these possibilities and barriers.[17]

In the era of its Revolution, Mexico represented multiple configurations of space: it was simultaneously a fixed place on the map, a place made meaningful relative to the places it bordered or was connected to through roads, rails, and ports, and it was also an imagined space upon which multiple competing fantasies were projected. The chapter considers the experiences of radicals who lived in, traveled to, or found themselves in Mexico during the during the fighting phase of the Revolution, 1910–20. The collective act of making new worlds, as they discovered, required a reckoning with the seductions of nationalism, the social relations of imperialism, and the spatial imaginaries of capital. Internationalism, in other words, had to be forged, not simply found. To do so, as this chapter shows, it had to compete with the enticements of the color line, the racist and gendered fantasies of the New Imperialism.

THE OTHER 1917

We would gain much, and human justice would gain much, if all the peoples of our America and all the nations of old Europe understood that the cause of revolutionary Mexico and the cause of Russia are the cause of humanity, the supreme interest of all oppressed people.

EMILIANO ZAPATA, 1918

In 1917, the Russian Bolshevik Revolution proposed to be the first of many revolutions to change the global order.[18] People all over the planet were swept up in the possibilities of the moment. What did it mean to be a Bolshevik? There were possibly as many paths as there were interpretations. For some, Bolshevism represented the culmination of already existing desires and activities. For others, it heralded unimagined possibilities of state power. *Völker hört die Signale* ("Peoples, hear the signals!") was the German translation of the refrain of "The Internationale." In Cuba, tobacco workers were moved by the concept of soviets and organized their workplaces accordingly. In Spain, radicals were largely swayed by what they perceived as an expanded practice of their already existing anarchism. Their international newspapers translated the Bolshevik Revolution as a victory of anarchism and syndicalism. For socialists, communists, and anarchists throughout the United States, it appeared that a new day had dawned. The possibilities were infinite.[19]

By the Bolshevik Revolution in 1917, the Mexican people had several years of fierce and bloody struggle behind them. After the successful overthrow of Porfirio Díaz's dictatorship and a succession of elected and unelected new leaders, acts of insurgency pervaded the entire country. Peasant leaders had seized land, organized communal holdings, and demanded revolutionary national redistribution schemes. Labor organizers had orchestrated massive strikes in industries as well as in semi-proletarianized spaces of capitalist agriculture, threatening foreign investments. Choruses of the dispossessed and exploited clamored for a total redistribution of wealth. Along with middle-class reformers and radicalized officials, they sought and won recognition of many basic rights and protections, enshrining them in the new Constitution. Throughout the country, *campesinos* also attacked symbols and practices of domination, mobilized class solidarity, and practiced an incipient form of international solidarity. Furthermore, they did this at the doorstep of US empire and in the shadow of its military.[20] These transformations doubtless exacted an enormous toll on the population, with around two million lives lost to war, starvation, and the collapse of basic services. The future was uncertain for the still-evolving Mexican state. Many possible revolutionary and counterrevolutionary paths lay before it.[21]

1917 marked the creation of Mexico's revolutionary Constitution, one of the most radical and comprehensive in modern political history for its nationalization of resources and sweeping land reforms. In cities like Orizaba, over a million copies of the Constitution were sold. Enshrined in law were provisions ensuring the nationalization of resources in defiance of US and British holdings, massive education programs, and proposals for sweeping land redistribution. Article 27, for example, declared that lands and water belonged to the nation, setting limits on the inviolability of private property. Article 123 offered dramatic protections for workers—guaranteeing their right to organize, their right to collective bargaining, as well as three months' maternity leave, an eight-hour day, a minimum wage, and equal pay for equal work, to be paid in cash, not company scrip. It obligated employers to provide clean, sanitary, and affordable housing to their workers, as tenant organizers well understood. It also restricted child labor, banned extorting practices of company stores and debt peonage, and set new regulations on employers' ability to fire workers. These shifts were reflected in popular culture, such as in Veracruz, where children were named after state laws that regulated the clergy and sanctioned the expropriation of private property. While many of these tenets wouldn't be enforced until much later, if at all, the promises of the new Constitution signified a great cultural shift. Radical articles enshrined ideals of a new society and gave authority to movements to push for their implementation. Radicals from around the world found themselves absorbed into this revolutionary atmosphere. One of them was M. N. Roy.[22]

NATIONAL AND COLONIAL QUESTIONS

When Narendranath Bhattacharya set sail from India in August 1915, he was seeking arms for the Independence movement to overthrow British imperial rule. By the time he returned in October 1920, he had changed his name to Manabendra Nath Roy and was fueled by the belief that India's fate was linked to subjugated people around the world. For M. N. Roy, the national liberation of India was no longer an end in itself but a necessary step toward global revolution.[23]

In his travels and studies, Roy had come to understand where and how the wealth of nations was produced. His early life in India, observing famine amid plenty under British rule, had made him a militant. In the Philippines, China, Korea, Malaysia, Java, Indonesia, and Japan, his crossings with national revolutionary leaders such as Sun Yat-sen, Ho Chi Minh, and Korea's Syngman Rhee forced him to reassess imperialism's devastating reach. In the New York Public Library, Roy read Marx and developed a critical language to explain how the epic violence moving people and things around the planet could be mundanely converted into Wall Street ticker tape.[24] In Mexico between 1917 and 1920, during the Mexican Revolution, Roy was transformed. There, in the "land of my rebirth," he began to see that "the overthrow of the capitalist system" was impossible without "the breaking up of the colonial empire." In 1920, he wrote, "Without the control of the extensive markets and vast fields of exploitation in the colonies, the capitalist powers of Europe cannot maintain their existence even for a short time." What allowed the imperialist bourgeoisie to maintain social control over Western workers, he argued, was the very existence of the colonies.[25]

Roy, in some circles, is best known for anti-colonial interventions he made within the Communist Party. In 1920, Vladimir Lenin presented his "Theses on the National and Colonial Question" at the 2nd International Congress of the Comintern. Lenin proposed that Communist Parties must "render direct aid to the revolutionary movements among the dependent and under-privileged nations," which included Ireland, India, and Black people in the United States, among others. In these nations, Lenin recommended that the Party "enter into a temporary alliance" with bourgeois nationalist elements, groups he believed could best marshal support and resources. While Lenin's original thesis recognized political actors from non-Western countries, it insinuated that these actors lacked sufficient consciousness and direction for revolutionary organization.[26]

Roy saw contradictions in this formulation. If the Party sought to foment a revolutionary overthrow of the capitalist system through the seizure of power by the working class, why would it compromise its principles and organize among the bourgeoisie in the colonies? Roy argued that the colonies possessed their own working classes with consistent revolutionary aims. He believed that authority needed to be given to the "masses of workers and peasants" and not the self-elected representatives who failed to represent their interests. He described the two struggles as fundamentally different, with the "bourgeois national democrats" striving to establish "a free national state," while the majority of people were revolting against the very system "which permits such brutal exploitation." These "contradictory forces," he wrote, "cannot develop together."[27]

Roy believed that the colonies were central to the struggle against capital-ism since, according to his logic, exploitation in the colonies provided the main source of wealth for industrialized nations. "The fountain head from which European capitalism draws its main strength is no longer to be found in the industrial countries of Europe," he wrote, "but in the colonial posses-sions and dependencies."[28] This argument drew attention to the effects of the color line in the Party's understanding of class struggle. Roy's analysis sug-gested the existence of a resistant consciousness among these populations, even if it often appeared unconsciously. He compelled the Party to recognize the Indian revolutionary movement as "a vital part of the world proletarian struggle against capitalism."[29]

Many delegates balked at Roy's argument. John Reed, the delegate from the US Communist Labor Party, vehemently disagreed, asserting that Black people in the US were a small, geographically contained population, seeking social equality rather than class struggle. A delegate from the British Socialist Party argued that British workers would not support an anti-imperialist uprising in India, since they would only see it as treason. It was commonly assumed that socialist revolution would lead to the automatic liberation of the colonies. It followed that the Communist Party would focus its revolutionary efforts on organizing the industrialized proletariat of the Western world. Roy challenged this configuration. He promoted the centrality of the colonized and racially subjugated world in the class struggle, and thereby countered the ideal of the classically conceived white industrial proletariat, an image reinforced by the color line. In doing so, Roy's intervention helped to reconfigure a struggle that many communists believed they well understood, and to which they had accordingly committed their lives.[30]

While arousing much consternation, Roy's comments were also met with a great deal of excitement. The twenty-five delegates from Asia, such as Lao Hsiu-Chao of the Chinese Socialist Workers Party, who were fighting for recognition in both their home countries and also in the Comintern, rejoiced at Roy's comments offering recognition and support to communist revolution in the East.[31] Roddy Connolly, son of the famed Irish internationalist revolutionary James Connolly and representing the Communist Party of Ireland, "enthusiastically endorsed" the recognition of the Irish anti-colonial struggle. The theses also gave America's Black Bolsheviks new authority. After being serially ignored in national leadership circles, "Black radicals found a podium and an audience in the new headquarters of international Communism." With this opening, other Black radicals, like poet Claude McKay and delegate Otto Huiswoud, would come to insist that the party foreground questions of racism and white supremacy in its analysis of labor, capital, and liberation.[32]

M. N. Roy's 1920 intervention is no musty detail dredged from the annals of Left history. Radicals nearly a century later continue to grapple with the implications of his arguments. They challenge many widely held beliefs, such as the idea that struggles for racial equality are discrete or separable from class struggle, that colonial struggles are incompatible with Marxist analyses, or that racism is a minor factor in producing spaces of capital accumulation. In Roy's writing we see an early iteration of the idea that the problem of the color line lies at the heart of the global class struggle. It was not in India or Russia where Roy came to this position, but in revolutionary Mexico.[33]

M. N. Roy entered Mexico in the fiery year of 1917 and was "sucked up" into "an atmosphere surcharged with great expectations." For Roy, along with all other "left-wing socialists" he was around in Mexico, it was a defiant moment of possibility. In Mexico, Roy experienced a "rise of the revolutionary temperature."[34] There, he was faced with the dilemma of squaring his newfound admiration for communism with his own nationalism. The Mexican Revolution gave him an opportunity to think anew about his political position. Not long after he arrived in the country, Roy was asked to pen some articles about the Indian struggle against British imperialism. The editor of the Mexican popular paper *El Pueblo* believed that such a story would find sympathetic ears in Mexico. Since Mexico had overthrown its own colonial rule but was still seeking actual independence, the editor reasoned that Mexican audiences would "benefit [from] a knowledge of your country and the struggle of its people for freedom." The assignment gave Roy pause. As he reflected in his memoir: "The spectacle of poverty of the Mexican people was no less grim than that of the Indian. To tell the Mexican all about the poverty of the Indian and its cause, British exploitation, etc., would be like carrying coal to Newcastle."[35]

Realizing that a standard anti-British tract might not compel a Mexican audience, Roy thought about how he could make Indian history legible and relevant. He turned to Marxism to make his case:

> In the articles I outlined the picture of India past and present, as a picture of class struggle. The poverty of the Indian masses was the result of economic exploitation by British imperialism and native feudalism. The liberation of the Indian masses, therefore, required not only the overthrow of British imperialism, but subversion of the feudal patriarchal order which constituted the social foundation of the foreign political rule. The corollary was that India needed a social revolution, not mere national independence.[36]

Roy was still sympathetic to the events that had brought him to a position of Indian nationalism, and he remained dedicated to opposing the racism, starvation, poverty, dispossession, and indignity that he had experienced in India. In Mexico, he was forced to broaden his analysis of power to account for the similarity of conditions he had experienced there. In the additional context of the Bolshevik Revolution, Roy began to wrestle with the role capitalism played in producing these conditions at a global scale. These early articles inaugurated Roy's "sudden jump from die-hard nationalism to communism." Triangulating the contexts of Russia, Mexico, and India, Roy began to think about the intersecting forces of racism, capitalism, and imperialism, as well as the logics that held them together. In this regard, he began to pay more attention to the country he was in and to the revolution amid which he was living.[37]

SPACES OF THE REVOLUTION

In Mexico, M. N. Roy began to perceive the enormous diversity of forms that the struggles of the Revolution had already taken. Just as the French Revolution was composed of different tactics, revolts, and targets from village to village, Mexico also possessed a great variety of regional interpretations, goals, and means. The revolution was, as some have suggested, "a constellation of local revolutions" that prefigured the foundation of the new state.[38] Since Mexico was not a hermetically sealed or culturally insulated territory but a product of global forces, within each region global relations were differently inflected. For Roy, these forces slowly came into view. Popular depictions of the Revolution often focused on the southern state of Morelos, where armed villagers led by Emiliano Zapata occupied sugar plantations and rose up against their large-scale landowners. In protesting the loss of their common land and water rights alongside their dispossession and exploitation, the villagers gave sugar company owners and administrators little alternative but to fulfill their revolutionary demands. Given these transformations, Zapata was able to understand how the modernization and dispossession of people in Morelos were linked to the investment of foreign capital. In his 1917 "Manifesto of the People," he declared his intention to "emancipate the country from the economic domination of the foreigner."[39]

Roy first came to Mexico with a letter of introduction directed to General Salvador Alvarado, socialist governor of the state of Yucatán. While Roy did not ultimately make that meeting, he had been inspired to visit the southern Mexican peninsula for its unique convergences of radical traditions. This region had a deep insurgent history. For a short time, Mayo Indians had set up an autonomous state in the southern part of Yucatán that had remained independent until 1902. General Alvarado had been swept into power by a revolt of the Mayo Indians, who installed a slate of self-professed socialists to their governing body. In 1912, the Casa del Obrero Mundial, the House of the

World Worker, an anarcho-syndicalist-inspired trade union that organized the country's emergent industrial working class, was founded in the region. The ideologies of the Casa had been inspired by Ricardo Flores Magón's organization the Partido Liberal Mexicano (PLM), which had articulated many of the key ideals of the Mexican Revolution, and the Industrial Workers of the World (IWW), a US-based anarcho-syndicalist organization whose interests overlapped greatly with the mission of the PLM in Mexico. Members were also influenced by the Russian anarchist Piotr Kropotkin and the Spanish anarchist Francisco Ferrer Guardia. The Casa itself was home to a number of radicals from throughout the country and beyond, including revolutionary artist José Clemente Orozco; his teacher, Dr. Atl, who had been inspired by his travels in European radical circles; and the Black radical from Dallas, Texas, Lovett Fort-Whiteman. Fort-Whiteman spent several years in the Yucatán peninsula. From the early years of the revolution until 1917, he witnessed leaders of the Revolution reform sex work, establish schools, fight the Catholic Church, and publicly punish landowners for crimes committed against their workers. He was inspired by these massive cultural shifts and the radical change they portended. After his time in Mexico, Fort-Whiteman would become one of the very first African Americans to sojourn to Moscow, pursuing a vision of global freedom through the Soviet project.[40]

In Mexico City, Roy would encounter other foreign radicals similarly opposed to US capitalist imperialism. Carleton Beals, Linn Gale, and Charles Phillips were some of the hundreds of American pacifist, anarchist, and socialist "slackers" who had escaped the draft and found it "more pleasant and profitable to be in Mexico than Leavenworth [Penitentiary]," according to Samuel Gompers.[41] There, they participated in Mexican politics, produced radical publications such as *Gale's Magazine,* and tried to advance a revolutionary socialist movement. Mexico offered them the unique opportunity to experience the brutality of US imperialism, an experience they were largely spared in the United States. Many were radicalized by the experience. For others, Mexico offered a "way station" of sorts where they could experiment with political ideas but where they ultimately felt little accountability. Nonetheless, many Mexican political organizations and presses were heartened by their presence and excited that people from the United States would take a stand against US imperialism in defense of Mexico. As a result of their agitation efforts and writings, more people in the United States became aware of the Revolution.[42]

The possibilities available in Mexico did not guarantee radical outcomes. As Roy would describe in his debate with Lenin, the sway of capitalist forces would not necessarily lend themselves to revolutionary ends. In fact, there was a good chance that aspiring bourgeois figures would reinforce the rule of capital through the color line—even those who had been victimized by it. For this reason, Roy did not believe that a transition through capitalism would produce a revolution of the color line. He implored his comrades from Western countries to "cease to fall victims to the imperialist cry that the masses of the East are backward races and must go through the hell fires of capitalistic exploitation to escape." Recognizing both the Indian and the Mexican struggles as part of the class struggle was essential for a global redefinition of revolution. Similarly, Roy understood the necessity of convincing those from colonized countries or under imperial rule that they were fighting more than a national struggle against racism. They had to overthrow capitalism as well. If not, the same conditions were guaranteed to persist.

Like Paris, Moscow, and Harlem, Mexico City was a place where desires could be imputed and the shape of new world could be imagined. Radicals like Roy encountered both the possibilities and limits of theory. In Mexico City, Roy gained his "first experience in practical politics" organizing with the Socialist Party and then heading "the first Communist Party outside of Russia." Inspired by the new Soviet project, Roy was involved with plans to form a Socialist Latin American Union, which would be a "powerful international instrument of mutual co-operation and common resistance to the overlordship of the northern colossus." In December 1918, several hundred delegates from across Mexico, as well as Central and Southern America, met to form a Latin America League. Banners at the conference proclaimed, "Down with Yankee Imperialism," "Petroleum Belongs to the Mexican People," "Long Live the Revolutionary Alliance of Latin American Republics," and "Long Live the Soviet Republic of Mexico." It was argued that because socialism was international, the Socialist Party could not be limited by the confines of a single country. Accordingly, at that conference, M. N. Roy was elected General Secretary of El Partido Socialista Regional Mexico.[43]

Subsequently, Roy was involved in the formation of the Mexican Communist Party. As he asked in his memoirs, "Until the middle of 1919, no Communist Party had been formed anywhere. Why should not Mexico, true to her revolutionary tradition, take the lead?"[44] In that same year, Roy helped form and headed the Latin American Bureau of the Communist International. In the conference establishing that party, a major highlight was the outline of a Communist Party platform, designed to back "up the anti-imperialist struggle of the oppressed and subjected people."[45] The platform became the supplements to the "Theses on the National and Colonial Question" that Roy would represent in Moscow a year later.

On leaving Mexico for Moscow, Roy reflected:

> I left the land of my rebirth an intellectually free man, though with a new faith. But the philosophical solvent of the faith was inherent in itself. I no longer believed in political freedom without the content of economic liberation and social justice. . . . But I had also learned to attach greater importance to an intelligent understanding of the idea of revolution. The propagation of that idea was more important than arms. With the new conviction, I started on my way back to India, round the world.[46]

M. N. Roy produced a unique synthesis between the color line and the class struggle. Because he saw capitalism as intrinsic to the project of imperialism and colonialism, he did not merely affix Marxist rhetoric to a project of national emancipation. By understanding the global class struggle as it actually unfolded rather than as it was prophesized, he defied the conviction that colonial struggles were discrete and secondary to the main objective of revolutionary communism. Roy's experience with the Mexican Revolution helped him comprehend the ways in which fates were linked and objectives were shared in the struggle against racism and capitalism. His experience in Mexico expanded his conception of a worldwide struggle for freedom. Global revolution could only come through such an understanding.

FREE SOIL OR WAY STATION

In the bloody year of 1919, marred by white mob race riots, famed Black boxer Jack Johnson became a cultural fixture in Mexico. As one of the most renowned celebrities of his day, he helped to popularize the jazz clubs, bars, and cabarets over the border, like the Newport Bar and the Main Event. Even the *New York Times* deemed Tijuana "Jack Johnson's Social Headquarters."[47] Johnson also gained fame for his boxing matches in Mexico, some of which were said to be funded by Pancho Villa. Other bouts were fought before huge crowds in bullfighting rings. Still others were fought in northern towns adjacent to the US–Mexico border. The proximity was not accidental. Johnson was invested in spreading the message that Mexico offered Black people freedom and prosperity. The US government believed that Johnson was "using Mexico as a beachhead of subversion." Indeed, Johnson wielded his celebrity in Mexico to encourage Black migration. As part of this project, he started a land company to facilitate settlement. Many heeded Johnson's call. A group of American Garveyites teamed up with investors to build a "Little Liberia" in Baja California. At twenty dollars an acre, they advertised that Black people who "want to be really free" could be "'sovereigns of [their] own labor.'"[48]

But as other Black people capable of moving across US borders often found, the promises of anti-racism could never hold in lands dominated by the capitalist system. Whereas some people would find their position elevated in Mexico, Mexicans of African descent were found among the poorest sectors of the population. Mexico's legacy in the slave trade was obscured by an emergent discourse of "*mestizaje*" which imagined the country as a righteous mix of Spanish colonial and Indigenous ancestry. Within this fiction, the actual differential and segregated treatment of the Indigenous and African-descended people was obscured in official narratives. Tribes like the Yaqui endured routine dispossession, disgrace, and dismemberment while the country professed a singular "mixed" national identity.[49]

To some degree, revolutionary Mexico did offer Black people from the United States respite from the brutal violence and exclusion in their own country. The Mexican press heavily promoted this image. A newspaper editor in Mexico City was kidnapped by the Klan because his writings about Black experiences over the border circulated so widely among sympathetic audiences. After the decoding of the Zimmermann Telegram, rumors circulated during World War I that the German military was recruiting Black people in Mississippi, Alabama, Missouri, South Carolina, and Texas, encouraging them to defect and to turn against the United States. According to rumors, the German government would send Black people to Mexico to train with German soldiers in a broader struggle against US racism. Government agents in Dallas had intercepted a message from Mexican recruiters promising Black people there the possibility of living "in peace and luxury" if they came to Mexico since "the white people are the cause of the Negroes being held down."[50]

Some Black people from the United States took advantage of a different form of leverage they enjoyed in the country. Writer Langston Hughes, in his memoir, *The Big Sea,* describes the travels of his father, who also went to Mexico during the Revolution. The elder Hughes went not to join a community of oppressed people but to acquire land and obtain the privileges of property ownership denied to him in the United States. Hughes's father came to own several properties, including a large ranch and several apartment buildings in Mexico City. As a young man visiting his father in Mexico,

Hughes began to reflect on the process of the color line, thinking deeply and critically about its elaboration as he witnessed his father's cruelty toward his Mexican workers and tenants. He recognized that his father had "a great contempt for all poor people" and thought "it was their own fault that they were poor." While he did not look like white property owners, Hughes's father was "just like the other German and English and American business men with whom he associated in Mexico" in his low opinion of Mexican people. Hughes wrote, "He said they were exactly like the Negroes in the United States, perhaps worse." It was while traveling by train to visit his father in Mexico and crossing over the Mississippi River that Hughes penned one of his most famous poems, "The Negro Speaks of Rivers." He reflected on his father's desire to escape to Mexico in order to leave the degraded position available to him in the United States:

> My father hated Negroes. I think he hated himself, too, for being a Negro. He disliked all of his family because they were Negroes and remained in the United States, where none of them had a chance to be much of anything but servants. My father said he wanted me to leave the United States as soon as I finished high school, and never return—unless I wanted to be a porter or a red cap all my life.[51]

From Hughes's astounding account of his father, we gain a portrait of a man fulfilling the same sad fictions of the New Imperialism in Mexico, defining his power in relationship to the Indigenous Mexican peasants who worked on his *haciendas* and identifying with old, embittered *señoras,* vestiges of a disappearing colonial order, through which the fantasies of power of the New Imperialism were routed. It was from these encounters that Hughes came to recognize the arbitrary desires for power that defined racism against Indigenous dispossessed peasants in Mexico and against his Black mother working as a waitress in Chicago. It was this pathetic spectacle, his father's imaginary, ruling over a fiefdom in an impoverished land, that Hughes reflected on, traveling over rivers—an understanding that would make him an internationalist.

COUNTERREVOLUTION OF THE NEW IMPERIALISM

The most famous chronicle of internationalism was arguably written by a young journalist from Oregon. John Reed's *Ten Days That Shook the World* offered a breathless first hand account of the 1917 Bolshevik Revolution. With no pretense of objective reportage, Reed described his book as "a slice of intensified history."[52] Readers at the time, ranging from sympathetic radicals to disgusted opponents, were fascinated by the Bolsheviks' bewildering seizure of power and the construction of their new revolutionary state. Reed represented the efforts of Russian workers to take over the government and reorganize their society through soviets—or councils—with unabashed enthusiasm. He not only chronicled the Bolshevik Revolution, he later returned to the Soviet Union as a delegate to the newly formed Communist International alongside M. N. Roy. As with Roy's contributions, Reed's 1919 comments at the Comintern were also punctuated with references to Mexico. Reed was also trying to make sense of the purported possibilities of internationalism presented by the Bolshevik Revolution as well as the challenges he had encountered during his time in Revolutionary Mexico.[53]

Years before Russia's revolutionary ten days, Mexico had ten shattering days of its own. La Decena Trágica, or the Ten Tragic Days, comprised the violent military coup that overthrew the new Mexican government in 1913. It had been orchestrated by Porfirio Díaz's loyalist forces, General Victoriano Huerta, and others in coordination with US Ambassador Henry Lane Wilson. This counterrevolution ultimately unseated Francisco Madero, the elected president who had ousted Díaz in the early phases of the Revolution. For ten bloody days in February 1913, Mexico City was racked with violence. The capital was bombarded, and hundreds of civilian lives were lost in the fighting. In the end, Madero was forced to resign, and General Huerta assumed the presidency. In a move that inflamed the entire country, Huerta's forces then executed the president alongside vice president José Pino Suárez. Factions throughout Mexico rose against "El Usurpador" Huerta, including followers of Zapata in the South and forces affiliated with Venustiano Carranza, Álvaro Obregón, and Pancho Villa in the North. John Reed traveled to Mexico in the wake of these events to chronicle the new phase of the Revolution.[54]

Metropolitan Magazine dispatched Reed to report on the Mexican Revolution as it mutated into a ferocious civil war. Reed, then twenty-six, came with his own set of questions. He had cut his teeth as a journalist reporting on militant labor strikes of the period, notably the famous 1913 IWW silk workers strike in Paterson, New Jersey. Jailed with the strikers, Reed had offered an intimate portrait of the immigrant workers, capturing the humor, fervor, and collective strength that they had realized through the strike.[55] Reed subsequently helped one thousand of the workers re-stage their strike before a large crowd at Madison Square Garden, a performance which ended with a singing of "The Internationale." A fixture in the bohemian milieus of Greenwich Village, New York, Reed was a friend to firebrands like anarchist Emma Goldman and prominent literary socialists like Max Eastman. He was also active in radical socialist politics himself. The assignment was therefore intriguing to Reed. Like many US radicals at the time, he was compelled by the multiple radical possibilities of the Mexican Revolution.[56]

Zapata's vision for revolutionary land redistribution resonated most with his own politics. Reed's first choice was to interview him. But, unable to obtain an audience, Reed was able to embed with Pancho Villa's Northern Division forces. His subsequent dispatches to *Metropolitan* represented Villa's followers with great empathy. Reed's articles gave readers a rare glimpse of the Revolution's fighters as fully formed and complex people, a respite from the crude and violent caricatures of Mexicans that were circulating in the mainstream English-language US press. While Reed did not completely escape the conceits of his day, he showed unusual care in his portraits of Mexican people, reproducing their jokes and their explanations of the revolution, and transcribing lyrics to their *corridos*. He sketched the hardened and dusty reality of battle life in camps and on trains and offered a sense of the fierce loyalty and camaraderie that assembled behind Villa. His articles also offered descriptions of people who lay beyond the frame of most war reporters: world-weary children who had experienced the chaos of regime change; *soldaderas,* the indispensable women on the front lines who prepared food, nursed soldiers, and set up camp before battle; and elderly and disabled *campesinos*.[57] As one older man reflected, "For the years of me, my father and my grandfather, the rich men have gathered the corn and held it in their clenched fists before our mouths. And only blood will make them open their hands to their brothers."[58] From Reed's articles, which eventually became his book *Insurgent Mexico* (1914), readers gained an appreciation of the unrequited rage that drove people to battle. Readers came to understand the chaos, violence, and hopes of the Northern Division: a range of Mexican perspectives seldom available to English-language audiences. Reed's more radical readers also gained a sense of an event that appeared to defy revolutionary projections.

The Mexican Revolution was difficult for many radicals in the United States to fully comprehend. For some this resulted from an inability to reconcile the occurrence of the revolution with the schemas of classical Marxist theory. Instead of an era of urban revolts led by an industrialized proletariat in Western countries, the New Imperialism unleashed an epoch of peasant uprisings and rebellions from semi-proletarianized rural spaces around the world. Fierce struggles against exploitation were conjoined with existential struggles for land, subsistence, and a general security of existence. Conceptualizing the unanticipated global struggles that were arising and converging across the capitalist landscape required a new synthesis of theory, one that perhaps not all radicals were ready to acquire.[59] Reed considered the persistent disbelief of many Western radicals as he reflected on the Bolshevik Revolution on its first anniversary. Many Western radicals believed that the country "must pass through the stages of political and economic development known to Western Europe, and emerge at last, with the rest of the world, into full-fledged Socialism."[60] In some instances, this faulty belief led radical movements in the United States to support imperialist regimes, as the Socialist Party did in 1914, believing that Mexico could only undergo true revolution if it first went through a capitalist phase. Often, radicals were caught in the sway of the same determinist developmental logic that capital itself had fostered, a geo-economic imagination that resonated broadly throughout American culture. In this imagination, a racial evolutionary logic was plotted on the planet, producing a hierarchy of cultures. For radicals to comprehend revolutionary advances in non industrialized Western nations by non-Western and non industrial workers, they needed to first unthink the logic of the color line. Toward this goal, Reed's reporting offered an important entry point.[61]

The development of US capital hardly represented a path toward liberal self-determination, let alone a step toward socialist revolution. The Revolution had thus far proved this. While reporting on the Mexican Revolution, Reed studied the operations of US capitalists and the arrogance transmuted to their functionaries and junior partners. In a 1914 article, he concluded that "American Business Men in Mexico are a degraded race." While they, along with US politicians, preached democracy and promised to help develop Mexico, Reed noted:

> They have a deep-seated contempt for the Mexicans, because they are different from themselves. They prate of our grand old democratic institutions, and then declare in the same breath that the peons ought to be driven to work *for them* with rifles. They boast in private of the superiority of American courage over Mexican, and then sneakingly buckle to whatever party is in power.[62]

These insights aligned with several fictionalized pieces about the Revolution that Reed wrote about Mexico. One of these, "Mac – American," was published in *The Masses* in April 1914. The short story depicts four men from the United States all getting drunk together in a Chihuahua bar during the Mexican Revolution. Of the four, only one character, Mac, is named. Reed's narrator describes Mac as "a breath from home, an American in the raw." The story was based on Reed's acquaintance with a man named Mac whom he met in Chihuahua City. Mac was likely a mechanic in a Durango mine turned gunrunner, surnamed McDonald, who surfaces in Reed's articles and book. As one author concludes, "Mac" likely provided Reed with early connections to Villa's troops. If McDonald was a fixer, Reed may have been forced to tolerate his otherwise intolerable behavior. This possible tension infuses the short story.[63]

Reed's narrator is a mostly silent observer in the story. He recounts the scene as three fellow Americans brag about their exploits in Mexico. At the beginning, these boasts are mostly sexual. The three disparage Mexican women with a range of insults. "'Mexican women,' said one, 'are the rottenest on earth. Why, they never wash more than twice a year.'"[64] The three men describe the women's bodies with a mixture of desire and revulsion, an eroticized engagement akin to Anne McClintock's notion of imperialist "pornotropics." Their professed familiarity with the country, expressed first as comprehension and apprehension of Indigenous Mexican women's bodies, underscores McClintock's observation that "knowledge of the unknown world was mapped as a metaphysics of gender violence."[65] The men work themselves up recounting the permissiveness of Mexican men. They imagine what they would do if any other man insulted their "American Woman" the way they insult Mexican women. "'I think I'd kill him,'" resolves Mac.[66]

Mac, twenty-five, nearly the same age as Reed at the time, is described as having had many jobs: "Railway foreman, plantation overseer in Georgia, boss mechanic in a Mexican mine, cow-puncher, and Texas deputy sheriff."[67] He also describes working in a lumber mill in Vermont, at an unspecified job in Kansas City, and having a brother who worked in the Canadian North-West Mounted Police. As the story proceeds, Reed offers an intriguing cognitive map of the New Imperialism. As narrated through the three men's stories, Mexico appears transposable, one site among many for these men's exploits. What is consistent and mutually affirmed is the role of these men in a community of hunters. In Mexico, they are hunting fortune; in the Canadian plains, "Indians"; around Georgia plantations, Black people; and in the borderlands with the Texas Rangers, Mexicans. As they sit in a Chinese bar named Chee-Lee's, with unseen Asian immigrants constantly refilling their drinks, Asians are absent presences, serving men who lust after the world while they themselves do not appear anywhere in it. There is hardly a pause between the description of the places and subordinations of the people within them. In some places, these men hunt as deputies of the state. In others, they hunt as vigilantes. Everywhere, they are hunting women.[68]

The "hunting" in the story is literal. "'Gar' said the first man. 'Northwestern Mounted Police! That must be a job. A good rifle and a good horse and no closed season on Indians! That's what I call Sport!'" Mac acknowledges the appeal of killing Indigenous people. He one-ups his companion by describing "the greatest sport in the world": "hunting" Black people. Mac goes on to discuss his job as an overseer on "a cotton plantation down in Georgia, near a place called Dixville."[69] He recounts falling in with a lynch mob, chasing an unseen and unnamed Black man with a pack of dogs:

We ran like crazy men, through the cotton field, and the woods swampy from floods, swam the river, dove over fences, in a way that would tire out a man ordinarily in a hundred yards. And we never felt it. The spit kept dripping out of my mouth—that was the only thing that bothered me. It was a full moon, and every once in a while when we came to an open place somebody would yell, 'There he goes!' and we'd think the dogs had made a mistake, and take after a shadow. Always the dogs ahead, baying like bells. Say, did you ever hear a bloodhound when he's after a human? It's like a bugle! I broke my shins on twenty fences, and I banged my head on all the trees in Georgia, but I never felt it.[70]

As he recounts the breathlessness of the chase, Mac narrates a shared blood-lust among the men. Bounding through the fields, woods, rivers, and over fences, alongside animals and like wild animals themselves, his story captures a heedless and thrashing movement of the mob through space. The hunt gives the lynch mob a collective force and purpose. The men move with the confidence of avengers, though they are deputized by no force other than the color line. Mac falls in with the twelve random men in the lynch mob only after hearing dogs give chase. He never knew what the mob's victim had supposedly done, and, as he continues, "I guess most of the men didn't either. We didn't care." Reed's story distills the purported camaraderie of anonymous men; the men in the lynch mob, like the nameless Americans around the table in Mexico, are all conjoined by an imagined solidarity, wrought through their collective capacity and authorization to enact racist and gendered violence. Reed is careful to recount their gratification as both grim and slender.[71]

"Mac – American" depicts rootless men. They have found themselves in Mexico not as heroes but as solitary and itinerant drifters. They drink together not as friends but as men with little holding them together beyond their purported Americanness. Their camaraderie is composed of swagger and violence. Mac tells another rollicking story of a fight between himself and his brother, with a cold coda. His brother rips Mac's ear to a stump, and Mac in turn blinds his brother's eye. After not speaking with his brother for years, Mac spurns his offer of affection, only to learn of his death shortly after. Without pause, another man immediately redirects the conversation back to the excitement of violence and the thrill of hunting non-white people. The turn underscores how starkly lonely the men are and, perhaps, how much they are trying to forget it.

Outside, it is just past midnight on New Year's Eve. Reed offers a glimpse of the street in Chihuahua where people are singing, shooting guns, and praying together. The new year is opening with a sense of possibility and warmth. Men sit around fires singing *corridos*. Women gather in the "pale red light" of the church "to wash away their sins." The narrator opens the story asking Mac if he wants to go into the cathedral to see the service. Mac is spooked. "There's too much risk in it," he says. Pressed, Mac haltingly explains, "'Why, when you die—you know. . . .' Now he was disgusted and angry."[72] Alongside his violence, Reed captures Mac's sense of being haunted. In a strange aside, Mac describes his initial response to hearing the hound dogs in Georgia before the chase:

> I don't know whether you fellows ever heard a hound bay when he's after a human. . . . Any hound baying in the night is about the lonesomest, *doom-ingest* sound in the world. But this was worse than that. It made you feel like you were standing in the dark, waiting for somebody to strangle you to death—*and you couldn't get away.*[73]

The New Imperialism, in John Reed's description of Americans in Mexico, had a dual character. Small and middling men like Mac could achieve previously denied forms of capitalist self-realization, such as the acquisition of property, the holding of small shares, or the mere possibility of achieving either. In this period, they could imagine themselves to be the small shareholders in the new spaces of global capitalist investment. To share the objectives and the spatial imaginaries of capital, particularly fractions of US capital, meant seeing the world as a site of acquisition and potential value production. These visions were consolidated through racist, anti-Indigenous, and gendered enactments of nationalist power. Shadow hegemony would arise through such apparent convergences of interest.

But in Mac and his compatriots, readers observe the haunted nature of these small men. While they profess swaggering satisfaction, Reed is careful to portray their doubt. In his story, they are not entirely convinced of their own violently wrested gains or their slim and borrowed authority. Some, like Mac, feel a dogged sense of guilt that eats at their conscience: they wait in the dark for their deserved reprisal. Despite the seductive appeals to heroism, they remain, in Reed's depiction, small and pitiable men. While the powerful subjectivities of the New Imperialism would be widely extended, there were no guarantees that they would root and take hold. Reed's story illustrates the contradictions and incompletion of this project. For those, like Reed, who sought to challenge this emerging hegemony, this incompletion was essential to comprehend as a political terrain. If the color line was learned, it could be unlearned. John Reed had faith that it could be.

When he returned from Russia in late 1918 after having published his book about Mexico, one of Reed's first assignments was in Chicago. There, he reported on men like Mac, who worked as longshoremen, wheat-binders, lumberjacks, and miners. These are the "kind of men the capitalist points to as he drives past.... There, he says, 'that's the kind of working-men we want in this country. Men that know their job, and work at it, instead of going around talking bosh about the class struggle.'" But these 101 men were precisely talking about class struggle. All 101 were on trial for obstructing the war effort. All 101 were members of the Industrial Workers of the World (IWW) and as Reed described, all "one hundred and one ... believe that the wealth of the world belongs to him who creates it, and that the workers of the world shall take their own." Fresh from his experiences in Mexico and the Soviet Union, Reed sat in the courtroom and believed he was witnessing the world turned upside down. Instead of the workers on trial, he thought as he heard their testimony of violence against organized labor, it was them putting the country on trial. "For a moment it seemed to me that I was watching the Central Committee of the American Soviets trying Judge Landis for—well, say counter-revolution."[74] While Reed's daydream would not come to pass in that Chicago courtroom, those same Wobblies would find ways to turn the world upside down alongside other global radicals and Mexican Revolutionaries—after they were found guilty and sentenced to Leavenworth Federal Penitentiary.

THREE

———

How to Make a University

RICARDO FLORES MAGÓN AND INTERNATIONALISM
IN LEAVENWORTH PENITENTIARY

[A]fter having suffered repeated incarcerations for my political
beliefs ever since I was seventeen years old, and having almost
miraculously escaped death at the hands of hired assassins on
several occasions, in that dark period of Mexican history ... I
decided to come to this country, which I knew to be the land of
the free and the home of the brave. . . .

RICARDO FLORES MAGÓN, LEAVENWORTH
FEDERAL PENITENTIARY, MAY 9, 1921

Authorized permit Megrim pantograph dormitory manlier
censor mummifying skitter drearily reaffirmed proportioning.
Arrange with Bagley satisfactory method for insectiverious tab
mummifying. PALMER

TRANSLATION: Authorized permit Kansas City office
Bureau of investigation censor mail socalled radical prisoners.
Arrange with Bagley satisfactory method for handling this mail.

ATTORNEY GENERAL A. MITCHELL PALMER, IN CODE
TO LEAVENWORTH WARDEN, JUNE 9, 1919

WHEN RICARDO FLORES MAGÓN FINALLY CROSSED back into his
beloved Mexico after nearly twenty years in exile, it was in a coffin. The train
carrying the revolutionary's body passed from El Paso, Texas, into Juárez,
Mexico, on January 5, 1923. Along rail lines that reached across the country's
interior, workers gathered to pay their respects. In Chihuahua, crowds
massed with doffed hats and red banners. In Torreón, a rally grew so fervent
that the nearby American consul locked himself inside. By the time it reached
Aguascalientes, many on the funeral train had lost their voices from all the
speeches and shouting along the way.[1] After its odyssey across the country,
the casket, draped with red and black flags and festooned with flowers and

lanterns, pulled into the Mexico City station. Hundreds solemnly received the body in a twenty-block-long procession organized by the railroad workers union.[2] Declared an "anarchist even in death," Flores Magón was laid to rest with fiery eulogies, songs, and red banners, under a mountain of flowers.[3] To orchestrate this elaborate cross-border burial, comrades had looked to the railway workers for aid, eschewing financial help from the Mexican government. Decades later, Ricardo Flores Magón's body would be disinterred and reburied at the national Rotonda de los Hombres Ilustres (Rotunda of Illustrious Men), a revolutionary anarchist paradoxically consecrated in the heart of the state.

But the fanfare for Flores Magón had not begun at the Mexican border. His body had been loaded onto a train in Los Angeles, California. This had followed a ceremony where nearly four hundred mourners had come out in the rain to the Breese Brothers Mortuary at 855 South Figueroa.[4] Anarchists, trade unionists, socialists, and other radical supporters had gathered there for a viewing. They sang the "Marseillaise" simultaneously in their own languages of Spanish, English, Yiddish, Russian, Polish, and Italian, as a paean to the much-loved internationalist.[5] The body had previously sat in a vault in Evergreen Cemetery in Boyle Heights, a largely Mexican working-class barrio in East Los Angeles. Here, Flores Magón and his comrades had once organized and agitated through their Spanish-and English-language radical paper, *Regeneración*.[6] From East LA, events were set in motion that would ultimately lead to the man's demise. But Flores Magón would not perish among friends and supporters in California. Far away, in a dank and fetid cell in Leavenworth Federal Penitentiary in Kansas, he would take his last breath. A fellow prisoner working in the Leavenworth hospital at the time witnessed orderlies carry the body out of the prison. As they lifted the heavy-laden stretcher, he heard them joke that it was "just another load of garbage for Peckerwood Ridge," a reference to the burial site for indigent prisoners whose bodies lay unclaimed. The man, Ralph Chaplin, removed his cap in silent ceremony until the body of Ricardo Flores Magón passed out of sight.[7]

After decades of publishing, organizing, and agitating, the Mexican revolutionary and visionary Flores Magón had been captured in what would be his final arrest in March 1918. A leader of the PLM (El Partido Liberal Mexicano), Flores Magón's calls for *tierra y libertad* ("land and freedom") had articulated the radical aims of the Mexican Revolution. Through his paper, *Regeneración*, he made clear that the struggle for freedom was global, extending throughout the borders of Mexico and beyond. What prompted this final arrest by US authorities was not a directive to Mexican revolutionaries or an attempt to organize Mexicans in Los Angeles. Rather, it was an appeal to people around the world. In midst of the First World War, Flores Magón and his comrade Librado Rivera published what they called a "Manifesto to the Anarchists of the Entire World and to the Workers in General."[8]

> The death of the old society is close, it won't be long in coming. . . . The citizen, who only yesterday considered the policeman his protector and supporter, now looks upon him with a grim gaze. . . . The workingman goes on strike, aware that it is no longer important that his action injures the country's interests, since the country is no longer his property but the property of the rich.[9]

The anarchist manifesto characterized workers' generalized disillusionment with the states that purported to represent them. It further implied that a latent insubordination smoldered in the hearts of people worldwide. For these suggestions, Flores Magón and his coauthor were deemed a threat to US national security and charged with violating the Espionage Act, a new piece of federal legislation that deemed it a felony to make "false statements" which might cause insubordination or disloyalty in the military.[10] After decades of surveillance, imprisonment, torture, and state repression on both sides of the US–Mexico border, it was for this crime that Flores Magón would die, or as some have argued, be killed, in Leavenworth Federal Penitentiary.[11]

Throughout his life, the repression of Flores Magón and his comrades was directly proportional to the popularity of their message among the poor and working class around the globe. In his speeches and writings, Flores Magón had commanded the world to witness, support, and join the struggle for freedom, especially the struggle of the Mexican Revolution, which he saw as a battle against US imperialism, racism, and capitalism. While a frail, older, and quite sickly man at the time of his arrest, Ricardo Flores Magón was deemed an enemy of the state because of his radical commitments, his belief in an international struggle, and the wide, warm reception of his ideas around the world.

The Espionage Act was part of a new set of federal legislation criminalizing dissent after the United States entered the First World War. Such laws were deployed within a new and broadened security infrastructure, designed to monitor, infiltrate, and suppress dissent increasingly located within the boundaries of US Empire. This moment of expanding domestic security and militarism also marked the global ascendency of US hegemony. In this context, social movements around the world, like the Mexican Revolution and the class-war anarchism of Ricardo Flores Magón, represented a dramatic and, up until that point, unrivaled challenge to the global capitalist economy. As the United States sharpened its capacities to control the social and political environments of capital accumulation within an expanding global sphere of influence, the opposition of Ricardo Flores Magón and others like him presented radical alternatives. Convicted under the new federal legislation, anarchists, socialists, communists, pacifists, and revolutionary nationalists, otherwise separated by deep ideological differences, increasingly found themselves bound together behind the walls of Leavenworth Penitentiary.

This chapter examines Leavenworth as a convergence space of radical internationalist traditions between 1917 and 1922. It observes that as the United States entered the First World War, Mexican revolutionaries like Ricardo Flores Magón joined other radicals and working-class military prisoners due to new federal laws regulating political dissent. It considers the multiple contradictions and possibilities produced by these encounters, as incarceration threw together prisoners of different nationalities, political orientations, and ideologies. Imprisoned for their resistance to militarism, capitalism, and racism, prisoners transformed Leavenworth into an organizing space, a laboratory for new ideas and tactics, or, as one federal surveillance file called it, "A University of Radicalism." In this way, insurgent prisoners repurposed the space of the prison to engage in the labor of radical knowledge production. Leavenworth in the late 1910s and early 1920s offers an episode in which the disciplinary mechanisms of capitalism unintentionally produced its own negation. Through a survey of prisoner writings, teachings, cultural productions, and prison records, it explores visions of internationalism that prisoners cultivated. It argues that the convergence spaces of Leavenworth Penitentiary offered a microcosm of political struggles in the period, reflecting how the color line and the class struggle were understood, experienced, and resisted.[12]

THE GLOBAL PRODUCTION OF THE PENITENTIARY

For most of the twentieth century, Leavenworth Federal Penitentiary served as the largest maximum-security federal prison in the United States. The struggles contained within the prison walls were prefigured in the production of the space itself. Built as a fort in the 1820s, Leavenworth first operated as an outpost for western conquest. The base offered military protection for settlers and merchants trading along the Missouri River, the Oregon Trail, and the Santa Fe Trail, the primary US trade route into Mexico. It became a central "staging area" for the US-Mexico War, a site where thousands of soldiers and volunteers were housed, equipped, and trained. The army divisions that captured Mexican cities like Santa Fe and Los Angeles were headquartered there. Later the Department of the Missouri organized many of its brutal Indian campaigns from the base. After the Civil War, the fort became home to regiments of "Buffalo soldiers," squads of Black soldiers who were variously stationed in the Plains, deployed against Indigenous forces, and later trained for overseas battle in the Philippines. When Leavenworth became a military prison in 1874, among its first prisoners were the original captives of US Empire: Native men from the Cherokee, Kiowa, Comanche, Cheyenne, Arapaho, and Nez Perce nations; Mexican men from the newly conquered territories; and Buffalo soldiers, many of whom were formerly enslaved or the children of slaves themselves.[13]

Given its readily available pool of prison labor, Ft. Leavenworth was authorized to become a federal penitentiary under the Three Prisons Act. Beginning in 1897, the military prisoners of Ft. Leavenworth were marched two and half miles every morning to the site of the future penitentiary. For twelve hours a day they dug, cleared brush, and extracted building materials from the surrounding environs. Under a blistering Kansas sun, prisoners cut grey stone from the high bluffs overlooking the Missouri River. Those who stepped out of line, slowed down, or stopped were punished with twenty-five-pound irons affixed to their legs. The building blocks of the penitentiary were consequently shaped, carried, and laid by prisoners themselves. From its foundation, Leavenworth's austere landscape was humanized as decades of imprisoned men built the literal walls around them. In addition to the construction work, maintenance, and clerical duties, other jobs like running the electrical generator and practicing medicine in the prison hospital all fell to Leavenworth's prisoners. To Congress's delight, this labor regime persisted for decades, keeping the costs of prison operations perennially low.[14]

For several years, steel for the remaining cellblocks lay untouched. Unwilling to hire skilled construction crews, prison officials halted the construction of the prison. In 1913, thirty-four ironworkers were convicted for their resistance to the National Erectors' Association, a brutal employer association. Their conviction was Leavenworth's gain. After fighting low pay, hazardous work conditions, and violent company thugs on the outside, the ironworkers found themselves erecting steel inside Leavenworth's walls, surrounded by armed guards in gun towers—which had themselves been built by prisoners under similar conditions of duress. Construction continued until 1927, with prisoners employing use of a penitentiary stone quarry, brickyard, carpentry shop, and stone sawmill among other advanced construction "offices."[15] So impressed was Henry Ford with the efficiency of the labor organization at Leavenworth, he commissioned Harry R. Hillier from the motion picture department of his Ford Motor Company to film the institution in 1919. Hillier assessed the situation, declaring: "I believe there is no community of the same size in the United States, which contains the amount of brains and even genius that the two thousand men in here have."[16] As the Ford Company's film approvingly described Leavenworth, "In the sunlight the prison looks like a prosperous banking institution."[17]

While maintaining its role as a military prison, Leavenworth Penitentiary became a unique space of control for political radicals after 1917 due to a series of new federal laws criminalizing dissent. In June of that year, Congress passed the aforementioned Espionage Act.[18] After the United States entered World War I, federal legislation increasingly focused on suppressing antiwar sentiment. New laws targeted individual draft dodgers as well as those organizing broader political opposition. Later amendments intensified the repression. The 1917 Selective Service Act mandated conscription and prosecuted those who avoided it. The Sedition Act of 1918 forbade the use of "disloyal, profane, scurrilous, or abusive language" about the US government, flag, military, and Constitution.[19]

In the wake of World War I, the ongoing Mexican Revolution, and the Russian Bolshevik Revolution in October 1917, these laws, as well as the creation of the first federal police system and the first major domestic intelligence program, produced a massive new security infrastructure. It also marked the first wartime instance when the government operated prisons to house its own legally defined "civilians." Over two thousand prosecutions occurred under the original Espionage Act, including those of Socialist spokesman and draft opponent Eugene V. Debs and anarchist intellectual Emma Goldman. In creating new state capacities to legalize the detention, repression, and imprisonment of thousands of Americans for their political beliefs and associations, the expansion of federal government capacities in this period laid the groundwork for the first Red Scare of 1919–20. As the largest and oldest of the three federal prisons, Leavenworth became a central node of this emergent security regime.[20]

The expansion of the prison system and the shifting capacities of the federal government responded to the contradictory movements of capital in the period.[21] The onset of the First World War was a boon to US industrial production, particularly as European powers increased their demand for US-produced war materials such as munitions, guns, and airplanes. By early 1917, Allied powers had purchased over two billion dollars of such equipment, helping to position the United States as the world's primary industrial power. Consequently, demand for production expanded, outstripping the available pool of labor. By 1918, with forty-four million people employed in the formal labor force, industrial production peaked, real wages rose, and workers dramatically enhanced their leverage. Strikes broke out across industries such as iron, steel, mining, lumber, textile, and a number of wartime concerns, significantly among East Coast shipbuilders.

Struggles in the period produced an emboldened labor movement, inspiring members of the Socialist Party, anarcho-syndicalist groups, and the Industrial Workers of the World (aka the Wobblies) to organize a class struggle across the color line. By 1919, approximately one in seven US workers went on strike, with as many as one in four in New York City. Various mechanisms were used to combat the real and potential growth of this class power, including employer subterfuge, raids, brutal strikebreaking by hired thugs, and surveillance by private detective agencies like the nefarious Pinkerton National Detective Agency. New state laws and new federal legislation such as the Espionage Act explicitly targeted labor militancy, giving local law enforcement new tools of repression.[22]

The 1917 Espionage Act in practice targeted three main groups (which were by no means mutually exclusive): World War I peace activists and war dissenters; labor organizers (especially foreign-born members of groups like the Wobblies); and Black workers, writers, and cultural producers organizing against Jim Crow racism. As Senator Lee Overman of North Carolina reasoned, the Espionage Act was necessary to stop papers from being circulated "through the South urging Negroes to rise up against white people." Though seemingly discrete actions, efforts to repress labor were deeply entangled with movements to suppress anti-racism and promote militarism.[23]

This movement of industrial capital was abetted by the geographic expansion of finance capital prior to and after World War I. Financial regulations significantly shifted, and in 1915 President Wilson lifted a ban on US creditors' ability to make private loans to Allied countries. As a result, US investments abroad nearly doubled—from $5 billion to $9.7 billion—between 1914 and 1919. The export of money and munitions and the decline of British solvency transformed the political economy of the country, making the United States, previously one of the largest debtor nations, into a creditor nation for the first time in its history. Thereafter, state entities were newly able to control capital and trade globally, and possessed the increased ability to dictate the terms of its loans and international investments. In this way the United States joined Britain as a major regulator of the world capitalist economy, and the central node of capitalist infrastructure began its shift from London to Wall Street. From this position, the United States was poised to overtake Britain and become the dominant economic, military, cultural, and political power in the world during what would later be called "The American Century."[24]

The export of both money and munitions securely tied the interests of US finance capital to an Allied victory and ultimately prompted the deployment of US soldiers to support the Allied nations. The peace movement challenged both the expansion of American finance capital overseas and the country's emergent global standing. Therefore, the criminalization of war dissenters by new federal legislation during the war was intended as much to punish individuals as to ensure investments of US capital abroad and the expanded sphere of US influence.

The opposing interests of various factions of capital appeared to crystallize with the onset of the war. This could be understood through the newly criminalized social movements of the period. Leavenworth Federal Penitentiary, a container of dissent against racism, capitalism, and militarism, became a site through which the fluidity of struggles within and across borders were made legible. Between 1918 and 1919, the prison population vastly expanded; it soon housed nearly two thousand men, almost four hundred of whom were foreign nationals. As many of Leavenworth's prisoners believed, the global regimes of capital were not inevitable. Prisoners came from the powerful social movements of the period and reflected a range of alternative visions. Though diverse and specific to their contexts, these global movements all held in common a desire for an equitable redistribution of wealth.[25]

The Bolshevik Revolution of 1917 clearly articulated this radical vision. By supporting efforts of self-determination and denouncing the social relations of private property, it offered a bold counter to capitalist visions. Revolutionaries around the planet were inspired to also imagine a new society. Labor radicals in Europe and the Americas were joined by Irish Catholic sheep-shearers in the "distant interior of Australia" as they "cheered" the Soviet workers' state. In Spain, the years between 1917–19 came to be known as "the Bolshevik biennium," even though most supporters were "passionately anarchist."[26] 1917 also marked the creation of Mexico's revolutionary Constitution, one of the most radical and comprehensive in modern political history for its nationalization of resources and sweeping land reforms. Meanwhile, the Ghadar movement against British imperialism in India was also growing with critical centers in the United States, especially in California and throughout the Pacific Northwest. Anti-colonial insurgents in Ireland took advantage of their new leverage during the First World War in order to launch a counterattack on occupying forces. By 1917, Irish forces were regrouping after the Easter Rising against British colonialism the prior year. In Niger, the Tuareg and Hausa people continued their extended rebellion against the French colonial army. In 1917, Marcus Garvey opened his first US chapter of the Universal Negro Improvement Association (UNIA). That year, Haitian Caco rebels continued their struggles against US military forces. African American papers like the *Messenger* would soon deem the US occupation of Haiti "America's India," "America's Corea [*sic*] and Ireland." According to the political economist Giovanni Arrighi such movements represented "the most serious wave of popular protest and rebellion hitherto experienced by the capitalist world-economy." Leavenworth Penitentiary offered a microcosm of these global waves of rebellion.[27]

UNIVERSITY OF RADICALISM

Between 1917 and 1922, Leavenworth was occupied by a motley crew of war dissenters, radical labor organizers, foreign-born radicals, and Black militants. Some key figures in this early post 1917 period included prisoners like Taraknath Das, an Indian leader in the US Ghadar movement; George Andreychine, a Bulgarian socialist and trade unionist who would go on to hold major positions in the Comintern; and Earl Browder, future general secretary of the Communist Party of the USA. Some of the most prominent political prisoners at the time were Wobblies. On September 28, 1918, ninety-seven members of the IWW were convicted of conspiring to obstruct the war by opposing the draft. Those sentenced included figures like "Big" Bill Haywood, a founding member and lead organizer of the IWW; Vicente Aurelio Azuara, a newspaper editor originally from Spain; Peter McEvoy, an ironmolder from Ireland; James Slovik, a fisherman from Russia; and Carl Ahlteen, a writer from Sweden.[28]

Ben Fletcher, an African American longshoreman, one of the most talented labor leaders of his time, was also among the convicted. In a period when few African Americans were permitted to join labor unions, Fletcher, one of the few Black Wobblies, attempted to shift the racial consciousness of the IWW and of the labor movement more broadly. In an op-ed he penned for the *Messenger,* Fletcher wrote, "Organized labor, for the most part be it radical or conservative, thinks and acts, in the terms of the White Race."[29] So concerned about his activities was J. Edgar Hoover, then head of the anti-radical General Intelligence Division of the Bureau of Investigation, who monitored Fletcher's mail for information about "Negro agitation." Imprisoned Wobblies also included those overlapping between the membership of the PLM and IWW, such as Mexican-born miner Tomas Martínez. The combination of these figures—Bulgarian communists, Indian Ghadarites, Mexican anarcho-syndicalists, and African American socialists—made for an unusual convergence of radical traditions. In September 1919, the *Liberator,* a socialist magazine out of New York, published an article by a Leavenworth prisoner that dubbed the prison a "school for revolution." The phrase is useful in describing the repurposing of space within the walls of Leavenworth.[30]

The prisoners wrote, edited, and published a newspaper called the *Leavenworth New Era.* The paper was an innovative source of information, including prison news, gossip, demographics, coverage of the prison baseball league, book reviews, poetry, and even excerpts from other prison newspapers. British Wobbly Charles Ashleigh wrote regularly about culture and politics. When he was not playing chess with IWW leader Big Bill Haywood or managing the prison baseball team, future CPUSA leader Earl Browder wrote about jazz, culture, and the fallacies of whiteness.[31]

Enrique Flores Magón, Ricardo's brother and fellow PLM member, published a regular column called "Mexican Kaleidoscope." In a series of short stories, he educated fellow prisoners about the Mexican Revolution. In one dramatic story entitled "The Invader," he described a fictionalized encounter in which elders in a Mexican village educated a young white American man about the causes of the revolution. "Why did you sell your land, your waters, your plows and your beasts?" asks the American. "They took it all away from us," replies one of the villagers. Following this exchange, a "long deep sobering sigh comes forth from the very bottom of [the villager's] heart; [a] sigh that finds echo in the bosom of all the others."[32] Perhaps such works transformed the thinking of other prisoners about Mexico and the plight of Mexicans in the United States. In an open letter to President Harding in 1922, fifty-two of the imprisoned Wobblies pleaded their case by making a poignant point about racist representation, saying, "In the capitalist newspaper the I.W.W. is like the Mexican in the movie show; he is always the villain."[33]

The cover story of the April 9, 1920, issue of the *Leavenworth New Era* describes the success of the Leavenworth night school, a minor university self-organized by the prisoners for the prisoners with the instructors being drawn from the ranks of the prison population itself:

> Over six hundred men gathered nightly in the great hall, to pursue their studies under the guidance of teachers, who were also their fellow prisoners. Yet, without any intervention by the officers of the prison, an admirable discipline prevailed. . . . The school is their institution; and they were responsible for its order and success.[34]

According to prisoner H. Austin Simons, the school emerged out of prisoners' organizing efforts. After first organizing strikes together and then organizing toward a greater "jail-democracy," prisoners began educating one another. Informal discussions about politics gave way to lectures by incarcerated teachers like Prof. Carl Hessler. Efforts transformed a place of "isolation" into a school of "revolution."[35] Classes included automobile mechanics, biology, English, Russian, French, logic, general electricity, Marxian economics, mechanical drawing, typewriting, and three classes in Spanish (one of which was taught by Enrique Flores Magón and another by Spanish Wobbly Vicente Azuara). Four out of five nights were devoted to study. On every Wednesday night, students were shown educational films or slideshows. Prisoners often wrote to the warden's office to order textbooks, foreign language dictionaries, notebooks, and other school supplies.[36]

Aside from the "formal" education of the night school, the prisoners educated each other in informal and innovative ways. Regular lectures were held in the wings of the cellblocks, with prisoners crowding corners or craning their ears down from tiers above to hear the lessons. Incarcerated lecturers like Allen Broms spoke about propaganda, sociology, Marxism and political economy. In good weather, Indian Ghadarite Taraknath Das would go outdoors to the "wobbly shed," joining Ralph Chaplin and Charles Ashleigh to discuss the Russian Revolution, poetry, the day's news, and medieval ballads, and he would sometimes deliver speeches about Indian Vedanta philosophy.

Das also introduced the Dewey Decimal System to the prison library, cataloguing over eight thousand volumes. Radical textbooks and pamphlets were brought in by any means possible. Some prison-issued copies of the Bible were taken by prisoners to the printing plant, gutted, filled instead with the *Communist Manifesto,* and rebound.[37]

Prisoners also read and passed around magazines like the *Liberator,* the *Messenger,* the *Industrial Worker, Regeneración,* the *Political Prisoner,* the *Nation, Arizona Labor Journal,* the *Globe,* the *Modern Review* from Calcutta, and *Workers' Dreadnought* out of London. The act of reading often provided a means of transfiguring the space of enclosure. "Books!" wrote J. A. McDonald in *The New Era.* "With Homer we are spectators at the Siege of Troy. We climb Olympus and listen to the congress of the gods. . . . We travel over fantastic seas to grotesque lands found only in the geography of the imagination."[38] Some books from Enrique Flores Magón's personal prison collection included *The Universal Kinship* by J. Howard Moore, *The Death of a Nobody* by Jules Romains, *Thought in the Russian Revolution* by Albert Rhys Williams, and *Russia in 1919* by Arthur Ransome.

One popularly circulated book was his copy of Louise Bryant's *Six Red Months in Russia,* the firsthand account of Bryant, an American socialist feminist, about the early years of the Bolshevik Revolution. Bryant recorded her conversations with many Bolsheviks, especially Russian feminists like Katherine Breshkovsky and Alexandra Kollontai, who made radical arguments about gender and sexuality, arguing, for instance, that until the revolution could fundamentally transform gender relations and liberate notions of sexuality it could not be truly transformative. Inside the prison copy of Bryant's book is Enrique Flores Magón's name and inmate number. On the next page is his note to his fellow prisoners: "Please take good care of this book, do not write in its pages, and return it to its owner as soon as you are through reading it, for there are others who want to read it and are waiting for their turn." Given the unusually generous (albeit contested) space the PLM gave to questions of feminism and gendered discourse, the inclusion of the book in Enrique's library was unsurprising. More remarkable is the book's apparent wide circulation, and the degree to which it was in demand by other prisoners.[39]

With this type of education, it is no surprise that radical action happened inside the walls as well. Strikes, work stoppages, and social protests occurred with frequency. On May Day in 1919, the prisoners held a march/celebration inside the prison. Successfully appealing to the warden that the first of May,

International Workers' Day, was as sacred to radicals as religious holidays were to practicing observers, the prisoners gained a May Day celebration with little interference. Prisoners turned their state-issued jackets inside out, exposing the red flannel lining. They hoisted images of Vladimir Lenin and Abraham Lincoln, cut from magazines, on broomstick handles. The day began with "The Internationale," an anthem that communists, socialists, anarchists, and all "prisoners of starvation" and "wretched of the earth" could sing together. The program also included a discussion of revolutionary methods, a quote contest between the anarchists and the socialists, and an open-air parade. The program gives a sense of the political tendencies within the prison as well as the camaraderie and political dialogues among the prisoners:

> 9am
> 1. "The International," by all Revolutionists.
> 2. "Dead March," by Russian chorus.
> 3. Address: "Karl Marx," by . . .
> 4. "The Red Flag," by all Reds.
>
> 12 noon
> 1. Open Air Parade Through Wire City.
> 2. "Hold the Fort," by I.W.W. choir.
> 3. Address: "The First of May," by . . .
> 4. "Stung Right," by all Reds.
>
> 6pm
> 1. Open Air Singing Between No. 6 and No. 7 Barracks.
> 2. I.W.W. vs. Socialist—Quotes Contest.
> 3. Address: "The American Way" by . . .
> 4. Discussion of Revolutionary Methods.
> 5. "The Marseillaise," by all Reds[40]

While the marches, night schools, lectures, and publications produced a unique political space, Leavenworth, of course, remained a punitive disciplinary institution. "The experience of being locked behind iron bars for a protracted period is a heavy shock," wrote Earl Browder in an unpublished memoir. "Many persons never recover from it and carry its spiritual and mental wounds and scars for the rest of their lives. It should not be prettified or painted in romantic colors."[41] Prisoners were indeed subjected to brutal treatment: malnourished, harshly disciplined, subjected to extended periods of solitary confinement, and routinely denied adequate medical care. Guards took out personal vendettas against prisoners for their political beliefs. The Wobblies were often subjected to weeks in what was referred to as the "torture chamber," otherwise known as "the hole," for their associations and protests. Men were particularly punished for their stance as conscientious objectors.

Labor and IWW leader Elizabeth Gurley Flynn recounted the gruesome treatment of a dozen Mennonite men who were serving long sentences for their "uncompromising opposition to warfare." Because of their refusal to join the military and wear army uniforms, they were disgraced and tortured by prison guards. Their beards were cut and buttons were affixed to their uniforms in defiance of their religious custom. They were made to sleep on the concrete with no blankets at night. During the day they were "manacled to bars so high they could barely touch the ground." With intense pressure, the cuffs dug into their wrists, swelling and eventually cracking the skin of their hands, spilling blood down their arms and upon them. Two of the men, Joseph and Michael Hofer, died as a result of this extreme torture. Adding insult to injury, the prison returned the bodies of the men to their pacifist Mennonite communities in South Dakota having dressed the corpses in the army uniforms the men had refused to wear in life. Their example illustrates the breadth of punishment in Leavenworth, from the extreme to the minute.[42]

There were other ways in which the prison itself was a disciplining institution, particularly in terms of race and gender. This was perhaps most clearly seen in the incarceration of the famed boxer Jack Johnson. Johnson had risen to fame in Black communities and reached notoriety in many white communities when he defeated the "Great White Hope" Jim Jeffries in 1910. In that defeat, the myth of white racial supremacy was profoundly ruptured. Films of Johnson overpowering white boxers were made illegal in some states because violent white mobs rioted across the country after viewing them. Johnson flouted his victory and his wealth in the face of white rage, openly dating and marrying white women, many of whom were sex workers.

Eventually, Johnson was convicted under the Mann Act in 1912, a law prohibiting the trafficking of "white slaves," particularly white women, across state lines for purposes of "prostitution or debauchery, or for any other immoral purpose." At this time, the regulation of sexuality through such laws criminalizing prostitution and interracial relationships enabled the growth of the federal prison system and local convict lease systems, and gave credence to deputized bands of vigilantes and lynch mobs.[43]

After his conviction, Johnson and his then-wife fled the country, eventually winding up in Mexico. There, Johnson also began to sympathize with the possibilities of revolutionary Mexico. He compelled other African Americans to follow suit to "Latin America, the garden of the world," which he reasoned "offers us all the golden privileges of a land that has never known racial prejudice." Mexico, he wrote, "was willing not only to give us the privileges of Mexican citizenship, but will champion our cause." According to FBI records, the 1919 films of Johnson in Mexico City, dressed to the nines, announcing that he, an African American man, was a member of the finest clubs in the city, caused jubilant celebrations and the possible "incitement" of African Americans in the United States. In face of Jim Crow segregation, the image of Johnson symbolically upending US racial codes fired people's imaginations. In crossing back across the Mexican border in 1920, Johnson was arrested and sent to Leavenworth.[44]

Jack Johnson's days in prison were full. He conducted daily financial affairs via telegram, wrote an autobiography, invented and patented a new tool, staged a public boxing exhibition in the prison with the blessing of the warden, and arranged his post-release boxing schedule. For a while, his official duty was to maintain the prison baseball yard. Through this work he would have encountered prisoners such as Roy Tyler. Tyler was much younger than Johnson. He became his sparring partner and developed a relationship that would carry on in letters after Johnson was released. On that baseball field, Tyler discovered his own athletic talent. He was effectively drafted into the Negro Leagues when the head of the organization became his parole sponsor. After his team lost a major championship, Tyler was marooned in Indiana and found work as a porter, a car washer, and other menial jobs. He was quickly picked up on a trumped-up charge and returned to Leavenworth for violation of his parole.[45]

Tyler was never listed as a "political prisoner," but perhaps this is a mistake. For Tyler was involved in another long-forgotten event in that global year of 1917. In August, the 3rd battalion of the 24th infantry mutinied against their officers in Houston, Texas. This was a regiment of Buffalo Soldiers, all Black men, one whose history reminds us of the United States' vast and contradictory imperial ambitions. The 24th infantry had been deployed to Cuba as part of the Spanish-American War in 1898. Later, the same infantry was sent to the Philippines as part of the Philippine-American War, where Black soldiers, or "smoked Yankees" as they were called, had to newly consider their support for waging an imperialist war against the Filipinos. In 1916, this regiment entered Mexico to assist General Pershing's search for Pancho Villa, where they might have encountered a number of African Americans who had defected to that country.[46]

In 1917, the battalion was stationed in Houston during construction of a base there. Racial tension in the city was high, with white Houstonians hostile to the Black regiment. On the evening of August 23, 1917, a Black soldier attempted to stop the assault of a Black woman by white officers and was subsequently arrested. Later that day, when another Black soldier, Charles W. Baltimore, inquired about the arrested man, he was brutally beaten by white officers. A rumor spread that Baltimore had been killed. Against the backdrop of violence, humiliation, threats of white mobs, and the specter of lynchings, this rumor set off anger and around one hundred and fifty members of the regiment took up arms. Marching to the center of town, they opened fire on the police station and killed fourteen people. For the crimes of murder and mutiny, nine soldiers were executed by hanging. Over forty were sentenced to Leavenworth. Like Tyler, many were young men. And like Tyler, many were paroled, picked back up, and sent back to Leavenworth at a higher frequency than other prisoners. Like many of the other men in his unit, Tyler's series of mug shots from each of his rearrests show him progressively aging, a haunting succession of images that illuminates the racist erosion of life by the prison.[47]

THE DEATH OF JOSÉ MARTÍNEZ

The documents for Roy Tyler's parole add a curious footnote to the story of Leavenworth Penitentiary. In support of his parole, Tyler was praised for protecting prison guards from other prisoners. In one instance, Tyler was credited with preventing "a gang of I.W.W. prisoners" from harming the deputy warden and other officers. In another, he was awarded special recognition for helping to capture another prisoner, José Martínez. The warden recounts the incident as follows:

> On November 14th, when Joe [sic] Martinez, a Mexican murderer, killed Captain Andrew Leonard and wounded six guards by stabbing them, [Roy] Tyler voluntarily entered the underground coal bunker and took a dagger from Martinez.[48]

For his help, the Warden offered Tyler "the highest commendation of the prison officials." Despite this praise, Tyler's parole was denied.[49] While the episode grew stale in the pages of Tyler's parole files, the particular entanglement between Roy Tyler and José Martínez highlights the unfortunate convergences enabled by the prison.

On November 14, 1922, Martínez "fashioned the knife" from a piece of steel and attacked several guards, including the captain, whose wounds proved fatal. The guards responded with gunfire. Injured by gunshot wounds, Martínez staggered off the prison yard into the penitentiary coal shed. A tense standoff ended after Roy Tyler entered the "bunker," disarmed Martínez, and enabled a guard to strike him in the head with a block of coal. Martínez was sent to the prison hospital while the captain was delivered to the morgue. The incident provoked a flurry of letters and telegrams. When a Montana deputy inquired whether his friend, Captain Andrew Leonard, had survived the attack, the Leavenworth warden curtly replied that Leonard had indeed been "fatally stabbed by [a] crazed Mexican."[50]

Martínez was a convicted murderer serving twenty-five years in Leavenworth Federal Penitentiary. He had killed the much feared and respected captain of the guards Andrew "Bull" Leonard, a Spanish-American War veteran employed at the prison since 1900. To a public accustomed to dime novels, silent films, and new detective fiction, the story of a violent convict attempting escape would have been exciting, albeit conventional. The fact that Martínez was Mexican enabled journalists to confirm readily available racial narratives about Mexican bloodthirst and sociopathy. Headlines declared "A Mexican Ran Wild and Killed," and "Mexican Shot After Stabbing Seven Guards." The story was both scintillating enough to land on the front page of the Kansas *Hutchinson News* and sufficiently mundane to be tucked in page six of the *New York Tribune*.[51]

Mexican people were increasingly maligned in the press and popular culture as US interests in Mexican land, resources, and labor expanded. Routinely depicted as bloodthirsty savages, prideful simpletons, or gun-toting madmen in need of pacification, this discursive violence profoundly shaped popular imaginaries just as it helped shape public policy. Prisoners in Leavenworth were not immune from its reach. One prisoner's account of the attack described Martínez as "a simple *pelado*" who snapped when asked by a guard to remove his hat. This observer suggested that the guard simply "didn't understand how proud a Mexican Indian can be of a hat, even a battered old prison-issue straw sombrero." Both inside and out of the penitentiary, mediated through such depictions, Martínez was not just a crazed prisoner but the fulfillment of a mass-produced fantasy: a wild, murderous representative of his race.[52]

Within days of the prison yard attack, this story disappeared from head-lines. While José Martínez lay dying in the prison hospital, another prisoner's dramatic story took its place. On November 22, 1922, Ricardo Flores Magón was found dead in his cell. Beloved by labor leaders, anarchists, socialists, and workers alike, Flores Magón's death received attention across the globe. From London to Mexico City to the White House, workers expressed outrage in articles, letters, and mass demonstrations. Flores Magón's closest comrade and political ally in prison, Librado Rivera, a fellow anarchist and PLM member, alleged that he had seen bruises around Ricardo's lifeless neck, sug-gesting that Flores Magón had been strangled to death. Rivera also noted that Flores Magón had been moved into a cell out of earshot the night before his corpse was discovered.[53]

While some doubted claims that Flores Magón was assassinated, others, like socialist labor leader Eugene V. Debs, accused the prison of committing slow murder. Writing in the *New York Call,* Debs echoed the concern of many of Flores Magón's friends and supporters, arguing that he had been killed as a result of medical neglect and the indifference of prison officials. An op-ed reprinted in several Mexican papers similarly described the circum-stances leading up to Flores Magón's death as simply *salvajismo inconcebible* ("inconceivable savagery").[54]

While separated by measures of public sentiment and international con-cern, the lives and fates of Ricardo Flores Magón and José Martínez were curiously linked. Flores Magón had been a leader and friend to many in the penitentiary, particularly to a growing number of Mexican prisoners like Martínez. He was regarded as a political mentor, a man who could compel-lingly lecture about philosophy, poetry, and Mexican history. He was also a much loved counselor, letter writer, and confidant for many men. A *Nation* article written during Flores Magón's incarceration at McNeil Island Federal Penitentiary, just prior to his transfer to Leavenworth, reported that "there was not a Mexican worker in that prison—and there were many—who would not have laid down his life to give Magón a free and easy hour."[55] This insight illuminates the likely solidarity between Ricardo Flores Magón and José Martínez.

There were multiple spaces where the two men could have encountered one another: in the Leavenworth library where Flores Magón worked as a librarian; in the prison yard where prisoners circulated; by the rock pile that Flores Magón and his comrades dubbed the "campus," where they gathered daily for debate and conversation, and where between November 25, 1919, and

February 3, 1920, Martínez was assigned to work; or possibly in the mess hall, where all the prisoners ate their meals together under heavy surveillance. Not long before Flores Magón's death and Martínez's attack, a strike broke out in the mess hall. The prisoners, fed up with a nauseating diet of boiled parsnips, first silently and then raucously expressed their disapproval. This "food riot" significantly upset the guards. Instead of responding directly to the protest, guards used the opportunity for retribution and sought ways to break the spirit of the prisoners.[56]

The guards selected prison leaders and educators, many of whom had nothing to do with the "riot." Flores Magón, an older man, in frail health with diminishing eyesight, was among those singled out for punishment. A former Mexican railroad worker, José Savás Reza, witnessed the assault. He recounted that Captain Leonard beat the enfeebled Flores Magón while José Martínez looked on helplessly. Days later, when Martínez attacked Leonard and several other guards, it was understood by Reza, and subsequently by other historians, as retribution for Leonard's attack on Flores Magón. Tellingly, Librado Rivera, Flores Magón's closest friend and ally, came to aid the injured Martínez during the attack. One eyewitness reported that Martínez even wept on Rivera's shoulder before he was taken to the prison hospital.[57]

According to his prison record, José Martínez was not the rash man driven by pride, the simple *pelado,* described in the press. In the years prior to the attack, he had incurred four minor violations: two for smoking a cigarette, one for not stopping when told, and another for not removing his clothes when ordered. A March 1921 physician's assessment found that Martínez "does not give any evidence of mental unbalance" and a February 1921 note from the Warden to the War Department indicates that his "conduct during confinement has generally been excellent." In a 1920 letter for clemency addressed to the Secretary of War, Martínez himself expressed doubt about his own survival, writing, "As for me, I very much doubt to outlive my sentence, as I have been very sick during my confinement in this prison." It is difficult to characterize José Martínez's decision to attack the Leavenworth guards as an impulsive response to a personal insult. Plausibly, the honor he was defending was not even his own.[58]

Martínez was brought to the infirmary with gunshot wounds to the knee and stomach and a severe head injury. His hospital record indicates that for five days he was administered the same treatment: aspirin. Not until the fifth day was he given the additional treatment of "ice bags to abdomen." After killing one guard and attacking six others, Martínez lay in the prison hospital with a growing fever and blood poisoning spreading throughout his system. He eventually succumbed to his injuries fifteen days later, with the official cause of death reported by prison officials as "septicemia, following gunshot wound, abdomen." In contrast to Flores Magón's case, there was no media scrutiny following the death of José Martínez. He was buried at Leavenworth, in the Kansas soil, alongside other prisoners with no family to claim them. On the note indicating who to contact in case of illness and emergency, the typist entered "noboyd" [sic].[59] There was no memorial for José Martínez, a common fate for many Leavenworth prisoners. In his poem "At the Grave of a Felon," fellow prisoner "Andy" Lockhart offered a eulogy for the many men like Martínez unceremoniously buried in the prison grounds:

> The poor wretched arms on the sunken breast . . .
> Perhaps in their day they helped to raise
> A fallen brother on the rough, hard ways . . .
> And as Life was bitter in the days long fled
> So Death may be sweet to the unmourn'd dead![60]

José Martínez had come to the United States from Chihuahua, Mexico, where Pancho Villa had briefly served as a provisional governor (1913–14) and where American publishing tycoon William Randolph Hearst owned the million-acre Babicora Cattle Ranch. A leatherworker by trade, he had been a bullfighter in his youth, a laborer in Sacramento, California, and El Paso, Texas, and possibly also a field hand in Plainview, Kansas. His immigration form asked if he was educated, healthy, and if he was an anarchist, a new category prompted by the growing popularity of Ricardo Flores Magón and fellow members of the PLM. Once in the United States, Martínez lived mainly in El Paso, a notoriously racist town with a large Mexican labor force and a history of rampant lynchings, beatings, and disappearances perpetrated by white civilians and deputized Texas Rangers alike. In 1916, twenty Mexican people were doused with kerosene and burned alive, an incident that incensed Mexicans on both sides of the border and provided the rallying cry for Pancho Villa's invasion of Columbus, New Mexico.[61]

Prior to his time in Leavenworth, Martínez himself had been a soldier of US Empire. He was incarcerated at Leavenworth after serving in Company M of the 125th Infantry, part of the Expeditionary Forces in France during World War I. Alongside many unwilling and suspicious Mexican workers in Texas, Martínez had enlisted with the US Army in 1917. Indeed, one of the few buildings in El Paso that did not carry a "No Mexicans Allowed" sign was the US Army draft office. In World War I, as in other wars, the contradictions of US racism came to bear on the sudden comradeship of sworn enemies. Americans served alongside Mexicans when, not long before, they had fought against them. In France, Martínez was involved in a fight with a superior officer, killing the officer in what he characterized as an act of self-defense. After being court-martialed in France, Martínez was sentenced to the military prison in Leavenworth, Kansas. There, to his surprise, he would come to meet and eventually defend Ricardo Flores Magón, in an unanticipated transnational alliance produced by this convergence space.[62]

José Martínez defended the Mexican Revolutionary figure who had offered one of the earliest and most trenchant critiques of US imperialism in the twentieth century. In doing so, Martínez had unwittingly entered a struggle with global dimensions. Ostensibly, there was much in common between José Martínez and Roy Tyler, the Houston Mutineer who disarmed him. Both men had enlisted in the defense of the United States. Both had faced racism from within and outside of the military. Both had consequently found themselves condemned to the same prison. But the common experience of incarceration did not ensure that they shared the same political commitments. While Leavenworth Penitentiary enabled a unique convergence of radical traditions and provided a space for productive and vibrant dialogue, this by no means guaranteed that all prisoners found common cause or shared affinities between themselves. Such alliances would have to be built and organized.[63]

ANTI-RACIST INTERNATIONALISM

In the years during and after World War I, radical movements inside and out of the prison were grappling with the parallel formations of racism and capitalism, although few large-scale movements could successfully theorize their congruity. However, revolutionaries like Ricardo Flores Magón were uniquely positioned to understand how capital crossed borders and linked the destinies of those it dispossessed.

In many respects, Flores Magón was like another imprisoned radical, his Italian contemporary Antonio Gramsci, who was imprisoned in fascist prisons for almost a decade starting in 1926.[64] Both men had been agitators for revolution in their respective countries. While Flores Magón was a leader in the PLM, Gramsci was a key figure in the Italian Communist Party. Both had been editors for radical periodicals: Flores Magón helped found *Regeneración* and Gramsci cofounded *Ordine Nuevo*. Like Flores Magón, Gramsci had been a key part of revolutionary movements by the industrial working class and articulated their need to form an alliance with the peasantry. Flores Magón's group, the PLM, had been instrumental in assisting the first two major Mexican industrial strikes of the twentieth century: one among the textile workers at the Rio Blanco manufacturing complex in Orizaba and another by the Cananea copper miners in Sonora. Gramsci had been a major proponent and chronicler of the council movement of the automobile factories in Turin. In both cases, these labor actions had the effect of mobilizing the working class in their countries, and were significant moments in the revolutionary movements of which the two men were key theorists.[65]

Both Gramsci and Flores Magón were invested in the production of revolutionary working-class intellectuals. Flores Magón believed that people certainly needed education, but not the dominant modes of education, "whose programs have been suggested or dictated by those with an interest in perpetuating the slavery of the poor for the benefit of the evil and brazen." Similarly, Gramsci saw that "traditional intellectuals" were characterized by the "specific conditions and specific social relations" in which they worked. Under capitalism, this meant that traditional intellectuals were tied to creating "the conditions most favorable to the extension" of the ruling class, however much they liked to believe that they operated under "autonomous and independent" conditions. Gramsci saw the working class challenge of developing "a new stratum of intellectuals," what he called "organic intellectuals" who would be tied to and representative of the interests of the proletariat.

Flores Magón anticipated Gramsci's insights. He saw that the "education of the masses, in order to be truly in their interests . . . must be in charge of the workers." This would be no easy task. As Gramsci realized, "Intellectuals develop slowly, much more slowly than any other social group, by their very nature and historical function." The precondition for the revolutionary education of the proletariat, Flores Magón insisted, was the production of material conditions enabling an "environment propitious for the education."[66] Specifically, he saw that the present conditions of the working class were antithetical to the formation of liberatory knowledge production:

The long hours of labor, the insufficient food, the hard conditions in the places of labor and habituation, make it so that the Mexican laborer cannot progress. Tired from long hours of work, he hardly has enough time to rest before he must return to his prison-like task. And of course this doesn't allow time to meet with his comrades from work and discuss and think over the common problems of the proletariat, nor does this allow him time to open a book or read a workers' newspaper. The laborer, thus, is absolutely at the mercy of voracious capitalism.[67]

Neither man suggested that prison was an ideal environment for supplying these preconditions. Prisons consciously impeded intellectual activity through methods such as surveillance, censorship of correspondence, isolation, regulation of reading time and material, denial of writing implements, destruction of personal writings, severe and arbitrary limitations on contact with other prisoners, and corporal punishment for reading material, writing, or verbal support of ideas deemed inappropriate by the prison administration. As scholars of incarceration suggest, the very fact of the prison produced its own "pedagogy," that is, prisons themselves demarcate the boundaries of freedom under capitalist social relations. However, as the writings and activities of Gramsci and Flores Magón during their respective confinements suggest, the prison also contained the potential for producing alternate pedagogies and more expansive definitions of freedom.[68]

In "The Southern Question," one of his final writings before his incarceration, Gramsci recognized that racial ideology had been successfully deployed to divide the industrial working class from the peasants in Italy. Gramsci suggested that in stories, folklore, and popular culture, the poverty and underdevelopment of the southern peasantry was made to seem natural, biologically induced, and separate from a class condition. Southerners were represented as "biologically inferior beings," sometimes "semibarbarians" or "barbarians by national destiny." Therefore, their poverty and underdevelopment did not appear as the "fault of the capitalist system, or any other historical cause" but as the result of the southerners' very nature: "lazy, incapable, criminal and barbaric." Amid a political drift toward fascism, Gramsci also recognized how southern peasants were being swayed by nationalist appeals. A powerful bloc of southern landowners and northern industrial capitalists sought to make their own alliance with the southern peasants through sentimental appeals to national regional identity. Unless these racist and nationalist ideologies could be ruptured, a peasant-worker class alliance could not come to fruition. As Gramsci correctly prophesized, the failure to unify in this class struggle rendered Italy vulnerable to the onset of fascism.[69]

Ricardo Flores Magón had been situated on both sides of the US–Mexico border and knew firsthand the difficulties of organizing transnational and interracial solidarities. He had witnessed the color line disfigure class solidarities both within and across borders. Beatings, lynchings, and mischaracterizations of Mexican and Black workers had wide implications. Such violence prevented class solidarity from forming among the entire working class. For Flores Magón, these racist divisions were not inevitable. The struggle for this identification among people, he believed, was simultaneously a struggle against capitalism. He wrote, "Capitalism foments racial hatred so that the peoples never come to understand each other, and so it reigns over them."[70]

Flores Magón recognized that a global revolutionary movement needed to simultaneously shatter the agreed-upon lies of racial hatred. Racism, in his analysis, was a conscious strategy by "the millionaires, the big businessmen, [and] the financial bandits" to "open abysses between the diverse races and nationalities, and in this manner to ensure their empire." In opposing international capital and practices of racialization, he proposed that the Mexican Revolution could inspire new global visions of liberation across the color line. Accordingly, he consistently sought to internationalize the struggle, which he believed had found an early expression in Mexico. He reminded the Mexican workers that their struggle, "the struggle of humanity" was global:

> Millions of intelligent eyes contemplate you from across the oceans, from other continents, from other lands, with the same emotion that awaits a life or death decision, because, know it well Mexican workers, because your triumph will be the dawn of a new day for all of the oppressed of the Earth, just as your defeat will result in the tightening of the chains on every worker on Earth.[71]

Flores Magón spent most of his final months writing to friends and allies, pleading for medical care to treat his illnesses and fading eyesight. In a chilling note to his lawyer, Harry Weinberger, Flores Magón compared his failing health and creeping blindness (the result of medical neglect) to the torturous conditions he had suffered during an earlier confinement in Mexico's Belén prison prior to the Mexican Revolution. "Once when I was young I was kept for several weeks in a dark dungeon, so dark that I could not see my own hands," Flores Magón remembers. "But," he writes, "I could suffer all that excepting the absence of light. I need light. I need light."[72] There was a diabolic symmetry between the international spotlight on Flores Magón and the darkness of his sequestration. As Michel Foucault has suggested, the more monstrous the criminal seemed, the more he was deprived of light and recognition: "He must not see, or be seen."[73]

Once, when he was too ill to speak for himself, Ricardo's brother Enrique addressed the federal court in Los Angeles, speaking on behalf of them both.

> The court has spoken of us as aliens to this country and its people. The court is in error. We are aliens to no country, nor are we aliens to any people on earth. The world is our country and all men are our countrymen. It is true that, by birth, we are Mexicans, but our minds are not so narrow, our vision not so pitifully small as to regard as aliens or enemies those who have been born under other skies.[74]

In his years at Leavenworth, Ricardo Flores Magón helped transform the federal penitentiary into a university of radicalism. Here, anarchists, communists, nationalists, and pacifists produced new affinities and new understandings. In the writing, reading, teaching, and friendships formed in this convergence space, Flores Magón and a number of other self-professed radicals, alongside imprisoned working-class soldiers of color, were able to confront the expanse and limitations of various radical traditions. But despite his hope for an alternate way of being, Flores Magón confronted the limits of solidarities produced within the confines of white supremacy. In one of his final letters, he recalls the beauty of the Mexican landscape, then concludes with the tragic lines, "I meant well, my blonde brothers, I meant well, but you could not understand me."[75] If the color line could penetrate prison walls, a movement confronting it would need to find ways to do the same. This was perhaps a thought that preoccupied Flores Magón at the end of his life. Before he died in a cold Kansas cell, he dreamt of the cliffs and skies of Mexico, hoping his brothers to the North could one day understand him.

SOMETHING ABOUT ROPE

AN ENCYCLICAL TO OUR
CUSTOMERS

OPES began to be used before history began to be written. Their origin is lost in the mists of the past. It may be that the apes, some species of which swing from tree to tree by means of vines and supple branches, or make living cables by climbing over each other's bodies, were the first rope makers. It is clear that the primitive races, however savage, must have felt the necessity of cordage. For the purpose of crossing streams, the ancient Peruvians used to twist together the strong fibers of the maguey, forming ropes sometimes as large as a man's body. The Chinese, who claim to have invented many modern necessities, undoubtedly made ropes of bamboo, of rattan, of flax, and perhaps of twisted hides, both raw and tanned, at very ancient periods.

FIGURE 1. Upson-Walton Company, *Something About Rope: An Encyclical To Our Customers* (Cleveland: Upson-Walton Company, 1902), 3.

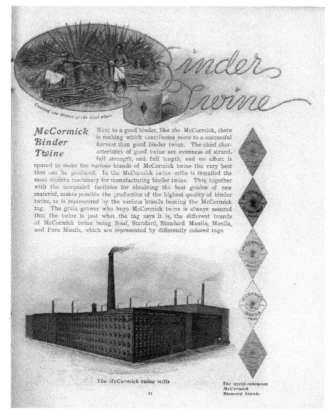

FIGURE 2. McCormick International Harvester, "A Model Machine Catalogue" (January 1903), 31.

FIGURE 3. F. Winold Reiss, "W. E. Burghardt Du Bois" (1925). Photo: Schomburg Center for Research in Black Culture, Manuscripts, Archives and Rare Books Division, The New York Public Library. New York Public Library Digital Collections.

FIGURE 4. Cover, *Regeneración* 192, Los Angeles, CA (June 13, 1914).

FIGURE 5. I.I. Brodskij, Portrait of Manabendra Nath Roy at the Second Congress of the Comintern in July 1920. Photo: International Institute of Social History, Amsterdam, The Netherlands.

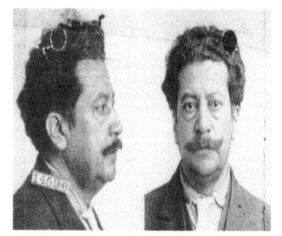

FIGURE 6. Ricardo Flores
Magón. Photo: National
Archives at Kansas City;
Record Group 129, Records
of the Bureau of Prisons;
Department of Justice.
Bureau of Prisons. US
Penitentiary, Leavenworth;
Inmate Case Files, 1895–
1952; National Archives
Identifier: 571125; Inmate
14596, Flores Magón,
Ricardo.

FIGURE 7. "Magón funeral photograph" (1922). Photo: MS 553, Harry Weinberger Papers,
Box 22, Folder 23, Manuscripts and Archives, Yale University, Sterling Memorial Library.

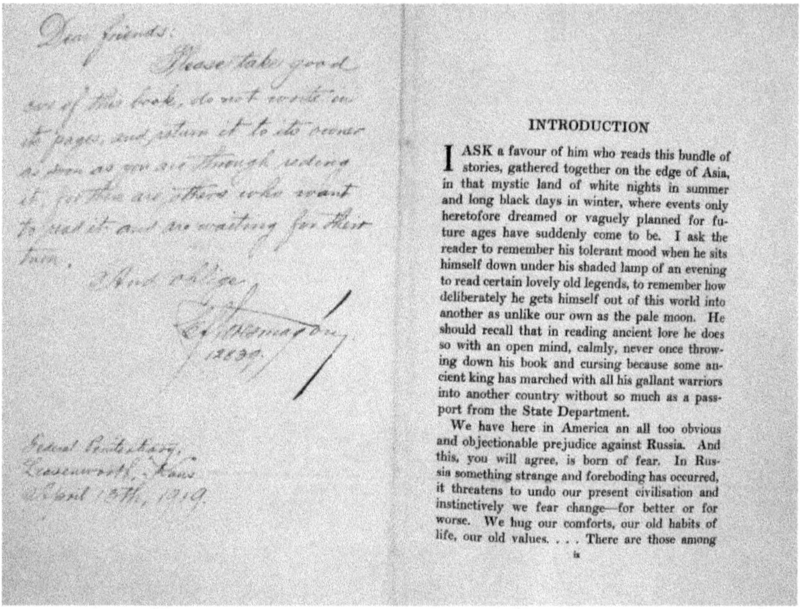

FIGURE 8. Flyleaf from Louise Bryant, *Six Red Months in Russia* (New York: George H. Doran, 1918). Photo: Leavenworth Libros, La Casa de El Hijo del Ahuizote Archivos, Mexico City.

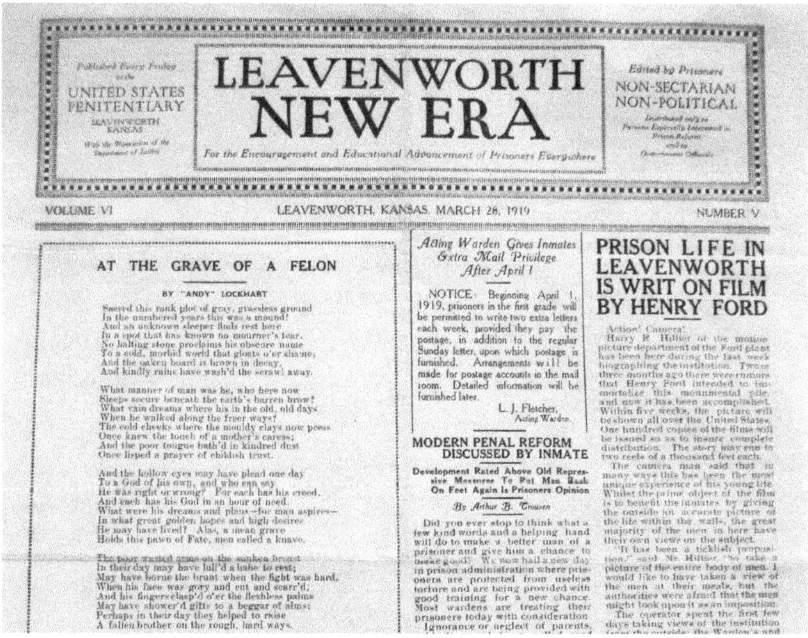

UNITED STATES
PENITENTIARY

LEAVENWORTH NEW ERA

For the Encouragement and Educational Advancement of Prisoners Everywhere

Edited by Prisoners
NON-SECTARIAN
NON-POLITICAL

VOLUME VI — LEAVENWORTH, KANSAS, MARCH 26, 1919 — NUMBER V

AT THE GRAVE OF A FELON

BY "ANDY" LOCKHART

Sacred this rank plot of gray, grassless ground
In the numbered years this was a mound!
And an unknown sleeper finds rest here
In a spot that has known no mourner's tear.
No halting stone proclaims his obscure name
To a cold, morbid world that gloats o'er shame;
And the oaken board is brown in decay,
And kindly rains have wash'd the scrawl away.

What manner of man was he, who here now
Sleeps secure beneath the earth's barren brow?
What vain dreams where his in the old, old days
When he walked along the freer ways?
The cold cheeks where the mouldy clays now press
Once knew the touch of a mother's caress;
And the poor tongue bath'd in kindred dust
Once lisped a prayer of childish trust.

And the hollow eyes may have plead one day
To a God of his own, and who can say
He was right or wrong? For each has his creed,
And each has his God in an hour of need.
What were his dreams and plans—for man aspires—
In what great golden hopes and high desires
He may have lived? Alas, a mean grave
Holds this pawn of Fate, men called a knave.

The poor wasted arms on the sunken breast
In their day may have lull'd a babe to rest;
May have borne the brunt when the fight was hard,
When his face was gory and cut and scarr'd,
And his fingers clasp'd o'er the fleshless palms
May have shower'd gifts to a beggar of alms;
Perhaps in their day they helped to raise
A fallen brother on the rough, hard ways.

Acting Warden Gives Inmates Extra Mail Privilege After April 1

NOTICE: Beginning April 1, 1919, prisoners in the first grade will be permitted to write two extra letters each week, provided they pay the postage, in addition to the regular Sunday letter, upon which postage is furnished. Arrangements will be made for postage accounts in the mail room. Detailed information will be furnished later.

L. J. Fletcher,
Acting Warden.

MODERN PENAL REFORM DISCUSSED BY INMATE

Development Rated Above Old Repressive Measures To Put Man Back On Feet Again Is Prisoners Opinion

By Arthur B. Trowen

Did you ever stop to think what a few kind words and a helping hand will do to make a better man of a prisoner and give him a chance to make good? We now hail a new day in prison administration where prisoners are protected from useless torture and are being provided with good training for a new chance. Most wardens are treating their prisoners today with consideration.

Ignorance or neglect of parents,

PRISON LIFE IN LEAVENWORTH IS WRIT ON FILM BY HENRY FORD

Action! Camera!

Harry R. Hillier of the motion picture department of the Ford plant has been here during the last week biographing the institution. Two or three months ago there were rumors that Henry Ford intended to immortalize this monumental pile, and now it has been accomplished. Within five weeks, the picture will be shown all over the United States. One hundred copies of the films will be issued so as to insure complete distribution. The story may run to two reels of a thousand feet each.

The camera man said that in many ways this has been the most unique experience of his young life. Whilst the prime object of the film is to benefit the inmates by giving the outside an accurate picture of the life within the walls, the great majority of the men in here have their own views on the subject.

"It has been a ticklish proposition," said Mr. Hillier, "to take a picture of the entire body of men. I would like to have taken a view of the men at their meals, but the authorities were afraid that the men might look upon it as an imposition."

The operator spent the first few days taking views of the institution

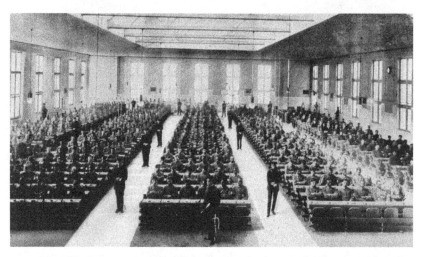

FIGURE 9. (Top) *Leavenworth New Era.* Photo: File #41751 Vol. VII: No VII (April 9, 1920), La Casa de El Hijo del Ahuizote Archivos, Mexico City.

FIGURE 10. (Bottom) "Dining Room," Federal Prison, Leavenworth, Kansas (circa 1910).

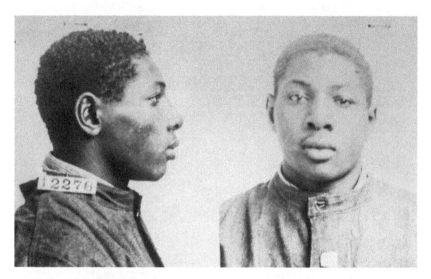

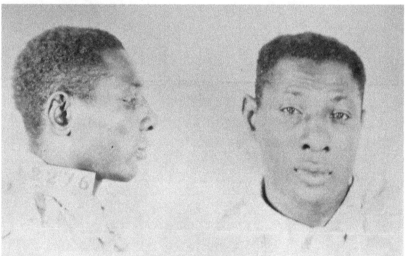

FIGURE 11 (Top). Roy Tyler, Inmate 12276, nineteen years old, 3rd Battalion, 24th Infantry, US Military, Received at Penitentiary: December 16, 1917. Photo: RG 129 Records of the Bureau of Prisons, United States Penitentiary, Leavenworth, Kansas.

FIGURE 12 (Bottom). Roy Tyler, Inmate 12276, thirty-four years old, Received at Penitentiary: September 7, 1932, for violating parole. Photo: RG 129 Records of the Bureau of Prisons, United States Penitentiary, Leavenworth, Kansas.

FIGURE 13 (Left). Portrait of Aleksandra Michajlovna Kollontai (Alexandra Kollontai). Photo: International Institute of Social History, Amsterdam, The Netherlands.

FIGURE 14 (Bottom). *Cincinnati Commercial Tribune* (Cincinnati, Ohio), November 14, 1926, page 1.

RUSSIA'S ENIGMA HEADS FOR MEXICO

Fascinating Feminine Machiavelli, Who Alternately Aided and Opposed Lenin and His Group and Became "Little Comrade" of the Reds, Now Comes as Soviet Envoy to the Hectic Central American Republic.

Mme. Alexandra Kollontai, brilliant woman diplomatist, chief representative of red Russia in the Western Hemisphere, with title of Envoy Extraordinary and Minister Plenipotentiary to Mexico.

By ALAN MACDONALD

FIGURE 15. "La Internacional," *El Machete* no. 496, Mexico City, Mexico, (October 24, 1937).

FIGURE 16. Elizabeth Catlett, *My role has been important in the struggle to organize the unorganized* (1947). Photo: © 2021 Mora-Catlett Family / Licensed by VAGA at Artists Rights Society (ARS), NY.

FIGURE 17. Elizabeth Catlett. Photo: Elizabeth Catlett papers Addendum II, Amistad Research Center, New Orleans, LA.

FIGURE 18 (Left). Elizabeth Catlett, *And a special fear for my loved ones* (1947). Photo: © 2021 Mora-Catlett Family / Licensed by VAGA at Artists Rights Society (ARS), NY.

FIGURE 19 (Bottom). Alfredo Zalce, *La dictadura porfiriana exalta demagógicamente al indígena* (1947). Photo: © 2021 Artists Rights Society (ARS), New York / SOMAAP, Mexico City.

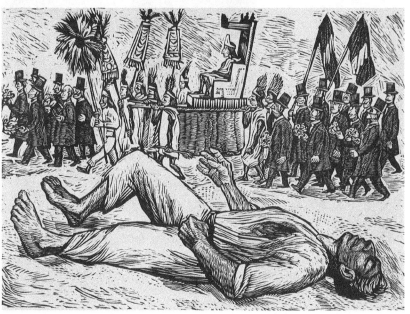

FIGURE 20. Elizabeth Catlett, *To pay for petroleum* (1947). Photo: © 2021 Mora-Catlett Family / Licensed by VAGA at Artists Rights Society (ARS), NY.

FOUR

How to Make Love

ALEXANDRA KOLLONTAI AND THE
NATIONALIZATION OF WOMEN

Alexandra Kollontai ... tells women that they are capable of a
new freedom, beautiful and untrampled. She is so carried away
by her enthusiasm that she is unmindful of how easily wings are
broken in this age of steel. But if her inspiration which aims to
lift women to the skies, lifts them only from their knees to their
feet, there will be nothing to regret. Civilization, in its snail-like
progress, is only stirred to move its occasional inch by the burning desire of those who will move it a mile.

LOUISE BRYANT, *MIRRORS OF MOSCOW*, 1918

The astonishing, beautiful lady Bolshevik has by the ears the
world that watches international complications. Kollontai in
Mexico! ... after hours, as you might say, she is reported to be
the heroine of tempestuous, whirlwind affairs of the heart.

ALAN MACDONALD, "RUSSIA'S MAGIC WOMAN IS
HEADING FOR MEXICO," *BOSTON DAILY GLOBE*,
NOVEMBER 14, 1926

PORT OF VERACRUZ

The crowd was intrigued long before they ever set eyes on the ambassador.
Gathered at the port, trade union leaders, members of the local militant renters' union, politicians, and a number of communists prepared to catch a
glimpse of their mysterious new visitor. Some bore gifts. Many waved red
flags. Musicians stood ready with their instruments. The revolutionary singer
Concha Michel waited with a song in her throat. The governor of Veracruz,
General Jeriberto Jara, prepared to offer his official reception while a coterie
of military officers readied themselves for formal introductions. As the welcoming party stood near the ship, their banners and flags caught the wind,

lifting their hair, their scarves, and their expectations. What would she look like? What would she say? What messages would the new ambassador bring to them from this still mysterious place, the Soviet Union?[1]

Alexandra Kollontai would later record in her diplomatic diary that the skies above Veracruz were not intense that day, but rather "pale" and milky, faded in the clouds that hung over the gulf.[2] Sailing into the harbor of "Mexico's most important" port city in December 1926, she noted the low-slung white houses, swaying palm trees, and the fortress "as white as sugar" burning against "the bright blue of the sea."[3] By 1926, this modern harbor was bustling with exports of Mexican oil and silver and with imports of foreign capital, much of which was invested in local real estate. This "badly smelling port, where the bourgeois exploit the people" and where they keep "its cocaine, its heroin, its marijuana" according to local anarchist housing organizer Hernán Proal, was a hotbed of radical activity.[4] A 1925 report indicated significant pro-communist and pro-Soviet sentiment among the largely Indigenous radical peasantry of Veracruz. To the dismay of the communists who reported it, these feelings had little formal relationship to communist doctrine or to the newly formed Mexican Communist Party.[5] After decades of dictatorship, state power was still largely associated with repression. Parties vying for political power were often viewed with suspicion.[6] Like many radicalized peasants throughout the country, *veracruzanos* found a resonance with the Bolshevik Revolution, routed through their own experiences of the Mexican state, land ownership, foreign capital, and indeed revolution. The terrain roiled with struggle as waves softly lapped against the shoreline.[7]

Kollontai, one of the first women to serve as a foreign diplomat, had much to contemplate before disembarking. Her reputation had preceded her, as she stepped into her role as Soviet ambassador to Mexico. She had recently discovered this in Cuba. During a brief refueling stop in Havana, she had prepared to meet with a group of local feminists and supporters. As the delegation waited for her with banners and flowers, Kollontai was brusquely confronted by police who climbed aboard. Citing an article of Cuban immigration law that prevented single women from entering the island, the officers barred the ambassador from coming ashore. Cuba, "a literal vassal" of the United States, was, to Kollontai's mind, only replicating US exclusions. Only a month earlier, Kollontai had been barred from passing through the United States. US Secretary of State Frank Kellogg had alleged that Kollontai's presence would foment Bolshevism throughout the United States and, indeed, throughout Latin America. Kollontai, a fifty-four-year-old diplomat and trade minister who had previously served as ambassador to Norway and was accustomed to interacting with counterparts from other diplomatic missions, considered these exclusions to be professional affronts. Her confinement in Cuba's harbor marked her rude awakening to the long reach of the United States into Latin America, a threat that would shadow all her activities in the region.[8]

Racing before her on the wind were stories about her wantonness, her impropriety, and her radicalism. She was, after all, not only a diplomat but a "sexually emancipated communist woman," as she titled her memoir drafted earlier that year.[9] Kollontai was an accomplished writer, theorist, and legislator, having served as Soviet Commissar of Social Welfare. In widely circulating writings, she had promoted new policies around motherhood, gendered labor, and social welfare. In fiction, she suggested how romantic relationships, friendships, and political organizing could transform the capitalist social relations that structured them. Her writings reached the eyes of radical feminists in North America and were even debated by the US Congress. Like her contemporaries Louise Bryant and Emma Goldman, Kollontai propagated unconventional notions of partnership and love. In her work and life, love was reimagined as a collective practice, the basis of her revolutionary platforms, and the ballast of her own personal relationships. Many at the port anxiously waited to see this revolutionary, this Bolshevik feminist, this cloud of rumors take shape upon the shore.[10]

Kollontai's predecessor as Soviet ambassador, Stanislav Pestkovsky, had arrived at the same port two years earlier. There, as in all of his inaugural addresses, he issued booming appeals to the Mexican workers and sent messages of unity from the Soviet Union.[11] He was received with a thunderous reception, especially in Mexico City, where he stood on the balcony of the Hotel Regis addressing the cheering crowd.[12] To his supporters' delight and to the great annoyance of the US ambassador, Henry Fletcher, Pestkovsky was greeted with enormous warmth and excitement. Pestkovsky, the first Soviet ambassador to Mexico, had inaugurated his position as one of internationalist solidarity between two revolutionary governments.[13] During his mission, the Soviet embassy in Mexico City, the first such embassy in the Western Hemisphere, served as the staging ground for this partnership, as well as a convergence space for radicals committed to revolutionary internationalism. From the Veracruz port, expectations were high that Madame Kollontai would do the same.[14]

After Kollontai's ship docked, the ambassador remained inside. To the surprise of Leon Gaikis, the first secretary of the Soviet Legation, she did not address the crowd as "Comrade Pestkovsky would certainly have greeted them."[15] Already, this initial decision marked a strategic choice. Her predecessor had been removed after complaints by the Mexican government, who found his presence as welcome as "a tack in a tire."[16] Among their concerns were his efforts to consort with communists in the country and region, thus incurring the suspicion of the US government. In her new position, Kollontai would be scrutinized by a less forgiving Mexican president, Plutarco Elías Calles, who was himself under intense scrutiny by the United States. With Mexican governmental anxieties, the surveillance of US officials, and the hopes of Mexican radicals and revolutionary feminists worldwide, expectations hovered above Kollontai before she ever stepped foot in the country.

Conspicuously absent at the port were representatives of the state-sponsored labor group, the Confederación Regional Obrera Mexicana (CROM). With its strong ties to the American Federation of Labor, the CROM occupied a complicated role relative to the Soviet Union. Mexican Labor Minister, and head of CROM, Luis Morones alleged that Mexican workers had "nothing in common" with Russian workers. Labor leaders were reportedly ordered to avoid welcoming Kollontai.[17] Their absence was not wholly inconvenient. Unlike Pestkovsky, Kollontai could not appear to support radical labor organizing. Her remit as ambassador was to encourage trade, share Soviet culture, and secure diplomatic relations with Mexico. She was not, in Soviet premier Joseph Stalin's stern words, to be seduced into revolutionary possibilities in Mexico that did not actually exist.[18] Neither conservative elements of the Mexican state nor her Soviet overseers wanted her to be seen propagating Bolshevism in Latin America. The US government further discouraged such affinities. If fully implemented, Mexico's radical 1917 Constitution would support Mexican labor rights and land redistribution, and directly threaten US interests in Mexico. US fears around labor organizing and the nationalization of Mexican land would merge with fears of Bolshevism and nationalization. These fears would soon nestle together in a distorted image of Kollontai and of her feminism.

Undeterred by these geopolitical concerns were the organizers, radicals, and left-leaning officials who had come to greet her that December day. As Kollontai stepped from the ship into buoyant music along the quayside, she saw women "with dark faces wearing calico dresses," with hair "thick and dark as a crow's wing" falling loose down their backs and lifted by the air. She noted men "in hats and overalls" nuzzle *sarapes* in the wind. Before them stood a tall Black man proudly waving a red scarf in greeting, beckoning the ambassador to address her supporters. Between the eager crowd, her vexed Soviet compatriots, anxious Mexican officials, impatient US agents, and the curious cluster of foreign journalists, many eyes were on the ambassador as she finally alighted onto Mexican soil.[19]

This chapter considers Alexandra Kollontai's brief time in Mexico as she served as Soviet ambassador between December 1926 and June 1927. Through an analysis of her diplomatic diary, correspondence, and periodical articles, as well as her political writings, it considers the imaginaries projected onto the ambassador during a tense period of US-Mexican relations. It recounts this period as a convergence of revolutionary as well as counterrevolutionary projections. These included the hopes radicals projected onto the Soviet Union and the negotiations of those hopes by Soviet officials who did not entirely share them. The US state projected its own fears of Bolshevism spreading throughout the Western hemisphere. Mexican officials, in turn, projected fears upon anything or anyone that might hasten US intervention. In Mexico, Kollontai found herself an unwelcome center of these manifold projections.

Kollontai was also ensconced in the aspirations of her radical feminist contemporaries. Through divergent paths and different vehicles, they sought to forge an internationalism rooted in a transformation of gender roles, sexual relations, and the fundamental organization of capitalist social relations. But the convergence space produced by Kollontai in Mexico, where these fears and these aspirations would collide, was ultimately tragic. This chapter traces how projected counterrevolutionary anxieties ultimately consolidated as a force against her feminism and against her person. Disparate fears around the organization of labor and the nationalization of land were displaced and given new shape by fears of Kollontai and the "nationalization of women." In this way, the chapter traces how Kollontai herself became a convergence space of hopes, aspirations, fears, and thwarted visions in this era of conflicting internationalist projects.

This chapter first considers the landscape of struggle in Mexico that Kollontai entered in 1926. It examines how Kollontai's socialist and feminist internationalism resonated with the projects she connected to in Mexico in the age of the New Imperialism. It then turns to the particular difficulties over the meaning of the Soviet embassy during this heightened period of US intimidation and worker insurgency. It finally describes her inglorious exit from the country as the fears of the US government, frustration of the Mexican government, and influence of the Soviet government converged in cynical and opportunistic interpretations of her feminism.[20]

Kollontai found herself in another complicated position as she set off from the port for the Soviet embassy in Mexico City. She could not be seen to enjoy the lavish accommodations of a traditional diplomat, representing as she did a worker's republic. This was according to the Soviet embassy secretary, Leon Gaikis, who made all the arrangements for the legation. Rather than a private coach or first-class cabin, Gaikis booked her on a third-rate train ticket to travel the long distance to Mexico City. In this way, he believed, she would be able to show that she was not "disgusted by traveling with the people." After her long sea voyage and stressful encounters, Kollontai found no joy upon "hard seats" of the third-class compartment. "The car was packed, it was hot, the air stifling and dusty," she wrote. She searched for water but found it was only available for passengers in the first-class dining cars. She made do and noted that she would talk to Gaikis about his "strange ideas" about democracy. For twelve hours under an "unforgiving sun," her head "was spinning" and her heart beat "painfully." On this difficult trek she would have traced a path through a landscape newly refashioned by social struggle.[21]

Over the port of Veracruz, where her journey began, international forces had jockeyed for power for centuries. Hernán Cortés had challenged Huastec, Otomíe, Totonac, and Olmec sovereignty in the region, inaugurating Spanish colonial rule in 1519. The city soon became New Spain's most important port, where silver, sugar, and enslaved African people were all profitably traded. In Veracruz's highlands, enslaved Africans and Indigenous people escaped to create maroon communities, securing the first free settlement in the Americas by 1618. From Veracruz, Antonio López de Santa Anna's forces defeated the Spanish Emperor of Mexico, decisively winning the republic's independence in 1822. During the brutal US-Mexico War, the port endured the largest amphibious invasion of the US Navy in 1847. Just over a decade later, Benito Juárez and his fellow Liberals ruled from the city during the War of Reform. In 1863, Napoléon III sent Archduke Maximilian von Habsburg to Veracruz to preside as Mexico's French Emperor. Though Maximilian was executed and French forces defeated, the insult of the short-lived invasion lingered. Deeply burning in living memory were the recent events of 1914, when the US military had occupied the port for six months. The US government still trained a covetous eye upon the opulent port. The swelling threat of invasion hung over the city and, indeed, over all of Mexico. According to Latin American and Soviet officials, all that was needed was a "pretext."[22]

Traveling from Veracruz in late 1926, Kollontai would have passed by red stars painted on the windows, walls, fences, and doors of tenements, signals of the city's protracted housing struggles. Beginning in 1922, local sex workers had organized rent strikes, the longest of which lasted thirty-eight months. Joining labor unions, tramway workers, and squatters, the sex workers formed the revolutionary renters' union or *Sindicato Revolucionario de Inquilinos*. Drawing on Article 123 of the Revolutionary 1917 Constitution, which obligated employers to provide clean, sanitary, and affordable housing, the union successfully argued for expanded state housing protections. The remnants of the union's collective actions and occupations were still visible, as was the poverty, slum housing, and homelessness against which they had organized, a landscape writhing in strife.[23]

Across the countryside, the ambassador might have seen the familiar sight of children, extremely poor, homeless, hungry, and often disabled due to malnutrition. Having also come from a country that had undergone revolution, extreme civil strife, famine, a pandemic, and the dislocation of established social structures, Kollontai would have been familiar with the sight. These children would have been similar to the thousands of the *besprizornost* (homeless waifs) that crowded railroad stations in major cities like Moscow. These were groups of children who had starved under the Tsarist regime and whose numbers had grown after the war and Bolshevik Revolution. Kollontai's work of reimagining of the state, civil society, and social relations revolved around managing and also preventing such massive suffering.[24]

As her train steamed toward neighboring cities, she would have passed coffee farms, textile mills, and tobacco plantations where recently proletarianized women who had migrated from the countryside were sharing newly learned skills in collective bargaining. As Kollontai's train cut through small rural areas, she would have witnessed spaces where upheavals, displacement, and migrations (disproportionately of men) had transformed gender roles, forcing women into previously unavailable positions of authority, such as heading households and fending for themselves and their children, and also leading campaigns as diverse as rent strikes, industrial agitation, suffrage movements, education reform, and school strikes.[25] A woman wearing a man's clothes, smoking, carrying a gun on her body, leading a strike, or even talking loudly in public—all represented radical cultural departures from repressive Catholic traditions.[26]

Unevenly throughout the interior, Kollontai would have passed through rural areas where national literacy campaigns were being implemented by female teachers who often incorporated lessons about the triplicate evils of "clergy, ignorance, and capital."[27] Article 3 of the Constitution called for secular education in schools. Thereafter, schools formerly named after saints or crony politicians were renamed for revolutionary heroes like Emiliano Zapata, Pancho Villa, Ricardo Flores Magón, and Karl Marx. A few years before Kollontai's arrival in 1923, the country experienced a dramatic shift in education through the Secretaría de Educación Pública (Secretariat of Public Education). Under the SEP, a mass federal education program sought to train teachers and dramatically increase student enrollments. With radical transformations, schools became centers where communities organized around issues of public health, child rearing, public sanitation, and later municipal projects such as road building, electrification, beautification of public spaces, etc. Teachers became linchpins of new social development, working as community organizers alongside campesino associations and worker movements.[28] Teachers like Concha Michel traveled through SEP cultural missions, collecting folk songs and "teaching women music and sewing during the day, organizing an evening theater festival, and teaching the men about political organizing and land reform at night."[29] Such transformations of gender roles, collective community projects, and spatial transformations served to unmask the "'counterrevolutionary' force of religion" upon education.[30]

Racing toward the capital in 1926, Kollontai might have sensed rumblings as divisions between the church and state were exploding in revolt. Tensions had mounted since President Calles implemented the articles of the 1917 Constitution promoting secularism. Article 130, for example, deprived the Church and clergy of the right to own property. Other laws, called the "Calles laws," closed religious schools, expelled foreign clerics, and banned public religious ceremonies. These laws were experienced as outrages. The massive social transformations of the Revolution, occurring in schools, homes, work sites, and towns, with their complementary challenges to gender norms and familial roles, had displaced the Church from its commanding role in civic life. Small protests that year gathered into a full-scale rebellion called the Cristero Rebellion. Coming from a country that had itself wrested political, economic, and social power from the Orthodox Church, Kollontai would have been familiar with the tensions. Her own reimagining of society required the upending of religious traditions, customs, gender norms, and entrenched family structures. Her efforts provoked backlash from comrades and counterrevolutionaries alike who were accustomed to a traditional gendered organization of power. As she well knew, building the new in the shell of the old was delicate and painstaking work.[31]

As Kollontai's train passed federal buildings, union halls, cultural centers, and schools at a good clip, she might have sensed how "new worlds" were being constructed "out of revolutionary devastation," as Jocelyn Olcott writes.[32] In eruptions of color and form, murals narrated new histories, symbols, and heroes of the revolution. José Vasconcelos, the first minister of education, had launched a national cultural movement in 1921, subsidizing public murals, most famously by Diego Rivera, David Alfaro Siqueiros, and José Clemente Orozco, known as *los tres grandes*. These murals denounced colonialism, imperialism, and brutality in the countryside. They celebrated long histories of struggle and offered images of possible futures. They depicted Indigenous people with consciousness and dignity and at the core of the country's past, present, and future. Though sometimes drawing on romanticized tropes and increasingly enlisted in revolutionary nationalist discourse, these murals counterposed official views of Indigeneity that had been promoted in political speeches, newspapers, and school textbooks. The dramatic visual language of murals imbued public walls with broad pedagogical functions. On the walls of the old world, visions of a new world were enshrined.[33]

Over the same railroad lines that carried a travel-weary Kollontai to the capital, *soldaderas*, women soldiers, had traveled during the fighting period of the Revolution. They often acted as saboteurs. They cared for and concealed soldiers, ran guns, and sometimes fought on the battlefield themselves. While by no means liberatory positions—in fact often violently coerced and exploited positions—these *soldaderas* "heralded a more open, mobile, experimental womanhood" and "assaulted Victorian morality and rules of sexual repression," as Mary Kay Vaughan describes.[34] But in riding the rails, Kollontai would encounter the source of her ultimate undoing in Mexico.

In 1926, workers went on strike against the National Railways of Mexico. By December 6, over five thousand machinists had stopped working. National and international forces had been jockeying for their loyalty and submission. The CROM and its close partner the AFL sought control over this critical segment of the working class. US businesses also sought intervention against their heavy losses. The railway workers maintained a perilous independence by organizing themselves into an unofficial union and drawing on Article 123, which affirmed their right to strike. Fifteen to twenty thousand workers would participate in the strike before its end, making it one of the era's largest labor actions. Pestkovsky had commiserated with the workers and arranged to send them solidarity aid from the Soviet Union. Critically, these funds would not reach strikers until his replacement's term was underway. Despite her immense caution, Kollontai would find herself at the center of an international scandal once those funds arrived. A conflagration of organized Mexican labor, international capital, US business unionism, and fraying diplomatic relations awaited her arrival. Unbeknownst to Kollontai, her train was delivering her swiftly to ignominy.[35]

As the ambassador's train traveled toward the capital, a clock was running down on foreign companies in Mexico. Article 27, one of the most radical of the 1917 Constitution, redefined private property, claiming that all land, subsoil, minerals, and resources belonged to the "nation." Concessions had previously been granted to foreign companies, preventing its implementation. These concessions were set to expire on December 31, 1926. The lapsing concessions threated to have a singular impact on the United States, which produced 75 percent of all of Mexico's imports and took in 65–85 percent of Mexico's exports. By the mid 1920s, US companies commanded 80 percent of all Mexican mineral production and close to 95 percent of all refinery production. Fears of Mexico's nationalization were expressed as fears of Mexico's relationship to Bolshevism. A few days before Kollontai's arrival, the Mexican government had recognized the radical government of Nicaragua. US ambassador James Sheffield was convinced this was evidence of "bolshevistic" elements in Mexico. On the day of Kollontai's arrival, Calles further antagonized the United States by proclaiming that Bolshevism was, in essence, a pursuit of Christian values, an agenda shared by all Mexicans. As US companies and state officials felt their interests threatened, their fears of Bolshevism would become anchored in the figure of Kollontai.[36]

When she finally arrived in the capitol, she was greeted by a crowd who welcomed her with banners proclaiming "viva Rusia soviética" and "viva la compañera Kollontai."[37] Many had waited all day, not knowing when her train would arrive. Just as in Veracruz, the expectant crowd was excited to meet the new ambassador. And just as she had on the shore, Kollontai stayed inside and contemplated the tightrope she was expected to walk. In her diplomatic diary, she described her conflicted feelings about the revolutionaries, who heartened her with their expressions of global solidarity, but with whom she could not publicly associate: "But I must not approach, I must not show that I am 'theirs.' I am just an ambassador."[38]

THE PROLETARIAT HAS NO FATHERLAND

US newspapers were gripped by Kollontai's time in Mexico. They wasted little time speculating about her character. According to the *Boston Globe*, "Kollontai is an inconsistent figure of challenge and crisis, of sudden masculine boldness, of swift feminine resignation and humility." US papers attempted to construe the ambassador as both conniving and shallow, infantilized and hypersexualized, and as a "dynamo of intrigue and passion" who was extremely vain.[39] The *New York Herald Tribune* explained her initial delay disembarking in Veracruz by asserting: "She kept every one waiting for some time while she finished dressing, appearing in the latest fashion."[40] The *Herald* would separately report on the extensive preparations being made at the Soviet embassy to accommodate Kollontai's trunks, "said to contain more than sixty dresses." While the ambassador had certainly brought her wardrobe, just as all diplomats were expected to do, the *New York Times* offered a correction entitled "Woman Envoy's Books Far Outnumber Gowns." It noted that she had actually brought a vast library of books in at least half a dozen languages. Indeed, Kollontai spoke eleven languages, a useful skill for a diplomat, trade minister, and person associated with the Soviet Union and the Communist International (Comintern), an association of global communist parties founded in 1919, which had often required her translation skills. In Mexico, Kollontai would begin to learn her twelfth language, Spanish. As she was serially maligned in the press, she was most often called upon to translate her own experiences from their cynical interpretations, a burdensome task for the careful diplomat.[41]

Kollontai came to Mexico City with established diplomatic as well as revolutionary credentials. She was an unusual figure in many respects. Born into an aristocratic family, her early socialist ideas and desire to resist bourgeois norms in her personal life put her at odds with her family and social circle. As a woman who defied gendered social norms of marriage and motherhood, she often clashed over her duties as wife and mother with her first husband. A feminist writer and theorist, she severely disagreed with fellow social democrats who failed to see feminism as anything but a series of bourgeois reforms. Initially a Menshevik, Kollontai joined the Bolsheviks in 1915 because of her opposition to World War I. She was one of the first officials appointed by Lenin after the October Revolution. As Commissar of Social Welfare, her feminist policies found broad support but also put her at odds with entrenched beliefs in Russian society held by the peasantry, her political foes, and fellow Bolsheviks. She had represented the Soviet Union as ambassador to Norway while also participating in the Left Opposition, resisting growing bureaucratization under Lenin and then Stalin. Conceivably, her post in Mexico was a punishment for political disloyalty. She brought extensive experience to Mexico of putting theory into practice while being opposed by powerful forces.[42]

In this, Kollontai was not alone. She had found her grounding as an internationalist among other brave socialist feminists. In 1914, Kollontai joined Clara Zetkin and Rosa Luxemburg in opposing the First World War. The Second International (SI), the organization within which socialists and global labor movements organized, had previously opposed wars that benefited the capitalist class. In the First World War, however, the SI encouraged workers to support the "national defense" of their own countries. Marx and Engels had declared that the proletariat had "no fatherland" in their *Communist Manifesto*. In this war, the "great men of the revolution," wrote Kollontai, were encouraging the proletariat to put their fatherlands before the class struggle. The SI's position authorized the working class to support wars in which they would be conscripted to kill one another. No class solidarity could develop under such conditions. How could the workers of the world unite while firing against each other in battle?[43] Kollontai described the stakes in 1915:

> In the distant future some historian shall picture the bloody year of horror, and describe the shattering crisis in the labor movement and the division and dissolution of the Socialist internationalism.[44]

Zetkin, Luxemburg, and Kollontai each took principled early stances against what they saw as a violent betrayal of internationalism. They appealed to other working-class women to join them. In 1914, Kollontai wrote a declaration calling for women to launch a "war on war." She foretold the "suffering, unemployment, and poverty" as well as "the cruelty, conquest, and degradation" that militarism inevitably brings.[45] Zetkin similarly addressed the "Women of the Working People" in 1915: "The men of the belligerent countries have been silenced. The war has dimmed their conscience, paralyzed their will and disfigured their entire being.... What are you waiting for in expressing your desire for peace and your protest against this war?"[46] In these appeals, Kollontai, like Zetkin, called back to the lyrics of "The Internationale," the official anthem of the Second International, which derided heads of state who "intoxicate us with gunsmoke."[47] Unseduced by the masculine appeals of nationalism, militarism, or the New Imperialism, they all rejected the conceits of the war. They were repulsed by the idea that a patriotic sense of belonging or a promise of restored manhood through militarism could be more redemptive than global worker solidarity. Arguably, their radical socialist feminism enabled them to be more clear-sighted internationalists.

Kollontai's anti-war work committed her to Bolshevism, the minority of the Russian Left opposition who also opposed the war. Bolshevik leader Vladimir Lenin warned Kollontai that abstract pacifism would simply disarm the proletariat and enhance their vulnerability. Just as "The Internationale" called for "peace amongst ourselves, war on tyrants," Lenin compelled the workers of the world to "transform" the imperialist war, where armed workers massacred each other, into a civil war against the bourgeoisie of each country. Kollontai's concept of "war on war" accordingly took on new meaning. She revised her thesis, asking in 1915, "Have the workers come to 'love' their own exploiters, their own tyrant masters so much during the war that they are willing to die to defend their profits and interests?!"[48] In their opposition to war, the Bolsheviks took the moral authority of the collapsed Second International, giving eventual rise to a Third International. When the Bolsheviks took power in Russia in 1917, Lenin appointed Kollontai to the Executive Committee, the first woman to hold such a prominent state office.[49]

From this position of power, Kollontai was able to observe and help shape multiple phases of the new Soviet state—from the ecstatic tumult of its early possibilities, the imaginative work of fusing theory and practice, the complicated tasks of state-building within the shell of a weak state, the sober years of civil war, mass starvation, the in-fighting, gradual bureaucratization, the repression of dissent, and attacks from without and from within. Though she only remained on the Executive Committee until 1918, she did not escape from these experiences unscathed.[50] As the Commissar of Social Welfare and the founder of the *Zjenotdel*, the Women's Section of the Communist Party, she had sought, above all, to challenge the social relations of capitalism. Central to all her efforts was a radical rethinking of love.

Love could not be contained in what Kollontai described as the "narrow framework" of capitalism.[51] This form of love, or "property love" as Michael

Hardt describes it, attempts to translate intimate social bonds into a limited set of recognizable propertied relationships.[52] Laws governing practices like marriage, patrimony, illegitimacy, divorce, and inheritance formalized property love and served to maintain class power and patriarchal authority. With the transmission of property determined through "family" units, wherein men were the primary owners, sellers, and beneficiaries of property, women were forced to tie their own survival and that of their offspring and often their extended family to property love. Kollontai saw how this gendered organization of power trapped women in prescribed roles of subservience and relations of unnecessary isolation. She saw propertied logic expressed as the exclusive "right to the absolute and individual possession of the beloved person."[53] Heterosexual partners were defined in a sanctified but exclusive relation to one another and isolated from any collectivity. The bourgeois family, she believed, mythologized its own self-sufficiency.[54]

Kollontai recognized how property love delimited the boundaries of care. Those who fell outside of the formal heterosexual family unit, including the unmarried, illegitimate, queer, orphaned, elderly, disabled, and widowed, were deemed undeserving of societal care, and suffered accordingly. Kollontai increasingly saw that the war-maimed, "the armless, the legless, the blind, the deaf, the mutilated," wandered through towns, not heralded as returning heroes but shunned as societal burdens.[55] In a truly revolutionary society, love would have to be redefined outside of capitalist, heterosexual, patriarchal, and militaristic relations. Love as a propertied relation disfigured those in its immediate thrall and, Kollontai argued, society as a whole.[56]

Kollontai believed that the foundation of a revolutionary society needed to be built through and toward an alternative definition of love. Three years before she departed for Mexico, she had published an essay entitled "Make Way for Winged Eros," where she offered a definition of her revolutionary notion of love, what she called "love-comradeship":

> For a social system to be built on solidarity and co-operation it is essential that people should be capable of love and warm emotions. The proletarian ideology, therefore, attempts to educate and encourage every member of the working class to be capable of responding to the distress and needs of other members of the class, of a sensitive understanding of others and a penetrating consciousness of the individual's relationship to the collective. All these "warm emotions"—sensitivity, compassion, sympathy and responsiveness—derive from one source: they are aspects of love, not in the narrow, sexual sense but in the broad meaning of the word.[57]

Love-comradeship incorporates these "warm emotions," shifting love away from individual, propertied, and isolated pairings, and into a collective sensibility. "Love," she observed, "is an emotion that unites and is consequently of an organizing character." This version of love had defined her policy work in the new Soviet state.[58]

Love-comradeship was Kollontai's central philosophy as Commissar of Social Welfare. Operationalizing this philosophy meant reconstructing society through a collectivization of previously individuated social functions. In place of private kitchens, for example, she helped to build public commissaries. Public laundries replaced private washrooms. In place of private homes, she built public homes for the elderly and sought to build public crèches where children could be watched, fed, and cared for, particularly while women were at work.[59] Kollontai envisioned a world where the burdens and expectations of highly gendered work were shifted to the state. As she explained in her 1920 essay "Communism and the Family," if the state could end the individuated labor of housework and childrearing, and transform traditional definitions of marriage, the family, and gender roles, it could enable new bonds forged through "affection and comradeship" to arise.[60] US journalist Louise Bryant appraised Kollontai's work:

> It is almost impossible that that institution which came to life through her enthusiasm and determination will ever cease to be. The laws I refer to are particularly those in regard to expectant mothers, orphans, illegitimate children and the state care of maternity hospitals, known as Palaces of Motherhood.[61]

A reconstruction of such social functions, Kollontai believed, would enable comrade-love to flourish.

But theory was difficult to align with the practice. The new Soviet experiment was built within the weak infrastructure of the Tsarist regime, which itself had been on shaky foundations before it was toppled. It also carried the vestiges of old traditions and values, unwilling to prioritize shifts in the social structure as the new state was under siege. Kollontai encountered these limitations in her capacity as Social Welfare Commissar. For example, she and her comrades were forced to deal with a massive number of children orphaned by war as starvation gripped the country. One solution had been to commandeer mansions of the old landed nobility to create centers or "colonies" where children could be fed, sheltered, and cared for, entering and exiting of their own free will. The thin resources available to coordinate this national effort could not address the scale of the need. The mansions had often been pilfered of all furnishings and partially destroyed. They lacked heat and plumbing, and they were perilous structures for children who had to dodge fallen ceilings and dangerously protruding beams. Trainloads of children were simply moved from one slum condition to another, with hardly enough supervision to make the centers viable in the way they had been imagined.[62]

Kollontai was also asked to find housing for the wounded veterans who eked out existence on the streets of Petrograd. One official recommended the nearly deserted Aleksandr Nevskii Monastery, formerly one of Russia's holiest shrines. This proposal was fiercely rejected by the monks who still occupied the monastery and refused to relent even after several rounds of negotiations. When a delegation of Soviet officials came to the monastery, the monks rang the church bells and called for help. An angry crowd soon formed, rejecting the sacrilegious use of space. Of her own accord, Kollontai called in members of the navy. In a chaotic standoff, sailors fired into the crowd, killing a monk in the process. The act scandalized religious officials, who saw it as an attempt to violently seize Church property. It also scandalized party members who had not approved of dispatching the sailors. Kollontai, then forty-five years old, subsequently married the navy officer in charge of the unit, who was twenty-eight. The scandal would plague Kollontai for years to come.[63]

Kollontai's crowning hope was a Palace of Motherhood, a sparkling hospital where women would be protected and cared for before, during, and after childbirth. Such a place, she believed, would elevate motherhood for working-class women, allowing their children to come into the world cared for and cherished, while they themselves were cared for and cherished. She sought to transform a former orphanage for this purpose. For a century, the foundling home in question had accepted illegitimate children through a discreet side window. Children were duly marked with numbers and added to an anonymous inventory of orphans. Kollontai felt there would be something beautiful about repurposing this space of shame and anonymity into a palace where working-class women and their children could be lovingly and safely cared for free of charge. The former orphanage staff were outraged by Kollontai's plan. For the old countess who had run the orphanage for years, honoring illegitimate births was an unforgivable disgrace. Ultimately, the Palace of Motherhood was not thwarted by the limitations of its physical structure or by political infighting; it was simply burned down. Kollontai suspected that the fire was intentional. After the protests of the monks and the burning of the palace, Kollontai had to admit she had underestimated the counterrevolutionary social forces of her opposition. In Mexico, she would continue to be dogged by similar adversaries.[64]

THE MEXICO CITY SOVIET EMBASSY

The Bolshevik Revolution found broad resonance around the world in its immediate aftermath. Movements against colonialism, imperialism, capitalism, and other forms of tyranny all took inspiration from this apparent workers' victory over autocracy. Some excitement came from careful watchers of the struggle, but some was due to an initial act of mistranslation. The radical Spanish press were among the first to report on the Bolshevik Revolution in 1917, which it interpreted in accord with its prevailing trends of anarcho-syndicalism.[65] The Mexican press, perhaps not entirely innocently, emphasized elements that would resonate with its Mexican readership, such as direct action, antimilitarism, workers' councils, and the "smashing of the state."[66] Barry Carr suggests that mistranslations which emphasized direct action and autonomous organizing not only appealed to the interests of readers but also suited the interests of the bourgeois press. There was great cynicism around state politics in Mexico at the time because, as Carr writes, "workers had gained little from politics" and the memory of state repression was still fresh.[67] Still, there was great excitement for communism as it was understood in different parts of the country. By 1926, there was a diffuse romanticism about the Soviet Union. As Kollontai reported to Soviet officials, she was often greeted by workers in the capital, who doffed their hats and yelled "Viva Rusia!" as she passed.[68]

Kollontai's primary contact was Leon Gaikis, the secretary of the Soviet embassy. Though they were officials from the same country, they had had different experiences of the Bolshevik Revolution and, subsequently, different interpretations of their missions in Mexico.[69] Kollontai had repeatedly explained to the foreign press weeks before her voyage that she believed diplomats should not interfere in the internal affairs of their appointed country. For this perspective, Gaikis would come to see Kollontai as something of a wet blanket.[70]

Gaikis had first served alongside Kollontai's predecessor Stanislav Pestkovsky when the Soviet embassy initially opened. Pestkovsky publicly bridged Russia and Mexico through appeals to the countries' respective revolutions. He drew links through further symbolic gestures, notably presenting his diplomatic credentials to President Obregón on the seventh anniversary of the October Revolution of 1917 and, afterwards, changing out of his tuxedo and donning less formal clothes to meet with workers in celebration of the Bolshevik victory. The newly established embassy of the newly established workers' state did not function as a traditional foreign embassy. As frequent embassy guest Bertram Wolfe observed, the embassy did not have much actual business to transact, so it devoted many resources to staging public gatherings. In a time of delirious creative ferment in Mexico City, the Soviet embassy under Pestkovsky was a center of rollicking activity.

In the 1920s, the exuberance of arts, culture, radical thought, transgressive experimentation, sexual expression, and revolutionary internationalism flowered among artists and intellectuals in Mexico City. The newly opened Soviet embassy became a central site where internationalists would converge. Here, people found new ways to articulate revolutionary national culture and communist currents. In addition to ostentatious workers' celebrations and revolutionary holidays, the recently formed Mexican Communist Party (PCM) held its meetings there. The nature of the party greatly shifted once the PCM decided to incorporate Mexican revolutionary cultural workers. By 1922, PCM-affiliated artists had organized themselves into the Sindicato de Obreros Técnicos, Pintores y Escultores (Mexican Union of Technical Workers, Painters, and Sculptors), with Siqueiros and Rivera in the leadership. Their weekly paper, *El Machete*, soon became the PCM's official organ, with funding from the embassy.[71] In 1923, Rivera was appointed to the party's Executive Committee while Siqueiros was appointed secretary of trade unions. The aims of the PCM were inadvertently subsidized by the state through the national mural program. As discussed in chapter 6, the era subsequently saw a flourishing of radical art through accessible forms, including linocuts, woodblock prints, easily reproducible lithographs, and murals adorning public walls, available for all to see.

Much of this high tide of Mexico City's radical energy, what Mauricio Tenorio-Trillo has called the "Cosmopolitan Mexican Summer," radiated from the Soviet embassy.[72] Diego Rivera appeared at embassy parties freshly splattered with paint after working on murals around the city or in his studio. The walls rang with music from Concha Michel's guitar. Boldly illustrated issues of *El Machete* were launched from the space. The journal's founder and Siqueiros's wife, Graciela Amador, would join artists like

Guatemalan painter Carlos Mérida or French-Mexican illustrator and muralist Jean Charlot in celebration. When there was "a vogue for all things Mexican," radical international artists, poets, thinkers, labor leaders, and filmmakers routinely passed through. US radical luminaries like Wolfe, Anita Brenner, photographer Edward Weston, and Weston's "pupil" and lover, the radical photographer Tina Modotti, all frequented the space. The embassy also drew regional connections and offered support to revolutionary movements in places like Nicaragua, Venezuela, and Cuba.[73] The secretary general of the Cuban Communist party, Julio Antonio Mella, also Modotti's partner, was able to conspire with other Cuban revolutionaries there. The embassy also hosted visiting Soviet artists like the great Russian poet Vladimir Mayakovsky, who was keen to understand what the Mexican Revolution had done for the country's most desperate people. (Not much, he concluded).[74]

In these ways, the embassy offered structure to an earlier movement of communists who had passed through the country and found possibilities there. Japanese revolutionary Sen Katayama had excitedly assessed that an organizing base in Mexico would "strike at the American capitalist imperialism a death blow" when he visited in 1921.[75] Swiss youth organizer Edgar Woog, aka Alfred Stirner, went from representing the Swiss Young Communist International to establishing the Mexican Young Communists in 1919. That year, the Mexican Communist Party was founded by former Indian nationalist M. N. Roy, as detailed in chapter 2. Internationalism was expressed through multiple celebrations: of Lenin's death, of Bolshevik victory, and May Day. In the tumult of strikes, radical activity, and celebrations of revolutionary culture, the embassy fostered a nascent internationalist culture and the ecstasy of possibility.[76]

These sentiments were tempered under the sober eye of Alexandra Kollontai. When Tina Modotti first entered the embassy at Kollontai's invitation, she was surprised to find bouquets of wildflowers, small pots of begonias, and tea served upon tables freshly laid with tablecloths. The embassy was cleaned and furnished, properly prepared to receive diplomats from other missions. Kollontai received Modotti with the warm greeting of a fellow feminist and practiced ambassador.[77] Kollontai understood her remit as maintaining and enhancing diplomatic relations between the two countries, encouraging trade of Russian exports like grain and even cultural products like film. Moreover, her job was to undo much of the influence of Pestkovsky: she was to stop threats of US aggression toward Mexico and the

Soviet Union. Kollontai brought an to end the party in the embassy, so to speak.

Kollontai and Gaikis sparred over everything. He scorned the new ambassador for behaving kindly toward diplomats of "hypocritical" countries such as England. While other diplomats had appointed cars waiting for them after meetings with the President at the National Palace, Kollontai recalled with embarrassment waiting until other delegates left in order to leave in her rented Ford. On other occasions, she had to pretend that she preferred walking, though she suffered in the heat and altitude and in her high-heeled shoes. She ultimately suffered a mild heart attack in January 1927 from the stress.[78]

Gaikis insisted that the Soviet legation reject the accoutrements of bourgeois culture and comfort. The embassy had precious little furniture since Gaikis found it "unnecessary." Coming from Norway, Kollontai could not conceive of how a diplomat could work without desks, typewriters, and most importantly, locked file cabinets. She furnished these things herself. While hosting teas and exhibitions to encourage greater trade and diplomatic relations with other countries, she felt strongly that the "Proletarians of the World, Unite" poster should not hang above the divan where she would entertain diplomats from other missions. On this and all other matters, she and Gaikis clashed.[79]

Beneath their disagreements lay different interpretations over what representing the Soviet Union meant—and at what stage the revolution was currently perceived to be. She wrote in her diplomatic diary that the embassy needed to "moderate" its "relations with local communists." To accomplish this, Kollontai believed that the embassy secretary might behave more like a diplomat and less "like a party organizer." Over this and many disagreements, Kollontai described her "friction" with Gaikis.[80] It was not that she did not desire such connections. She described her excitement at meeting local intellectuals, one of whom had even read her book. The meeting was a warm and welcome one. But she concluded with regret that she could not be seen to have too close contact with communists, and therefore could not continue the meetings as she would have liked. While she limited public meetings with high-profile communist leaders, she did meet with delegations of women workers. She sympathized with their desire to push for more radical feminist reforms. As Concha Michel would later reflect, many feminists in Mexico consorted with Kollontai to gain *orientadas* (direction) from the Bolshevik feminist.[81]

Kollontai knew from experience that integrating socialist feminist principles into state projects was complicated. Advances came through working women's direct confrontations with capital and the state. She traced the "awakening of the class self-consciousness" to revolts by Russian women textile workers beginning in 1872. Legislation supporting women and children only came about as concessions to their great strike waves. Available theory was scant, save for texts like *The Origin of the Family, Private Property, and the State* by Friedrich Engels, himself a textile heir, who was radicalized observing textile workers in Manchester, England. At the turn of the century, Kollontai had begun developing her own materials to share with textile workers in Germany and later the Russian Union of Textile Workers. Escaping tsarist repression, she disguised her talks as sewing circles.[82] This was a sly reference to Nikolai Chernyshevsky's 1863 radical feminist novel *What Is to Be Done?*, about a woman who rejects bourgeois love to form a sewing collective with friends who pool resources to care for each other. The book influenced a generation of radicals like Emma Goldman and Lenin, who famously riffed on its title. To escape tsarist censors, it was written as romantic fiction, a tactic Kollontai would later employ. Kollontai believed she had found herself in a feminist revolution while visiting Paterson, New Jersey, in 1913. She reportedly shouted, "A revolution has happened!" when she saw the mostly women immigrant silk workers take to the streets during the famous strike. Her affection for Mexican women who attempted to weave together women's liberation and socialism was not surprising.[83]

As she consorted with Mexican feminists, she was increasingly under attack from the conservative Mexican and US press. Increasingly anxious about Mexican oil concessions, Mexican support for radical Latin American governments, and the Mexican railway workers' ongoing strike, reporters often blamed Bolshevik influence upon the Mexican government. They increasingly identified Kollontai as the source. Just a few weeks into her post, she concluded that she was their "target."[84] By March she noted that the "press attacks on the embassy and on me are in full swing. . . . I live in constant agitation."[85] Later that month, she wrote, "Every day without exception there are attacks in the press. . . . It terribly affects my weak heart."[86] From the time of her appointment to Mexico, the US press particularly fixated on her. This was not only due to the rabid anti-communism of figures like Secretary of State Kellogg, but also due to the fact that she had been so warmly received on her earlier visits to the United States, where her ideas about motherhood and state protections of women and children, and nascent ideas around love-comradeship, were embraced.

She had been warmly received on two speaking tours of the United States, where she had joined socialists like Eugene Debs and Wobblies like Big Bill Haywood. Her pamphlet "Communism and the Family" had been translated and published in the United States in 1920. This was celebrated by a range of feminists looking for increased state support for women, children, and families. In 1920, the Federal Children's Bureau issued a report on maternity benefits admittedly inspired by Kollontai's work. It called for "free medical and nursing care for mothers and infants at home or at a hospital when necessary."[87] In 1929 hearings before the Committee on Interstate and Foreign Commerce concerning the Child Welfare Extension Service, Kollontai and the publication were disparaged by congressmen:

> Alexandra Kollontay [sic] is now Soviet Minister to Norway again, after a hectic career which has included eight husbands, two positions as people's commissar.... The State Department refused her permission even to pass through the United States on her way to her post as Soviet Minister to Mexico in November, 1926.... Prof. Pitrim Sorokin, an eyewitness of the Russian revolution, contends that Kollontay has had a dozen husbands ... and Sorokin adds: 'I wish she might come under the observation of Freud and other psychiatrists. She would indeed be a rare subject for them.'[88]

This was not the first time Kollontai's name was smeared in the US Congress. During the Overman Committee hearings, otherwise known as the 1919 *Hearing on Bolshevik Propaganda,* witnesses were repeatedly questioned about Kollontai's plans to "nationalize" women. Bessie Beatty, editor of *McCall's* magazine, was questioned about Kollontai's plans.

> MR. HUMES: What do you know about the nationalization of children, or the taking over by the state of children of certain ages, for the purposes of education?
>
> MISS BEATTY: I know that when I talked to Alexandra Kollontay, who is commissar of public welfare, she told me a great deal, at length, as to what her social program was, and there was nothing of that sort in that program. Her idea was that an orphanage was a bad place in which to keep children, and that it was best to get them away from that sort of control. In order to make it possible for women to keep their own

children, they formulated a plan by which a mother should have eight weeks of liberty from her factory position previous to the birth of her child and immediately after.

MR. HUMES: That is in order to encourage woman labor; in order to protect and encourage woman labor in the factories?

MISS BEATTY: No; these are the women who always had to work, just as our women work in factories, whether they have children or not. This was to protect the woman from hurting herself before and after the birth of her child.

MR. HUMES: Is it true that this Madame Kollontay married the man whom she did marry, and with whom she went to the Scandinavian countries, because of these regulations or requirements for the nationalization of women and compulsory marriage?

MISS BEATTY: I am quite sure that she never did anything under compulsion.[89]

Throughout the hearing, and in press reports that circulated long after, Kollontai's character was questioned. Her ideas about employing love-comradeship through the reconfiguration of the state were deliberately misrepresented as efforts to "nationalize" women, in other words, to force young women into positions of sexual servitude administered by the state; an imagined redistribution of sexual labor. This grotesque imaginary played to counterrevolutionary fears. Just as conservative forces in the United States construed any anti-racist, anti-lynching, anti-Jim Crow agitations as threats to the social order, so too did those forces construe any radical movement, especially radical feminist movements, as a threat to the sanctity of the monogamous family. These deliberate falsifications were renewed during Kollontai's time in Mexico.[90]

By April 1927, once the solidarity funds for striking railway workers in Mexico authorized by Pestkovsky had arrived, the backlash was intense. Despite her protestations, Kollontai was blamed for orchestrating foreign state support for an illegal strike. All suspicions hovering around the ambassador appeared to be confirmed: she was a cunning Bolshevik who sought to use diplomatic cover to undermine the Mexican government, to disrupt its main transportation sector, threaten US economic and geopolitical interests, inflame dissent nationally, and thereafter spread Bolshevism throughout Latin America. Whatever thin patience conservative forces in the United States and Mexico had had for this woman quickly dissipated in the scandal. For the remainder of her time in Mexico, accusations against Kollontai took on utterly misogynist tones. The press insinuated that Kollontai's true, prurient objective was to nationalize women, a warping of US fears around the 1917 Mexican Constitution's promised nationalization of its land and resources.[91]

Adding to her misfortunes, a pirated and mistranslated version of her 1923 short fiction "Bolshiaia liubov," or "A Great Love" was published against her wishes. As in Chernyshevsky's *What Is to Be Done?*, Kollontai had attempted to use the form of a romance novel to popularize feminist theories of love-comradeship. The story was given a scintillating cover and the suggestive title *Amor Rojo* ("*Red Love*"). Despite her best efforts, Kollontai was crushed under the weight of reaction. She requested and was granted permission to quietly leave Mexico.[92]

Unlike her arrival into the country, Kollontai's departure from Mexico in early June 1927 was quick and unceremonious. She was forced to leave many of her belongings behind, not wanting to alert the press or even the embassy secretary, Gaikis. But, as she sailed away from Mexico, she recounted that she had kept a few things in her possession. Radical workers had given her small objects made out of wax, clay, and henequen. Members of the textile workers union had gifted her a *sarape* with her initials woven into it. Mexican labor organizers had also given her a coconut into which the following inscription was carved:

> *Para la camrada Kollontai. Los imperialistas te odian, los revolucionarios te quieren. Viva en nuestros corazones la amistad de México y Rusia.*
>
> To Comrade Kollontai. The imperialists hate you, the revolutionaries love you. Long live the friendship in our hearts between Mexico and Russia.[93]

In her time as ambassador to Mexico, Alexandra Kollontai herself became a center where projected fears around Bolshevism, nationalization, feminism, and internationalism were aimed. She was also a focal point around whom these possibilities converged but were ultimately thwarted. Her brief time in the country offers an opportunity to consider the significance of what she called love-comradeship. What had clarified her own internationalism, sharpened her conception of a revolutionary state, and determined her understanding of radical collectivity was her evolving interpretation of how to make love. In order for an internationalist consciousness to be made, she believed that the social relations of capital had to be undone, the traditionally gendered organization of power reorganized, and a new conception of relationality imagined.

As she sailed away from Mexico, her thoughts continually drifted back to the country. There was unfinished work to do and certainly much more to be done. Before she left, she had started an article entitled "La tierra cambia de piel" ("The Earth sheds its skin"). We find ourselves in the center of a changing world, she wrote. "Todo ha cambiado, se mueve lentamente." Everything has changed. It moves slowly.[94]

FIVE

How to Make a Living

DOROTHY HEALEY AND SOUTHERN CALIFORNIA
STRUGGLES FOR RELIEF AND REVOLUTION

Arise, you prisoners of starvation!
Arise, you wretched of the earth!

¡Arriba, parias de la Tierra!
¡En pie, famélica legión!

THE INTERNATIONALE (*LA INTERNACIONAL*)

THE WOMEN IN THE JAIL cell were singing. The jail, a dusty facility in the farming town of Brawley, California, twenty-five miles north of the Mexican border, was full of striking lettuce pickers, their wives, and supporters. Crammed together in the women's section were a number of Mexican women who had been arrested in the strike and one brassy white teenager. The teen couldn't speak Spanish because, as she later lamented, "I [was] a backward, stupid, provincial Anglo." To pass the time, the women taught each other songs. The teenager, Dorothy Healey, a Communist organizer from Los Angeles, tried teaching radical labor songs. The women, "part of that generation of Mexicans who had grown up with the Mexican Revolution," bested the young organizer. In Spanish, they sang the "Internationale," a song that commanded the "prisoners of starvation" and the *parias de la Tierra* ("wretched of the earth") to arise. In the early 1930s, this song was still an anthem that socialists, anarchists, communists, and fellow travelers could sing together. This song, remembered Healey, "bridged all the countries of the world." Having lived through the Mexican Revolution, a struggle variously derided as the chaos of an underdeveloped nation while also praised as the first major social revolution of the twentieth century, the women knew the lyrics well.[1]

Brawley, a small town in California's Imperial Valley, was one of many rural areas on fire in the early years of the Depression. In 1933, a year before general strikes would rock docks, mines, mills, and shop floors across the country, California's fields exploded in rebellion. Santa Clara cherry pickers, Lodi grape cutters, Yolo County orchard pruners, and Oxnard sugar beet harvesters, among others—close to fifty thousand workers in total—went on strike, accounting for half of all US farmworker strikes that year. More than eighteen thousand workers walked away from cotton fields across the San Joaquin Valley in what was then the largest strike in agricultural history. Spanning over a hundred miles and affecting 65 percent of the state's crops, these thirty-seven strikes represented an unprecedented insurgency in the California fields.[2]

By 1935, half of all fresh fruit in the Unites States and 70 percent of all the country's canned fruit came from California. According to the 1935 Agricultural Census, a scant 2 percent of California "farmers" controlled a third of all agricultural production in the state. The "farmers" in question could more accurately be described as corporate agribusiness owners, given the nature of their consolidated land monopolies and networks of processing, canning, and marketing companies. The struggle for dignified labor in the California fields by some of the country's worst paid and most expendable workers was therefore no provincial matter. With the interests of major corporations and banks threatened, the strikes represented significant affronts to national and international financial interests.[3]

California farmworkers fought for a closed shop, better wages, safer working conditions, and the ability to unionize, demands consistent with the industrial strikes of the period. While they faced conditions similar to industrial workers, they had scant chance to organize alongside them since the American Federation of Labor refused to organize "unskilled" workers. Overrun with racism and rampant nativism, the AFL had historically opposed including Black, Asian, and many immigrant workers in its ranks and categorically opposed the inclusion of Mexican workers in their unions. In addition to these structural exclusions, California's mostly Mexican farmworkers contended with unique factors that hampered their organizing efforts and sustained their vulnerability.[4] The state's agricultural labor regime required a floating reserve army of labor, available for work during harvests but subject to dispersal, deportation, or arrest during growing seasons—in other words, "an unemployed pool available on call, much in the manner of water or electricity."[5] Toward this end, California's farmworkers were violently disciplined by forces such as racism, incarceration, and deportation, as well as the punitive dispensation of local, state, and federal relief forces coordinated across the US–Mexico border. Against these conditions of sustained vulnerability, farmworkers and their families rebelled.[6]

In December 1933, striking lettuce workers in the Imperial Valley traveled two hundred miles northwest to Los Angeles to seek organizing aid from the Communist Party (CP). The CP had assisted farmworkers in most of the strikes across the state that year (twenty-four out of thirty-seven) and had also participated in earlier strikes in the Imperial Valley, so it was no surprise that the lettuce workers again sought its assistance. Healey agreed to accompany the striking workers. In driving the long highway between Los Angeles and the Imperial Valley, the group traced an urban-rural continuum across the capitalist landscape, where migratory workers, crops, and capital moved in symbiotic circulation. For Los Angeles–based entities such as the new Bank of America, the Los Angeles Chamber of Commerce (LACC), and the Los Angeles Police Department (LAPD), it was a path well-trod. Throngs of migrant workers had also made this trek after harvest seasons. As Carlos Bulosan would write of Filipino migrant workers like himself, "All roads go to California and all travelers wind up in Los Angeles."[7]

Before joining the lettuce workers, Healey had been a leader in the Los Angeles Unemployed Councils, a CP-led project that organized unemployed workers for relief long before the New Deal promised any such federal provisions. In leaving the unemployed movement in Los Angeles to assist the strikers in the fields, Healey had unwittingly joined the forefront of a shared struggle. In rural areas like the Imperial Valley, workers were striking for wage increases, union recognition, clean water, transportation, and improved living conditions, then considered the worst in the state.[8] In Los Angeles, unemployed workers were being thrown off relief rolls and often coerced into the fields to break the farmworkers' strikes. The state's management of relief preempted regional solidarity and attempted to turn workers against one another across the urban-rural divide. Confronting these conditions required the nimble capacity to organize farmworkers in the fields and unemployed workers in the city. During the Depression, the CP provided the organizational structure for such organizing across space.

The revolutionary struggle for relief in Depression-era Southern California uniquely connected organizing efforts across the capitalist landscape. Between the Unemployed Councils in Los Angeles and the agricultural strikes in places like the Imperial Valley, the struggle represented a distinct convergence of radical movements. Workers from revolutionary traditions—

in particular anti-imperialist Filipinos; militant Okinawan and Japanese laborers; anti-colonial South Asians; militant Black workers from the US South; and, significantly, radical Mexican workers, emerging from the Mexican Revolution—were able to organize together. They subsequently brought strategies, tactics, and militant beliefs to the California struggle for relief and against repression.

The struggle for relief by workers in the fields and unemployed workers in the city was a regional confrontation with class power. "Relief" took many forms. As unemployment insurance, food aid, and rent supplements, as well as expenditure for heat, education, and subsistence, relief offered workers and their families the material basis to reproduce their lives and labor. Relief was also strategic. In sparing people from the ravages of starvation, homelessness, and destitution, relief enabled them not only to survive but also to challenge their conditions. With relief, workers could extend strikes, expand their organizing efforts, and elevate their political horizons. The struggle for relief promoted a class consciousness wherein individualized notions of success and failure were replaced with collective demands to radically redistribute resources. In these ways, the working-class struggle for relief addressed immediate material needs and offered robust ideological provocations.

In the hands of growers—the regional representatives of global capital—relief had different strategic meanings and uses. It could be used to undermine organizing efforts. For example, relief could be withheld to punish key leaders and their associates. Such efforts hampered organizing efforts and also threatened potential sympathizers. Relief could be strategically denied or supplied in efforts to starve out strikers, recruit scabs, and break strikes.[9] The absence of relief could produce conditions such as homelessness or vagrancy that would trigger other levers of the state, such as police aggression or deportation efforts. These insecurities were compounded in the Imperial Valley, rife as it was with some of the most ferocious vigilante violence in the state.[10]

Encompassing multiple geographical and political dimensions, the struggle for relief cut to the heart of ongoing national and international debates. During the Great Depression, as millions lost their jobs and millions more found themselves in various states of utter destitution, many began to question the priorities of the state. How could so many starve and go without work, shelter, or hope of a future without any type of intervention or relief?

The conditions forced organizers to raise new questions about the nature of struggle: Where, in this deformed landscape, was the class struggle being fought out? Could the unemployed and marginally employed organize an alliance for survival and political change? Who would lead such an alliance? How could leaders be identified? In this unprecedented economic crisis, how could they take advantage of the fundamental questions being raised about the nature of capitalism and the limits of human suffering to build an organization capable of confronting class power?

This chapter suggests how rebellions in the cities, factories, and the fields were part of interlinked radical struggles rather than spontaneous cycles of protests that emerged suddenly in the early 1930s. The chapter first explores the political economy of Southern California agriculture in the era in order to situate farmworker organizing in the Imperial Valley. It then examines Unemployed Council organizing in Los Angeles as part of a continuum of struggle. By examining how a struggle for relief aligned with revolutionary struggles across the capitalist landscape, this chapter offers an example of how internationalism was made in a regional confrontation with class power.[11]

RELIEF AND THE OPEN SHOP

A combination of regional, national, and international capitalist interests coalesced to shape the Southern California landscape. Successful organizing efforts in heavily unionized coastal cities such as Portland, Seattle, and San Francisco had achieved higher wages and improved labor conditions. In response, capitalists envisioned Los Angeles as an industrial city that would buck the red trend on the Pacific coast. By the 1920s, major industrialists such as Harrison Gray Otis and Henry Ford, as well as the heads of Firestone, Bethlehem Steel, and Procter and Gamble, had devised plans to maximize production efficiency and diminish barriers to capital accumulation in the region. Their plans stressed strident anti-unionism, low taxes, and strong police departments, all central elements to establishing and maintaining a thoroughly exploitative labor regime. Companies such as the B. F. Goodrich Company, Continental Can, Pittsburgh Plate Glass, Willard Storage Battery, American Maize-Products, and US Steel further contributed to the surge of investment in Los Angeles. The city's industrial capacity grew faster than that of any other area of the country in the 1920s. While these businesses competed fiercely against each other, they were willing to collaborate to maintain the one thing that had brought them to the Golden State: a cheap, unorganized, and terrorized labor force, a large segment of which was kept permanently unemployed to depress wages and ambitions.[12] Under the aegis of the Los Angeles Chamber of Commerce, these interests aligned to pursue an "open shop" model, in which employers could conduct business "free from interruption and interference" of labor organizing. Capitalist forces sought to achieve in Los Angeles what had been impossible in other major US cities: the "open shop citadel of America."[13]

The principal agency charged with implementing this vision was the Los Angeles Police Department, specifically a unit called the Red Squad. By the early decades of the twentieth century, these "archangels of the Open Shop" were notorious for their repression of organized labor and harassment of unemployed workers.[14] With the backing of the police commission, the courts, and the mayor, the Red Squad infiltrated labor groups, broke up legal and peaceful picket lines, disrupted meetings, bashed meeting places, tortured protesters, and illegally monitored organizers with impunity. Hailed as an unparalleled success across the state, the Red Squad extended its reach outside of Los Angeles. The Red Squad facilitated a tight interdependence of regional control, dispatching officers to surrounding rural areas to help break strikes and target organizers. Representatives from the Chambers of Commerce of places like the Imperial Valley and San Joaquin Valley sought the LAPD's expertise in their own labor conflicts, given the ties between their agricultural economies and the city's. Raw materials such as Acala cotton, for example, were farmed in these rural industrial-agricultural spaces and then transported for use in the city's manufacturing industry. Preserving the open shop meant stretching police resources across this geography of accumulation and repressing labor at each phase of valorization. Tellingly, the head of the Red Squad maintained a special office inside the headquarters of the Los Angeles Chamber of Commerce, a center of anti-labor repression.[15]

From the point of view of the region's capitalists, an open-shop model had largely been realized on California's agribusiness farms in the form of a vulnerable, precarious, racially segregated, and largely unorganized labor force. Farmworkers were "treated as so much scrap when it was needed."[16] By the onset of the Depression, most of California's migrant agricultural laborers came from Mexico. Mexican immigrants, as well as Mexicans who were US citizens, were broadly condemned by ferocious nativist racism. Growers contended that all Mexican workers would move back to Mexico after completing a job, leaving nothing behind but profit.

For over a century, Mexicans had been depicted as "uncivilized" and unfit to "mix their labor properly with the land"—an imaginary intrinsic to US expansionism since the nineteenth century.[17] The prevailing racist belief structure encompassed multiple contradictions. In his Congressional testimony in favor of limiting Mexican immigration, Roy L. Garis argued that Mexicans had an unfair advantage: "White Americans cannot live in competition with peons trained by 400 years of Spanish oppression and political and economic exploitation, to live on next to nothing in the way of subsistence and shelter." Mexican people, in such an imaginary, were disciplined by colonialism to accept degraded conditions of existence, and simultaneously deemed unassimilable because of it. Such contradictions were not always easy to perceive.[18]

The bucolic imaginary of rural landscapes often obscured the labor regimes of large-scale industrialized capitalist agriculture. Carey McWilliams, a labor advocate and California state commissioner of immigration and housing in the late 1930s and early 1940s, coined the term "factories in the field" as a corrective to help reimagine the fields as factories and reinterpret farmworkers as workers within them. He also dispelled the myth that farms were owned and operated by small independent famers, revealing that, in fact, half of all agricultural lands in California were owned by Bank of America (then called the Bank of Italy). California's corporate agricultural interests, organized into a group called Associated Farmers, bore little resemblance to small family farms. Associated Farmers included industrial, railroad, utility, and banking interests, with corporate donors such as Southern Pacific Railroad, Bank of America, and Pacific Gas and Electric. A government commission would observe later that while farmers were depicted as rugged, sympathetic, salt-of-the-earth patriots, the actual owners of the farms were genteel capitalists who "track[ed] very little earth into their parlors."[19]

Within this rural labor regime, capitalists, in collusion with the state, cultivated multiple mechanisms to control the movement of Mexican people. The Border Patrol, first established in 1924, evolved to enforce immigration laws as a form of labor control. While individual Border Patrol agents were influenced by contradictory and competing notions of manhood, whiteness, belonging, and empire, broad interpretations of immigration laws and enforcement priorities were often determined by the Southern California regional power bloc. In different periods of need, the Border Patrol unevenly permitted Mexican laborers to cross the US–Mexico border and work in the California fields. Agents simultaneously kept their eyes trained on Mexican workers, ensuring that they neither left jobs before the end of harvests nor attempted to stick around afterwards, once their labor was no longer needed. Local police departments operated toward similar ends. They could redouble growers' controlling mechanisms by, for example, evicting workers and their families from company-owned homes if they dared to challenge working conditions. They could also evict people who lived in tent-city "Hoovervilles" or "hobo jungles" adjacent to the fields, claiming that such encampments posed public health hazards. Given the supple definition of vagrancy laws, nearly anyone was vulnerable to arrest, particularly if they were found to be participating in strike meetings. Threats of arrest and deportation freighted every choice Mexican people made in and around the California fields, as the Border Patrol and police officers sought to keep workers terrorized and unorganized.[20]

Alongside immigration and local police forces, vigilante groups operated with relative impunity in the fields. As the *Daily Journal* noted in 1934, in Los Angeles jails, police "do their own assaulting," but in the Imperial Valley, "the police put prisoners outside and let the populace assault them." Vigilante groups, organized through clubs such as the American Legion or the Kiwanis, often operated as informal extensions of local law enforcement. These groups of "armed men," Healey remembered, would "beat up the strikers and the strike leaders . . . [then] go into the community and carry on the same as the Ku Klux Klan." Local law enforcement agencies openly and actively colluded with private vigilantes, enabling terroristic activities such as night rides, burning crosses, tar and feathering, mutilation, bombings, gassing, and clubbing. A 1934 LAPD manual (later adopted by the statewide California Peace Officers Association) instructed the police to cultivate local citizens' groups and encourage them to attend "special training schools" to learn "corrective measures" that police officers could not use legally. Across the state, labor organizers observed that "vigilantes attack 'independently'—but conveniently without police interference." California's reputation as a haven for vigilantism grew in the 1930s. In the words of a national antifascist pamphlet, the "West Coast saw the greatest and most consistent rise in the corrupt vigilante movement," with the Imperial Valley specifically identified as a "festering cancer of vigilantism."[21]

While deportation, policing, and vigilante violence operated as clear instruments of repression, one less-obvious mechanism was also crucial to this regime:

the dispensation of relief at local, state, and federal levels. Racist caricatures of Mexican people aligned with this mechanism of control. Espousing a commonly held belief, agribusiness leader Charles Collins Teague declared in 1928 that itinerant Mexican laborers were ideal for work in the California fields because they did not need "to be supported through the periods when there was no work to do." Such racist characterizations had material consequences. According to a California State Emergency Relief Administration study, most Mexican agricultural workers had employment for an average of six months a year, making survival solely on wages nearly impossible, especially as wages declined during the Depression. When asked about this situation, Harold E. Pomeroy, executive secretary of Associated Farmers, testified to a Senate subcommittee that Mexican workers were often "satisfied" with their earnings during the shorter period and thereafter able to enjoy what he called a "rather long holiday." Speaking for thousands of agricultural workers like him, Juan Serrano starkly noted at a 1931 statewide public hearing on unemployment that "my family is facing starvation."[22] Farmworker Innocentio Mendez, father in a household of ten, added, "I am in danger of having my gas and water shut off, and also in danger of losing my home." For workers and their families who faced immediate threats of starvation, untreated illness, homelessness, and extreme poverty, these intervening months hardly constituted a "holiday."[23]

Relief had been previously used by Mexican state entities, working in collaboration with regional US capitalists, to divert workers into narrowly based mutual aid societies. These societies were cynically engineered to rearticulate class grievance into nationalist injuries in order to break workers' solidarity. Previous attempts to corral workers in this way had derailed organizing efforts in the multiracial Imperial Valley. Working against the international collusion of capitalist and state entities, farmworkers and their families had learned that the class struggle was decidedly internationalist and, by necessity, waged across the capitalist divisions of the color line.[24]

To survive after the harvest season, workers and their families cobbled together informal work (often gendered labor in the garment industry), mutual aid, and paltry but accessible forms of relief. In Los Angeles, where workers largely congregated, available relief took the meager forms of private charity administered through the Catholic Welfare Bureau or emergency relief from the Los Angeles County Outdoor Relief Division. Prior to the New Deal, urban areas absorbed much of the off-season cost of supporting agricultural workers from rural areas. Some Los Angeles agencies and nativist groups opposed such a distribution of relief, arguing that it constituted an informal subsidy to agribusiness. While relief indeed reduced rural employers' costs for sheltering, feeding, clothing, and generally reproducing workers, Southern California growers were not overly concerned about workers' access to resources beyond their control. Rather, through the expansive spatialization of productive relations in Southern California, growers were invested in maintaining and reproducing a vulnerable and mobile workforce. Both workers and employers therefore recognized the centrality of relief to broader struggles over production and reproduction.[25]

The vulnerability of Mexican workers on relief intensified alongside the expansion of mechanisms for arrest and deportation, especially as the economic crisis deepened. Formal measures made it increasingly difficult for farmworkers to receive aid. In August 1931, the state legislature passed the Alien Labor Act, which prohibited companies doing business with the government from employing "alien" workers on public jobs. In the same year, the legislature passed residency requirements for public relief, requiring applicants to prove that they had resided in the state for three years and within a particular county for one year. These new provisions excluded many itinerant Mexican workers. In addition, the absence of relief could lead to confinement or deportation. Louis Barros, who picked peas in Castroville for fifteen cents a basket, barely made enough to cover his nightly board of $1.25. He traveled to Los Angeles, where he soon found himself arrested for vagrancy. "Reaching Los Angeles too late one evening for the soup line," he wrote, "I was picked up by a detective and jailed." In a 1932 editorial, Barros explained that imprisonment was the "penalty workers pay for being unable to find jobs which do NOT exist." For workers like Barros, the inability to locate relief could easily translate into imprisonment and, often, deportation.[26]

As relief grew scarce, public sentiment turned sharply against migrant workers receiving aid, especially in Los Angeles. Charles P. Visel, director of the LA Citizens Committee on Coordination of Unemployment Relief, helped to accelerate the process, arguing that "it would be a great relief to the unemployment situation if some method could be devised to scare these people out of our city." By coordinating local police and federal immigration agents in surrounding states, Visel arranged a large-scale roundup of Mexican workers in February 1931. Through political pressure and other scare tactics, local and federal agents worked with relief and welfare agencies to raid the city's Mexican communities and to drive approximately fifty thousand people, many of whom were US citizens, south of the border. All in all, nearly half a million Mexican workers were forcibly and illegally "repatriated" during the Great Depression as deportation emerged as a central tool to manage labor and relief.[26]

Through the conjoined practices of deportation, policing, vigilante violence, and relief policies, Mexican workers were among the most exploited and vulnerable of Southern California's laborers. The prospect of deportation put extreme pressure on them to accept reduced wages and abysmal living conditions. Repatriation in the early 1930s, however, produced unintended and contradictory consequences, namely the disappearance of a skilled labor force experienced enough to meet the growers' needs.[27]

With this newfound leverage, Mexican workers began to challenge the terms of their employment with greater frequency and militancy. By the early 1930s, the heads of agribusiness grew worried that their fields were becoming fertile grounds for radicalism—and many of them blamed access to relief. "The Mexican on relief is being unionized and is being used to foment strikes among the few still loyal Mexican workers," George Clements of the Los Angeles Chamber of Commerce warned. "The Mexican casual labor is lost to the California farmer unless immediate action is taken to get him off relief." To a meeting of the Farmers Union, *San Francisco Chronicle* editor Chester Rowell announced, "Make no mistake about it, if you yourselves do not settle this question of the migratory laborer, the Communists will." In the capitalist landscape of Southern California, relief and radicalism arose together.[28]

MEXICAN REVOLUTIONARY TRADITIONS

Communists such as Healey did, in fact, help migrant workers organize against agribusiness capitalists, but they did not introduce Mexican workers to this fight. For many Mexican farmworkers in California, their struggles represented an ongoing confrontation with capital. The Mexican Revolution was itself a struggle against many of the transformations wrought by US capital. In the years following World War I, US capital continued to dominate the Mexican economy, as it had since the beginning of the twentieth century. In the 1920s, 65 to 85 percent of all of Mexico's exports went to the United States, and nearly 75 percent of all of Mexico's imports came from the United States. In addition, US companies commanded 80 percent of all Mexican mineral production and close to 95 percent of all refinery production by 1929. Throughout the 1920s and into the Great Depression, the

United States looked to Mexico for economic relief as a market for its manu-factured goods, a source of raw materials, and a site for production. Individuals from Los Angeles invested more capital in Mexico than residents of any other city in the United States.[29]

The expansion of US investment, extraction, production, and transporta-tion in Mexico also led to the expansion and radicalization of the working class there. By the early 1930s, Mexican workers were enveloped in dramatic revolts. In 1933, more than seventeen thousand people walked off their jobs demanding better wages, housing, schools, and medical services. In 1934, Mexico saw a rash of major strikes launched across various industries. Strikes were mostly organized against foreign-owned companies such as the Huasteca Petroleum Company (owned by US Standard Oil) and the Mexican Telephone and Telegraph Company (an allied company of American Telephone and Telegraph). By the following year, over one hundred thousand workers were on strike from industries as diverse as mining, oil, railroad, telephone, and sanitation, representing one of the largest industrial strike waves in Mexico's history.[30]

Many of these strikes grew out of everyday indignities. The Huasteca strikes, for example, sprang from unrest over decrepit housing for workers. Workers protested unsanitary conditions and insufficient space for their children at company-run schools. Although demands for better housing and schools were not on their face revolutionary, workers' organizing for their basic rights and dignity informed the broader struggle for control over pro-duction, ownership of national resources, and eradication of exploitative conditions. The strike wave across industries and revolts across the country-side forced the Mexican government to implement the most radical tenets of the 1917 Mexican Constitution. The 1930s witnessed the nationalization of the oil and railroad industries, the revoking of foreign capitalist interests, massive national education and literacy programs, and the most sweeping land redistribution programs in the history of the Americas.[31]

These experiences circulated in the California fields. Recalling his encoun-ter with Mexican workers in the 1933 cotton strike, organizer Pat Chambers noted how workers discussed the "many revolutions and wars" waged so that "the Mexican people might be free, have some land of their own," and "have the right to live without fear of starving to death."[32] Such perspectives and backgrounds had profound effects on the militancy of farmworkers in California and upon those who had direct and indirect relationships to the revolution. Communist organizers came to realize the value of this experience. In the Imperial Valley, Healey soon noticed that her radical appeals were met with patient indulgence. While she talked about strategy, the workers explained to her, "Of course we're ready for revolution. When the barricades are ready, we'll be on the barricades, but don't bother us with meetings all the time. We know what to do, we know who the enemy is. . . . Just tell us when the revolution is ready. We'll be there."[33]

The Mexican strikers drew on a consciousness of tactical alliances they had gained during the revolution. As Devra Weber's generative research demonstrates, the revolution operated as "a model of a collective struggle" that inspired the strategies and symbols of the strike. Former military officers organized patrols and sentries with other veterans. Within the strike camps, workers named streets after revolutionary heroes and sang revolutionary *corridos*. They reminisced about friends and relatives who had participated in revolutionary strikes. "The Mexican people are revolutionary as it is," insisted organizer Leroy Parra. With their knowledge, he argued, they were better able to see "the exploitation here in this country." While workers maintained different and conflicting feelings about the Mexican Revolution, these differences appeared to be "submerged" during the strike. Instead, the workers' memories of the revolution stressed shared historical opposition to the United States. For working people long exposed to the unrestrained incursions of US capital in Mexico, unity through antipathy became common sense.[34]

This shared history made a deep impression on the striking workers. In his coverage of the cotton strike, Joe Evans observed that white workers and other workers of color learned that "Mexican workers were not 'greasers' as portrayed by Hollywood films." In the process of struggle, they came to see them instead as "courageous, determined, intelligent workers." "Never has there been greater courage shown," reported Evans, "than that of the Mexican workers in the course of this strike." Workers, in turn, developed a deep sense of solidarity and affinity. When growers at Corcoran tried to intimidate them, setting up loudspeakers and demanding that the leaders come forward, a "spontaneous shout" came back proclaiming, "We are all the leaders!"[35]

Amid the 1933 agricultural strikes, a bloc of growers, financiers, and local government officials across California united to stem the tide of radicalism. Discovering that strikers were receiving relief through the New Deal's Federal Emergency Relief Administration with few stipulations, they immediately sought to cut off access. While growers exerted disproportionate control over local relief, they had no control over federal aid. As Paul Taylor and Clark Kerr concluded in a report for a Senate subcommittee, the 1933 cotton strike effectively became the first large labor conflict in the United States in which a federal agency offered support to striking workers. In this case, the federal government had specifically supported striking workers through food aid. This form of relief allowed strikers to feed themselves and their families, enabling the strike to persist.[36]

After the 1933 strike wave, agribusiness leaders (including cotton and walnut growers, Sunkist, and the Western Growers Protective Association) quickly organized. These regional capitalists convened a special labor committee of the Los Angeles Chamber of Commerce to wrest control over relief from the federal government, as a Senate investigation into California labor abuses later revealed. Once relief was administered by state and local agencies sympathetic to agribusiness, farmworkers remained at the mercy of growers. Collaborating with Los Angeles public agencies, charities, and government offices, California growers increased their pressure on relief officials. Soon, unemployed workers were being removed from local and state relief rolls and forced to work in the fields during strikes. Los Angeles relief recipients, particularly Mexican workers, were given an ultimatum: scab in the fields or relinquish eligibility for relief. Relief officers were instructed to offer jobs with guarantees of free transportation and sometimes an advance of one bag of groceries. Instructions to relief workers concluded with this admonition: "If [relief recipients] refuse, do not threaten them, only state that they need not expect any more favors from Los Angeles County."[37] By compelling workers into the fields and dictating the terms of their employment, state and local relief agencies operated as de facto strike-breakers for agribusiness.[38]

An October 1933 editorial by a Mexican worker who withheld his name in fear of reprisal described how workers were being turned against each other:

> We go to the fields in the hot sun and work long hours—at 15c an hour. It is too little. . . . Our children get hungry, our women get sick. We cannot buy medicine. Then we try to get more wages—just a little more, to live on, not to get rich. What happens? The sheriff comes with lots of men. They have clubs, pistols, machine guns. They beat us with the clubs. They throw the gas that burns our eyes. Then the courts—they issue injunctions. . . . It means we cannot strike. They put us in jail. . . . They tell us there is a job for us in the country. We go there—and there is a strike going on. WE must break the strike to keep the workers from getting more wages.[39]

Employers and law enforcement agents continued to work hand in hand to create an "open shop" in Southern California.

By 1935, the Los Angeles Chamber of Commerce and the state relief administration were working with agribusiness to tailor relief rolls according to the needs of growers. Between August and October 1935, seventy-five thousand workers were dropped from the rolls and forced into the fields. These local developments reflected national power struggles. Southern California agribusiness added its voice to a powerful bloc of Southern capitalists, Dixiecrats, and other landowners. The federal government responded by denying agricultural workers equal protection in New Deal legislation such as the National Labor Relations Act, the Social Security Act, and the Fair Labor Standards Act. The status of Mexican farmworkers in California held national significance. "California is today the testing ground for fascism in this country," a *New Republic* commentator surmised. "If the present program of oppression and terrorism can be launched with active success in California, it can be utilized in other states as well." To confront the machinations of capital, organizing efforts had to operate across regions, in urban and rural areas, with a concrete consideration of the global scale. Accordingly, workers in the fields posed an important question to their "comrades in the big cities." What would they do "to help smash the vigilantes' murder gangs and the policy to starve them back to work"?[40]

LOS ANGELES UNEMPLOYED COUNCILS

California was a key destination for desperate job seekers during the Depression. With few jobs to be had, the Golden State quickly became the "transient capital of America." In 1931 alone, upward of twelve to fifteen thousand hopefuls a day drove, hitchhiked, jumped trains, and otherwise made their way across state lines from the Dust Bowl, northern Mexico, the Pacific Northwest, the Pacific Islands, and the Jim Crow South. Los Angeles became home to most of California's job seekers and half of the state's jobless population. Unemployment reached crisis levels, with one out of five Angelenos unable to find work. Those lucky enough to secure employment were surrounded by the growing masses crowded into the city's shelters, relief offices, jails, and peripheries. On the outskirts of downtown and on the banks of the culverted Los Angeles River, a new landscape had cropped up, a veritable jungle of shantytowns and ramshackle tent cities bearing the president's name: Hoovervilles. Squat shacks and lean-tos rendered poverty publicly visible. Men hired by the city to sweep streets and clear brush in these outlying areas could barely finish a day's work and regularly fainted from malnutrition. The health board would soon recommend that the unemployed hunt pigeons for sustenance.[41]

In the early years of the Depression, there was no national unemployment insurance, no provisions for direct relief, and no federal legislation to help the millions without jobs. State-level assistance was paltry, inefficient, and discriminatory. To receive aid, people often needed to qualify as mentally or physically disabled. Only a fraction of those in need qualified. In 1931 unemployment hovered around 28 percent in Southern California, with rates as high as 50 percent for Black and Mexican workers in Los Angeles. Racist administration by state and regional agencies often meant that the smallest grants went to Black and Mexican families. Public relief operated as a disciplinary measure, dispensed to few and intended to demean recipients to discourage their reliance upon it. Oftentimes, relief was administered through the auspices of the police department, an arrangement that drove away many applicants. As late as 1934, receiving relief deprived citizens of the right to vote in fourteen states. The disciplinary power of the relief system, both federal and state-sponsored, generally lay not in an outright refusal of relief but in the systematic degradation of those who received aid.[42]

The official silence around mass suffering was deafening. The poor, falling beyond the purview of the president, politicians, labor leaders, and social scientists, carving out existence on the peripheries of public consciousness, seemed invisible to all but "the doctor, the judge, the gravedigger, and bumbailiff."[43] Herman Boren, an unemployed milling operator from San Francisco, wrote that "the way that homeless unemployed men have to live is worse than the way animals and insects live." Writer Meridel Le Sueur observed that, in desperation, "A woman will shut herself up in a room until it is taken away from her, and eat a cracker a day and be as quiet as a mouse so there are no social statistics concerning her." If the poor were willing to suffer silently, there seemed no incentive for the government to intervene. Herbert Benjamin, national leader of the Unemployed Councils, told a Senate committee in 1931 that no real help would be forthcoming "until every man in Congress is shivering in his very pants because he thinks the unemployed are going to engage in struggle."[44]

With nearly a third of the US labor force out of work, Unemployed Councils spread quickly across the country. They demanded recognition and resources, giving voice, expression, and mobilization to an otherwise unrecognized surplus population that had grown exponentially since the stock market crash of 1929. They became the nation's first poor people's organization, representing one of the first large-scale protest movements to emerge amid the economic crisis. In contrast to segregated American work sites, Unemployed Councils produced spaces where working-class people of different backgrounds could engage in a common struggle for radical social change.[45] Unemployed Councils had several objectives: to organize the unemployed for immediate relief by door-to-door outreach, to develop new leadership from the rank and file through block committees, and to bring groups of people in need to welfare offices to demand jobs and relief.

The Los Angeles Unemployed Councils coordinated an impressive range of activities. Before the New Deal legislation, they organized at charities and welfare bureaus for relief, demonstrated at City Hall, and negotiated with the Board of Supervisors to implement citywide increases in relief. Once federal relief became available through the New Deal, they organized locals of the Relief Workers' Protective Union. They protested racially discriminatory hiring in public jobs. They called for an end to foreclosures, challenged evictions in courthouses, and moved furniture back into the homes of the evicted. They organized in shelters against rotten food and for the right of all residents to have beds. They defended squatters living in Hoovervilles and forced officials to find them alternative housing. They allied with movements to demand housing and bonus pay for starving World War I veterans. They fought for free medical care, public utilities, and transportation for the unemployed. The Councils protested the incarceration of their members and the deportation of Mexican workers, thus tying their movement to broader revolutionary demands—including a tax on the rich to end the Depression.[46]

Local organizing efforts in different Los Angeles neighborhoods, such as Boyle Heights, Echo Park, Hollywood, Huntington Park, and Long Beach, converged to produce citywide Hunger Marches in the plaza downtown. Later, the Councils coordinated statewide demonstrations in Sacramento. On caravan trips to the state capital, members would stop in small towns, recruiting new members along the way. The same process was replicated across the country, leading up to the Hunger Marches on Washington. With their efforts, "marching columns of unemployed became a familiar sight." Observer Len De Caux wrote, "The communists brought misery out of hiding in the workers' neighborhood." The unemployed were refusing to suffer in silence.[47]

On March 6, 1930, the Unemployed Councils held an International Day of Struggle Against Unemployment. More than 1.2 million people came out in cities and towns across the United States and around the world. On that day, "the unemployed and homeless—poor farmers, Black workers and share-croppers in the deep South, miners in Appalachia all became a strategic political force to be reckoned with," according to Los Angeles Unemployed Council member Elaine Black. In Los Angeles, the protest drew a crowd of five to ten thousand to the plaza, one of the biggest demonstrations in the city's history. Three years later, in 1933, the Hunger March drew an even bigger crowd of nearly forty thousand. Nationwide, these protests helped convert unemployment into a front-page issue that was impossible to ignore.[48]

Like many city residents, Elaine Black witnessed hundreds of people—demonstrators and spectators alike—arrested and beaten, some "almost clubbed to death." The Presidential Commission on Law Observance and Enforcement later corroborated her statement, describing the attack on the Los Angeles demonstration as "an eight-hour clubbing party." Truncheons, brass knuckles, tear gas, rifles, blackjacks, blades, and impunity allowed the LAPD's Red Squad to act as a brutal force against demonstrators and onlookers as well. The violence drove some away, but many more were transformed by the obvious injustice of police brutality and emboldened to join Unemployed Councils. An unsympathetic *Los Angeles Record* article agreed, opining, "In the existing unemployment situation, they can count on making recruits among jobless men made desperate by hunger and indignant by senseless police cossackism."[49]

In 1931, Dorothy Healey moved to predominantly Mexican East Los Angeles, on Soto Street near Hollenbeck Park. There she organized block committees of Unemployed Councils. She recalled, "You could go anywhere and knock on doors and you were going to find the unemployed." Council organizers went house to house in working-class neighborhoods setting up meetings and convincing the unemployed to form block committees with their neighbors. In effect, they became an "informal neighborhood association" for the "destitute." Women emerged as critical leaders and participants in these efforts—women like housewife Mildred Olsen, who had been unable to feed her children or afford rent or gas bills before local Unemployed Councils demonstrated with at the local relief office. To a California State Commission on Unemployment she testified, "We could go hungry; we could live in basements and skirmish in ash cans and our children go hungry; but by organized pressure we got our demands met."[50]

The Unemployed Councils attracted and transformed women of different backgrounds. In addition to Elaine Black, a daughter of Russian Jewish immigrants, and Healey, prominent figures of the movement included

Japanese American organizer Mary Hatsuko Imada and African American organizer Adele Young.[51] Though Healey would go on to have a five-decade career in the Los Angeles Communist Party, she found her work in the Unemployed Councils revelatory and exemplary. There she saw "fragmented" and "atomized" unemployed participants "start to feel a consciousness." She recalled the transformation of participants in the organizing process:

> We didn't just agitate. People joined an organization, and those people, those unemployed, would lead the next demonstration, and you'd go on and set up a new block committee a block away that would meet every week and take its delegations down. You'd keep doing that so that you were constantly developing new leaders . . . with new talents that were latent before but then became explicit.[52]

The struggle for relief opened up new political possibilities and coalitions.

RADICAL INTERNATIONALISM AND THE GLOBAL STRUGGLE FOR RELIEF

Alfred Wagenknecht, head of the Communist Party's relief arm, complained that while "thousands of unemployed workers were kept intact," the ranks of the party did not increase proportionally as a result of the Unemployed Councils. Tens of thousands of people streamed through the ranks, but fewer became CP members. This was particularly true for Mexican workers. Although commentators have proposed that there was a fundamental incompatibility between Mexican nationalism and Communism or, alternately, that Mexican workers were predisposed to anarcho-syndicalism, such observations tend to overlook examples to the contrary. Mexican workers were very active in Communist and socialist organizations and campaigns, including El Congreso, a radical California coalition of Latino labor and civil rights activists, and later the Congress of Industrial Organizations (CIO) and the Cannery and Agricultural Workers Industrial Union (CAWIU).[53]

In a 1932 editorial, Irving Kreitzberg wrote that there was great support among Mexican workers for CP campaigns, especially when the CP made efforts to include them and published flyers in Spanish. Even absent these efforts, Mexican workers often spoke at rallies and spontaneously joined demonstrations. Mexican workers who did join the Party, like Jose Arispe, regularly organized with other Mexican workers. In 1939 Emma Tenayuca, a Communist organizer and Unemployed Council leader in Texas, considered this point in an article she cowrote titled "The Mexican Question in the Southwest." While she recommended that the Party pay greater attention to the specific needs of Mexican workers—recognizing that they formed distinct communities affected by racial, cultural, and political discrimination—she argued that their liberation was tied to a broader radical movement. Tenayuca's claims help to explain the significance of the struggle for relief to the CP. Although it did not necessarily increase recruitment, it intensified the struggle against racism, expanded opportunities for participation of non-white communities, and crucially expanded the dimensions of class struggle.[54]

While expressly organizing and raising consciousness around unemployment, the Unemployed Councils helped expose the unwaged relations that permanently structured the processes of capital accumulation. As Karl Marx had noted nearly a century earlier, the accumulation of capital requires a "constant transformation of a part of the working population into unemployed or semi-employed 'hands.'" A permanent surplus labor population functioned to pressure the employed segment of the working class into accepting lower wages and more exploitative conditions. In Southern California, this surplus labor population was disproportionately composed of people of color. Although hunger and unemployment were becoming newly recognizable as national conditions during the Depression, they had long structured the lives and labors of workers of color, in particular migrant farmworkers, female domestic workers, and industrial workers who were racially excluded from trade unions. What had been deemed "exceptional" for these sectors of the working class soon became a generalizable condition for much of the country. The economic crisis only deepened the trenches of class struggle already established along the color line.[55]

Throughout the Depression, the CP experienced a major upsurge in participation and membership. Its western division attributed this jump to two primary campaigns: farmworker organizing through the CAWIU and the advent of the Unemployed Councils. Outgrowths of the new Trade Union Unity League (TUUL), an independent organization that sought to organize workers traditionally excluded from trade unions, found their greatest successes in California. The CAWIU and Unemployed Councils achieved particular success in Southern California, ironically because of state and local restrictions placed on labor organizing. The open-shop policies of the region, coupled with the American Federation of Labor's unwillingness to share organizing space with the CP, meant that factories and white factory workers were largely out of reach, particularly in Los Angeles. In turn, the Party sought new constituencies. In the notoriously sectarian Third Period of 1928 to 1935, the Party was able to reach people of color who were farmworkers and unemployed workers, half of whom were women. In Southern California, these organizing efforts broadened the struggle against capitalism to include sites such as fields, homes, food banks, jails, deportation centers, and relief offices, in addition to factories and other points of production. Given its new constituencies, the Party became more attentive in its organizing to the intersections between the color line and the class struggle.[56]

The struggle for relief forged meaningful internationalist alliances between workers of various backgrounds to facilitate discussions of racial and class dynamics at local, national, and international scales. Pettis Perry, for example, who would become one of the most influential African American Communists in the country, had formative experiences organizing in Southern California. Perry had left Alabama, barely escaping the clutches of Jim Crow racial terror. He worked in auto plants, canneries, and packinghouses and eventually found harvesting work in the Imperial Valley. There, in the California fields, he encountered radical Mexican farmworkers alongside Communist organizers. He later joined the movement in Los Angeles, working as a full-time organizer around unemployed struggles. He became one of the Party's foremost critics of white supremacy and capitalism, concluding, "The working class will never come to power unless there is a relentless struggle against white chauvinism."[57]

The Unemployed Councils were one of several new vehicles that generated greater participation of working-class people of color in radical politics. Other Communist campaigns in this period included the defense of the Scottsboro Boys in Alabama, support for jailed Unemployed Councils leader Angelo Herndon, opposition to Japanese imperialism, and support for striking farmworkers. In multiethnic Los Angeles, these campaigns created greater spaces within which people of color could operate. Official membership in the CP tripled and the ranks of sympathizers grew exponentially, drawing increasingly from the Black, Mexican, Japanese, and Chinese communities, as well as from already established Russian, Jewish, and poor white communities. Meetings often required interpretation into Spanish, Italian, and Japanese.[58]

Japanese American organizer Karl Yoneda helped coordinate a Japanese branch of Unemployed Councils in Los Angeles. As a worker and organizer of farmworkers, fruit-stand workers, waiters, and newspaper writers in the early Depression years, Yoneda had become acquainted with Mexican, Black, Filipino, Japanese, and white workers, encounters that helped to shape his analysis of race and class in the labor movement. Recognizing the complex position that Japanese farmworkers occupied in the early 1930s, he appealed to berry pickers in El Monte "not to scab!" but to "join their Mexican and Filipino brothers in strike." Similarly, he condemned Japanese American boarding-house owners, growers, and scab providers for being on the wrong side of the class struggle. With Party members like Yoneda, movements for unemployment relief were meshed with calls to free the Scottsboro Boys and demands such as "Hands Off China" and "Down with Japanese Imperialism!" A radical internationalist spirit thereby infected the local work of Unemployed Councils.[59]

Otto Huiswoud, one of the first Black members of the CP in the United States, believed that the Depression presented an opportunity for a "broad campaign among the Negro masses on the basis of everyday demands for a united revolutionary struggle of the entire working class against Yankee Imperialism."[60] Leading Pan-Africanist and Communist George Padmore agreed. Addressing Black workers throughout the colonized world in his magazine *The Negro Worker,* Padmore instructed his readers to follow the example of the Unemployed Councils:

> The gigantic hunger marches of the unemployed workers in the USA— colored and white united—in England, and other European countries have struck deep fear in the hearts of the bosses and have caused a halt to the tide of many contemplated anti-working class measures in these countries. These splendid examples of proletarian mass action should serve as an inspiration to the unemployed colonial toilers to do likewise.[61]

As Padmore's observations suggest, the struggle against hunger and unemployment was decidedly international. At the core of this struggle was an understanding that racism was repressing the working class as a whole. As a journalist writing about the case of the Atlanta Unemployed Council, organizer Angelo Herndon concluded, "Maintenance of the color line is the core of anti-labor policy." Through their struggles, members of the Unemployed Councils came to see their work as a part of a worldwide class struggle.[62]

The California strikes occurred amid a global wave of radicalism brought on by the Depression. By 1934, strikes were being staged by sugarcane workers in Puerto Rico, unemployed workers in Trinidad, miners in northern Spain, and thousands of workers across Mexico, as well as sharecroppers, longshoremen, domestic workers, and unemployed workers in the United States. The struggles for relief and against racism in the California fields, Los Angeles Unemployed Councils, and Mexican industries exemplified and expanded a militancy that was proliferating across the world.

With their diverse composition, the farmworker strikes and Unemployed Councils in Southern California enabled a critical conceptualization of geographies of capitalism. Organizing simultaneously in spaces such as the agricultural fields and among the urban unemployed enabled a view of how capitalism was developing across regions and around the globe. These Southern California movements for relief and against repression integrated considerations of racism and imperialism in confronting capitalism. Taken together, they demonstrate how convergences of radical traditions emboldened the global anti-racist class struggle in the 1930s and beyond.

SIX

How to Make a Dress

ELIZABETH CATLETT, RADICAL PEDAGOGY, AND
CULTURAL RESISTANCE

HOW TO MAKE A MEXICAN DRESS

"At 3 o'clock on the afternoon of the ball, Miss Catlett had not the faintest idea of what her costume would be."[1] So wrote the *Chicago Defender* in its coverage of the 1941 Artists and Models Ball. For this grand event on Chicago's South Side, over 3,500 people crowded into the Savoy Ballroom, where "'everybody who is anybody'" could be seen. The *Defender* had heavily publicized the gala and subsequently devoted a full-page spread to photos of lively dancers, sultry singers, and the crowning of the coveted "Queen of the Ball." The glamorous event was declared to have "established itself definitively as an institution." The Artists and Models Ball was the fourth annual fundraiser for the South Side Community Art Center (SSCAC), a beloved community art space serving the South Side's Black community. As a former SSCAC teacher, Elizabeth Catlett had agreed to be a last-minute replacement queen. The event's "Pan-American" theme was fateful. Her charge: to model a dress that might embody "Mexico itself."[2]

Arriving by train from New Orleans shortly before the event, Catlett found herself with little time to acquire an "authentic" Mexican dress. She scavenged the closets of her friends within Chicago's radical Black arts community. The young writer and future playwright Lorraine Hansberry loaned Catlett a shoulder-baring Mexican blouse and shawl. Hansberry had spent time in the country following her father, Carl Hansberry, who had wanted to relocate his family away from the "howling mobs" of US white supremacy.[3] Her shawl was a traditional *rebozo,* a long cloth worn as a wrap, scarf, or sling by Mexican women, but as Catlett later reflected, "I didn't know it yet." From Charles White, the Chicago-born muralist who would soon become her husband, Catlett borrowed some wax fruit, taken from White's mother's home. White had been deeply influenced by Mexican muralists, taking technical, stylistic, and political inspiration from the milieu. Catlett straightened her hair and tied a basket to her head, filling it with fruit to match the hyperstylized images of Mexican "peasant" women appearing on calendars, fruit labels, and travel posters.[4] In need of a skirt, she removed the striped curtains from SSCAC cofounder Margaret Burroughs's home, then "doubled them over and gathered them around the top," cinching them with a belt to mimic a Mexican-style wrap-around skirt. As a final touch, she wore sandals "like huaraches," completing her improvised version of a Mexican "peasant dress."[5]

Arriving at the ballroom, Catlett was bemused by her competition. Wearing mink coats atop elaborate bespoke costumes, they lounged elegantly after having been promenaded across the city. At work with the other event organizers, Catlett observed the queens in their pleated gowns from Veracruz, their lavish hats and ornate dresses "with ruffles all around" to represent South American countries like Chile and Argentina. A few queens emulated the popular Pan-American archetype Carmen Miranda, midriffs bared and towers of fruit affixed to their heads. To open the show, the Boogie La Conga chorus dedicated a dance number in honor of "danseuse" Katherine Dunham. As journalist Diana Briggs observed, "The girls were so lovely and 'boogied' so scintillatingly that one person was heard to remark, 'Goodness I'm certainly glad my husband couldn't be here tonight,'" a comment open to multiple interpretations. In another number, models took the stage while White, Burroughs, and other artists sketched them on a huge canvas. In the background, singer Elizabeth Hunt belted "Frenesí," a popular big band hit. The song, written by Mexican songwriter Alberto Domínguez, arranged by Black composer William Grant Still, and recorded by Jewish clarinetist Artie Shaw after his return from Acapulco, begins, "Some time ago, I wandered down into old Mexico."[6]

Clad in her modest borrowed blouse and belted curtain skirt, Catlett was carried out in a basket by two muscular men. While other queens confidently sashayed in high heels, Catlett stumbled along the ramp in sandals without her glasses, nervous that the wax fruit would tumble off her head. At last, she took her place in line alongside the other contestants while the judges appraised them. The queens were assessed according to how "authentically" they represented their assigned country. Miss Roxie Joynes from New York received a dress as a prize for her ruffled representation of Argentina. Miss Maxine Tanner from Maywood, Illinois, was given a new housecoat for her representation of Mexico. Praying that she would not be the only one without an award, Catlett was stunned when the judges awarded Queen of the Ball to "that little lady from New Orleans, Miss Elizabeth Catlett."[7]

Internationally acclaimed for her graphic prints and signature sculptures, Elizabeth Catlett, the "Dean" of Black women artists, would go on to have a long and storied romance with Mexico. Because she would spend sixty-five years in her "adopted" country, every early biographical encounter, including being crowned Queen in her "Mexican dress," seems ripe with premonition. But the Ball contained poignant and competing meanings. It was a staging ground for commercialized and gendered "Pan-American" representations of Latin America. It was also a site of engagement for radical Black internationalist artists with deeper political ties to Mexico. As such, the Ball foretold a number of convergences and divergences that would be critical to Catlett's own political formation.[8]

The Artists and Models Ball was meant to celebrate the "warm passionate beauty of the Pan American countries" and, implicitly, their hemispheric political and economic cooperation with the United States.[9] Amid the alarming spread of fascism during the Second World War and concerns about the possible spread of Communism, the US State Department coordinated a hemispheric counteroffensive. Organized by the Department's Cultural Relations Division and Nelson Rockefeller's Office of the Coordinator of Inter-American Affairs, "Pan-American" cooperation was both a diplomatic ideal and a potent cultural project. In order to "sell" Latin America to the US public, its goods saturated department stores, expositions, and popular culture. Hypersexualized figures like Carmen Miranda, with her bountiful tower of Latin American produce, loomed large, as did motifs of Indigenous Mexican peasant women. Such gendered fantasies of Indigenous Latin America imagined its peoples trapped in a romanticized past, simultaneously simple, pliant, and available, particularly for forces of US economic development. With its exaggerated feminized caricatures and stylized tropes of Indigeneity, the Artists and Models Ball uncritically reproduced many of these Pan-American fantasies.[10]

At the same time, the event highlighted a parallel but more subversive Left-labor alliance between Mexican and US-based organizers, a project critically built by Black radical artists. If Mexico was a site of projected imperial fantasies in commercial culture, it was also a "Mecca" for Black artists on the Left. The actual and imagined spaces of Revolutionary Mexico, particularly Mexico City, offered much to the radical Black artists based in the United States, serving as a source of inspiration, a site of refuge, and a nodal point of internationalist culture. These artists converged with Mexican artists in style, form, and commitment to anti-racist, anti-fascist, and anti-imperialist politics. Sheltered under the auspices of Pan-American cooperation, the radical internationalism of this convergence flourished, finding ultimate expression in the early life and work of Elizabeth Catlett.[11]

Catlett's name is scattered throughout histories of the Black Left in the 1930s and 1940s. There, she is mostly mentioned in relation to her one-time husband, Charles White, another radical artist of great prominence. If she is referenced on her own, it is mostly as a friend and "fellow traveler" of other self-declared radicals. Biographies and scholarly texts often downplay or minimize Catlett's politics. This is in no small part due to an image that Catlett cultivated herself in a later Cold War context, and one her biographers conceivably respected since the viability of her professional career was contingent upon such political distance. As Mary Helen Washington describes, this biographical performance was often necessary for the survival of Black artists organizing on the Left in the Cold War—particularly Elizabeth Catlett.[12]

Catlett, in art historian Melanie Herzog's words, was "one of the most important American artists of the past century." While much has been written about her artwork and on the general contours of her biography, there are few sustained studies of her politics. Her affiliations can be ascertained in other ways. Walking into homes of older radical activists in the United States, one is likely to encounter her original artwork. In memoirs, children of radicals describe Catlett's powerful presence in Mexico. Diana Anhalt recalls tracing the soft contours of Catlett's sculptures that graced her home and homes of other Cold War exiles in Mexico.[13] Catlett's name surfaces in the biographies of radicals who sought refuge in Mexico in the postwar era. In his autobiography, *Black Bolshevik,* Harry Haywood describes Catlett as a friend, a relationship confirmed by Catlett, her son, and Gwendolyn Midlo Hall, Catlett's friend and Haywood's former wife.[14] When Marvin X, teacher of Huey Newton and cofounder of the Black Arts Theater, escaped persecution in California, he found shelter with Catlett in Mexico City. As she said upon receiving him, "Mexico has always given refuge to revolutionaries from around the world." Catlett clearly assisted many seeking refuge in Mexico, including Black radicals fleeing US state repression along with others escaping McCarthyism in the US, Franco's fascism in Spain, and repressive regimes throughout the world. The convergence of revolutionary traditions sequestered together in Mexico had an undeniable effect on her art and political work. As Catlett noted in a 1975 interview with Raquel Tibol, "The revolutionary atmosphere in which I developed in Mexico was determinant in my development and projection."[15]

In the 1940s, Mexico became Catlett's adopted home and also the site of the first FBI office outside the United States. Catlett was a persistent presence on the FBI's watch list and under the surveillance of agents in its Mexico office. At the height of the Red Scare, she was classed an "undesirable alien" by the US State Department and held in a Mexican jail for several days. Under the Immigration and Nationality Act, the US government could refuse entry to any person perceived to be a communist, and this, as her 1964 FBI file demonstrates, is what she was suspected of being. Because of this perception, she was repeatedly denied a visa to return to the United States, even while her mother was dying.[16] Drawing upon original and archival oral histories conducted with Catlett and her friends, as well as interviews, memoirs of her contemporaries, her writings, and her own artwork, this chapter offers a new portrait of Catlett, one at odds with the image of an ingenue who happened to wander into some of the most charged radical political scenes of the late 1930s and early 1940s. In the words of Gwendolyn Midlo Hall, "It is time to tell the truth" about this exceptional artist, teacher, and organizer.[17]

Catlett initially traveled to Mexico to study with the Taller de Gráfica Popular (TGP), an internationalist art collective based in Mexico City. There she found a like-minded group of artists who collaborated with labor unions, anti-fascist forces, Left political organizations, and other radical anti-racist groups agitating for change in Mexico, the United States, and internationally. The TGP, a convergence space of radical politics, was an extension of other internationalist convergence spaces that had shaped Catlett and that she, in turn, had been critical to shaping in the United States. The South Side Community Art Center in Chicago offered one such space, as did the George Washington Carver School in Harlem. Recovering the life of Elizabeth Catlett through the convergence spaces of Chicago, Harlem, and Mexico City unearths not only an overlooked biography but also a submerged theory of internationalism. In her artwork, teaching, and thinking, Catlett placed Black working-class women, particularly domestic workers, at the heart of an internationalist imaginary. By situating Catlett within the radical milieus that produced her and that she in turn helped to produce, the radical anti-racist feminist internationalist politics of her work can be reassessed. To recognize Catlett's radical contributions to pedagogy and culture is to follow

Tiffany Ruby Patterson-Myers's injunction to bring the "gendered and class contours of internationalism out of the shadows."[18]

MEXICAN WPA

For José Clemente Orozco, "the first signs of the revolution appeared in Mexican art." In the immediate lead-up to the Revolution, he and other young artists began to explore "the wretchedest barrios" around Mexico City for inspiration. Soon, "on every canvas there began to appear, bit by bit, like a dawn, the Mexican landscape . . . a first and still timid step toward liberation from foreign tyranny." In 1910, official state celebrations were being prepared for the centenary of El Grito de Dolores, the 1810 declaration of Mexican Independence from Spain. The Academia de San Carlos planned an Exposition of Contemporary Spanish Art. Academy art students like Orozco were outraged. "Why did they give us, the Mexicans, nothing, when it was precisely our Independence that was being celebrated?" Students had already begun rebelling. By scouring their neighborhoods and depicting the people and scenery that surrounded them, they were bravely rebuffing colonial aesthetics. Collectively, they were also developing "a sense of our own being and our destiny." They organized their own counter-Exposition of Mexican Painting. Instead of a jury, they hoisted their paintings before a crowd who "accepted or rejected" them with hisses or exuberant applause. Their selected paintings filled the patio, halls, and corridors of the Academy. Each, on its own, offered a powerful aesthetic rebuttal. Taken together, they expressed a defiant new collective spirit. "There has never been another such showing in Mexico," wrote Orozco. The exhibition was held in September 1910. Rumblings of defiance exploded that November with the outbreak of the Mexican Revolution.[19]

Mexican artists had long articulated popular grievances. The beloved illustrator José Guadalupe Posada was a central inspiration. During the Porfiriato, Posada's cartoon *calaveras* (skeletons) had whimsically caricatured the daily pleasures, pains, and fears of the masses. They also seditiously mocked the excesses of Mexican elites and foreign capitalists.[20] His broadsheets, mass-produced on cheap paper, marked, as one scholar has noted, the "dawn of urban mass popular culture in Mexico City."[21] Posada famously produced his engravings out of his ground floor office before an enormous window that faced the street. Orozco grew up watching Posada work. As a child, he would sneak into the office and quietly pocket metal shavings from the artist's desk.

Orozco's murals and the revolutionary mural tradition he helped inspire, carried traces of Posada's popular democratic aspirations within them.[22]

In 1924, radical Mexican muralist David Alfaro Siqueiros published his manifesto for the Mexican Union of Technical Workers, Painters, and Sculptors, which served as a mission statement for the revolutionary Mexican art movement. The art of this movement, it declared, "is great because it surges from the people; it is collective." Rather than the "bourgeois individualism" that defined most professional artistic endeavors, Siqueiros defined the alternate aim of "socializ[ing] artistic expression."[23] Like Posada's broadsheets, this movement saw the flourishing of democratic art forms like linocuts, woodblock prints, and lithographs, all cheap and easy forms to mass produce. Most accessible were new murals adorning public walls, available for all to see for free. Diego Rivera, the most famous Mexican muralist, observed in 1932 that "the importance of an artist can be measured directly by the size of the multitudes whose aspirations and whose life he serves to condense and translate."[24] Rivera, Orozco, and Siqueiros together made up *los tres grandes,* or "the three greats" of the Mexican mural movement. With the popularity of their work, Mexico's national cultural infrastructure became one of the Revolution's most innovative and internationally inspiring developments. By the 1920s, the Mexican government was subsidizing the work of artists, in effect "giving them walls" on which to inscribe the new ideals of the revolution. The country's cultural awakening had profound effects on the rest of the world.[25]

Starting in 1921, the Mexican government began to subsidize cultural work, including a prominent public mural program. This national effort effectively reframed artists as "cultural workers" in service to the public.[26] State officials like José Vasconcelos, head of the Secretariat of Public Education, foresaw how public murals could inculcate a new national identity within the new Mexican state. The effects were dramatic. As a friend of Franklin Roosevelt's recounted to the then-President:

> The Mexican artists have produced the greatest national school of mural painting since the Italian Renaissance. Diego Rivera tells me that it was only possible because [President] Obregon allowed artists to work at plumber's wages in order to express on walls of government buildings the social ideals of the Mexican Revolution.[27]

Influenced by Mexico's program, the US government made the bold move to subsidize similar national public art programs in the United States. The

Works Progress Administration (WPA) and its short-lived predecessor the Public Works of Art Project (PWAP) were the first New Deal experiments to employ artists. The projects embraced a principle, remarked Charles White, "practically unheard of up to then in United States history—that the arts were socially useful work."[28]

This decision to arm artists in the United States with paintbrushes had profound implications for a world convulsing with radical activity. In this late interwar period, radical sentiment in the United States resounded with revolts occurring globally, with general strikes in Mexican railroads and oil fields to US docks and factories. Social struggle and newly imagined future worlds could be seen in the federally commissioned murals that adorned schools, post offices, and libraries. They depicted scenes of integrated classrooms, multiracial workers reading revolutionary literature together or organizing strikes, and even warmongers surrendering to mutinying soldiers.[29] The powerful dialectic between art and revolutionary practice was expressed in WPA projects as it had also been in Mexican murals.

The WPA project put murals in "public possession," as Holger Cahill, head of the Federal Art Project, believed, making art "the property of all rather than the hobby of the few."[30] Murals hung in public buildings and became public entities that could not be sold to private buyers. For WPA muralists, a "gratifying new spirit" entered their work with the realization that their art was meant for public viewing and appreciation rather than private consumption after private commission.[31] The influence of the Mexican artists was so strong that Edward Bruce, head of the Fine Arts in the WPA, vowed to stop the radical content appearing in the early murals by preventing the "Mexican invasion on the border."[32] By the 1930s, Catlett, like many Black radical artists, had been inspired by the art of the Mexican Revolution.[33] As Catlett's biographer would later note, "To emulate the Mexican artists was not only an aesthetic choice. It was also a political decision with lasting repercussions."[34]

PEDAGOGY AND PROTEST

"I was radical since I was young," declared Catlett in a later oral history. Her first arrest came as a high school student in her hometown of Washington, DC. Standing before the Supreme Court, she had protested lynching while wearing a noose around her neck, an experience that foretold her obstinacy to injustice.[35] Catlett was exposed to the murals of Diego Rivera through a mural assignment for the PWAP in 1934.[36] She was soon fired from the project because, as she later recalled, she spent less time working on the mural and more time buying fabrics and making dresses for herself. While studying art at Howard University, she was hired to paint the basement party room of a local DC abortionist. The doctor, named Dr. Goodloe, had requested a mural in the style of Miguel Covarrubias, a Mexican artist who had spent a significant amount of time in Harlem, and famously depicted its jazz scene in prints, book covers such as Langston Hughes's *The Weary Blues* (1926), magazines, and compilations like *Caricatures of Harlem* (1929). She recalled the story to Covarrubias with glee when she later met him later in Mexico.[37]

Catlett lived at home while she attended college. She was soon "fed up" with the elite "Washington society," color prejudice, and sorority culture at Howard, and found an alternative cultural scene. She began spending time with one of her mother's borders, Pauline Meyers, a Howard graduate student and young communist. Catlett and Meyers were part of the Liberal Club and participated in anti-war demonstrations together. Meyers would organize meetings and give speeches against racism, colonialism, and fascism. She also brought many young radicals to the house. Catlett recalls how one young African man would come and revere Catlett's grandmother, saying, "I'm sitting at your feet, grandmother, tell me about slavery." From these experiences, Catlett came to learn more about her family's history than anyone in her family had ever discussed. Meyers also exposed her to theories of communism, anti-colonialism, and Marxism, things Catlett said she had "never learned in school."[38]

Out of college during the Great Depression and unable to find work in Washington, Catlett found a job as a high school teacher in Durham, North Carolina, from where her mother's family hailed. Here Catlett learned how pedagogy and protest could align. During the Depression, she was horrified to see working-class Black students, especially girls, being cheated of their education: most were trained to make socks for a nearby factory. In the segregated town, Catlett quickly encountered racial disparities in teaching facilities, funding available for students, and teacher pay. Catlett helped organize a teacher protest, an effort that was quickly quashed. She soon came to understand the corruption of local officials and their entanglements with city government and local Black elites. In Durham, known for decades as the "Capital of the Black Middle Class" and the "Black Wall Street of America," Catlett gained her first experience of what she called "Black monopoly capital."

Observing local class power within Durham's elite Black community, Catlett quickly understood how North Carolina Mutual Bank held a "monopoly on the city." This key financial institution exerted local control by either granting or withholding investments in local business and public services. It also held sway over local civil rights organizations and political groups.[39] Catlett witnessed the bank crush her uncle, an independent contractor who was denied loans for his contracting materials. His small business foundered, and he was forced to accept a position with the Bank. Catlett was eager to leave because, as she cryptically noted, "any single girl was prey for the North Carolina Mutual." "I learned a lot of things in Durham," she recounted.[40]

Catlett escaped to study art at the University of Iowa, where there was no out-of-state tuition. She began working with Grant Wood, painter of the iconic *American Gothic* (1930). Wood was famous for depicting the rural Iowa landscapes he knew best. He encouraged Catlett to depict what she best understood, so she began painting, and later sculpting, working-class Black women, particularly Black domestic workers in uniform and Black mothers. This was perhaps a tribute to her own mother, who had taken on many jobs, including as a seamstress, a truant officer, and later a domestic worker to provide for Catlett, her siblings, and her grandmother. It was also possibly in recognition of the local Black women in Iowa who helped her find odd jobs, housing arrangements, and food when she could not afford it. She socialized with them, played in their bridge games, and enjoyed their company. She won a major prize for her thesis sculpture, *Mother and Child,* carved in limestone. When she graduated in 1939, Catlett became one of the first people ever to earn an MFA in Fine Arts and the first Black woman to do so at the University of Iowa. Before graduation, she was hired in the art department at Dillard, a historically Black university in New Orleans.[41]

Before starting the position, Catlett took a summer job teaching design to home economics students at Prairie View College, northwest of Houston, Texas. There she encountered buildings with three separate entrances: main doors for white people, side doors marked "Coloreds," and others marked "Mexicans." She and her friends were stopped by authorities, chased by speeding cars, and threatened by local racists. Texas segregation was for her a "revelation."[42] In each of these experiences Catlett came to develop a sense that teaching meant making political decisions about the world one lived in, and the world one chose or refused to reproduce.

As an art professor at Dillard, Catlett developed a reputation as a local firebrand. She lived at 426 Dauphine Street in the French Quarter, among very poor white families, Black and white sex workers, and a staggering countess "who looked like something out of a Streetcar Named Desire."[43] Only her new colleague, the famous sociologist St. Clair Drake, would visit her.[44] Drake came by after several Black Dillard students were arrested, accused of removing the signs demarcating the segregated sections on a bus. Such signs were constantly removed by people in the city, including Catlett herself, who was fondly remembered for always tearing them down. Catlett contacted Raymond Tilman, local NAACP secretary and head of the Transport Union. Tilman was also part of a New Orleans Marxist group that Catlett was briefly affiliated with. He agreed to represent the students. The case was quietly resolved since the Chair of Dillard's Board of Directors, it appeared, was also chief stockholder of the bus company.[45] Administrators later divulged that they had planned to fire Catlett for bringing a "CIO Communist lawyer on campus." Though short-lived, Catlett's time at Dillard left a lasting impression on the global imagination of her students.[46]

In 1941, Catlett famously desegregated the Delgado Museum of Art, later the New Orleans Museum of Art, by having a bus drive 160 Black students from Dillard to the museum's front door to see a Picasso exhibit. The experience was formative; most of her students had never been inside an art museum, even though many were studying art. Some, like Samella Lewis, Catlett's student, friend, and later biographer, would credit their own journey to becoming artists as beginning on that day.[47] Famed New Orleans artist Willie Birch, who grew up in the city, described how this act reverberated for students in New Orleans for generations. Students stayed at the Delgado for hours, wandering the gallery, amazed to see the art, and studying, in particular, Picasso's famous 1937 painting *Guernica*.[48]

Catlett's political development was forged within the struggle against racism and fascism, a struggle that was keenly being fought out in visual culture. *Guernica* depicted the fascist firebombing of a Basque town, a three-hour ordeal where Nazi and Spanish fascist planes rained down tons of incendiary bombs. This brazen act of civilian slaughter through new war technologies was a prelude to the systematized mass murder to come. When the *London Times* reported on the attack, William Lang described the air raid using a phrase that would come to dominate the lexicon of twenty-first-century war: *weapons of mass destruction*.[49] Catlett once described *Guernica* in a scathing response to a scholar who called "revolutionary art" a meaningless description. She wrote in the Mexican paper *El Dia*:

Who would dare scorn ... the genius of Picasso, moved to shout his anger against inhumanity in the mural of Guernica? This tendency is evidence of the intentions to neutralize and control the power of art, to deny art one of its most sacred functions, and artists one of their greatest responsibilities, to hold up the mirror of truth and to reveal to the eyes of humanity the repulsive presence of the exploitation of man by man.[50]

SOUTH SIDE COMMUNITY ART CENTER

In the early 1940s, the struggle against racism and fascism, particularly among the Black Left, was largely led by women. In Chicago, Margaret Burroughs, director of the South Side Community Art Center, brought Catlett into the fold. While Catlett had advanced training in art, the SSCAC offered her something new. In war time, Burroughs observed that Black artists had "our own plans for a defense—a defense of culture." In the ferment of Chicago, Catlett's consciousness about art's relationship to radical internationalist politics would radically transform.[51]

During the Chicago Renaissance, as it was sometimes called, figures like dancer Katherine Dunham, poet Gwendolyn Brooks, photographer Gordon Parks, scholar Horace Cayton, and organizer Harry Haywood all flourished at the intersections of art and politics.[52] Many were able to cultivate their talents independently or through the alliance of labor and civil rights organizations known as the National Negro Congress (NNC), as well as through Communist Party–affiliated John Reed Clubs. Black artists in this scene connected local struggles against racism and poverty to the global fight against colonialism, imperialism, and fascism, particularly in the Spanish Civil War. After returning from Spain, Haywood helped to organize large anti-fascist peace mobilizations, twenty thousand marchers strong.[53] Through these relationships, participants in Chicago's cultural scene connected local struggles to a global context, developing support for the global fight against fascism and in support of the Mexican, Nicaraguan, and Haitian peoples' fights against US imperialism.[54]

In 1932, a group of visual artists formed the Arts and Crafts Guild on Chicago's South Side. Given that there were few easily accessible venues for Black artists to receive formal training or exhibit their work, artists like Burroughs, George Neal, William McGill, and Bernard Goss began their own organization. The group met every Sunday, alternating between one another's homes. Later, the Guild rented a garage as a studio, which doubled as a home for some of the artists. Neal, who was enrolled in the highly respected Art Institute of Chicago, was the only member of the collective receiving formal training. During the Guild's Sunday sessions, he would share what he had learned the previous week in class, offering guidance and technical instruction.

Just as Orozco and his fellow students at the Academy of San Carlos had, members of Chicago's Arts and Crafts Guild took the radical step of painting and drawing the world around them. The predominantly Black South Side was one of the areas in the country hardest hit by the Depression. In 1931 alone, the Chicago bailiff's office had thrown 1,400 families out of their homes. Relief offices were filled. Schools were closed. The poverty existing prior to the financial crash intensified. The Guild illustrated scenes that were rarely depicted in Chicago's art galleries.[55] Noted Burroughs, "It was not from our imagination that we painted slums and ghettos, or sad, hollow-eyed black men, women and children. They were the people around us."[56]

In the beginning, Guild artists practically had to "lasso" audiences to view their exhibitions, which were held "in whatever spaces were available," as Burroughs recalled. These spaces included church basements, the YMCA, Boys Clubs, and occasionally vacant lots. The Guild gained popularity over time. With small fundraising parties, which would later morph into the elaborate Artists and Models Balls, the Guild began to grow. "Scholarships" covered the costs for one member to attend night classes at the Art Institute. In the tradition George Neal had started, the scholarship recipient would return to share what they had learned with the other members. Through this model, spaces of art production simultaneously became spaces of organizing and instruction. The Arts and Crafts Guild branched out toward becoming a more formalized space. Its base and its subjects were one and the same. Artists from the community sought to represent their community.[57]

Charles White joined the Guild in 1932 after reading about it in the *Chicago Defender*. At fourteen, he had sheared his education from the corners of available public resources. While his mother was at work as a domestic worker, White went to the public libraries and learned to draw from books. He wandered the public galleries of the Art Institute. At the park, he would set up paints within earshot of the Institute's students, listening in on their lessons and sheepishly asking for instruction. He was quickly recognized for his talent, winning awards in school. He was hired by a sign painter, who exploited his talent and non-union status. White remembers that he was "unconscious of trade unions" since his schools certainly "never mentioned them."[58] His experience with the Guild was to be the first of many with organized artists. Like him, they made time after work as bellhops, cooks, maids, dishwashers, and porters and carved out time on Sundays to produce art. Artists like Mitchell Siporin and Edward Millman, who had been to Mexico and studied with *los tres,* would later help White comprehend how aesthetic choices were inextricably developed through one's political consciousness.[59] White would come to protest the WPA's failure to hire a sufficient number of qualified Black artists. He recalled, "We picketed the project. Finally we won. And so my first lesson on the project dealt not so much with paint as with the role of unions in fighting for the rights of working people."[60]

Critical to the WPA's success was the development of an artistic culture, one that funded artwork and also created spaces wherein people could be exposed to art, celebrate it, and produce it themselves. The WPA-sponsored Community Art Centers Project, part of the Federal Art Project, offered federal subsidies to make more permanent structures for art production and instruction.[61] The WPA would provide funding for a space if a community could demonstrate their organizational capacity by selecting an administrative board, raising the initial funds, and finding a suitable location. In this way the Arts and Crafts Guild became the WPA-sponsored South Side Community Art Center. Funding was found locally not only through the annual Artists and Models Ball and exhibitions but also by community outreach. A "mile of dimes" campaign raised over twenty thousand dollars from across the community. Teachers and artists joined gamblers, sex workers, and white uptown gallery owners as contributors, all of whom felt invested in the project. David Ross, speaking on behalf of the other members, said at the SSCAC's official opening, "Here was our chance to stop shining shoes all week and painting on Sundays. This gave us a means of learning as well as earning our living as artists."[62] With free art classes, exhibition space, and a place for artists to discuss and develop their own work, the SSCAC was "tremendous for the community."[63]

That summer, Elizabeth Catlett was able to develop her skills alongside other Black artists in a thriving radical environment.[64] She studied ceramics at the Art Students' League, lithography at the SSCAC, and in her garage studio attached to Burroughs's home, she worked on her own stone carvings. She engaged in political debates about the meaning of art, representation, and global political struggles.[65] White, Burroughs, and many of her friends were in the Communist Party and "were trying to recruit me." She liked them but she did not join. The Center had begun to operate as a celebrated community space, hosting lectures from figures like Lorraine Williams, one of many artists who had gone to Mexico, as well as club meetings of groups like the Negro Press Club, performances from the Negro People's Theater, and events like the National Negro Congress's "Cultural Fiesta." The ferment of these events helped produce a collective radical vision of art and culture in Chicago. This vision was decidedly not about individual advancement.[66] As Margaret Burroughs pointedly described the importance of Black art developed through the SSCAC:

> We were not then and are not now complimented by the people who had the romantic idea that we liked to live in garrets, wear off clothes and go around with emaciated faces, painting for fun; living until the day we died and hoping that our paintings would be discovered in some dusty attic fifty years later and then we would be famous. . . . We believed that the purpose of art was to record the times.[67]

From Chicago, Catlett gained a sense of collective cultural production that could articulate radical political aims while being responsive and accountable to the Black community. In her first summer at the Center, she began dating Charles White. "Theoretically we fell in love," she said flatly upon reflection. Their relationship would soon take them out of Chicago and into the rich cultural milieu of Harlem.[68]

HUNGER FOR CULTURE

Newly married to Charles White, Catlett moved with him to New York City in 1942. The two were immediately wrapped up in Harlem's art and cultural scene, encountering an internationalist cultural infrastructure very similar to the one they had left in Chicago. They moved into the apartment of the actor Kenneth Spencer, who was in Hollywood filming *Cabin in the Sky* (1943). Their apartment building at 409 Edgecombe Avenue was a familiar address for Harlem's luminaries, variously housing figures like W. E. B. Du Bois, Duke Ellington, and Thurgood Marshall.[69] Quickly, Catlett and White would come to meet a broader New York scene including Aaron Douglas, Langston Hughes, Jacob Lawrence, Shirley Graham Du Bois, Harry Belafonte, and Louise Thompson—artists, activists, and cultural workers who considered themselves and their work in a radical global context.[70]

In Harlem, Catlett and White became familiar with organizing spaces for cultural resistance. Augusta Savage's Studio of Arts and Crafts, for example, had become the Harlem Art Workshop, offering free instruction to around seventy-seven students in 1933. This space, located at 306 West 141st Street, came to affectionately be known as "306." Artist Charles Alston moved in, making 306 his home and studio as well as a salon for cultural workers living in or passing through. Poet Claude McKay became a special influence. McKay's wife, the artist Selma Hortense Burke, was influenced by Savage's training and spaces. Other luminaries like Countee Cullen, Ralph Ellison, Walter White, Alain Locke, Eugene O'Neill and Aaron Douglas came to 306. They discussed social issues of the day, some eventually forming a Harlem Artists Guild, similar to Chicago's Artists' Union, but with a greater focus on the particular exclusion of Black artists in the WPA. With Savage's lobbying efforts and the help of artists like Alston, she secured WPA funding, transforming the Workshop into the Harlem Community Art Center. In 1936, this Center was teaching 1,500 students in drawing, painting, sculpture, printmaking, and photography.[71]

From Harlem, Catlett worked in multiple spaces of labor, Left, and cultural resistance. She worked at an interracial family camp, Camp Wo-Chi-Ca, short for Workers Children's Camp, organized by the radical Furriers' Union.[72] She was listed as a "staff illustrator" for the National Negro Congress newsletter, though NNC records and archives of her correspondence shows that she was actually a persistent organizer. In one note, she wrote to W. E. B. Du Bois in her capacity as Executive Secretary of an art initiative in Detroit organized by the NNC and the *New Masses*. She asked Du Bois to serve as co-chair to "combat the campaign of racial antagonism that is being carried on in Detroit by followers of Gerald L. K. Smith and other American Firsters" (a local fascist organization). "May we hear from you soon?," she asked sweetly at the end of the letter. Du Bois agreed. One learns from the NNC correspondence of Catlett's relationships to Harlem's radical Black left, perhaps even a sense of her tenacity within it.[73]

Catlett was a shrewd writer as well as a visual artist. In 1946, she reviewed the exhibit "The Negro Artist Comes of Age," organized at the American Federation of Arts at the Brooklyn Museum, for *The New Masses*. "The title in itself is an insult," she began. "Negro artists have contributed to American culture since the late eighteenth century." While she approved of the work of the "well known" Black male artists included in the exhibit—Romare Bearden, Eldzier Cortor, Ernest Crichlow, Sargent Johnson, Jacob Lawrence,

Hughie Lee-Smith, Charles White, John Wilson, and Hale Woodruff—their "wide diversity of style" left her unconvinced that there was any theme organizing the curation, as would befit most art exhibitions. "There seems to be little purpose in such a separate exhibit," she concluded.

> There is in my mind, and possibly in those of the majority of young Negro artists, no reason for such all-Negro art exhibits, unless to show, in some way, the continuous struggle of Negro artists against tremendous economic and cultural barriers.[74]

She found the Federation's single exhibition patronizing, ultimately denying Black artists the "cultural equality of opportunity." In other efforts in New York, Catlett would help build alternative cultural spaces while also educating new audiences about equality of opportunity.

RADICAL PEDAGOGY

Between 1923 and 1957, "possibly the largest system of adult education in America" was the network of adult education schools organized by labor unions and the Communist Party.[75] These were the "functional equivalent of a university" for the working class, who could both learn a vocation and also enter "the world of ideas" even if they were kept out of formal elite institutions of higher education. In his magnificent *The Cultural Front*, Michael Denning quotes a Croatian immigrant named Stjepan Msaroš—foreign born and poorly educated, like most of the students who passed through. "The radical movement was our teacher," Msaros said. "It was a great step forward to be drawn together in a group to talk and listen, to be induced to read and study. Where else could we get that opportunity?"[76]

During World War II, this network of schools vastly expanded. In the Popular Front era, which emphasized national unity against fascism, schools drew on nationalist patriotic culture. Boston's school was called the Samuel Adams School, Chicago's was named after Abraham Lincoln, and Philadelphia's for Tom Paine. In New York, the main school was the Thomas Jefferson School at 575 Sixth Avenue. The Jefferson School's first publication used unapologetic language to describe its classes and forums, terming them "mass weapons, as sharp and decisive as bullets in the struggle against fascism."[77]

In 1944, Catlett joined the staff of the George Washington Carver School, also known as "A People's Institute," at 57 W. 125th Street in Harlem.[78]

If other schools were named after so-called American heroes, Harlem's was named after a Black agronomist and botanist who made extraordinary advances in soil cultivation after Reconstruction. Carver had brilliantly developed farming methods to enliven the fallow earth. His methods introduced new crops with high protein content that not only nourished communities but also replenished soil that had been stripped and depleted by excessive cotton cultivation. His findings allowed new worlds to grow out of brutal grounds, making his a prophetic name for a radical school.[79]

The school itself was a product of the NNC and drew heavily from the ranks of organized workers, specifically the longshoremen and the Marine Cooks and Stewards Union, which historian Allan Bérubé describes as having their own radical anti-racist, anti-sexist, and anti-homophobic politics (their slogan was "No red baiting, no race baiting, no queer baiting," since members knew that if they could be divided along any of these lines, they could be defeated).[80]

The Carver School tied them to the space of Harlem. One board member, Ben Davis, Harlem's communist councilman, was active in supporting radical Black Left institutions. Other members, such as Du Bois and Paul Robeson, were simultaneously part of the Council on African Affairs, an anti-colonial solidarity organization, arguably one of the first, supporting African struggles against colonialism and apartheid. William Patterson, head of the International Labor Defense (ILD), was one of many organizers with the Civil Rights Congress (CRC) in the global political campaign to free the Scottsboro Boys. Catlett describes moving between spaces and thinking about Harlem, police violence, the poverty and debt of its residents and the gendered vulnerabilities they experienced, all in the context of global anti-fascist and anti-colonial struggle.[81]

World War II also had the unintended consequence of enhancing women's leadership, especially in the Black Left and particularly in Harlem. As Erik S. Gellman writes, "A younger group of black women took over much of the NNC's operation in NYC."[82] Louise Thompson Patterson, Esther Cooper Jackson, Claudia Jones, Marvel Cooke, Augusta Savage, and Eslanda Robeson, to name a few were all in decisive leadership positions. Catlett should be firmly elevated to the ranks of these leaders, alongside her friend and the Carver School's director, Gwendolyn Bennett. Through Catlett's relationship with Bennett in Harlem, similar to her relationship to Margaret Burroughs, one gains a sense of how these women's relationships were critical components of their organizing effectiveness.[83] Dayo Gore's collective political biography recounts how these women's shared work "took shape at the crossroads of the fights for Black liberation, women's equality, workers' rights, and the US left," an early model of revolutionary intersectionality.[84]

In the ferment of Harlem in the 1940s, where, as Harold Cruse described, "nobody gave a damn who you were [or] what your politics were," debates raged between communists, Black nationalists, anti-communists, and liberals at places like the YMCA. Cruse, later a fierce anti-communist, said of the time, "Anybody that couldn't argue Marx or Engels was considered a god damn dummy." Cruse took his first class with Du Bois at the Carver school. He also took a class on philosophy taught by Howard Selsam, a former professor at Brooklyn College.[85]

Selsam had been dismissed by the New York Rapp-Coudert Committee investigation, which purged suspected leftists from their teaching jobs. Many teachers at Carver had been victims of this early Red Scare hysteria, which was an unfounded assault on public education. Usually it was students who were much more radical on campus than their teachers. They often only learned that their teachers were on the Left after hearing they'd been killed in the Spanish Civil War. As one substitute teacher in Harlem described, if you were drawn to the people who worked hardest to change things for students, you inevitably found yourself with the communists. They were the ones who looked out for their coworkers, and who fought against the exploitation and repression faced by students, staff, or local neighbors.[86] Mark Starr, who was avowedly not a communist but head of worker education for the International Ladies' Garment Workers' Union (ILGWU), formed a committee to combat Red Scare attacks on education. "Talk of subversive and immoral activities," he wrote, "is nothing but a smokescreen behind which the enemies of public education seek to destroy the economic and intellectual foundations of our school system."[87] While many talented teachers lost their jobs in the Red Scare, places like the Carver School gained the benefit of their labor.

TREMENDOUS HUNGER

Initially Carver's students cut a wide swath across Harlem's social classes. But after an article by Westbrook Pegler denounced the school as a "Red Front," most of the middle-class students left. As a result, the students of Carver were the cooks, maids, janitors, elevator operators, garment industry workers, and domestic workers of New York City, who took courses for three dollars apiece.[88] The students quickly transformed the place into their own. Young artists painted the originally "dreary" walls of the school. A volunteering minister "rolled up his sleeves and glued together chairs" for students to sit on. McCrory's Five and Ten Cent Store up the block donated a grand piano. In the first term, 157 people came from trade unions, fraternal organizations, youth groups, and churches.[89] After three years, enrollment rose to 702 students. In a 1946 *Chicago Defender* article, student Katherine Hennant describes her experience:

> I wondered why I was receiving such valuable and capable guidance at so small a fee. How was this possible? [I thought about my teacher and why] he must have been interested in the problems of the working class since he used politics to illustrate the meaning and use of words. / I then began to wonder about other teachers . . . whether they too were interested in the problems of workers. I decided that the Carver School must be a school for the fair thinking people of this community. Why. Because black and white were serving side by side to aid those of us who sought a better understanding of life and problems.[90]

The curriculum was developed according to what the students needed. Popular classes included Black history, taught by Alain Locke and E. Franklin Frazier. Irwin Freundlich of Juilliard taught music appreciation; Dorothy Homer, head librarian at the 135th Street New York Public Library branch, held a class on "Current Books and Social Classes." A local head of price control taught a course called "Your Dollar and How to Spend It." Students jokingly suggested that they would rather have a class called "Your Dollar and How to Get It."[91] Classrooms offered students opportunities to discuss politics as they unfolded in Harlem. As Catlett recounts:

> Some cops shot a soldier in the back in a hotel when La Guardia was mayor. And the people cleaned out of 125th Street and everything. Yeah, well we analyzed that in our school, why that happened.[92]

Catlett later recalled one particularly memorable evening. "About 350 of us were squeezed into a small room, sweating on a hot June night, with the windows closed and the shades drawn (because of the World War II blackout). [It was] most uncomfortable, [and we were] listening to Shostakovich's 7th Symphony."[93] Dimitri Shostakovich's symphony, titled "Leningrad," was written during the devastating Nazi siege of his hometown in 1941. This symphony had been smuggled out of Russia on microfilm by a US agent in 1942. It was then flown to Tehran, driven through the Middle East and into Cairo, flown to Brazil and then to DC, where the agent almost forgot it on a lunch tray but recovered it just before it was tossed into the trash. After the music was transcribed and performed by musicians in New York, it was broadcast across the country, offering people in the United States an intimate vision of the brutal Nazi assault. During the siege of Leningrad, over a million people were cut off from food, heat, and contact with the outside world. Many of the musicians who originally performed it in Russia regularly fainted from hunger and even died during rehearsal. The symphony was said to be so compelling that when it was broadcast over loudspeakers in Leningrad, even Nazi soldiers were affected. Years later, one remarked on the "slow but powerful effect" the symphony had: "We began to see that there was something stronger than starvation, fear and death—the will to stay human." According to M. T. Anderson, the song marked a decisive turn in the siege and in the war. Its force was not lost on US audiences.[94]

This was what Catlett and the others had packed into the room to listen to on that hot June night. As she recalled, "A professor from Juilliard's Music School had come to play his tape for our students who were mostly from Harlem's people—janitors, day workers, laundresses, cooks, elevator operators, and so on—poor black people who served others."[95] In the middle of the eighty-minute symphony, the professor stopped the record. Said Catlett:

> When the first movement ended the professor explained that since the second movement was very long we could take a break to refresh ourselves with some cold punch. Our students politely refused. They said no, the break can wait. We want to hear it all together. Now, ignorant me! I had thought they weren't interested in classical music.[96]

Catlett told this anecdote in many interviews to illustrate what she described as her new awareness of a "tremendous hunger for culture."[97] This hunger, she said, "made me realize that artists should create art for everyone, not just an elite."[98] The students she encountered in Harlem were "domestic workers, people that worked in the dress trades, people that served other people. . . . Their interests and their desire to lean about literature and art and economics and history and so forth was great."[99] At the Carver School, Catlett was enlivened to think and learn with them. To do this through teaching art posed a specific challenge. "The main method of denial," as she later explained, "was then and continues to be the fostering of an elitist art which further widens class distinctions."[100] Her experiences teaching in Harlem, she said in 1998, made her "realize that I had to work for people. . . . Up until then, I guess I didn't have any artist's philosophy about what I was doing and why." At the Carver School, Catlett developed a new fusion of culture and politics through the specific interaction with her students, who were largely the Black domestic workers of New York City.[101]

HOW TO MAKE A DRESS

The most popular class at the Carver School, as the *Chicago Defender* described, "was the one called 'How to Make a Dress.'"[102] The class was originally conceived to help the mostly women workers sew their own dresses on furnished sewing machines. Catlett taught this popular class. Here she would come into the closest and most regular contact with Black domestic workers in Harlem, who were at the center of the class struggle. Lessons about dressmaking would accordingly adopt broader dimensions. Catlett recalled common conversations she would have about it when people would ask:

> "How do you teach Marxism making a dress?" And I said, Well, while we're sewing, we talk. And when a lady says, "I have to leave early to get my news," I say, "Do you know what the news thinks of you and black people?" And we'd get into a discussion of why newspapers are printed, and who reads them, what they support, what they don't support. . . . It was the way that we worked.[103]

The question of Black domestic workers occupied the organizing efforts, writing, and theory of Black radical feminists in Harlem in this period. The writer Alice Childress would go on to devote much of her *Freedomways* column "Conversations from Life" to the lives of Black domestic workers. Marxist Claudia Jones would devote a four-page section of her 1949 essay "An End to the Neglect of the Problem of the Negro Woman" to "The Domestic Worker."[104] As Jones explained, Black women's triple oppression of race, class, and gender meant that the exploitation of Black domestic workers was the "crassest manifestation of trade union neglect."[105] Marvel Cooke would also write a series of articles about their struggle. In 1935, Cooke and young organizer Ella Baker coauthored the article "Bronx Slave Market," describing the humiliations of Black domestic workers huddled on the street corner in early morning hours, awaiting inspection from middle-class women for potential labor for the day. Baker and Cooke emphasized the role of clothing as critically enabling or preventing employment. It marked ability, social class, and level of desperation, and often signaled the form of labor the wearer was willing to undertake. "Rain or shine, cold or hot—you will find them there . . . women, old and young, sometimes bedraggled, sometimes neatly dressed—but with the invariable paper bundle, waiting expectantly."[106] Catlett took the bus often; surreptitiously sketching the Black domestic workers aboard.[107]

For Black domestic workers, dresses were not just objects of fancy but necessary for confronting the complexities of their employment. Catlett's material engagement helped elaborate the multiple forms of valorization happening through the dress. These articles of clothing were class signifiers, prerequisites for entrance into different spaces and places of employment. Their style, color, and upkeep became unstable markers of employability: they needed to be clean and signal reliability to potential employers and stylish enough to make the wearer a conspicuous object of servitude, able to impress friends and neighbors of the white women who hired them. These were also objects of utility, necessary to clothe the body. They needed to be sturdy, flexible, and durable enough to work in. As Catlett recounted, "It was easier to have navy blue, or brown, or black that didn't show dirt so much." These were, after all, not just costumes but uniforms. In early morning hours and throughout long days, they needed to be warm enough for their wearers to endure interminable hours of working or of waiting. These dresses had to be understood, too, as a potential liquid asset that could be sold in desperate conditions. Catlett understood these conditions. During one cold winter in Iowa, she had been forced to sell her own coat in order to afford rent and food.[108]

Critically, these dresses had to subtly convey the wearer's availability or unavailability for sex work. While it was more often wealthy white women who did the hiring, as Baker and Cooke noted, their husbands, sons, and brothers, "under the subterfuge of work offer worldly-wise girls higher bids for their time."[109] These scenes underscored the ways in which complex realities of race, gender, and class collided for Black domestic workers, forcing them to negotiate a wide range of vulnerable entanglements. Accordingly, clothes had to be complex vectors of communication, their wearers aware of the racialized, classed, gendered, and sexual codes simultaneously communicated with every transaction.

"How to Make a Dress" was perhaps one space where the complex politics of Black working-class women's daily lives could be untangled. Catlett even described learning about how clothing reflected her students' housing conditions, since women "didn't have bathrooms, or they shared them with somebody." These spatial constraints also determined where and how often dresses could be washed and mended.[110] The class was a unique space for exploring the complex relations that went into the commodity of the dress, the commodity of the labor power of these women, and an understanding of capital not as an abstraction but a practice, a determinate set of social relations in which the inseparability of racism, patriarchy, and class could be understood. But if these dresses signaled the vulnerability of their wearers, they could also become, as Peter Stallybrass writes, the "materialization of class resistance."[111] New York City, after all, had the highest rates of unionized Black domestic workers, as Esther Cooper Jackson, future editor of *Freedomways* magazine, described in her 1940 Master's thesis.[112] Such organizing was necessary, for as Du Bois would argue in *Darkwater,* "as long as domestic service was the rule for Black people, emancipation would always remain a conceptual abstraction."[113]

In these ways the Carver school gave Catlett the transformative opportunity to better understand the position of Black working-class women in relation to global struggles for socialism. It also helped her understand how art could be responsive to their lives and political and social movements. With this in mind, she proposed a series about the lives of Black working-class women, submitting an application to the Rosenwald Fellowship to go to Mexico.

WHY MEXICO?

Throughout their time in New York, Catlett and White remained in the orbit of Mexican art, just as artists in Mexico City kept abreast of the New York cultural scene as it was regularly reported on in José Juan Tablada's *Nueva York de día y noche* ("New York by Day and Night") column in the Mexican newspaper *El Universal.*[114] The presence of Diego Rivera and José Clemente Orozco was still fresh in the murals they had painted around New York City. While some had been destroyed, others—for example, Orozco's 1931 murals at the New School, including *Homecoming of the Worker of the New Day* and *Table of Universal Brotherhood,* and Rivera's 1933 murals, including *Mussolini, Modern Industry,* and *Proletarian Unity* at the New Workers' School—still stood.[115] Black artists in New York had come into regular contact with *los tres.* In 1933, Charles Alston had observed Rivera as he painted *Man at the Crossroads* at Rockefeller Center. Jacob Lawrence had observed Orozco as he painted a mural for the Metropolitan Museum of Art.[116] When Catlett studied lithography at the New York Art Students League, she met the artists Raúl Anguiano, José Chávez Morado, and Ignacio Aguirre of the Taller de Gráfica Popular. Aguierre would invite her to be a part of the TGP and Morado would later give her and Charles White the address of Siqueiros's mother-in-law, who ran a boardinghouse in Mexico City.[117]

The 1930s had also seen a number of exhibitions featuring Orozco, Siqueiros, and Rivera, as well as a number of artists who had been to Mexico to work with them. Shows hosted by the American Artists' Congress Against War and Fascism (1936), the NAACP (1935), and the Communist Party (1935) featured their artwork against racial violence. The NAACP and the CP hosted competing exhibitions protesting lynching. Both exhibits featured Orozco's lithograph *Hanged Negroes* (1930), a haunting image of four lynched Black men being consumed by fire. Art historians have observed the stylistic similarities between Orozco's depictions of lynching and the earlier series he had done about violence suffered during the Mexican Revolution.[118] Also participating in these shows were members of the Taller de Gráfica Popular (who appeared in the American Artists' Congress show) and American artists who had traveled to Mexico, such as Japanese American Isamu Noguchi, who displayed his work in both anti-lynching exhibits.[119] Noguchi's haunting sculpture, *Death,* or *Lynched Figure* (1934), was based on a photograph of a contorted body after a lynching that had been published by the International Labor Defense. Noguchi's twisted figure is similar to an element in Diego Rivera's *Modern Industry,* one of the frescos he had recently completed at the New Workers' School in New York. Also present in the NAACP exhibit was Hale Woodruff, a mural artist who had gone to Mexico in 1936 to study with *los tres* and subsequently painted a three-paneled mural commemorating the *Amistad* slave rebellion in Alabama's Talladega College Savery Library upon his return.[120]

In 1946, Catlett and White traveled from New York City to Mexico City. Catlett had received a Rosenwald grant to complete a series on Black women there. Just as in Chicago and Harlem, they were soon caught up in the revolutionary ferment of Mexico City. This scene was anchored by the TGP, a radical collective composed of like-minded Mexican and international artists. Catlett brought her experiences of space making, pedagogy, and internationalism to the TGP. She observed the working of the collective in their collaborative critiques.

At the end of the day, the artists would gather their work and affix it to the walls. Moving slowly as a group, they would stop at each other's drawings and discuss, a process called *críticas colectivas,* or collective critiques. Some comments revolved around style, others around purpose and clarity. Artists were firm but encouraging.[121] Catlett recounts:

> [A]t the *taller* we all worked more or less collectively; everyone was interested in your project. Each artist would select a theme, go home, and do a drawing. Then the drawings were brought in and put up so we could see how they related to the assignment. The criticism was always constructive. 'I think the symbolism is very good,' someone might say, 'but the drawing is weak. To make it a stronger work, you could improve the way you drew that hand, which you slurred . . . when you were focusing on the face.'[122]

The success of the image was the shared intention of the collective. Could the image convey its message to the other artists present? Could it illustrate the specific elements of the campaign for which striking students, trade unions, or other anti-fascist movements had enlisted the TGP's help? How might it disrupt prevailing assumptions about power and inequality? Could it, in turn, communicate these visions to the majority of the people in Mexico and beyond?[123]

During Catlett and White's first visit, the TGP artists were in the middle of producing their series on the history of the Mexican Revolution. The *Estampas de la Revolución Mexicana* was a series of eighty-five linocuts graphically illustrating the history of the Revolution. Catlett was clearly moved by what she saw and was compelled to incorporate elements into her own work. Her Rosenwald application stated her intention to produce a print series celebrating the lives of Black working-class women. Her subsequent series, *The Negro Woman* (later titled *The Black Woman*), did just that.

The Black Woman consists of fifteen linograph prints. Placed together, the titles can be read as a poem:

> I am the Black woman
> I have always worked hard in America
> In the fields
> In other folks' homes
> I have given the world my songs

In Sojourner Truth I fought for the rights of women as well as Blacks
In Harriet Tubman I helped hundreds to freedom
In Phillis Wheatley I proved intellectual equality in the midst of slavery
My role has been important in the struggle to organize the unorganized
I have studied in ever increasing numbers
My reward has been bars between me and the rest of the land
I have special reservations
Special houses
And a special fear for my loved ones
My right is a future of equality with other Americans.[124]

The TGP's inspiration is evident in her series. Both *The Black Woman* and the *Estampas* feature several portraits of key historical figures. In the TGP's series, Emiliano Zapata and Pancho Villa are given heroic depictions, while in Catlett's series, famous Black leaders such as Sojourner Truth and Phillis Wheatley are featured. Significantly, both series also celebrated the experiences of ordinary men and women, and their lives as workers, musicians, grievers, fighters, and organizers.[125] Placed side by side, the stylistic similarities and political resonance between the two series becomes apparent.

One piece in the TGP's series, *La Dictadura Porfiriana Exalta Demagógicamenta al Indígena* ("The Porfirian Dictatorship Demagogically Exalts the Native") [Figure 18] by Alfredo Zalce, depicts a scene leading up to the Mexican Revolution. An impoverished Indigenous Mexican man lies prostrate on the ground while a procession of foreign capitalists parade in the background, seemingly over his body. In the center of their procession is an exalted Indigenous figure in costume, seated on a throne carried by other men.

Zalce's image reflects actual parades held in Mexico City on the eve of the Revolution. Celebrating President Porfirio Díaz's reelection in 1910, thousands witnessed a historical pageant meant to link Indigenous history to Díaz's modern Mexico. In the procession, Indigenous figures were extolled as national symbols. Zalce's panel highlights the hypocrisy of this act. Indigenous people suffered greatly under Díaz. Few were even allowed to get close to the parade. As one historian describes, "All beggars, ragged-trousered peasants, and any who did not obey an unwritten sumptuary code were expelled from the central section of the capital."[126] This irony played out throughout the country as the Mexican state tried to claim pre-Hispanic Indian ancestry for itself while at the same time expropriating the land and labor of Indigenous Mexicans.[127] Arbitrary laws and violent disciplinary measures were put in place to suppress the Indigenous masses. The shadow of the prison hung over the land, checking disobedience.[128] The existence of some Indigenous groups, like the Yaqui, threatened the expansion of railroads and subsequent capital accumulation. Accordingly, they endured some of the most barbarous persecution.[129] In Zalce's image, the exalted Indigenous figure is flanked on either side by white men in top hats holding French and American flags, representatives of the foreign capital invested in the entire spectacle.

Zalce's image did not only show the Porfirian Mexican state's violent and contradictory relationship to Indigenous people in the lead-up to the Revolution. In the postrevolutionary period, Indigenous people were cunningly depicted as part of a nationalist cultural project. From the 1920s on, Indigeneity was conceived as part of a unique Mexican amalgamation of *la raza cósmica* ("the cosmic race"), an imagined identity of colonial Spanish and Indigenous, one that conspicuously excised all mention of African ancestry (and therefore denied all relation to the Atlantic slave trade). The postrevolutionary state sought to incorporate Indigenous people as mixed or *mestizo* subjects in the name of revolutionary nationalism. Zalce's image of the falsely exalted Indigenous person demonstrates how both forms of national culture consciously obscured stark divisions between the poor, dispossessed, and violently repressed Indigenous populations and the owners of wealth and controllers of capital in the country. The prostrate Indigenous man in his image is therefore a poignant representation of both prerevolutionary and postrevolutionary nationalism's vexed relationship to Indigeneity.[130]

Elizabeth Catlett's image *And a special fear for my loved ones* [Figure 19] illustrates a similar scene from a different time and place. The image depicts a Black man who has been lynched, his body on the ground and a noose around his neck. The feet surrounding him appear, at first glance, to belong to a lynch mob. When compared with Zalce's image, a few elements are thrown into different relief. The lynched man's hand is outstretched like the Indigenous man's in Zalce's image. What is different is that his eyes are open, looking up at the figures surrounding him. It is unclear whether those eyes indict the figures above him or look sympathetically at them. As in Zalce's image, the foregrounded figure presses one part of his body to the base of the page. In both images, ill-defined horizons make the background figures appear to float. In Zalce's piece, this contrast successfully conveys the symbolism of the procession, contrasting the extolled myth of Indigenous ancestry and the actual suffering of Indigenous people during Díaz's reign.

Catlett's image is similarly composed. The man with the noose around his neck has his foot placed at the base of the page. An ill-defined horizon, exaggerated by Catlett's shifting lines, destabilizes the ground. Instead of standing above him, the feet surrounding the man also appear to be floating. The feet of the purported lynch mob could be alternately interpreted. They might instead be the feet of other men who have also been lynched but are still floating above the ground. The feet appear at the top of the picture as the only visible part of their bodies. The ambiguity of perspective in the picture shifts the intention away from singular indictment. Lynching, from this perspective, is simultaneously an act of racist terror that takes the life of its victim and an act that destroys the humanity of the perpetrator. Freedom as the abstract capacity to suppress another's life is not freedom at all. Catlett's piece underscores the long line of abolitionist thought that no one can be free in a society premised on the violent exclusion of another.[131]

As Catlett found her place in the TGP, she contributed a piece that would ultimately become a part of the TGP's Mexican Revolution series. Her print, which appears to be a collaboration with her soon-to-be husband, Francisco "Pancho" Mora, is entitled *To pay for petroleum* [Figure 20]. The scene depicts popular support for the nationalization of Mexican oil. In 1938, the Mexican government under President Lázaro Cárdenas had scandalized foreign investors by implementing Article 27, the most radical tenet of its 1917 Constitution, and nationalizing the country's oil reserves. This move was led by the country's trade unions and Left-wing political movements, with the support of US trade unions, communists, and allies. In the background of the print, oil wells are all adorned with the Mexican flag. In the foreground, Mexican *campesinos* bring livestock, small coins, and crops to the table as donations for the effort. In the center of the image is a woman donating what she has to offer to the cause: a sewing machine. Here, in this image designed by Catlett, is the culmination of struggles for feminism and internationalism, articulated through the nationalist struggles of the Mexican Revolution. The tools to make a dress are here intertwined with a radical alternate vision of revolution.

CODA—HOW TO MAKE INTERNATIONALISM

In 1942, while still in New York, Catlett began taking private classes with Ossip Zadkine, an accomplished Russian-born Jewish sculptor who had fled the Nazis in Paris. In his cold-water Greenwich Village studio, Zadkine and

Catlett discussed internationalism. Motivated by the fight against fascism, Zadkine's angular modernist sculptures took on themes of suffering, the destruction of cities in war, and universal pain. He asked why Catlett insisted on sculpting images of Black women and children, a theme, he asserted, that was "limited" and not internationalist. She pushed Zadkine on his definition of internationalism. Why couldn't people identify with a Black mother and child in the same way? What made him assume that her artwork was limited instead of universally identifiable? And why did he presume that his sculpture of a male poet adorned with a French poem was somehow universal and internationalist?[132] Years later, Catlett would clarify: "It does not need revolution as its subject in order to be revolutionary."[133] Indeed, her art and collaborative work challenges many presumptions of what it means to be revolutionary. To recover the political life of Elizabeth Catlett is to reclaim the feminist and anti-racist spaces where internationalism has been collectively struggled over, and where it can be made.

Conclusion

HOW TO MAKE HISTORY

Arise ye prisoners of starvation,
Arise ye wretched of the earth:
For justice thunders condemnation,
A better world's in birth.
No more tradition's chains shall bind us,
Arise ye slaves, no more in thrall;
The earth shall rise on new foundations,
We have been naught, we shall be all.

"THE INTERNATIONALE," 1888

The hungry in the United States, the French outcast, the Russian
slave, the British serf, the disinherited of all countries could take
a lesson from their brother, the Mexican worker.

RICARDO FLORES MAGÓN, *REGENERACIÓN*, MAY 1914

Yet the rich world is wide enough for all, wants all, needs all.

W. E. B. DU BOIS, *BLACK RECONSTRUCTION IN AMERICA,*
1860–1880, 1935

IN THE HEART OF THE WORKSHOP of the Taller de Gráfica Popular sat
a treasured printing press engraved with the number 1871.[1] According to
TGP lore, the press had been smuggled to Mexico City from Paris, where
Eugène Pottier, a transport worker, had organized his own artists' group. The
Fédération des Artistes was a radical international collective of artists and
artisans, an early precursor to the TGP. There, Pottier and his comrades
joined paint, ink, clay, wood, fabric, and the "bonds of solidarity" to visually

express the wild experimental spirit of the Paris Commune.[2] In June 1871, Pottier wrote a poem. "Arise ye starvelings from your slumbers," it began. Pottier dedicated the poem to his fellow communards, thirty thousand of whom had just been slaughtered by the French military. Survivors who had escaped death and arrest were forced into exile, with some, like Pottier, stealing away to England and then the United States. The communards' crime: forging a temporary workers' government. Observers at the time were shocked by the volume of blood spilled on Parisian streets. Some recognized that the "ferocity" of this domestic massacre had incubated in French colonial wars and expansionist ventures in places like Algeria, Crimea, Vietnam, Senegal, and Mexico.[3] The global dimensions of revolution and counterrevolution were not lost on Pottier. His poem referred to an International, the International Working Men's Association, formed in 1864 in London, where Pottier had been in attendance.[4] The Association, also known as the First International, represented a convergence of international labor struggles, abolitionist movements, and anti-colonial and anti-imperialist currents, as discussed in the first chapter. Belgian composer Pierre Degeyter set the poem to music in 1888. The song soon spread as widely as the struggles forged in its name.

By the outbreak of the Mexican Revolution in 1910, "The Internationale" had been adopted as the standard for international workers' movements. Its lyrics were published in songbooks and woven throughout the text of radical newspapers. At the famous Bread and Roses strike in 1912 organized by the Industrial Workers of the World, the lyrics were translated into Italian, Portuguese, French, German, Hungarian, Polish, and Syrian, and sung at once by the immigrant textile workers, mostly women, in Lawrence, Massachusetts. Into the teens and twenties, the song became the lingua franca of anarchists, socialists, communists, radical labor organizers, and self-professed revolutionaries, including those who found themselves in revolutionary Mexico, as described in the second chapter. It echoed in spaces of confinement, like Leavenworth Penitentiary, where Mexican revolutionaries sang with incarcerated radicals from around the world, as described in chapter 3. The Bolshevik Revolution of 1917 deepened the appeal of the song, as Soviet ambassador Alexandra Kollontai learned when greeted with the anthem throughout her time in Mexico in the 1920s, as described in chapter 4. By the 1930s, militant communists like Dorothy Healey and Mexican women farmworkers took the song as their own as they fought conjoined struggles for relief and revolution in Southern California, inspired by the Mexican Revolution, as recounted in chapter 5. When Elizabeth Catlett joined the TGP in Mexico City, the lyrics and symbology of the song figured heavily into the collective's artistic work, as described in chapter 6. Since the turn of the century, millions have sung "The Internationale," the definitive anthem of internationalism, with varying interpretations of its meaning, but with some shared faith in a better world to come.[5]

Over the long twentieth century, writers have also turned to Pottier's lyrics to reckon with the political struggles fought in internationalism's name. Historian Melvyn Dubofsky titled his comprehensive study of the anarcho-syndicalist Industrial Workers of the World, *We Shall Be All.* Stalwart anti-fascist and former Communist Party member Jessica Mitford named her memoir *A Fine Old Conflict* after her youthful misconstruction of the lyrics "'Tis the final conflict." Frantz Fanon famously excerpted the song's second line in the title for his book *The Wretched of the Earth,* in which he reflected on anti-colonial struggles in and beyond colonized French Algeria. A few months after Dorothy Healey resigned from the Communist Party, she expressed her desire to write a book entitled *Tradition's Chains Have Bound Us,* a slight adaption of the song's lyrics. The title, she believed, would signal the need for revolutionary movements to "constantly keep alive that challenging, questioning and probing of the real scene around it," freed even from the bounds of its own "traditions." Healey's far-reaching oral history, conducted by Maurice Isserman, ultimately carried her title.[6] This small sampling offers a sense of the writers and the scope of struggles fought in internationalism's name. While disparate in their visions and their reckonings, they all plumbed the lyrics of "The Internationale" and found new meaning in Pottier's words.

Arise! is written in this tradition. It shares the spirit of reflection and urgency, taking the song's first word as its title. This book has traced the history of internationalism in the early twentieth century as a way of negotiating its legacy in the present. Alongside these other texts, it recognizes that the study of internationalism is always a reckoning with an unbidden inheritance. This reckoning, to paraphrase Fanon, is the responsibility of each generation to fulfill or to betray.[7] The inheritance of internationalism is neither straightforward nor directly transferable. Each successive generation has interpreted, enlivened, and/or deformed the tradition, with wide variances within. The accretion of this history is dense. All the hopes, thwarted dreams, and betrayals, the unfinished and inchoate longings weigh, as one might say, like a nightmare on the brain. Anyone who confronts the nastiness of the world must challenge, question, and probe the traditions of struggle they find they have inherited. There is no way around or apart from this history of radical struggle—only, somehow, through.[8]

In seemingly impossible times, history can be a guide. Alternately, it can be a powerful palliative, a source of mere "pleasure and amusement." In the misery of the Great Depression, W. E. B. Du Bois warned of the ways that history can gratify readers with a false but seductive "sense of accomplishment." During the Depression, he brought to light the obscured histories of the Reconstruction era. His magnum opus *Black Reconstruction in America* presented the culmination of abolition, the overturning of slavery by enslaved people during the Civil War, and the subsequent era of Reconstruction, "the finest effort to achieve democracy for the working millions which this world had ever seen." Racist historians had propagated the idea that Black people possessed neither the will nor the capacity for such action. They had so maligned and censored this history that its mere presentation was revelatory. Du Bois's final chapter, "The Propaganda of History," offered a direct rebuttal to this dominant school of thought. Both embittered readers of the conquered South and embarrassed readers of the North had agreed upon a version of slavery's history where "nobody seems to have done wrong and everybody was right." This history, wrote Du Bois, was propaganda, "lies agreed upon" to exculpate a nation and educate new generations in a blithe but empowering ignorance.[9]

Du Bois took specific aim at the scholarship emanating from one of the nation's most elite educational institutions, Columbia University. William Dunning, history professor and founder of the reigning historiography of the Reconstruction era, had trained generations of scholars, many from the US South, who had not grown up in the "arrogant bluster of the slave oligarchy" but with the resentment of a "conquered people" in the bloody aftermath of Redemption and the economic panic of 1873. The scholarship of the Dunning school offered absolution in the form of omission: Black people's leadership under Reconstruction and their alliance with poor white people toward equality became, in its historical works, "incomprehensible." Dunningites contrived racist palliatives into historical fact.

The embittered Dunning scholars were men who believed themselves to be the "small shareholders" of empire, the imagined beneficiaries of the New

Imperialism. Their racist fictions, propagated as histories of Reconstruction, were inextricable from the racist fictions imagined on a global scale, what Du Bois had elsewhere called a "color line." But it was not to the adherents of the Dunning school that Du Bois directed his final chapter. Rather, it was to their students and to all those who had inherited such racist versions of history and adopted complimentary visions of themselves within it. Du Bois beheld the world produced by this false knowledge like a curse.

One of his book's final images is of "a teacher sit[ting] in academic halls, learned in the tradition of its elms and its elders." Du Bois describes the teacher, looking "into the upturned face of youth" and choosing to teach the student a lesson in the impossibility of equality. Here Du Bois quotes the same words he had selected for his observations about the US intervention in Mexico in 1914, as described in the introduction. Once this lesson of impossibility is delivered, Du Bois conjures the ways that torture, rape, and violence are "immediately" spread around the globe: "In Africa, a black back runs red with the blood of the lash; in India, a brown girl is raped; in China, a coolie starves." Du Bois ends his book by linking the pedagogical and the political. To "sneer" at movements toward equality in the past makes their future realization nearly impossible.[10]

I have been moved by Du Bois to write a book against impossibility. I wrote it in part on the campus of Columbia, where the Dunning school once reigned and where Du Bois's lessons about the propaganda of history and the global color line have motivated a renewed inquiry. At the time of this writing, impossibility continues to be a feature of elite education. Histories of past struggles are taught cautiously and selectively. If heroic, they are more often narrated as circumscribed and small. Mass struggles are less appraised for the conditions they confronted and more often decried as victims of their own overreach, idealism, or theoretical blindness. This is the propaganda of history now. This is not to say that there should be no reckoning with history. There must. But cruel fictions that dissuade people from fully comprehending histories of mass struggle preclude many from ever engaging in them. Such fictions allow elites to be charmed by their own disenchantment, dazzled by the portentousness of their sneers. They encourage students to arrive prematurely at the hardboiled certainty of impossibility and comport themselves to murderous settlements, disguised as objectivity. From this perspective, the prison of the present seems inescapable. But this path is contrived. As this book has shown, and as present events have demonstrated, when radical questioning is made impossible, violent reaction is made inevitable.

As Du Bois observed, when workers were abandoned from any revolutionary vision, they were most susceptible to the seductive fantasies of the New Imperialism and its racist and spatial imaginaries. Racism, in other words, is not inevitable. His argument about the potential for global class alliances across the color line was in keeping with Frederick Douglass's own assessment:

> But is this color prejudice the natural and inevitable thing it claims to be? If it is so, then it is utterly idle to write against it, preach, pray, or legislate against it, or pass constitutional amendments against it. Nature will have her course, and one might as well preach and pray to a horse against running, to a fish against swimming, or to a bird against flying. Fortunately, however, there is good ground for calling in question this high pretension of a vulgar and wicked prepossession.[11]

Douglass and Du Bois were both keen observers of the global capitalist economy and the struggle against it because they understood the instability of the racial regimes that underlay it. They saw the color line as a political project rather than an ontological condition. It had been organized and so, they believed, it could be organized against and overcome. Following their lead, this book argues that the color line is less a physical demarcation to be traced and more a political project to be overcome. It calls for a different form of making.

INTERNATIONALIST CONVERGENCES

This book observes that the Mexican Revolution staged a significant set of convergences within which internationalism was "made." It tracks groupings of people thrown together in the tumult of the revolution and the chaos of global capital, who were forced to make meaning together in different spaces and struggles. These include migrant workers, cultural workers and intellectuals, self-declared revolutionaries, ambassadors, and organizers, among others. In observing disparate spaces of making, it contends that the internationalist consciousness, forged in the era of the Mexican Revolution, posed particular challenges to emergent US hegemony in this era of the New Imperialism.

This book has tried to rethink this tradition of internationalism for the present moment. It makes several interventions critical to this task. First, it recognizes that a political economic basis, the internationalization of capital, produced the conditions for internationalist consciousness in the late nine-teenth and early twentieth centuries. Through an analysis of thinkers like Ricardo Flores Magón, W. E. B. Du Bois, Frederick Douglass, and Giovanni Arrighi, it considers the specific development of global capital in the period.

I take from Arrighi my consideration of the overlapping period within which US hegemony came to slowly displace British hegemony as the domi-nant systemic cycle of accumulation. I periodize this era through Du Bois's analysis of the "New Imperialism," that is, a period that carried the vestiges of the old forms of empire while presenting itself through the seemingly more democratized language of finance. As Du Bois and Douglass both contended, the New Imperialism's appeals to the aspiring class of Western capitalist countries were made across an imagined global color line. Such appeals ena-bled "white" people (and others seduced by propertied fantasies) to believe that the gains of new imperial forays were their own. As Flores Magón under-stood, the sharpest gains of ascendant US hegemony in the age of the New Imperialism occurred in Mexico. *Arise!* argues that the United States's role within the New Imperialist era was largely shaped in relation to Mexico. In relation to Mexico's revolution, it further observes that internationalist resistance was constructed. Global capital has always produced its own con-tradictions. This is a story of how.

THE MAKING

E. P. Thompson's *The Making of the English Working Class,* W. E. B. Du Bois's *Black Reconstruction,* and the broader traditions of history from below that such works fomented, are significant influences on this book. My interest in "making" refers to the messy assemblages of people unevenly cast together by the chaos of this evolving global system, alternately subjugated, seduced, or radicalized by it. The convergence spaces of strikes, prisons, embassies, and art collectives offer an overview of how people forced together often found their fates linked and their struggles conjoined. It observes how they devel-oped new syntheses of their struggles accordingly. From the social history of revolutionaries in the period—those who came to internationalist conscious-ness through different routes—we see how internationalism was made in this era of the New Imperialism. The book argues that shifts in the global capital-ist economy produced the conditions that would, in turn, produce interna-tionalist consciousness.

Conditions, of course, do not produce consciousness alone. They are the raw materials, so to speak, that require refinement through political organization. The forms of organization described in *Arise!* are multiple. The routes traced might appear eccentric. Ricardo Flores Magón, an anarchist; John Reed, a communist; Elizabeth Catlett, a fellow traveler. It is not a history of any one sectarian group or political tendency. As the archive of social movements in the period demonstrates, these traditions are interlinked and interrelated. John Reed made his name covering the IWW strike in Paterson, New Jersey, where Alexandra Kollontai, the Soviet ambassador, happened to be present. Reed, who would cover some of the fighting phase of the Mexican Revolution in Northern Mexico, would end up buried in the Kremlin, a devoted communist. Ricardo Flores Magón and other members of the PLM would organize across the US border with members of the IWW like Joe Hill as well as the Western Federation of Miners. M. N. Roy would transform from a committed Indian nationalist struggling against British colonialism into the founder of the Mexican Communist Party. Soviet official Alexandra Kollontai stood at odds with Stalin and never saw her feminist policies incorporated into the Soviet project, yet she remained a party member until her death. In each of these places, the red flag was raised and "The Internationale" was sung, suggesting that internationalism was never singularly of any one party or political formation but was a practice continually contested, arrived at, fought over, discovered, expanded—in other words, a process of continual becoming.

Following these various routes helps us understand something about the slipperiness of politics in the period. Political formations one hundred years ago were themselves not hardened or fully formed. Only in retrospect—often in the historiography and propaganda of different political formations—are histories presented as possessing nascent coherence, always becoming the thing they became (or seek to become). This foreclosure of meaning often makes history into hagiography and politics into causes to which fidelity is pledged, rather than a process that is continually ruptured, undone, and remade. The righteous presentation of such history offers palliatives but never cures. The propagandist's bracing language of certitude commands a blind obedience to partial histories. It further distorts our ability to comprehend the present as we attempt to make sense of the world we have inherited. Indeed, this book is driven by questions rather than answers. How do we make sense of the world in struggle? What shall we do with this inheritance? How will we find our way to something better?[12]

There are no easy answers, no transhistorical traditions, no unblemished heroes, and no easy victories. Asserting that any historical process is merely the result of historical precedent unwittingly transforms analysts into apologists for power.[13] The inheritance is a question rather than an answer. Here is a future where we might arrive. How shall we get there from here? As this book observes, the makers of nineteenth- and twentieth-century internationalism were shaped by where they came from, what they saw, who they met, what they experienced, and how they came to understand the world anew. To recognize this process is an invitation to do the work of making, to make collective sense of the world in struggle, to defy its otherwise meaningless singular suffering.

It is not by moral outrage alone that people have lent their lives to the struggle for better worlds. Neither is it by the purity of instruction from theory. There is certainly no royal road, only the one made by walking. Many have walked, many have been forced to move, many have found roads while walking with others. This book has attempted to map some of that movement in the hope of making future roads possible. History is not a guide but a map drawn in the stars of past lights. Out of the prison of the present is a recognition: We have been warmed by other fires that we have not built. What warmth and light shall we leave behind?

ACKNOWLEDGMENTS

Two decades ago, Ruth Wilson Gilmore set my mind on fire. In a course called Carceral Geographies, she walked students through the portal of radical theory. We entered with anecdotal knowledge of the California that had raised us. We walked out with new eyes blinking, seeing a landscape deformed by prisons, abandonment, and premature death. In that light, we also saw ourselves anew, blithe young conscripts trained to condone brutality as though it were inevitable. The course recast our comprehension of space and reframed our understanding of politics. Things could be otherwise, we learned, and we could be too. When *Golden Gulag* was published, I read Ruthie's acknowledgments with amazement. She thanked her students, which meant, abstractly, that I was a part of her book. Even more stunning was the sprawling list of organizers, activists, artists, journalists, scholars, and thinkers she thanked as co-conspirators. With that book burning in my hands, I read about a life I wanted, one where I could engage all the smart, creative, angry, and organized people who wanted to break down and rebuild all that enraged them. Everything since has been inspired by her work and, to my great fortune, by her guidance, including the making of this book.

Robin D. G. Kelley is a master of his craft and a keeper of a radical flame. He showed me the tenets of social history: to have utter faith in the ability of the working class to change the world while amassing the overwhelming evidence to prove it. Also, the prose had to sing. Reading W. E. B. Du Bois together, he would dare me: *Write like that.* Robin taught me about grounding, how to keep one foot in the world, while slipping another into the archives. They are, of course, the same world, one shaping the interpretation of the other, ad infinitum. In this dance, he showed me how radical traditions could become guardrails against cynicism, idealism, and despair. He taught me to never stop learning. He showed me how to be still and know. He asked that I remain open to the Marvelous. The sparks of hope that flash up from the past can only be fanned with open and agile hands. He makes it all look effortless.

Moving between intensely policed Los Angeles neighborhoods and the University of Southern California campus, I found mentors who created critical space from the tension. Laura Pulido never let me forget that the city was made from accretions of struggle. She taught me as much about racism and space as she did critical mentorship. Nothing forced me to work harder than her admonition: "I am not convinced." Quietly generous, she left articles in my mailbox and offered babysitting gigs when research costs became prohibitive. Before she passed, María Elena Martínez was an advisor and a door-opener. She tutored me in the history of the Mexican Revolution and pushed me to think about competing forces in hegemonic struggles. She introduced me to a network of transnational scholars in Tepoztlán, Mexico, an experience that singularly transformed my project. Meetings with Robeson Taj Frazier were pure joy. In our discussions about internationalism, culture, and radicalism, I found both a guide and kindred spirit. Conversations with David Lloyd were nothing short of dazzling. Through them I came to appreciate aesthetics, cultures of resistance, and the global legacies of James Connolly anew.

For their help at various stages in the project, thanks also to Macarena Gómez-Barris, Jack Halberstam, Lanita Jacobs, Kara Keeling, Viet Thanh Nguyen, Akira Lippit, John Carlos Rowe, and George J. Sanchez in USC's Department of American Studies and Ethnicity. There, I was fortunate to learn with Deborah Al-Najjar, Heather Ashby, Umayyah Cable, Jolie Chea, Jih-Fei Cheng, Amee Chew, Michael Cucher, Jennifer DeClue, Treva Ellison, Max Felker-Kantor, Laura Fugikawa, Jeffrey Govan, Analena Hope, Kai M. Green, Priscilla Leiva, Sharon Luk, Álvaro Daniel Márquez, Mark Padoongpatt, Monica Pelayo, Haven Perez, Nic John Ramos, Anthony Rodriguez, Orlando Serrano, Sriya Shrestha, Tasneem Siddiqui, David Stein, Gretel Vera-Rosas, and Yushi Yamazaki. My deep thanks to Jujuana Preston, Kitty Lai, Sonia Rodriguez, and Sandra Hopwood.

Through the School of Unlimited Learning (SOUL) led by Jordan T. Camp, George Lipsitz, and Clyde Woods at UC Santa Barbara, I discovered a shadow committee alongside Thomas Carrasco, Daniel Olmos, Steven Osuna, and Damien Sojoyner. Gary Colmenar and John Munro educated me in anti-colonial histories. I found laughter, warmth, and counsel around Cedric and Elizabeth Robinson's dining room table. As Clyde, George, Cedric, and Jordan helped me link housing struggles in Los Angeles to Ivory Perry's St. Louis, post-Katrina New Orleans, and Haiti after its 2010 earthquake, I learned to see insurgent space-making practices in anti-racist struggle.

At the Center for Place, Culture, and Politics, I received extraordinary feedback from Anthony Alessandrini, Loïse Bilat, Padmini Biswas, Tara Burk, Sujatha Fernandes, Ruthie Gilmore, Saygun Gökarıksel, David Harvey, Peter Hitchcock, Steve McFarland, Jarrett Martineau, Don Mitchell, Keith Miyake, Alf Gunvald Nilsen, Preeti Sampat, Eva Tessza Udvarhelyi, and John Whitlow. At the CUNY Graduate Center, I found guidance and support from Kandice Chuh, Duncan Faherty, Cindi Katz, and Eric Lott. Héctor A. Rivera, Denisse Andrade, Deshonay

Dozier, Malav Kanuga, Kaitlin Noss, Marlene Ramos, Nathaniel Sheets, and Tommy Wu stretched my spatial imagination. Once, I had been a student of Neil Smith. I was glad to find a way back to the Graduate Center to take up his provocations about capital, space, and struggle on my own terms.

My comprehension of racism and capitalism has been shaped by many conversations, including those curated between Cedric J. Robinson, Hakim Adi, Angela Y. Davis, Thulani Davis, Gina Dent, Jack O'Dell, Avery Gordon, Robin D. G. Kelley, S. Ani Mukherji, Paul Ortiz, Barbara Ransby, Elizabeth Robinson, Nikhil Pal Singh, Danny Widener, and Françoise Vergès at "Confronting Racial Capitalism: The Black Radical Tradition and Cultures of Liberation," a 2014 conference Jordan T. Camp, Ruthie Gilmore, and I organized in honor of Cedric's work. Kazembe Balagun, Raechel Bosch, Deborah Cowen, Nikhil Pal Singh, and Mary Taylor all offered support.

I am deeply indebted to many people for organizing spaces and sharing critical insights about my work, including Yui Hashimoto, Mona Domosh, and Pamela Voekel at Dartmouth College (Society of Fellows, Department of Geography); Ayça Çubukçu at the London School of Economics (Centre for Human Rights) and Princeton University (Fung Global Fellows Program); Daniel Martinez HoSang, Lisa Lowe, Leah Mirakhor, and Stephen Pitti at Yale University (Center for the Study of Race, Indigeneity, and Transnational Migration; Department of American Studies); Anne Cheng, Jordan Dixon, Sarah Malone, and Reagan Maraghy at Princeton University (Department of American Studies); Keeanga-Yamahtta Taylor, April Peters, and Dionne Worthy at Princeton University (Department of African American Studies); Yousuf Al-Bulushi at University of California, Irvine (Institute for International, Global and Regional Studies); Yesenia Barragan, Jeffrey Berryhill, and Leo Valdes at Rutgers University (Department of History); Tyler Wall and Parastou Saberi at the University of Tennessee, Knoxville (*Antipode* workshop); Mark Overmyer-Velázquez and Chris Vials at the University of Connecticut (El Instituto; American Studies Program); Françoise Vergès and Marcus Rediker (Collège d'études mondiales); Alejo Stark at the University of Michigan, Ann Arbor (Department of American Culture); and Nicole M. Guidotti-Hernández and Michael Cucher at University of Texas at Austin (Center for Mexican American Studies).

Flávio Almada, Rui Estrela, Craig Gilmore, Ruthie Gilmore, and Maíra Zezun gave incredible feedback along with instructions for leaving readers with the proper "taste." Rachel Buff, Mike Davis, Thulani Davis, Betsy Esch, Kristin Hoganson, Andy Hsiao, Moon-Ho Jung, Robin D. G. Kelley, Peter Linebaugh, George Lipsitz, Paul Ortiz, Vijay Prashad, David Roediger, Jay Sexton, and Devra Weber all offered exceptional critiques. Allison Brown and Sarah Grey shared superb editing advice. Anthony Alessandrini, Lisa Brock, Jason Oliver Chang, Mary Coffey, Alessandro De Giorgi, Cynthia Greenlee, Noura Erakat, Nick Estes, Dana Frank,

Niklas Frykman, Alan Gómez, Jane Gordon, Dayo Gore, Sandy Grande, Nicole Guidotti-Hernández, Zoe Hammer, Rebecca Hill, Mingwei Huang, Michael Innis-Jiménez, Leslie James, Nisha Kapoor, J. Kēhaulani Kauanui, John Lear, Marisol LeBrón, Austin McCoy, Laura McTighe, Laurel Mei-Singh, Andrea Morrell, S. Ani Mukherji, José Navarro, Mark Neocleous, Eric Porter, Ben Rubin, Stuart Schrader, Elizabeth Sine, Dean Spade, Waqas Tufail, Diren Valayden, Danny Widener, Brian Williams, Barbara Winslow, and Melanie Yazzie all gave amazing notes. Kevan A. Aguilar, Peter Cole, Michael R. Gonzales, Tariq Khan, David Struthers, Steve Thornton, and Kenyon Zimmer keep the spirit of the IWW alive. Thanks to Allan Pred who did the same for Walter Benjamin.

At Barnard College, thanks to my colleagues Elizabeth Bernstein, Tina Campt, Vrinda Condillac, Abosede George, Beck Jordan-Young, Manu Karuka, Gale Kenny, Colin Leach, Celia Naylor, Shayoni Mitra, Anu Rao, Anoo Siddiqi, Paul Scolieri, and Alex Watson. Special thanks to Lila Abu-Lughod, Bernard Harcourt, Saidiya Hartman, Audra Simpson, Amy Starecheski, Paige West, and Catherine LaSota for their kindness at Columbia. It was a joy to collaborate with Avi Cummings, Hope Dector, Che Gossett, Tami Navarro, Miriam Neptune, Pam Phillips, Michelle Rowland, and Martha Tenney. I am grateful to Bud Gankhuyag, Allison Guess, Bernie Mendoza, Hannah Pullen-Blasnik, and particularly Jay Gundacker and Toby Shore, for their amazing work. My deep admiration and respect go to Grey Berkowitz, Hannah Cohen-Sidley, Kalina Ko, Michaela Lindsey, Sara Morales, and Hannah Wyatt, who persevered while the world was on fire. During the darkest days of the pandemic, they found their voices and helped me find mine.

I am blessed to know Davarian Baldwin as a mentor, colleague, and friend. It is an honor to return to Trinity College to work with him and my brilliant colleagues Tanetta Andersson, Zayde Antrim, Ciaran Berry, Janet Bauer, Jeff Bayliss, Sonia Cardenas, Robert Cotto, Pablo Delano, Judy Dworin, Sheila Fisher, Scott Gac, Cheryl Greenberg, Chris Hager, Kifah Hanna, Isaac Kamola, Josh King, Serena Laws, Laura Lockwood, Seth Markle, Reo Matsuzaki, Priscilla Meléndez, Karen Li Miller, Garth Myers, Diana Paulin, Mitch Polin, Bishop John Selders, Maurice Wade, Tom Wickman, Hilary Wyss, Johnny Eric Williams, and many others. Ben Carbonetti has made me more human. What a dream to be able to think and scheme with Diana Aldrete, Jordan T. Camp, Amanda Guzmán, Mary McNeil, Juliet Nebolon, Leniqueca Welcome, along with Davarian, in our Entangled Histories cluster. Christina Bleyer, John Dlugosz, Cait Kennedy, Mary Mahoney and Dave Tatum have been incredible collaborators on public and digital archives. Veronica Zuñiga keeps everything afloat. Anida Yoeu Ali, Joan Hendrick, Alex Manevitz, Linda Tabar, and Prabhakar Venkateswaran are all greatly missed. Thanks, above all, to my students who have shaped my thinking and writing. Look out world! Domonique Griffin, Jake Villarreal, and Renita Washington are all making moves.

For exceptional assistance, I am indebted to the following archivists: Lisa Moore and Christopher Harter at the Amistad Research Center, Tulane University; Hugo Sergio Sánchez Mavil at La Casa de El Hijo del Ahuizote; Randall K. Burkett at Emory University; Stephen Spence and Lori Cox-Paul at the National Archives, Central Plains Region; Guha Shankar at the American Folklife Center, Library of Congress; Kristie French at University Library, California State University, Long Beach; Peter Blodgett and Sue Hodson at the Huntington Library; Gerben van der Meulen at the International Institute for Social History; Michele Welsing at the Southern California Library for Social Studies and Research; Shannon O'Neill at the Special Collections Center, NYU; and the archival staffs of the Library of Congress; El Centro de Estudios del Movimiento Obrero y Socialista A.C.; Archivo General de la Nación de México; Schomburg Center for Research in Black Culture; Special Collections, Smith College; Charles E. Young Library, UCLA; Bentley Historical Library, University of Michigan; Doheny Memorial Library, USC; Bancroft Library, UC Berkeley; and the Sterling Memorial Library, Yale University. Christopher K. Starr helped me access archives at the University of the West Indies, St. Augustine. Gwendolyn Midlo Hall shared astounding reflections from her and Harry Haywood's time in Mexico. Thanks to the late Michael Nash for advice in the Tamiment Library and Wagner Labor Archives. Laura Browder, S. Ani Mukherji, and April Merleaux all generously shared sources. In Mexico, Juan Manuel Aurrecoechea, Jacinto Barrera Bassols, Olivia Gall, and Diego Flores Magón all offered invaluable resources and conversations. Before she passed, Elizabeth Catlett was kind enough to meet and speak with me about her life and work in Cuernavaca. Barry Carr, David Mora, Devra Weber, and Suzi Weissman all helped to make this research possible.

Support for this project was provided by the Columbia University Center for the Study of Social Difference; Barnard College Office of the President; Barnard College Office of the Provost; Barnard College Inclusive Pedagogy Fund; Trinity Institute for Interdisciplinary Studies; Trinity College Faculty Research Committee; W.M. Keck Foundation, Huntington Library; Davis-Putter Scholarship Fund; USC Donald and Marion James Montgomery Endowed Scholarship; USC Grayson and Judith Manning Endowed Fellowship; USC Asian Pacific Alumni Association Karen Wong and Scott Lee Leadership Scholarship; and the Knollwood Institute.

This work developed out of longstanding collaborations with organizers on works for popular and political education. Housing organizers like Eric Ares, Paul Boden, Becky Dennison, Steve Diaz, General Dogon, Gerardo Gomez, Lisa "Tiny" Grey-Garcia and her late mother, Dee, Mara Raider, Grant Sunoo, and Pete White, have all been formative to my thinking. It has been my fortune to strategize with members of the Los Angeles Community Action Network, including Sonni Abdel, Esther Alejandro, Deacon Alexander, Bilal Ali, Deborah Burton, James Porter, Al Sabo, Karl Scott, Joe Thomas, Lydia Trejo, Pam Walls, and the late great Wesley Walker.

The pirates, witches, and smugglers of the Bristol Radical History Group shaped my understanding of radical social history, particularly Roger Ball, Kev Davis, Johnny Evans, Rich Grove, Rachel Hewitt, Jim McNeill, Mark Steeds, and Ruth Syminster, along with the Easton Cowboys and Cowgirls. Their work on water projects in Mexico was critical to my own understanding of internationalist traditions of the Revolution. My gratitude goes to Zoey Exley, Helen McArthur, Jane Nicholl, Jess Orlik, Mark Sands, Will Simpson, Kate and Ben, the Pauls, Peace, Punky, Ru, Toby, Yaz, and Jayne Dentith, who was the fiercest of the Red Hot Frilly Kickers. Kindest regards to Ian Bone for keeping E. P. Thompson alive in more ways than one.

For teaching me how to conjoin struggles, thanks to the Ronnie Nakashima Committee, the Asian American Drug Abuse Program, the Asian Vietnam Vets Organization, the Asian Prisoner Support Committee, and their supporters, including Debbie Flood; Ray Hamaguchi; Scott Handleman; Audee Holman; Judi and Staci Itomura; Cindy and Henry Kato; Eddie Kochiyama; Sandy Maeshiro; Marlene Murakami; Nick, Wendy, and Remy Nagatani; Dean Nakanishi; Mike Nakayama; Mo Nishida; Rahimah Shah; Dave Suga; Ben Wang; Mike Watanabe; Evelyn Yoshimura; and Eddy Zhang. Special thanks to Art Ishii who kept me accountable. This study was guided by the spirits of Tara Inouye-Hill, Jon Kingi, Yuri Kochiyama, and Victor Shibata.

In difficult times, Rod Ferguson reminded me to not lose focus. I owe him, Lisa Lowe, and Chandan Reddy heartfelt gratitude for their support. Justin Akers Chacón, Kandice Chuh, Thulani Davis, Jason Ferreira, Laleh Khalili, Neetu Khanna, Peter Linebaugh, George Lipsitz, David McNally, Don Mitchell, Paul Ortiz, Marcus Rediker, Judah Schept, Dean Spade, Keeanga-Yamahtta Taylor, and Angela Zimmerman help me keep the faith. Ujju Aggarwal, Mizue Aizeki, Amna Akbar, Diana Aldrete, Anida Yoeu Ali, Benjamin Balthasar, Rachel Buff, Lisa Chen, Trexy Ching, Jim Davis, Martín Espada, Kade D. Griffiths, Mike Duncan, Treva Ellison, Diane Gamboa, Jeff Govan, Rachel Herzing, Rohini Khanna, Arun Kundnani, Johari Jabir, Léopold Lambert, Sasha Lilley, Laura Liu, Ben Mabie, Álvaro Márquez, Erik Matsunaga, Alessandra Moctezuma, Jack Norton, Isaac Ontiveros, Reynaldo García Pantaleón, Jane Power, Elizabeth Robinson, Najda Robinson-Mayer, Russell Rodríguez, Brett Story, Sónia Vaz Borges, Tyler Wall, Tiffany Willoughby-Herard, Craig Willse, Ari Wohlfeiler, Diana Yoon, and Eddie Yuen all make magic out of miserabilism. Zumi, Ann, Tien, Leilani, Jay, Diana, Walter, Dana, Camille, and Ayame have gotten me through it. Thanks to Kaz and Henrik for saving the future, Leila and Amani for rat-sitting, Gloria for the sharks, Biko for being brave, Bean, Tendayi, Zuri, Jacob, Nishad, Maceo Fidel, Sadie Rose, Idgie, Clara and Roland, Miro and Gracie, Minara, Qatari, and Hana, and to Rei for walking with thunder.

It has been a delight to work with the American Crossroads series at the University of California Press. I thank my editor, Niels Hooper, for seeing early promise in the project and for offering patience and support while it developed into something bigger. Naja Pulliam Collins has been an absolute joy to work with. Catherine R. Osborne is a copy editor nonpareil. I'd say it twice if she'd allow it. Huge thanks to Emily Park, Katryce Lassle, and Teresa Iafolla for exceptional work on production and marketing to bring this book into the world. My deep appreciation to Dana A. Kopel for proofreading and Cynthia L. Savage for indexing.

Thanks to my family for bringing the history of internationalism and the Imperial Valley to life. My great aunts, Michi Miyada and Angel Nishinaka, showed me Okinawa in the California desert where their sister, my grandmother Susie, once stood. Thanks to Mary Yamashiro and to Dusty Yamashiro for his story about Pancho Villa that inspired this project. Kathy Cerra Itomura, Rick Itomura, Mark Nishinaka, and Wesley Nishinaka helped me get to the Chocolate Mountains. To the Inouye, Nishinaka, Espinoza, Itomura, Miyada, Sugimoto, Mizokami, Nakama, Yamashiro, Folick, Peck, Heatherton, Camp, and McGee families, and to my fiercely tough and wonderful Bakanakas, I offer my deepest thanks. The kindness of my many "aunts" and "uncles"—Jimmy, James, Yas, Elizabeth, Steve, Cathy, Alex, Nancy, Ginny, Ed, and Patricia—has sustained me. I will never not look up to my Uncle Daro. If they had lived to read this, my grandfather Kazuo would have flicked the back of my head and laughed and my Uncle Bryan would have lovingly asked if I might have jumped out of a plane instead. I would like to think that my grandmother Susie Itomura Inouye would be proud.

My great thanks go to Tom, the pride of Itawamba County, who soundly came to the rescue in more ways than he will ever know. Ms. Bernay has been a constant source of kindness, laughter, and grace. My father Dick and stepmother Lucy have been unfailingly loving and supportive. I am so grateful for their presence in my life, which I count meatball by spicy meatball. My Aunt JJ has been a second mother. Any charm I can claim is a cheap imitation of her generosity of spirit. My magnanimous sister Dana has always been my biggest supporter. I hope one day she will realize that I am hers as well. My mother Linda gave me the sage advice that if I couldn't explain myself in two sentences, I probably didn't know what I was talking about. Here is a book of sentences that will prove her right, one way or another. I owe her absolutely everything.

The day I met Jordan T. Camp, time was reset, and my life was forever changed. He helped me see that the stakes of the work were bigger than my personal anxieties could ever be. To bring a new world into being meant becoming a person suitable for that world. He showed me that the only way to overcome the nastiness was to have the conviction to write, think, and organize against it. To my extraordinary collaborator, editor, partner, and friend, I hope to show you that I have been paying attention.

· · ·

Parts of Chapter 1, "How to Make a Flag," appeared in, "Making the First International: Nineteenth-Century Regimes of Surveillance, Accumulation, Resistance, and Abolition," *in Cambridge History of America in the World,* eds. Kristin Lee Hoganson and Jay Sexton (Cambridge: Cambridge University Press, 2021), 295–315.

Chapter 3, "How to Make a University," first appeared as "University of Radicalism: Ricardo Flores Magón and Leavenworth Penitentiary." Copyright © 2014 The American Studies Association. This article first appeared in *American Quarterly, Special Issue: Las Américas Quarterly* 66:3 (Fall 2014): 557–581.

Chapter 5, "How to Make a Living," first appeared as "Relief and Revolution: Southern California Struggles Against Unemployment, 1930–1933," in *The Rising Tides of Color: Race, State Violence, and Radical Movements across the Pacific,* ed. Moon-Ho Jung (Seattle: University of Washington Press, 2014), 159–186.

NOTES

INTRODUCTION

1. Upson-Walton Company, *Something About Rope: An Encyclical to Our Customers* (Cleveland: Upson-Walton Company, 1902), 10.

2. "Mask and Manilla: Lynching of Three Negroes Accused of the Indiana Butchery—An Eye-Witness Account of the Affair," *Chicago Tribune*, Nov 22, 1871; Carl E. Kramer, *This Place We Call Home: A History of Clark County, Indiana* (Bloomington: Indiana University Press, 2007), 204; Michael J. Pfeifer, introduction to *Lynching Beyond Dixie: American Mob Violence Outside the South* (Urbana: University of Illinois Press, 2013), 8. The men's ages are given in "The Indiana Ku-Klux: Particulars of the Late Lynching of Three Colored Men—One Hundred Masked Men in the Field—Systematic Jail Breaking and Lynching," *The Sun* (Baltimore), November 23, 1871, 1; "The Park Tragedy: A Negro Confesses and Implicates Two Others The Guilty Parties Arrested and Lodged in Jail Interview with the Prisoners—Conflicting Stories Property of the Victims Found in the Houses of the Accused Threats of Lynching," *Louisville Courier Journal*, November 15, 1871, 4; "Mob Law: The Hanging of the Three Murderers of the Park Family," *Indiana Press*, November 22, 1871, 1.

3. Frederick Douglass, "John Brown," in *Frederick Douglass: Selected Speeches and Writings*, ed. Philip S. Foner (Chicago: Chicago Review Press, 2000), 633–48; Jack Shuler, *The Thirteenth Turn: A History of the Noose* (New York: Public Affairs, 2014), 107–8.

4. J. R. McCulloch, *A Dictionary, Practical, Theoretical, and Historical, of Commerce and Commercial Navigation* (Philadelphia: Carey and Hart, 1849), 1:759; Shinzo Hayase, "Manila Hemp in World, Regional, National, and Local History," *Journal of Asia-Pacific Studies* 31 (March 2018): 172; Arturo Giraldez, *The Age of Trade: The Manila Galleons and the Dawn of the Global Economy* (Lanham, MD: Rowman and Littlefield, 2015), 124–25.

5. Murad M. Saleeby, *Abaca (Manila Hemp) in the Philippines* (Manila: Bureau of Printing, 1915); *Official Catalogue of Exhibitors: Division of Exhibits, 1915—*

Panama-Pacific International Exposition (San Francisco: Wahlgreen Company, 1915); Hayase, "Manila Hemp," 172–74.

6. Waterbury Company, *General Catalogue and Price List* (New York: Waterbury Company, 1920), 28.

7. Upson-Walton Company, *Something About Rope,* 10; Rebecca Tinio McKenna, *American Imperial Pastoral: The Architecture of US Colonialism in the Philippines* (Chicago: University of Chicago Press, 2017); Norman G. Owen, *Prosperity without Progress: Manila Hemp and Material Life in the Colonial Philippines* (Berkeley: University of California Press, 1984); Manila Merchants' Association, *The Philippines, Treasure House of the Tropics, Manila, Pearl of the Orient* (Manila: n.p., 1911); *Official Catalogue of Exhibitors, 1915—Panama-Pacific International Exposition;* Shinzo Hayase, "American Colonial Policy and the Japanese Abaca Industry in Davao, 1898–1941," *Philippine Studies* 33, no. 4 (1985): 505–17. For an overview of strikes, insurgency, and resistance to US rule, see Alfred McCoy, *Policing America's Empire: The United States, the Philippines, and the Rise of the Surveillance State* (Madison: University of Wisconsin Press, 2009) and E. San Juan, Jr., *U.S. Imperialism and Revolution in the Philippines* (New York: Palgrave Macmillan, 2007).

8. Gilbert Michael Joseph, *Revolution from Without: Yucatán, Mexico, and the United States, 1880–1924* (Durham, NC: Duke University Press, 1987), 76; Channing Arnold and Frederick Frost, *The American Egypt: A Record of Travel in Yucatan* (London: Hutchinson, 1909), 324. See John Kenneth Turner, *Barbarous Mexico* (Chicago: Charles H. Kerr, 1910), and Shelley Streeby, *Radical Sensations: World Movements, Violence, and Visual Culture* (Durham, NC: Duke University Press, 2013), 151–74, for debates around Turner's work. See also Sterling D. Evans, *Bound in Twine: The History and Ecology of the Henequen-Wheat Complex for Mexico and the American and Canadian Plains, 1880–1950* (College Station: Texas A&M University Press, 2013), 59.

9. Guillermo Bonfil Batalla, *México Profundo: Reclaiming a Civilization,* trans. Philip A. Dennis (Austin: University of Texas Press, 1996), 99.

10. For "vast federal prison," see Evans, *Bound in Twine,* 56, 68. Generally, see Allen Wells and Gilbert M. Joseph, *Summer of Discontent, Seasons of Upheaval: Elite Politics and Rural Insurgency in Yucatán, 1876–1915* (Stanford, CA: Stanford University Press, 1996), see specifically 55–92; Lee J. Alston, Shannan Mattiace, and Tomas Nonnenmacher, "Coercion, Culture, and Contracts: Labor and Debt on Henequen Haciendas in Yucatán, Mexico, 1870–1915," *Journal of Economic History* 69, no. 1 (March 2009): 104–37; Gary Y. Okihiro, *The Columbia Guide to Asian American History* (New York: Columbia University Press, 2001), 38. On the radical possibilities of the "motley crew," see Peter Linebaugh and Marcus Rediker, *The Many Headed Hydra: The Hidden History of the Revolutionary Atlantic* (London: Verso, 2000), 27–28.

11. Albert Bacon Fall, *Investigation of Mexican Affairs: Preliminary Report and Hearings of the Committee on Foreign Relations, United States Senate, Pursuant to S. Res. 106, Directing the Committee on Foreign Relations to Investigate the Matter of Outrages on Citizens of the United States in Mexico,* Senate Committee on Foreign

Relations (Washington, DC: U.S. Government Printing Office, 1920); Patrick Wolfe, "Settler Colonialism and the Elimination of the Native," *Journal of Genocide Research* 8, no. 4 (2006): 400. Wolfe writes of the Dawes Act: "In the half-century from 1881, the total acreage held by Indians in the United States fell by two thirds, from just over 155 million acres to just over 52 million." See Evans, *Bound in Twine;* Gordon M. Winder, *The American Reaper: Harvesting Networks and Technology, 1830–1910* (Routledge, 2016), 108–12; Toni Gilpin, *The Long Deep Grudge: A Story of Big Capital, Radical Labor, and Class War in the American Heartland* (Chicago: Haymarket, 2020), 38; Joseph, *Revolution from Without*, 37; Alston, Mattiace, and Nonnenmacher, "Coercion, Culture, and Contracts"; Alan Knight, "Mexican Peonage: What Was It and Why Was It?," *Journal of Latin American Studies* 18, no. 1 (1986): 41–74.

12. Quoted in Evans, *Bound in Twine,* 61.

13. Rebecca Hill, *Men, Mobs, and Law: Anti-Lynching and Labor Defense in US Radical History* (Durham, NC: Duke University Press, 2008), 70–72; David R. Roediger, "Mother Jones and Haymarket in Mexico," in *Haymarket Scrapbook,* ed. David R. Roediger and Franklin Rosemont (Chicago: Charles H. Kerr, 1986), 213. The quote is from Paul Avrich, *The Haymarket Tragedy* (Princeton, NJ: Princeton University Press, 1984), 393.

14. Mother Jones, *Autobiography of Mother Jones* (Chicago: Charles H. Kerr, 1977), 12. For a discussion of the relationship between Haymarket and the Mexican Revolution, see Streeby, *Radical Sensations,* 35–110; Colin Maclachlan, *Anarchism and the Mexican Revolution: The Political Trials of Ricardo Flores Magón in the United States* (Berkeley: University of California Press, 1991), 107–8; "Mother Jones to John Fitzpatrick and Ed Nockles, Mexico City, May 16, 1921," in *The Correspondence of Mother Jones,* ed. Edward M Steel (Pittsburgh: University of Pittsburgh Press, 1985), 227; James R. Green, *Death in the Haymarket: A Story of Chicago, the First Labor Movement and the Bombing That Divided Gilded Age America* (Toronto: Anchor Books, 2007), 305; John Hart, *Anarchism and the Mexican Working Class, 1860–1931* (Austin: University of Texas Press, 1987), 119; Avrich, *Haymarket Tragedy,* 393; James R. Green, "The Globalization of a Memory: The Enduring Remembrance of the Haymarket Martyrs Around the World," *Labor: Studies in Working-Class History of the Americas* 2, no. 4 (2005): 12.

15. Peter Linebaugh, *The London Hanged: Crime and Civil Society in the Eighteenth Century* (London: Verso Books, 2006 [2003]), 111.

16. Alan Knight, *The Mexican Revolution, Volume 1* (Cambridge, UK: Cambridge University Press, 1987), 171; William D. Carrigan and Clive Webb, *Forgotten Dead: Mob Violence against Mexicans in the United States* (Oxford, UK: Oxford University Press, 2013), 81–83, 118–20; Monica Muñoz Martinez, *The Injustice Never Leaves You: Anti-Mexican Violence in Texas* (Cambridge, MA: Harvard University Press, 2018), 30–75.

17. Wells articulates this in many places, including in her description of the petty jealousies and property rivalries that led to the lynching of Thomas Moss. See Ida B. Wells, *Crusade for Justice: The Autobiography of Ida B. Wells,* ed. Alfreda M.

Duster (Chicago: University of Chicago Press, 2020), 42–26; Paula K. Giddings, *Ida: A Sword Among Lions: Ida B. Wells and the Campaign Against Lynching* (New York: Harper Collins, 2008), 175–89.

18. Jacqueline Jones Royster, ed., *Southern Horrors and Other Writings: The Anti-Lynching Campaign of Ida B. Wells, 1892–1900* (New York: Bedford/St. Martin's, 2016); Hazel Carby, "'On the Threshold of Woman's Era': Lynching, Empire and Sexuality in Black Feminist Theory," in *Feminist Postcolonial Theory: A Reader,* ed. Reina Lewis and Sara Mills (New York: Routledge, 2003), 222–38; Stuart Hall, "Race, Articulation, and Societies Structured in Dominance," in *Sociological Theories: Race and Colonialism,* ed. UNESCO (Paris: UNESCO, 1980), 305–45.

19. Ricardo Flores Magón, "The Repercussions of a Lynching," *Regeneración,* November 12, 1910; Martinez, *The Injustice Never Leaves You,* 30–75.

20. Frederick Douglass, "The Color Line," in *Frederick Douglass,* ed. Foner, 654.

21. W. E. B. Du Bois, "To the Nations of the World," in *W. E. B. Du Bois: Writings* (New York: Library of America, 1986), 639.

22. Du Bois struggled before he came to a resolute understanding of the movement and operation of the color line. His definitions over the first three decades of the twentieth century are understandably varying and contradictory. In these turbulent years, the world changed and so too did theories attempting to explain it. In *Black Reconstruction,* he analyzed the color line within a study of the social struggles, transformation of the state, shifting modes of production, ruptures in social relations, and forces that took hold of state power before, during, and after the period of Reconstruction in order to better understand his own period and freedom struggles globally. See W. E. B. Du Bois, *Black Reconstruction in America 1860–1880* (New York: Free Press, 1992), 17; see also Du Bois, "Jefferson Davis as a Representative of Civilization," in *W. E. B. Du Bois: A Reader,* ed. David Levering Lewis (New York: Henry Holt, 1995), 17; Ruth Wilson Gilmore, "Race, Prisons, and War: Scenes from the History of U.S. Violence," *Socialist Register* 45 (2009): 73–87; Richard Drinnon, *Facing West: The Metaphysics of Indian-Hating and Empire-Building* (Norman: University of Oklahoma Press, 1997).

23. Du Bois, *Black Reconstruction,* 711; Du Bois, "The Color Line Belts the World," in *W. E. B. Du Bois,* 42–43; Douglass, "The Color Line"; Edward W. Said, *Culture and Imperialism* (New York: Vintage, 1994), xiii. See Cedric J. Robinson, *Forgeries of Memory and Meaning: Blacks and the Regimes of Race in American Theater and Film Before World War II* (Chapel Hill: University of North Carolina Press, 2007), xii. The relationship between race-making and space-making in colonial Mexico is thoughtfully explored in Daniel Nemser, *Infrastructures of Race: Concentration and Biopolitics in Colonial Mexico* (Austin: University of Texas Press, 2017), 1–24.

24. Robinson, *Forgeries of Memory and Meaning,* xii–xiii.

25. On the class composition of the Klan, see Nancy MacLean, *Behind the Mask of Chivalry: The Making of the Second Ku Klux Klan* (New York: Oxford, 1994), especially 52–97.

26. Ida B. Wells, "Mob Rule in New Orleans," in *Collected Work of Ida B. Wells-Barnett* (Charleston, SC: Bibliobazaar, 2007), 70

27. W. E. B. Du Bois, "The Souls of White Folks," in *W. E. B. Du Bois: Writings* (New York: Library of America, 1986), 927.

28. W. E. B. Du Bois, "Mexico," *The Crisis,* June 1914, 79.

29. Du Bois, "The African Roots of War," *The Atlantic Monthly,* May 1915, 707–14; Du Bois, "The Negro Problem," 49; Du Bois, *Black Reconstruction,* 17. His insights about the dividends of whiteness were a precursor to his observations about the "psychological wage" of whiteness, developed in *Black Reconstruction* two decades later. See David R. Roediger, *The Wages of Whiteness: Race and the Making of the American Working Class* (New York: Verso, 2007). For Giovanni Arrighi and Beverly Silver, hegemony describes the additional leadership powers accrued to dominant groups who successfully present their interests as in the general interest, an interpretation of Antonio Gramsci's definition. See Giovanni Arrighi and Beverly J. Silver, "Capitalism and World (Dis)Order," *Review of International Studies* 27 (2001): 257–79; Antonio Gramsci, *Selections from the Prison Notebooks,* ed. and trans. Quintin Hoare and Geoffrey Smith (New York: International Publishers, 1971), 182.

30. V. I. Lenin, *Imperialism, the Highest Stage of Capitalism: A Popular Outline* (New York: International Publishers, 1939 [1917]).

31. Du Bois, "The Souls of White Folks," 932.

32. Du Bois, "The African Roots of War"; Giovanni Arrighi, *The Long Twentieth Century: Money, Power, and the Origins of Our Times* (New York: Verso, 2010). On the distinction between geopolitics and geoeconomic power, see Deborah Cowen and Neil Smith, "After Geopolitics? From the Geopolitical Social to Geoeconomics," *Antipode* 41, no. 1 (2009): 22–48. In their read, geopolitics "entwine political power to the territorially demarcated system of national states" wherein social, cultural, and economic factors align within preordained territorial divisions. Geoeconomic conceptions, by contrast, recognize how the geopolitical is "recalibrated" by market logics. Further, it enables scalar analyses of the tensions between social, cultural, and economic forces within, between, and across states forms and at supranational levels.

33. Arrighi, *Long Twentieth Century,* 60.

34. The question of the new imperialism has been famously debated by economic historians around the scholarly interventions of John Gallagher and Robin Robinson, concerning the forms of "informal empire" developed by Britain in the nineteenth century. See John Gallagher and Robin Robinson, "The Imperialism of Free Trade," *Economic History Review* 6, no. 1 (1953): 1–15. These insights have been productively considered by French historians of the Second Empire such as David Todd, "A French Imperial Meridian, 1814–1870," *Past and Present* 210 (February 2011): 155–86, and in discussions of the expanding economic geography of US control such as Chris Grocott and Jo Grady, "'Naked abroad': The Continuing Imperialism of Free Trade," *Capital & Class* 38, no. 3 (2014): 541–62. Also see Arrighi, *Long Twentieth Century,* 28–73; Neil Smith, *American Empire: Roosevelt's*

Geographer and the Prelude to Globalization (Berkeley: University of California Press, 2004), 31; Richard Seymour, *American Insurgents: A Brief History of American Anti-Imperialism* (Chicago: Haymarket Books, 2011), 60. This book adds Du Bois's underappreciated and underutilized contributions to these debates.

35. Mario Barrera, *Race and Class in the Southwest: A Theory of Racial Inequality* (Notre Dame, IN: University of Notre Dame Press, 1979), 11–13; John Mason Hart, *Empire and Revolution: The Americans in Mexico Since the Civil War* (Berkeley: University of California Press, 2002), 91; Greg Grandin, *Empire's Workshop: Latin America, the United States, and the Rise of the New Imperialism* (New York: Metropolitan Books, 2006), 17; John Mason Hart, *Revolutionary Mexico: The Coming and Process of the Mexican Revolution* (Berkeley: University of California Press, 1997), xviii. While historians disagree about the degree to which Mexican revolutionaries explicitly targeted and demonstrated against American interests, most concur that the Revolution arose as a response to transformations brought about by the country's rapid integration into the global economy, a process intensified by US trade, enterprise, and investment. For an overview of debates, see Daniel Nugent, ed., *Rural Revolt in Mexico: U.S. Intervention and the Domain of Subaltern Politics* (Durham, NC: Duke University Press, 1998).

36. Peter Dicken, "Global Shift—The Role of United States Transnational Corporations," in *The American Century: Consensus and Coercion in the Projection of American Power,* ed. David Slater and Peter J. Taylor (Malden, MA: Blackwell Publishers, 1999), 36–37; Cyrus Veeser, *A World Safe for Capitalism: Dollar Diplomacy and America's Rise to Global Power* (New York: Columbia University Press, 2013), 1–5; Thomas J. McCormick, *America's Half-Century: United States Foreign Policy in the Cold War and After* (Baltimore: Johns Hopkins University Press, 1995), 17–21.

37. Sam Gindin and Leo Panitch, *The Making of Global Capitalism: The Political Economy of American Empire* (New York: Verso, 2012), 2–9; Smith, *American Empire,* xviii. Amy Kaplan troubles the "central geographic bifurcation" common to histories of US imperialism which narrate the early twentieth century as the watershed moment when the United States first became a formal imperial power. Such a narration serves as a "denial of empire," obscuring the histories of conquest, expansion, and dispossession that preceded this moment (*The Anarchy of Empire in the Making of U.S. Culture* [Cambridge, MA: Harvard University Press, 2002], 17).

38. Odd Arne Westad, *The Global Cold War: Third World Interventions and the Making of Our Times* (Cambridge, UK: Cambridge University Press, 2007), 29.

39. Peter J. Taylor, "Locating the American Century: A World-Systems Analysis," in *The American Century,* 1–6; Akira Mizuta Lippit, *Atomic Light (Shadow Optics)* (Minneapolis: University of Minnesota Press, 2005), 109.

40. This concept is in dialogue with Mona Domash's "geoeconomic imagination" as the "meanings, cultures, and places constitute the discursive field which capitalist spatial expansion produces and is produced by" ("Geoeconomic Imaginations and Economic Geography in the Early Twentieth Century," *Annals of the Association of American Geographers* 103, no. 4 [July 2013]: 944–66). It intends to

avoid confusion with discussions of the New Imperialism related to the global war on terror.

41. See conversation between Jodi Byrd, *Transit of Empire: Indigenous Critiques of Colonialism* (Minneapolis: University of Minnesota Press, 2011), xxiv–xxv, and Lisa Lowe, *The Intimacies of Four Continents* (Durham, NC: Duke University Press, 2015), 10–11. "Hegemonic shadows" is a gloss on a broader discussion of hegemony over systemic cycles of accumulation. See Arrighi and Silver, "Capitalism and World (Dis)Order," 270.

42. Paco Ignacio Taibo II, *The Shadow of the Shadow,* trans. William I. Neuman (El Paso, TX: Cinco Puntos Press, 1991).

43. The concept of the shadow is influenced by Lisa Lowe and David Lloyd's discussion of the "limits" of an "international proletarian formation." The shadow denotes sites that fall "'below' the level of the nation, and across national sites," a conceptual space "in contestation, and 'in difference'" to capitalism, a space of theorization wherein "feminist, antiracist, and subaltern struggles" can enliven oppositional cultural politics. See Lisa Lowe and David Lloyd, Introduction to *The Politics of Culture in the Shadow of Capital,* (Durham, NC: Duke University Press, 1997), 1–32.

44. This analysis is indebted to Robin D. G. Kelley's concept of "other streams of internationalism," Marxist traditions that have arisen from anti-imperialist, anti-colonial, and anti-racist struggles, particularly in the early twentieth century. See Robin D. G. Kelley, "How the West Was One," and "A New Look at the Communist Manifesto," *Race Traitor* 13–14 (Summer 2001): 135–39. It also offers a friendly rejoinder to Arrighi's analysis. Arrighi defines a key variable unattended to in his study, class struggle (*Long Twentieth Century,* xiv). As Beverly Silver, Arrighi's longtime collaborator, notes, a charting of capital's evolution without attendance to organized, spontaneous, and unanticipated forms of struggle offers an incomplete portrait. Class struggle has been determinate in directing capital's evolution. See Beverly Silver, "Class Struggle and Kondratieff Waves, 1870 to the Present," in *New Findings in Long-Wave Research,* ed. Alfred Kleinknecht et al. (London: St. Martin's Press, 1992), 279–95.

45. Mark Wasserman, *Everyday Life and Politics in Nineteenth Century Mexico: Men, Women, and War* (Albuquerque: University of New Mexico Press, 2000), 133–200; William H. Beezley, *Judas at the Jockey Club and Other Episodes of Porfirian Mexico* (Lincoln: University of Nebraska Press, 2018).

46. This overview summarizes literature from multiple sources, including James D. Cockcroft, *Mexico's Hope* (New York: Monthly Review Press, 1998); Adolfo Gilly, *The Mexican Revolution* (New York: New Press, 2005); Adam David Morton, *Revolution and State in Modern Mexico: The Political Economy of Uneven Development* (Lanham, MD: Rowman and Littlefield, 2011); Nora Hamilton, *The Limits of State Autonomy: Post-Revolutionary Mexico* (Princeton, NJ: Princeton University Press, 1982).

47. Ramón Eduardo Ruíz, *The Great Rebellion: Mexico, 1905–1924* (New York: Norton, 1980). Gilbert M. Joseph and Daniel Nugent discuss the "marked tendency

to isolate and privilege the revolution as event . . . rather than to study it as a culturally complex, historically generated process" ("Popular Culture and State Formation in Revolutionary Mexico," in *Everyday Forms of State Formation: Revolution and the Negotiation of Rule in Modern Mexico,* ed. Gilbert M. Joseph and Daniel Nugent [Durham, NC: Duke University Press, 1994], 5.) See also Mark Wasserman, "The Mexican Revolution: Region and Theory, Signifying Nothing?," *Latin American Research Review* 25, no. 1 (1990): 231–42; Nicole M. Guidotti-Hernández, *Unspeakable Violence: Remapping U.S. and Mexican National Imaginaries* (Durham, NC: Duke University Press, 2011); Heather Fowler-Salamini, *Working Women, Entrepreneurs, and the Mexican Revolution: The Coffee Culture of Córdoba, Veracruz* (Lincoln: University of Nebraska Press, 2013); Michael R. Gonzales, "Rebellion and Repression in Colorado's Coalfields: The 1927–1928 Wobbly Coal Miners' Strike" (PhD diss., University of Wisconsin-Milwaukee, Department of History, in progress).

48. The human toll of the Revolution should not at all be minimized. After many phases of fighting, and counting over two million deaths due in part to war, famine, and disease, as well as a mass migration out of the country, the Mexican Revolution also represented the, "greatest demographic catastrophe of the twentieth century" (Robert McCaa, "Missing Millions: The Demographic Costs of the Mexican Revolution," *Mexican Studies/Estudios Mexicanos* 19, no. 2 [2003]: 397).

49. Alan Knight, "The United States and the Mexican Peasantry, circa 1880–1940," in *Rural Revolt in Mexico: U.S. Intervention and the Domain of Subaltern Politics,* ed. Daniel Nugent (Durham, NC: Duke University Press, 1998), 25–63; Knight, *Mexican Revolution,* 1:311–15, 1:485; Friedrich Katz, *The Secret War in Mexico: Europe, the United States, and the Mexican Revolution* (Chicago: University of Chicago Press, 1981), 78–80; Joseph, *Revolution from Without,* xx–xxii, 41–60; John Foran, "Reinventing the Mexican Revolution: The Competing Paradigms of Alan Knight and John Mason Hart," *Latin American Perspectives* 23, no. 4 (Autumn, 1996): 120.

50. As John Cockcroft noted: "The countryside resembled not so much the feudal manor as the company store, and Mexico as a whole not so much a nation as a company country" (*Mexico: Class Formation, Capital Accumulation, and the State* [New York: Monthly Review Press, 1983], 93). See also Hart, *Revolutionary Mexico;* Jessica M. Kim, *Imperial Metropolis: Los Angeles, Mexico, and the Borderlands of American Empire, 1865–1941* (Chapel Hill: University of North Carolina Press, 2019); Mark Wasserman, *Persistent Oligarchs: Elites and Politics in Chihuahua, Mexico, 1910–1940* (Durham, NC: Duke University Press, 1993), among others.

51. For an overview of the debates, see Nan Enstad, "The 'Sonorous Summons' of the New History of Capitalism, or, What Are We Talking about When We Talk about Economy?," *Modern American History* 2, no. 1 (2019): 83–95. Zach Sell notes that the seeming "new" history of capitalism produced "a binary between the new and the old," where we might benefit from studies of the old, such as those by Du Bois. See Zach Sell, *Trouble of the World: Slavery and Empire in the Age of Capital* (Chapel Hill: University of North Carolina Press, 2021), 8. See also John Tutino,

The Mexican Heartland: How Communities Shaped Capitalism, a Nation, and World History, 1500–2000 (Princeton, NJ: Princeton University Press, 2017), 1–28.

52. For example, since the opening of Soviet archives in 1991, scholars have translated key materials, thereby building upon Barry Carr's foundational study of Marxism and Communism in Mexico. Daniela Spenser has dramatized decisions of the Mexican Communist Party, demonstrating its early "stumbling." Alongside Daniel Kent Carrasco's research on M. N. Roy, Spenser's work offers a complicated portrait of the Indian-born Mexican Communist Party founder, as discussed in chapter two. Rina Ortiz Peralta's scholarship on Alexandra Kollontai has uncovered a surprisingly intimate story of the Soviet ambassador. Read alongside María de Lourdes Cueva Tazzer, Stephanie J. Smith, and Jocelyn Olcott, one gains a sense of the uneasy practice of radical feminism in the period, as discussed in chapter four. The book also draws on narrative histories, notably Taibo's resurrection of the lifeworld of *Los Bolshevikis* and Elena Poniatowska's recovery of the Mexican internationalist orbits within which Italian photographer and radical Tina Modotti existed, a period Mauricio Tenillo Trillo has called the "cosmopolitan Mexican summer." See Barry Carr, *Marxism and Communism in Twentieth-Century Mexico* (Lincoln: University of Nebraska Press, 1992); Daniela Spenser and Rina Ortiz Peralta, *La Internacional Comunista en México: Los Primeros Tropiezos: Documentos, 1919–1922* (Mexico City: INEHRM, 2006); Daniela Spenser, *Stumbling Its Way Through Mexico: The Early Years of the Communist International,* trans. Peter Gellart (Tuscaloosa: University of Alabama Press, 2011); Daniela Spenser, *The Impossible Triangle: Mexico, Soviet Russia, and the United States in the 1920s* (Durham, NC: Duke University Press, 1999); Rina Ortiz Peralta, "La Embajadora Roja: Alexandra Kollontai y México," *Relaciones Estudios de Historia y Sociedad* 38, no. 149 (2016): 13–38; Rina Ortiz Peralta, *Alexandra Kollontai en México: Diario y Otros documentos* (Xalapa: Universidad Veracruzana, 2012); Daniel Kent Carrasco, "México en las Memorias de M. N. Roy: Nostalgia, Devoción Política e Historia," *Autobiografías y/o Textos Autorreferenciales,* ed. Alicia Sandoval (Puebla: Benemérita UNAM de Puebla, 2019), 95–118; María de Lourdes Cueva Tazzer, "Textos y Prácticas de Mujeres Comunistas En México, 1919–1934" (PhD diss., UAM-I, 2009); Stephanie Smith, *The Power and Politics of Art in Postrevolutionary* Mexico (Chapel Hill: University of North Carolina Press, 2017); Jocelyn Olcott, "'A Plague of Salaried Marxists': Sexuality and Subsistence in the Revolutionary Imaginary of Concha Michel," *Journal of Contemporary History* 52, no. 4 (October 2017): 980–98; Paco Ignacio Taibo II, *Los Bolshevikis: Historia Narrativa de los Orígenes del Comunismo en México, 1919–1925* (Mexico City: J. Mortiz, 1986); Elena Poniatowska, *Tinisima,* trans. Katherine Silver (Albuquerque: University of New Mexico, 2006); Mauricio Tenorio Trillo, "The Cosmopolitan Mexican Summer, 1920–1949," *Latin American Research Review* 32, no. 3 (1997): 224–42; Justin Akers Chacón, *Radicals in the Barrio: Magonistas, Socialists, Wobblies, and Communists in the Mexican American Working Class* (Chicago: Haymarket Books, 2018).

53. This rethinking draws from Catherine Hall, "Gendering Property, Racing Capital," *History Workshop Journal* 78, no. 1 (2014); Himani Bannerji, "Building from Marx: Reflections on Class and Race," *Social Justice* 32, no. 4 (2005): 144–60.

54. Henri Lefebvre, *The Production of Space,* trans. Donald Nicholson-Smith (Malden, MA: Blackwell, 1991) and David Harvey, "Geography of Class Power," in *Spaces of Capital: Towards a Critical Geography* (New York: Routledge, 2012), 369–93. See also Seung-Ook Lee, et al., "Geopolitical Economy and the Production of Territory: The Case of US–China Geopolitical-Economic Competition in Asia," *Environment and Planning A* (2017): 1–21.

55. See Ruth Wilson Gilmore, "Fatal Couplings of Power and Difference: Notes on Racism and Geography," *The Professional Geographer* 54, no. 1 (2002): 15–24, and Marion Werner, et al., "Feminist Political Economy in Geography: Why Now, What is Different, and What For?," *Geoforum* 79 (2017): 1–4, for discussions on method.

56. Walter Rodney, *History of the Guyanese Working People, 1881–1905* (Baltimore: Johns Hopkins University Press, 1982 [1981]), 179.

CHAPTER 1. HOW TO MAKE A FLAG

1. Stephen A. Townsend, *The Yankee Invasion of Texas* (College Station: Texas A&M University Press, 2006), 3–9; John A. Adams, Jr., *Conflict and Commerce on the Rio Grande: Laredo, 1755–1955* (College Station: Texas A&M University Press, 2008), 91; A. C. Greene, *Sketches from the Five States of Texas* (College Station: Texas A&M University Press, 1998), 71–72; Hart, *Empire and Revolution,* 9–14.

2. Hart, *Revolutionary Mexico,* 107–15; David Correia, "Making Destiny Manifest: United States Territorial Expansion and the Dispossession of Two Mexican Property Claims in New Mexico, 1824–1899," *Journal of Historical Geography* 35 (2009): 87–103.

3. Greene, *Sketches,* 72; Amy S. Greenberg, *A Wicked War: Polk, Clay, and the 1846 U.S. Invasion of Mexico* (New York: Vintage, 2012), xvii.

4. Hart, *Revolutionary Mexico,* 109–15.

5. Hart, *Revolutionary Mexico,* 109–14; Townsend, *The Yankee Invasion of Texas,* 3–9; Joseph Contreras, *In the Shadow of the Giant: The Americanization of Modern Mexico* (New Brunswick, NJ: Rutgers University Press, 2009), 192; David Montejano, "Mexican Merchants and Teamsters on the Texas Cotton Road, 1862–1865," in *Mexico and Mexicans in the Making of the United States,* ed. John Tutino (Austin: University of Texas Press, 2012), 141–70.

6. Hart, *Revolutionary Mexico,* 109–15.

7. Hart, *Revolutionary Mexico,* 109–15.

8. Marilyn McAdams Sibley, "Charles Stillman: A Case Study of Entrepreneurship on the Rio Grande, 1861–1865," *The Southwestern Historical Quarterly* 77, no. 2 (October 1973): 227–40; C. L. R. James, *Mariners, Renegades, and Castaways: The Story of Herman Melville and the World We Live In* (Hanover, NH: University Press of New England, 1989 [1953]).

9. On "false innocence" and the active processes of silencing history, see Michel Rolph-Trouillot, *Silencing the Past: Power and the Production of History* (Boston: Beacon, 1995).

10. Cedric J. Robinson, *Black Marxism: The Making of the Black Radical Tradition* (Chapel Hill: University of North Carolina Press, 2000), 26.

11. This point was powerfully made by Anna Julia Cooper: "If your own father was a pirate, a robber, a murderer, his hands are dyed in red blood, and you don't say very much about it. But if your great great great grandfather's grandfather stole and pillaged and slew, and you can prove it, your blood has become blue and you are at great pains to establish the relationship" (*A Voice from the South: By a Black Woman of the South* [Chapel Hill: University of North Carolina, 2017], 102).

12. Gilbert G. González, *Mexican Consuls and Labor Organizing: Imperial Politics in the American Southwest* (Austin: University of Texas Press, 1999), x.

13. Katz, *The Secret War in Mexico*, 16.

14. For details of the Bank's investments, see Domosh, "Geoeconomic Imaginations"; Robert Mayer, "The Origins of the American Banking Empire in Latin America: Frank A. Vanderlip and the National City Bank," *Journal of Interamerican Studies and World Affairs* 15, no. 1 (February 1973): 60–76; Peter James Hudson, "The National City Bank of New York and Haiti, 1909–1922," *Radical History Review* 115 (Winter 2013): 91–114.

15. Neil Smith, *American Empire: Roosevelt's Geographer and the Prelude to Globalization* (Berkeley: University of California Press, 2003).

16. Arrighi, *Long Twentieth Century*, 28–73. This formulation is also in dialogue with internationalism as it is developed by Glenda Sluga, *Internationalism in the Age of Nationalism* (Philadelphia: University of Pennsylvania Press, 2013) and Christy Thornton, *Revolution in Development: Mexico and the Governance of the Global Economy* (Oakland: University of California Press, 2021).

17. John M. Belohlavek, *Patriots, Prostitutes, and Spies : Women and the Mexican-American War* (Charlottesville: University of Virginia Press, 2017), 141; Peter Guardino, *The Dead March: A History of the Mexican-American War* (Cambridge, MA: Harvard University Press, 2017), 110, 229–300; Hart, *Revolutionary Mexico*, 107–115; Clare Sears, *Arresting Dress: Cross-Dressing, Law, and Fascination in Nineteenth Century San Francisco* (Durham, NC: Duke University Press, 2014), 28; Greenberg, *A Wicked War*.

18. Frederick Douglass, "The War with Mexico," *The North Star,* January 21, 1848.

19. Guardino, *The Dead March,* 250–65; Douglass, "The Present Condition and Future Prospects of the Negro People," in Foner, ed., *Frederick Douglass,* 256.

20. Ulysses S. Grant, *Personal Memoirs of Ulysses S. Grant* (New York: Cosimo Classics, 2006), 25–27.

21. Karl Marx, *The Eighteenth Brumaire of Louis Bonaparte* (New York: International Publishers, 1963), 15–19, 44; Michael Denning, "Impeachment as Social Form," *New Left Review* 122 (March/April 2020): 70–72.

22. Christina Carroll, "Imperial Ideologies in the Second Empire: The Mexican Expedition and the Royaume Arabe," *French Historical Studies* 42, no. 1 (February 2019): 67–100; Du Bois, *Black Reconstruction,* 88; Kristine Ibsen, *Maximilian, Mexico, and the Invention of Empire* (Nashville: Vanderbilt University Press, 2010),

1–29; David Todd, "A French Imperial Meridian, 1814–1870," *Past and Present* 210 (February 2011): 155–86; Steven C. Topik, "When Mexico Had the Blues: A Transatlantic Tale of Bonds, Bankers, and Nationalists, 1862–1910," *American Historical Review* 105, no. 3 (June 2000): 714–38.

23. Karl Marx, "The Intervention in Mexico," November 8, 1861, in Karl Marx and Friedrich Engels, *The Civil War in the United States* (New York: International Publishers, 1937), 26.

24. Hart, *Empire and Revolution*, 1–72; Gilbert G. González, *Culture of Empire: American Writers, Mexico, and Mexican Immigrants, 1880–1930* (Austin: University of Texas Press, 2004), 19–31.

25. Karl Marx and Friedrich Engels, *The Communist Manifesto* (New York: Penguin, 2002); Marx, *Eighteenth Brumaire*, 19; Angela Zimmerman, ed., *The Civil War in the United States: Karl Marx and Friedrich Engels* (New York: International Publishers, 2016), xiii.

26. Marx, *The Eighteenth Brumaire;* Angela Zimmerman, "From the Second American Revolution to the First International and Back Again: Marxism, the Popular Front, and the American Civil War," in *The World the Civil War Made,* ed. Gregory Downs and Kate Masur (Chapel Hill, NC: University of North Carolina Press, 2015): 304–36.

27. Jeremy Bentham, *An Introduction to the Principles of Morals and Legislation* (1789), quoted in Ole Spierman, *International Legal Argument in the Permanent Court of International Justice: The Rise of the International Judiciary* (Cambridge, UK: Cambridge University Press, 2005), 50–52; Mark Mazower, *Governing the World: The History of an Idea, 1815 to the Present* (New York: Penguin, 2013), 19–23; David R. Armitage, "Globalizing Jeremy Bentham," *History of Political Thought* 32, no. 1 (2011): 63–82.

28. Linda Colley, "Empires of Writing: Britain, America and Constitutions, 1776–1848," *Law and History Review* 32, no. 2 (May 2014): 237–66.

29. William Hazlitt, *The Spirit of the Age* (New York: Derby & Jackson, 1859), 3; Colley, "Empires of Writing"; Annie L. Cot, "Jeremy Bentham's Spanish American Utopia," in *Economic Development and Global Crisis: The Latin American Economy in Historical Perspective,* ed. José Luís Cardoso, et al. (New York: Routledge, 2004), 34–47; Aaron Burr, *The Private Journal of Aaron Burr* (Rochester, NY: Post Express Printing Co., 1903); C. L. R. James, *The Black Jacobins: Toussaint L'Ouverture and the San Domingo Revolution* (New York: Vintage, 1989), 24.

30. Prussian advisor Frederich von Gentz, quoted in Mazower, *Governing the World,* 6.

31. John Tutino, "The Americas in the Rise of Industrial Capitalism," in *New Countries: Capitalism, Revolutions, and Nations in the Americas, 1750–1870,* ed. John Tutino (Durham, NC: Duke University Press, 2016), 25–70; Leland Jenks, *The Migration of British Capital to 1875* (New York: Alfred A. Knopf, 1938), quoted in Arrighi, *Long Twentieth Century,* 217.

32. For a critique of Bentham's liberal internationalism, see Lowe, *The Intimacies of Four Continents,* 45. See also David Harvey, *Spaces of Neoliberalization: Towards a Theory of Uneven Geographical Development* (Wiesbaden: Franz Steiner Verlag, 2005), 80.

33. Michel Foucault, *Discipline and Punish: The Birth of the Prison* (New York: Vintage, 1995), 195; Linebaugh, *The London Hanged,* 371–74.

34. Linebaugh, *The London Hanged,* 371–401.

35. Karl Marx, "The East India Company—Its History and Results," *New York Daily Tribune,* July 11, 1853; Arrighi, *Long Twentieth Century,* 271.

36. Stephanie Smallwood, *Saltwater Slavery: A Middle Passage from Africa to American Diaspora* (Cambridge, MA: Harvard University Press, 2007), 33–64; Ian Baucom, *Specters of the Atlantic: Finance Capital, Slavery, and the Philosophy of History* (Durham, NC: Duke University Press, 2005), 138.

37. Karl Marx, "Debates on the Law on Thefts of Wood," *Rheinische Zeitung* 303, October 30, 1842; Peter Linebaugh, "Karl Marx, the Theft of Wood, and Working-Class Composition: A Contribution to the Current Debate," *Social Justice* 40, no. 1–2 (2014): 137–61.

38. Karl Marx, "Proceedings of the Sixth Rhine Province Assembly, Third Article: Debates on the Law on Thefts of Wood," *Rheinische Zeitung* 298, October 25, 1842, quoted in Linebaugh, "Karl Marx, the Theft of Wood."

39. Quotes from Frederick Douglass, "The Revolution of 1848," *The North Star,* August 4, 1848. Shark quote from Frederick Douglass, "[Letter], Edinburgh, Scotland, July 30, 1846. To William A. White," in Philip S. Foner, ed., *Life and Writings of Frederick Douglass* (New York: International Publishers, 1950), 1:181; Manisha Sinha, *The Slave's Cause: A History of Abolition* (New Haven, CT: Yale University Press, 2016), 339–80; Paul Ortiz, *An African American and Latinx History of the United States* (Boston: Beacon, 2018), 46–53.

40. Michael Craton, *Testing the Chains: Resistance to Slavery in the British West Indies* (Ithaca, NY: Cornell University Press, 2009), passim and 334–38; Douglass, "Revolution of 1848."

41. James, *The Black Jacobins;* Laurent Dubois, *Avengers of the New World: The Story of the Haitian Revolution* (Cambridge, MA: Harvard University Press, 2005), 91–96.

42. Peter Linebaugh, "All the Atlantic Mountains Shook," *Labourite Travailleur* 10 (Autumn 1982): 87–121; Peter Linebaugh, *Red Round Globe Hot Burning: A Tale at the Crossroads of Commons and Closure, of Love and Terror, of Race and Class, and of Kate and Ned Despard* (Oakland: University of California Press, 2019), 183, 179–92.

43. Frederick Douglass, "Lecture on Haiti," in *African Americans and the Haitian Revolution: Selected Essays and Historical Documents,* ed. Maurice Jackson and Jacqueline Bacon (New York: Routledge, 2013), 202–11; Robin Blackburn, "Haiti, Slavery, and the Age of the Democratic Revolution," *The William and Mary Quarterly* 63, no. 4 (October 2006): 643–74.

44. Douglass, "Revolution of 1848."

45. Julia Gaffield, ed., *The Haitian Declaration of Independence: Creation, Context, and Legacy* (Charlottesville: University of Virginia Press, 2016); Dubois, *Avengers*, 298–301.

46. Erick Langer, "Indigenous Independence in Spanish South America," in *New Countries: Capitalism, Revolutions, and Nations in the Americas, 1750–1870*, ed. John Tutino (Durham, NC: Duke University Press, 2016), 350–75; Amanda T. Perry, "Becoming Indigenous in Haiti, from Dessalines to La Revue Indigène," *Small Axe* 21, no. 2 (July 2017): 45–61; José Carlos Mariátegui, "On Studying the Peruvian and Indo-American Reality," in *Jose Carlos Mariategui: An Anthology*, ed. and trans. Harry E. Vanden and Marc Becker (New York: Monthly Review Press, 2011), 78.

47. Julius S. Scott, *The Common Wind: Afro-American Currents in the Age of the Haitian Revolution* (New York: Verso, 2020), 210; Ada Ferrer, "Haiti, Free Soil, and Antislavery in the Revolutionary Atlantic," *The American Historical Review* 117, no. 1 (2012): 40–66; John Rydjord, "The French Revolution and Mexico," *Hispanic American Historical Review* 9, no. 1 (February 1929): 60–98.

48. Ferrer, "Haiti, Free Soil, and Antislavery"; Scott, *Common Wind*, 210; Deborah Jenson, *Beyond the Slave Narrative: Politics, Sex, and Manuscripts in the Haitian Revolution* (Liverpool: Liverpool University Press, 2011), 177–79, 161–93.

49. Sean Kelley, "'Mexico In His Head': Slavery and the Texas-Mexico Border, 1810–1860," *Journal of Social History* 37, no. 3 (Spring 2004): 709–23.

50. "Abolition of Slavery in Mexico," *Liberator*, May 19, 1832. See also Alice L. Baumgartner, *South to Freedom: Runaway Slaves to Mexico and the Road to the Civil War* (New York: Basic Books, 2020). Quote from Karl Jacoby, *The Strange Career of William Ellis: The Texas Slave Who Became a Mexican Millionaire* (New York: W. W. Norton & Company, 2016), 15.

51. Quoted in Dubois, *Avengers of the New World*, 225.

52. Robert D. Bush, *The Louisiana Purchase: A Global Context* (New York: Routledge, 2013); Dunbar-Ortiz, *An Indigenous Peoples' History*, 95–96.

53. Thomas Jefferson to William Henry Harrison, Governor of Indiana Territory, February 27, 1803, quoted in Francis Paul Prucha, ed., *Documents of United States Indian Policy*, 2d ed. (Lincoln: University of Nebraska Press, 1990), 22–23; John Grenier, *The First Way of War: American War Making on the Frontier, 1607–1814* (Cambridge, UK: Cambridge University Press, 2005), 214–15.

54. Karl Marx, *Capital: A Critique of Political Economy*, Volume 1, trans. Ben Fowkes (New York: Penguin, 1990), 919–20. See also Emily S. Rosenberg, *Financial Missionaries to the World: The Politics and Culture of Dollar Diplomacy, 1900–1930* (Cambridge, MA: Harvard University Press, 1999).

55. Sven Beckert, *Empire of Cotton: A Global History* (New York: Alfred A. Knopf, 2014), 214; Deborah Cowen, "Following the Infrastructures of Empire: Notes on Cities, Settler Colonialism, and Method," *Urban Geography* 41, no. 4 (2020): 469–86.

56. Scott Reynolds Nelson, *A Nation of Deadbeats: An Uncommon History of America's Financial Disasters* (New York: Alfred A. Knopf, 2012), x, 31, 36–38, 41, 51; Jay Sexton, *Debtor Diplomacy: Finance and American Foreign Relations in the Civil War Era, 1837–1873* (New York: Oxford University Press, 2005).

57. Scott A. Sandage, *Born Losers: A History of Failure in America* (Cambridge, MA: Harvard University Press, 2005), 110–11.

58. David R. Roediger, *How Race Survived US History: From Settlement and Slavery to the Obama Phenomenon* (London: Verso, 2008); Alexander Saxton, *The Indispensable Enemy: Labor and the Anti-Chinese Movement in California* (Berkeley: University of California Press, 1971), passim; Giovanni Arrighi, *Adam Smith in Beijing: Lineages of the Twenty-First Century* (London: Verso, 2007), 221; Reginald Horsman, *Race and Manifest Destiny: The Origins of American Racial Anglo-Saxonism* (Cambridge, MA: Harvard University Press, 1981), 1–6, 229–49; Ronald Takaki, *Iron Cages: Race and Culture in 19th-Century America* (New York: Oxford University Press, 2000), 11; Silvia Federici, *Caliban and the Witch: Women, the Body, and Primitive Accumulation* (Brooklyn: Automomedia, 2004), 12–19.

59. Du Bois, *Black Reconstruction,* 89. On English looms, see Karl Marx, "English Public Opinion," *New York Daily Tribune,* February 1, 1862.

60. Marx, "English Public Opinion."

61. Frederick Douglass, "The Slave's Appeal to Great Britain," *The Saturday Press,* November 29, 1862.

62. Philip S. Foner, *British Labor and the American Civil War* (New York: Holmes & Meier, 1981), 58; David Featherstone, *Solidarity: Hidden Histories and Geographies of Internationalism* (London: Zed Books, 2012), 1–4.

63. Frederick Douglass, "The Meaning of July Fourth for the Negro," in Foner, *Frederick Douglass,* 188–206.

64. International Working Men's Association, "To the People of the United States of America," *The Workman's Advocate,* October 14, 1865; Karl Marx, "Inaugural Address of the Working Men's International Association," in Zimmerman, *The Civil War in the United States,* 179–82, 187.

65. Cockcroft, *Mexico's Hope,* 72; John Womack, Jr., *Zapata and the Mexican Revolution* (New York: Vintage, 1969), 44; Gilly, *The Mexican Revolution,* 4, 40; Nugent, *Rural Revolt in Mexico,* 16.

66. David Walker, "Porfirian Labor Politics: Working Class Organizations in Mexico City and Porfirio Diaz, 1876–1902," *The Americas* 37 (1981): 257–89; Paul Vanderwood, "The Mexican Revolution: Region and Theory, Signifying Nothing?," *Latin American Research Review* 25 (Winter 1990): 231–42; John Coatsworth, "Railroads, Landholding, and Agrarian Protest in Early Porfiriato," *Hispanic American Historical Review* 5, no. 1 (1974): 48–71; Friedrich Katz, *The Secret War in Mexico: Europe, the United States, and the Mexican Revolution* (Chicago: University of Chicago Press, 1981), 4–27.

67. Katz, *Secret War in Mexico,* 3; Grandin, *Empire's Workshop,* 17; Hamilton, *Limits of State Autonomy,* 51; Cockcroft, *Mexico's Hope,* 85; John Foran, "Reinventing

the Mexican Revolution," 120; Jonathan C. Brown, *Oil and Revolution in Mexico* (Berkeley: University of California Press, 1993); Hart, *Revolutionary Mexico,* xviii, 146.

68. Thomas F. O'Brien, *Making the Americas: The United States and Latin America from the Age of Revolutions to the Era of Globalization* (Albuquerque: University of New Mexico Press, 2007), 92–93; Gene Z. Hanrahan, ed., *The Bad Yankee: American Entrepreneurs and Financiers in Mexico,* vol. 2 (Chapel Hill, NC: Documentary Publications, 1985); Barrera, *Race and Class in the Southwest,* 11–13.

69. Hart, *Empire and Revolution,* 1–72; Mario Gill, *Nuestros Buenos Vecinos* (Mexico City: Editorial Azteca, 1964), 2–8, cited in González, *Mexican Consuls,* ix.

70. See Hudson, "The National City Bank of New York and Haiti"; Louis A. Pérez, *Cuba and the United States: Ties of Singular Intimacy* (Athens: University of Georgia Press, 2003).

71. Ricardo Flores Magón, "Todavía es tiempo," *El Colmillo Público,* June 24, 1906, 382–83; Flores Magón, "La debilidad de la dictadura," *El Colmillo Público,* April 15, 1906, 223.

72. Ricardo Flores Magón, "Mexican Manifesto," *Regeneración,* June 13, 1914.

CHAPTER 2. HOW TO MAKE A MAP

1. Marx, *Capital,* 926; Rosa Luxemburg, *Accumulation of Capital* (London: Routledge, 2003); David Montgomery, *Fall of the House of Labor: The Workplace, the State and American Labor Activism, 1865–1925* (Cambridge, UK: Cambridge University Press, 1987), 70; John Tully, *Devil's Milk: A Social History of Rubber* (New York: Monthly Review Press, 2011); Arthur Conan Doyle, *Crime of the Congo* (London: Hutchinson & Co., 1909); Christopher Hill, *The World Turned Upside Down: Radical Ideas During the English Revolution* (New York: Viking Press, 1972).

2. Quotes come from Paul Shinsei Kōchi, *Imin No Aiwa (An Immigrant's Sorrowful Tale),* trans. Ben Kobashigawa (Los Angeles: Privately printed, 1978). There are minor differences between this version and the version written in June 1938 and republished as Shinshei Kōchi, "Sad Tale of an Immigrant: Dedicated to the Souls of the Departed," in *History of the Okinawans in North America,* trans. Ben Kobashigawa (Los Angeles: Okinawan Club of America and the Asian American Studies Center, University of California, 1988), 524–40. Where relevant, these differences are noted.

3. In the 1978 publication of *Imin no Aiwa,* Kōchi describes setting off: "At four in the afternoon on September 2 in the 7th year of the Taishō era (1918), we rebels boarded the Taigimaru bound for Kobi" (19). But the 1988 edition describes the graffiti Kōchi scribbles on the wall of the Salina Cruz detention center as a note signed "November 1917" and later a message on a rock dated "December 1917" (528, 532).

4. On "backwardness" and "savage" and for debates on Okinawa's colonial status, see Alan S. Christy, "The Making of Imperial Subjects in Okinawa," in *Formations of Colonial Modernity in East Asia,* ed. Tani E. Barlow (Durham, NC: Duke

University Press, 1997), 141–70, and Julia Yonetani, "Ambiguous Traces and the Politics of Sameness: Placing Okinawa in Meiji Japan," *Japanese Studies* 20, no. 1 (2000): 15–31. For a discussion of Japan in the context of Gramsci's "Southern Question," see Harry Harootunian, "Some Reflections on Gramsci: The Southern Question in the Deprovincializing of Marx," in *Gramsci in the World,* ed. Fredric Jameson and Roberto M. Dainotto (Durham, NC: Duke University Press, 2020), 140–57.

5. Kōchi, *Imin No Aiwa,* 20; Chushichi Tsuzuki, *The Pursuit of Power in Modern Japan, 1825–1995* (Oxford, UK: Oxford University Press, 2000), 192; Chushichi Tsuzuki, "The Changing Image of Britain among Japanese Intellectuals," in *The History of Anglo-Japanese Relations, 1600–2000: Social and Cultural Perspectives,* ed. Gordon Daniels and Chushichi Tsuzuki (London: Palgrave Macmillan, 2002), 17–40.

6. Kōchi, "Sad Tale of an Immigrant," 526.

7. Kōchi, *Imin No Aiwa,* 21, 33; Mamoru Akamine, *The Ryukyu Kingdom: Cornerstone of East Asia,* trans. Lina Terrell, ed. Robert N. Huey (Honolulu: University of Hawai'i Press, 2016), 140; Richard Siddle, "Colonialism and Identity in Okinawa Before 1945," *Japanese Studies* 18, no. 2 (1998): 121–22; James E. Roberson, "Singing Diaspora: Okinawan Songs of Home, Departure, and Return," *Identities* 17, no. 4 (2010): 430–53; J. Kēhaulani Kauanui, *Hawaiian Blood: Colonialism and the Politics of Sovereignty and Indigeneity* (Durham, NC: Duke University Press, 2008); Edith Mitsuko Kaneshiro, "'Our home will be the five continents': Okinawan Migration to Hawaii, California, and the Philippines, 1899–1941" (PhD diss., University of California, Berkeley, 1999), 116; Adria L. Imada, "'Aloha 'Oe': Settler-Colonial Nostalgia and the Genealogy of a Love Song," *American Indian Culture and Research Journal* 37, no. 2 (2013): 35–52; Michael Denning, *Noise Uprising: The Audiopolitics of a World Musical Revolution* (New York: Verso, 2015), 35–67.

8. Mae M. Ngai, *Impossible Subjects: Illegal Aliens and the Making of Modern America* (Princeton, NJ: Princeton University Press, 2004), 18.

9. Kōchi, *Imin No Aiwa,* 33. For intertwined histories of immigrant exclusion and settler colonialism see Roxanne Dunbar-Ortiz, *Not "A Nation of Immigrants": Settler Colonialism, White Supremacy, and a History of Erasure and Exclusion* (Boston: Beacon, 2021). On refusal to consent to colonial mappings and occupations of territory, see Audra Simpson, *Mohawk Interruptus: Political Life Across the Borders of Settler States* (Durham, NC: Duke University Press, 2014), 128. Mahmood Mamdani suggests placing US settler-colonialism into a "global-historical" standpoint as a precursor to decolonization in *Neither Settler nor Native: The Making and Unmaking of Permanent Minorities* (Cambridge, MA: Harvard University Press, 2020), 98–99.

10. Priyamvada Gopal, *Insurgent Empire: Anticolonial Resistance and British Dissent* (London: Verso, 2019), 209.

11. Grace Peña Delgado, *Making the Chinese Mexican: Global Migration, Localism, and Exclusion in the U.S.-Mexico Borderlands* (Stanford, CA: Stanford University Press, 2013); Edith M. Kaneshiro, "Communists, Christians, and Japanese Imperial Subjects: Okinawan Immigrants within the Japanese Diaspora, 1899 to

1941," in *Studies in Pacific History: Economics, Politics, and Migration,* ed. Dennis O. Flynn, Arturo Giráldez, and James Sobredo (London: Routledge, 2018), 170–87.

12. Kōchi, *Imin no Aiwa,* 23. Since there is a discrepancy over the date of the voyage, the nature of the quarantine is unclear. If the trip occurred at the end of 1917, the quarantine would have been for typhus. If it occurred at the end of 1918, it would have been for the Spanish Flu pandemic. See Ryan M. Alexander, "The Fever of War: Epidemic Typhus and Public Health in Revolutionary Mexico City, 1915–1917," *Hispanic American Historical Review* 100, no. 1 (2020): 63–92; Ryan M. Alexander, "The Spanish Flu and the Sanitary Dictatorship: Mexico's Response to the 1918 Influenza Pandemic," *The Americas* 76. no. 3 (July 2019): 443–65.

13. Kōchi, *Imin no Aiwa,* 23.

14. Kōchi, "Sad Tale of an Immigrant," 528.

15. Kōchi, *Imin No Aiwa,* 35, 39.

16. For the debates about the disjuncture between nineteenth-century revolutionary political predictions and twentieth-century revolutionary conditions, see Cedric J. Robinson, *An Anthropology of Marxism* (Aldershot, UK: Ashgate, 2001), 153; Mike Davis, *Planet of Slums* (London: Verso, 2007), 174; Mike Davis, *Late Victorian Holocausts: El Niño Famines and the Making of the Third World* (London: Verso, 2002), 207–9; Mike Davis, "Old Gods, New Enigmas," *Catalyst* 1, no. 2 (2017): 7–40. For a discussion of the insufficiency of the "transnational" designation, see Arif Dirlik, "Performing the World: Reality and Representation in the Making of World Histor(ies)," *Journal of World History* 16, no. 4 (December 2005): 391–410. Dirlik notes, "Ethnic and diasporic spaces are prime examples in our day of such spaces that are often described, somewhat misleadingly in my opinion, as 'transnational' spaces. Such spaces preceded in their existence the emergence of nations; they may not be of equal significance to all parts of the nation, in which case they may help undermine its unity and homogeneity, and they are quite likely to outlast the nation as we have known it" (397).

17. For many Asian immigrants like Kōchi, especially many Chinese people, the question of internationalism in relation to the Mexican Revolution was a vexed one. East Asians were unevenly incorporated into state-building and capitalist development projects. As Jason Oliver Chang notes, Chinese immigrants were largely regarded as disposable labor or *motores de sangre* (engines of blood) under the Porfiriato and then later reimagined as threats to the state and killable subjects at different points during the Revolution. See Jason Oliver Chang, *Chino: Anti-Chinese Racism in Mexico, 1880–1940* (Champaign: University of Illinois Press, 2017), 8, 71–87; Robert Chao Romero, *The Chinese in Mexico, 1882–1940* (Tucson: University of Arizona Press, 2012); María Elena Ota Mishima, *Destino México: un estudio de las Migraciones Asiáticas a México, siglos XIX y XX* (Mexico City: Colegio de México, Centro de Estudios de Asia y África, 1997).

18. Zapata (epigraph) is quoted in Spenser, *Stumbling Its Way Through Mexico,* 36.

19. Dan La Botz, "American 'Slackers' in the Mexican Revolution: International Proletarian Politics in the Midst of a National Revolution," *The Americas* 62, no. 4 (2006): 575; Eric Hobsbawm, *The Age of Extremes: A History of the World, 1914–1991* (Vintage: New York, 1995), 65–66; M. N. Roy, *Memoirs* (Delhi: Ajanta Publications, 1984), 59; Barry Carr, *Marxism and Communism in Twentieth-Century Mexico* (Lincoln: University of Nebraska Press, 1992), 18.

20. Spenser, *Stumbling Its Way Through Mexico,* 2.

21. Robert McCaa, "Missing Millions: The Demographic Costs of the Mexican Revolution," *Mexican Studies/Estudios Mexicanos* 19, no. 2 (2003): 367–400.

22. Joe C. Ashby, *Organized Labor and the Mexican Revolution under Lázaro Cárdenas* (Chapel Hill: University of North Carolina Press, 1967), 10–12; Andrew Grant Wood, *Revolution in the Street: Women, Workers, and Urban Protest in Veracruz, 1870–1927* (Wilmington, DE: Scholarly Resources Books, 2001), 29; Gilly, *Mexican Revolution,* 233–35; Alan Knight, "The Working Class and the Mexican Revolution, c. 1900–1920," *Journal of Latin American Studies* 16, no. 1 (May 1984): 51–79.

23. Samaren Roy, *The Restless Brahmin: Early Life of M. N. Roy* (Bombay: Allied Publishers, 1970), 59–81.

24. Roy, *Memoirs;* Satyabrata Rai Chowdhuri, *Leftism in India, 1917–1947* (New York: Palgrave, 2007), 42–135.

25. Sibnarayan Ray, ed. *Selected Works of M. N. Roy* (Delhi: Oxford University Press), 165–66.

26. V. I. Lenin, "Preliminary Draft Theses on the National and Colonial Questions," in *Collected Works* (Moscow: Progress Publishers, 1966), 31:144.

27. M. N. Roy, "Draft Supplementary Theses On the National and Colonial Question, 2nd Congress Communist International," in *Documents of the History of the Communist Party of India,* ed. G. Adhikari (New Delhi: People's Publishing House, 1971), 1:179.

28. Roy, "Draft Supplementary Theses," 184, 186–88.

29. On the ways in which Marxism provided "the conscious expression of the unconscious historical process" see Leon Trotsky, *My Life* (New York: Pathfinder Press, Jun 1, 1970), 334; M. N. Roy, "An Indian Communist Manifesto," in *Selected Works of M. N. Roy,* 1:164.

30. Roderick D. Bush, *The End of White World Supremacy: Black Internationalism and the Problem of the Color Line* (Philadelphia: Temple University Press, 2009), 102–3; Kevin McDermott and Jeremy Agnew, *The Comintern: A History of International Communism from Lenin to Stalin* (New York: St. Martin's Press, 1996), 162–63. In "An Indian Communist Manifesto" Roy had explicitly called on the British working class to stage a "simultaneous general strike" to deal a "vital blow to imperialistic capitalism at home and abroad" (161). See also Ranajit Guha, "Historiography of Colonial India," *Subaltern Studies I: Writings on South Asian History & Society,* ed. Ranajit Guha (New Delhi: Oxford University Press India, 1982), 77.

31. Josephine Fowler, *Japanese and Chinese Immigrant Activists: Organizing in American and International Communist Movements, 1919–1933* (New Brunswick, NJ: Rutgers University Press, 2007), 17–18; Robert C. North and Xenia J. Eudin, *M. N. Roy's Mission to China: The Communist-Kuomintang Split of 1927* (New York: Octagon Books, 1977), 1; Minkah Makalani, *In the Cause of Freedom: Radical Black Internationalism from Harlem to London, 1917–1939* (Chapel Hill: University of North Carolina Press, 2011), 80–81.

32. J. C. Johari, *M. N. Roy, The Great Radical Humanist: Political Biography and Socio-Political Ideas* (New York: Sterling Publishers, 1988), 64; Robin D. G. Kelley, *Freedom Dreams: The Black Radical Imagination* (Boston: Beacon, 2002), 46–47; Kate A. Baldwin, *Beyond the Color Line and the Iron Curtain: Reading Encounters Between Black and Red, 1922–1963* (Durham, NC: Duke University Press, 2002), 28–42.

33. See Kelley, *Freedom Dreams*, 47. The insights of this chapter are influenced by Bruno Bosteels's injunction to rethink the Mexican Revolution outside of two separate trends: an empirically minded history of the Communist Party in Mexico and the more standard histories of the Revolution, which tend to focus on key figures like Zapata and Pancho Villa. He describes two trajectories as "parallel tracks that rarely meet" and instead proposes that we observe the missed encounters among political traditions, ones that rarely fall neatly into prescribed political formations but often intersect in unintended and generative ways. Bruno Bosteels, "The Mexican Commune," Historical Materialism Conference, New York City, April 26, 2013.

34. Victor Serge quoted in La Botz, "American 'Slackers,'" 575; Hobsbawm, *The Age of Extremes*, 65–66; Roy, *Memoirs*, 59.

35. Roy, *Memoirs*, 71, 75–6.

36. Roy, *Memoirs*, 76.

37. Roy, *Memoirs*, 59.

38. Joseph and Nugent write that histories of the Revolution have "suffered from a marked tendency to isolate and privilege the revolution *as event*—as the supreme moment of popular resistance in Mexican history—rather than to study it as a culturally complex, historically generated process." See Gilbert M. Joseph and Daniel Nugent, "Popular Culture and State Formation in Revolutionary Mexico," in *Everyday Forms of State Formation: Revolution and the Negotiation of Rule in Modern Mexico*, ed. Gilbert M. Joseph and Daniel Nugent (Durham, NC: Duke University Press, 1994), 5. See also James Scott, "Foreword," in *Everyday Forms of State Formation*, ed. Joseph and Nugent, viii, ix; Wasserman, "The Mexican Revolution."

39. Womack, *Zapata and the Mexican Revolution*, 87; Paul Hart, *Bitter Harvest: The Social Transformation of Morelos, Mexico, and the Origins of the Zapatista Revolution, 1840–1910* (Albuquerque: University of New Mexico Press, 2006), 175; Arturo Warman, "The Political Project of Zapatismo," in *Riot, Rebellion, and Revolution: Rural Social Conflict in Mexico*, ed. Friedrich Katz (Princeton, NJ: Princeton University Press, 1988), 321–37; Robert P. Millon, *Zapata: The Ideology of a Peasant Revolutionary* (New York: International Publishers, 1969), 78.

40. Kris Manjapra, *M. N. Roy: Marxism and Colonial Cosmopolitanism* (London: Routledge, 2010), 32; Enrique Montalvo Ortega, "Revolts and Peasant Mobilizations in Yucatán: Indians, Peons and Peasants from the Caste War to the Revolution," in *Riot, Rebellion, and Revolution,* ed. Katz, 295–317; Linn A. E. Gale, "Socialism in Yucatan," *Gale's Magazine,* March 1920, 7; José Carlos Mariátegui, "Mexico and the Revolution," in *The Heroic and Creative Meaning of Socialism: Selected Essays of José Carlos Mariátegui,* ed. and trans. Michael Pearlman (Atlantic Highlands, NJ: Humanities Press, 1996), 124; Daniela Spenser, "Radical Mexico: Limits to the Impact of Soviet Communism," trans. Richard Stoller, *Latin American Perspectives* 35, no. 2 (March 2008): 60; Devra Weber, "Keeping Community, Challenging Boundaries: Indigenous Migrants, Internationalist Workers, and Mexican Revolutionaries," in *Mexico and Mexicans and the Making of the United States,* ed. John Tutino (Austin: University of Texas Press, 2012), 208–35; Glenda Gilmore, *Defying Dixie: The Radical Roots of Civil Rights, 1919–1950* (New York: W. W. Norton, 2008), 33–34.

41. Quoted in Spenser, *Stumbling Its Way Through Mexico,* 94.

42. La Botz, "American 'Slackers'"; Spenser, *Stumbling Its Way Through Mexico,* 38; Turner, *Barbarous Mexico;* Van Gosse, *Where the Boys Are: Cuba, Cold War America and the Making of a New Left* (London: Verso, 1993), 14–34; Curtis Marez, "Pancho Villa Meets Sun Yat-sen: Third World Revolution and the History of Hollywood Cinema," *American Literary History* 17, no. 3 (Fall 2005): 486–505.

43. Roy, *Memoirs,* 107, 108, 143.

44. Roy, *Memoirs,* 204.

45. Roy, *Memoirs,* 211.

46. Roy, *Memoirs,* 219–20.

47. Catherine Christensen Gwin, "'The Selling of American Girls': Mexico's White Slave Trade in the California Imaginary," *California History* 99, no. 1 (2022): 41.

48. Gerald Horne, *Black and Brown: African Americans and the Mexican Revolution, 1910–1920* (New York: New York University Press, 2005), 32–37; Delores Nason McBroome, "Harvests of Gold: African American Boosterism, Agriculture and Investment in Allensworth and Little Liberia," in *Seeking El Dorado: African Americans in California,* ed. Lawrence B. de Graaf, Kevin Mulroy, and Quintard Taylor (Seattle: University of Washington Press, 2001), 161; Karl Jacoby, "Between North and South: The Alternative Borderlands of William H. Ellis and the African American Colony of 1895," in *Continental Crossroads: Remapping U.S.-Mexico Borderlands History,* ed. Samuel Truett and Elliott Young (Durham, NC: Duke University Press, 2004), 209–40.

49. Olivia Gall, "Identidad, Exclusión y Racismo: Reflexiones Teóricas y Sobre México," *Revista Mexicana de Sociología* 4, no. 2 (2004): 221–59; Guidotti-Hernández, *Unspeakable Violence,* 177–280.

50. "Mexico City Editor Seized," *New York Times,* August 28, 1923; Theodore Kornweibel, Jr., *"Investigate Everything": Federal Efforts to Compel Black Loyalty*

During World War I (Bloomington: Indiana University Press, 2002), 40–41, 42, 45, 57, 58, 68, 70, 244.

51. Langston Hughes, *The Big Sea* (New York: Hill and Wang, 1940), 40.

52. John Reed, *Ten Days That Shook the World* (New York: Penguin, 1977), 9.

53. Barry Carr, "Marxism and Anarchism in the Formation of the Mexican Communist Party, 1910–19," *The Hispanic American Historical Review* 63, no. 2 (May 1983): 295.

54. Alan Knight, *The Mexican Revolution* (Lincoln: University of Nebraska Press, 1990), 2:1–70. Also see Renato Leduc, "Preface to the New Edition," in John Reed, *Insurgent Mexico* (New York: International Publishers, 1969), 14.

55. John Reed, "War in Paterson," *The Masses*, June 1913.

56. Eric Homberger, *John Reed* (Manchester, UK: Manchester University Press, 1990), 27–57.

57. Reed, *Insurgent Mexico;* Hector Agredano, "Rails to Revolution: Railroads, Railroad Workers and the Geographies of the Mexican Revolution" (PhD diss., CUNY Graduate Center, 2019).

58. Reed, *Insurgent Mexico,* 166–67.

59. Davis, *Planet of Slums,* 174. Also see Erez Manela, *The Wilsonian Moment: Self-Determination and the International Origins of Anticolonial Nationalism* (New York: Oxford University Press, 2007).

60. Reed, *Ten Days,* 12.

61. Mike Davis, "Old Gods, New Enigmas: Notes on Revolutionary Agency," in *Old Gods, New Enigmas* (New York: Verso, 2018), 1–154; Robinson, *An Anthropology of Marxism,* 153.

62. John Reed, "What About Mexico?," *The Masses*, June 1914.

63. "American" here is used in line with Reed's designation, the colloquial expression for someone from the United States. John Reed, "Mac – American," in *Adventures of a Young Man* (San Francisco: City Lights, 1975), 51; Robert A. Rosenstone, *Romantic Revolutionary: A Biography of John Reed* (New York: Vintage, 1975), 158; Daniel Wayne Lehman, *John Reed and the Writing of Revolution* (Athens: Ohio University Press, 2002), 105–11.

64. Reed, "Mac – American," 52.

65. Anne McClintock, *Imperial Leather: Race, Gender and Sexuality in the Colonial Context* (New York: Routledge, 1995), 22.

66. Reed, "Mac – American," 53.

67. Reed, "Mac – American," 53.

68. Fredric Jameson, "Cognitive Mapping," in *Marxism and the Interpretation of Culture,* ed. Cary Nelson and Lawrence Grossberg (Urbana: University of Illinois Press, 1988), 347–60.

69. Reed, "Mac – American," 55.

70. Reed, "Mac – American," 55.

71. Reed, "Mac – American," 56.

72. Reed, "Mac – American," 52.

73. Reed, "Mac – American," 55, emphasis original.

74. John Reed, "The Social Revolution in Court," *Liberator,* September 1918.

CHAPTER 3. HOW TO MAKE A UNIVERSITY

Epigraphs: Letter to Harry Weinberger, Yale Sterling Memorial Library, Harry Weinberger Papers, Group no. 553, box 22; Department of Justice, CPUSA Mss 21, 966 Files 77–94, Reel 14. Translation in original.

1. Claudio Lomnitz, *The Return of Comrade Ricardo Flores Magón* (New York: Zone Books, 2014), 505.

2. Lomnitz, *Return,* 502–4; W. Dirk Raat, *Revoltosos: Mexico's Rebels in the United States, 1903–1923* (College Station: Texas A&M University Press, 1981), 289.

3. "Anarchist Even In Death," *Los Angeles Times,* January 6, 1923.

4. "Tribute Paid 'Scorpion': Sympathizers With Ricardo Flores Magon Gather at His Bier for Final Act of Devotion," *Los Angeles Times,* November 27, 1922.

5. Lomnitz, *Return,* 497.

6. Colin M. MacLachlan, *Anarchism and the Mexican Revolution: The Political Trials of Ricardo Flores Magón in the United States* (Berkeley: University of California Press, 1991), 108.

7. Ralph Chaplin, *Wobbly: The Rough-And-Tumble Story of An American Radical* (Chicago: University of Chicago Press, 1948), 310.

8. Ward S. Albro, *Always a Rebel: Ricardo Flores Magón and the Mexican Revolution* (Fort Worth: Texas Christian University Press, 1992); William Owen, "Death of Ricardo Flores Magón," *Freedom,* December 1922; Emma Pérez, *The Decolonial Imaginary: Writing Chicanas into History* (Bloomington: Indiana University Press, 1999), 56. According to the editor of the English edition, William Owen, "When I succeeded John Kenneth Turner as editor of the English section of *Regeneración* the circulation was about 17,000 and the paper must have been making money. Every cent of it was spent on spreading the propaganda. We had between 600 and 700 papers on our free exchange list, and got extraordinarily full notices throughout the Latin American world. Our great aim was the uniting of Latin opinion, in Mexico, Central and South America, against invasion by the Plutocracy, and the creation in the United States of a sentiment strong enough to hold in check the intervention perpetually threatened. I believe Ricardo regarded this last as *Regeneración*'s special task, and that on this account, he opposed the transfer of the paper to Mexico, a step I at one time urged" ("Death of Ricardo Flores Magón," *Freedom,* December 1922).

9. Reprinted in Chas Bufe and Mitchell Cowe Verter, eds., *Dreams of Freedom: A Ricardo Flores Magón Reader* (Oakland, CA: AK Press, 2005), 145.

10. Norman Caulfield discusses the manifesto as a call for workers to "act in solidarity with Mexicans as they fought to shake off the yoke of capitalism" and clarifies that "Mexican workers' fight was not a national one, but universal, because the cause of the 'wage slave' has no frontiers. Magón also warned the American

worker of the dire consequences if the revolution failed. If Mexico's workers lost, Flores Magón predicted, the nation would become an ideal land for business because of low salaries, and American workers would find their firms and factories there instead of the United States because it would be more profitable to employ Mexicans" (*Mexican Workers and the State: From the Porfiriato to NAFTA* [Fort Worth: Texas Christian University Press, 1998], 1). See also Paul W. Keve, *Prisons and the American Conscience: A History of U.S. Federal Corrections* (Carbondale: Southern Illinois University Press, 1991), 7.

11. For debates around Flores Magón's death, see Andrew Grant Wood, "Death of a Political Prisoner: Revisiting the Case of Ricardo Flores Magón," *A Contra corriente* 3, no. 1 (2005): 38–66; Harrison George, "Ten Acres of Hell" *Liberator,* August 1923.

12. Quoted in Theodore Kornweibel, *"Seeing Red": The Federal Campaign against Black Militancy, 1919–1925* (Bloomington: Indiana University Press, 1998), 160. The conceptualization of a "university of radicalism" is indebted to key texts in American and Ethnic Studies, including Alan Eladio Gómez, "'Nuestras Vidas Corren Casi Paralelas': Chicanos, Independentistas, and the Prison Rebellions in Leavenworth, 1969–1972," *Latino Studies* (2008): 64–96; Sarah Haley, "'Like I was a Man': Chain Gangs, Gender, and the Domestic Carceral Sphere in Jim Crow Georgia," *Signs: Journal of Women and Culture in Society* (Autumn 2013); Laleh Khalili, *Time in the Shadows: Confinement in Counterinsurgencies* (Stanford, CA: Stanford University Press, 2012). Critical works that frame transnational struggles related to the Mexican Revolution include Streeby, *Radical Sensations,* and David Luis Brown, *Waves of Decolonization: Discourses of Race and Hemispheric Citizenship in Cuba, Mexico, and the United States* (Durham, NC: Duke University Press, 2008).

13. Mary Bosworth, *Explaining U.S. Imprisonment* (Los Angeles: Sage, 2010), 58; Barrera, *Race and Class in the Southwest,* 11–16; Jessica Enoch, *Refiguring Rhetorical Education: Women Teaching African American, Native American, and Chicano/a Students, 1865–1911* (Carbondale: Southern Illinois University, 2008), 77; David Wallace Adams, *Education for Extinction: American Indians and the Boarding School Experience, 1875–1928* (Lawrence: University Press of Kansas, 1995), 36–38; Spencer C. Tucker, *The Encyclopedia of North American Indian Wars, 1607–1890: A Political, Social, and Military History* (Santa Barbara: ABC-CLIO, 2011), 289; Irene Schubert and Frank N. Schubert, *On the Trail of the Buffalo Soldier II: New and Revised Biographies of African Americans in the U.S. Army, 1866–1917* (Lanham, MD: Scarecrow Press, 2004), 16, 49, 211, 286; Willard B. Gatewood, *"Smoked Yankees" and the Struggle for Empire: Letters from Negro Soldiers, 1898–1902* (Fayetteville: University of Arkansas Press, 1987), 228; Byrd, *The Transit of Empire,* 148, 222.

14. Keve, *Prisons and the American Conscience,* 36, 53–56, 141; Tapan K. Mukherjee, *Taraknath Das: Life and Letters of A Revolutionary in Exile* (Calcutta: National Council of Education, Bengal, 1998), 144–45; "The Dynamiters Convicted," *The Independent* 74 (January-March 1913): 3.

15. Louis Adamic, *Dynamite: A Century of Class Violence in America, 1830–1930* (London: Rebel Press, 1984), 110–14; Marilyn D. McShane and Frank P.

Williams III, eds., *Encyclopedia of American Prisons* (New York: Garland, 1996), 342–43.

16. "Prison Life in Leavenworth Is Writ on Film by Henry Ford," *Leavenworth New Era*, 6.5 (March 28, 1919), la Casa de El Hijo del Ahuizote, Mexico City, (CHA) File # 41738.

17. "At the cross roads," Ford Motor Company, 1919.

18. Zaragosa Vargas, *Crucible of Struggle: A History of Mexican Americans from Colonial Times to the Present Era* (New York: Oxford University Press, 2001), 189; Mukherjee, *Taraknath Das*, 143–44; Stephen M. Kohn, *American Political Prisoners: Prosecutions under the Espionage and Sedition Acts* (Westport, CT: Praeger, 1994), 7; Keve, *Prisons and the American Conscience*, 7.

19. Kohn, *American Political Prisoners*, 7–9.

20. Bosworth, *Explaining U.S. Imprisonment*, 56–57; Kohn, *American Political Prisoners*, 7; Keve, *Prisons and the American Conscience*, 141.

21. This materialist analysis of prison expansion follows the lead of Ruth Wilson Gilmore, *Golden Gulag: Prisons, Surplus, Crisis, and Opposition in Globalizing California* (Berkeley: University of California Press, 2007).

22. Richard Hofstadter, *The American Political Tradition and the Men who Made It* (New York: Vintage, 1989), 341–42; Barbara Foley, *Spectres of 1919: Class and Nation and the Making of the New Negro* (Urbana: University of Illinois, 2003), 8–36; Jeremy Brecher, *Strike!* (Cambridge, MA: South End Press, 1997), 116; Melvin Dubovsky, *We Shall Be All: A History of the Industrial Workers of the World* (Urbana: University of Illinois Press, 1988), 376–425; Westad, *The Global Cold War*, 16–17.

23. Bosworth, *Explaining U.S. Imprisonment*, 56–58, quoted in Kohn, *American Political Prisoners*, 8.

24. Hofstadter, *The American Political Tradition*, 341–50; Stephen Broadberry and Mark Harrison, *The Economics of World War I* (New York: Cambridge University Press, 2005), 334; Robinson, *Forgeries of Memory and Meaning*, 237; Howard Zinn, *A People's History of the United States* (New York: Harper Collins, 2010), 362–64.

25. Robinson, *Forgeries of Memory and Meaning*, 237.

26. S. Ani Mukherji, "The Anticolonial Imagination: Migrant Intellectuals and the Exilic Productions of American Radicalism in Interwar Moscow, 1919–1939" (PhD diss., Brown University, 2011); Hobsbawm, *The Age of Extremes*, 66.

27. Maia Ramnath, *From Haj to Utopia: How the Ghadar Movement Charted Global Radicalism and Attempted to Overthrow the British Empire* (Berkeley: University of California Press, 2011); Seema Sohi, "Echoes of Mutiny: Race, Empire, and Indian Anticolonialism in North America" (PhD diss., University of Washington, Seattle, 2008); Gilmore, *Defying Dixie*, 24; Priscilla Metscher, *James Connolly and the Reconquest of Ireland* (Minneapolis: University of Minnesota, 2002), 182–200; Kimba Idrissa, "The Kawousan War Reconsidered," in *Rethinking Resistance: Revolt and Violence in African History*, ed. Jon Abbink, Mirjam de Bruijn, and Klaas

van Walraven (Leiden: Koninklijke Brill, 2003), 191–217; Arrighi, *Long Twentieth Century*, 65; Silver, "Class Struggle and Kondratieff Waves," 279–95.

28. National Archives, Central Plains Region (NA), RG 129 Records of the Bureau of Prisons (BP), Boxes 510, 525, 526, 534, 554.

29. Kornweibel, *"Seeing Red,"* 157–59; Irwin Marcus, "Benjamin Fletcher: Black Labor Leader," *Negro History Bulletin* 35 (October 1972): 131–40.

30. NA, BP Box 510, 12895; Socialist CO, "May Day in Ft. Leavenworth," *The Liberator* 2, no. 6 (June 1919).

31. My thanks to Laura Browder for sharing "The Horrors of Leavenworth," a draft for her forthcoming study of her grandfather, Earl Browder; Earl Browder, "Values in Music," *Leavenworth New Era* 5, no. 7 (February 20, 1920): 41746, CHA.

32. Enrique Flores Magón, "The Invader," *Leavenworth New Era* 5, no. 7 (February 20, 1920): 41746, CHA.

33. Industrial Workers of the World, *An Open Letter to President Harding. From 52 Members of the I.W.W. in Leavenworth Penitentiary Who Refuse to Apply for Individual Clemency* (Chicago: General Defense Committee, 1922).

34. Superintendent, "Our School," *Leavenworth New Era* 7, no. 7 (April 9, 1920): 41751, CHA.

35. H. Austin Simons, "The U.S. Revolutionary Training Institute," *Liberator* 19 (September 1919): 42–44.

36. Superintendent, "Our School"; NA, BP, Box 510, 525, 526, 534, 554.

37. Raat, *Revoltosos*, 285; Simons, "The U.S. Revolutionary Training Institute," 42–44; Mukherjee, *Taraknath Das*, 150, 147.

38. J. A. McDonald, "The White Magic of Books" *Leavenworth New Era* 5, no. 488 (January 30, 1920): 41745, CHA; Box 2, 10, 16, 17, 18, CHA.

39. Pérez, *The Decolonial Imaginary*, 63–71. For a broader context in which these conversations did and did not occur, see Guidotti-Hernández, *Unspeakable Violence*, 11.

40. Socialist CO, "May Day in Ft. Leavenworth."

41. "Prison," from Earl Browder, "A Political Autobiography," unpublished memoir. Notes shared with author by Laura Browder, granddaughter of Earl Browder, materials for biography. Phillip Jaffe papers, Emory University, box 40, folder 1.

42. Elizabeth Gurley Flynn, *The Rebel Girl: An Autobiography, My First Life (1906–1926)* (New York: International Publishers, 1973), 255; Mukherjee, *Taraknath Das*, 146; Paul Alexander, *Peace to War: Shifting Allegiances in the Assemblies of God* (Telford, OR: Cascadia Publishing House, 2009), 135–36.

43. NA, BP Box 2, Inmate 15461; Randy Roberts, *Papa Jack: Jack Johnson and the Era of White Hopes* (New York: Free Press, 1983); Theresa Runstedtler, *Jack Johnson, Rebel Sojourner: Boxing in the Shadow of the Global Color Line* (Berkeley: University of California Press, 2012), 232–33; Khalil Gibran Muhammad, *The Condemnation of Blackness: Race, Crime, and the Making of Modern Urban America* (Cambridge, MA: Harvard University Press, 2010), 133.

44. Horne, *Black and Brown*, 33.

45. NA, BP, Box 467, File 12276.

46. Robert V. Haynes, *A Night of Violence: The Houston Riot of 1917* (Eunice: Louisiana State University Press, 1976); Gatewood, *"Smoked Yankees."*

47. Martha Greuning, "Houston," *The Crisis,* November 1917.

48. "Case Summary of Federal Parolee" (September 13, 1932); NA, BP, Box 467, File 12276.

49. "Case Summary of Federal Parolee" (September 13, 1932).

50. "A Mexican Ran Wild and Killed," *Hutchinson News,* November 14, 1922, 1; "Mexican Shot After Stabbing Seven Guards," *Baltimore Sun,* November 15, 1922, 9; "Convict Kills Guard, Stabs 6 Others; Dying," *New York Tribune,* November 15, 1922, 6; Telegram from Biddle to G. E. Herron, Deputy Sheriff, Havre Montana, November 16, 1922, NA, BP, Box 554, Inmate 13396.

51. Kenneth M. LaMaster, *U.S. Penitentiary Leavenworth* (Charleston, SC: Arcadia Publishing, 2008), 100; Robinson, *Forgeries of Memory and Meaning;* Nan Enstad, *Ladies of Labor, Girls of Adventure: Working Women, Popular Culture, and Labor Politics at the Turn of the Twentieth Century* (New York: Columbia University Press, 1999); Michael Denning, "Cheap Stories: Notes on Popular Fiction and Working-Class Culture in Nineteenth-Century America," *History Workshop* 22 Special American Issue (Autumn 1986): 1–17.

52. Streeby, *Radical Sensations,* 74, 89, 129, 137, 165; Tomás Almaguer, *Racial Fault Lines: The Historical Origins of White Supremacy in California* (Berkeley: University of California Press, 2009); Ken Gonzales-Day, *Lynching in the West: 1850–1935* (Durham, NC: Duke University Press, 2006); quoted in Chaplin, *Wobbly,* 277–80.

53. Bufe and Verter, *Dreams of Freedom,* 99; Juan Gómez-Quiñones, *Sembradores: Ricardo Flores Magón y el Partido Liberal Mexicano: A Eulogy and a Critique* (Los Angeles: Chicano Studies Center, Aztlan Publications, UCLA, 1973), 68; Wood, "Death of a Political Prisoner," 38–66; Raat, *Revoltosos,* 287; Ethel Duffy Turner, *Ricardo Flores Magón y el Partido Liberal Mexicano* (Mexico City: Comisión Nacional Editorial del CEN, 1984), 341.

54. Eugene V. Debs, "The Assassination of Magón," *New York Call,* December 3, 1922; "Salvajismo Inconcebible," *C.R.O.M.,* May 1, 1923; Yale Sterling Memorial Library, Harry Weinberger Papers, Group no. 553, Box 22, Folder 24.

55. Gilbert O'Day, "Ricardo Flores Magón," *The Nation,* December 20, 1922, 689–90.

56. NA, BP, Box 554, Inmate 13396; Bufe and Verter, *Dreams of Freedom,* 97; Raat, *Revoltosos,* 285.

57. Turner, *Ricardo Flores Magón,* 342–43; Gómez-Quiñones, *Sembradores,* 68; Raat, *Revoltosos,* 288; Chaplin, *Wobbly,* 278–81; "Salvajismo Inconcebible," *C.R.O.M.;* NA, BP, Box 554, Inmate Number 13396.

58. NA, BP, Box 554, Inmate Number 13394–13401.

59. NA, BP, Box 554, 13396. José Martínez's death is a subject of minor dispute among historians. See for example, Gómez-Quiñones, *Sembradores,* 68; Raat, *Revoltosos,* 288; Chaplin, *Wobbly,* 277–80; and Turner, *Ricardo Flores Magón,* 342–43.

60. "Andy" Lockhart, "At the Grave of a Felon," *Leavenworth New Era*, March 28, 1919, CHA, File 41738.

61. NA, BP, Box 554, Inmate 13396; "Un Mexicano Preso Q' Muere De Sus Heridas," *El Heraldo De Mexico*, December 1, 1922; Frank McLynn, *Villa and Zapata: A Biography of the Mexican Revolution* (London: Jonathan Cape, 2000), 323.

62. NA, BP, Box 554, Inmate 13396; Cynthia E. Orozco, *No Mexicans, Women, or Dogs Allowed: The Rise of the Mexican American Civil Rights Movement* (Austin: University of Texas Press, 2009), 52–53.

63. On the struggle to build a "purposeful social movement," see Gilmore, *Golden Gulag*, 191–96.

64. Gramsci was released to a clinic shortly before his death in 1937. Antonio Gramsci, *Letters from Prison*, ed. Frank Rosengarten, trans. Raymond Rosenthal (New York: Columbia University Press, 1994), 400.

65. Gwyn Williams, *Proletarian Order: Antonio Gramsci, Factory Councils and the Origins of Italian Communism, 1911–1921* (London: Pluto Press, 1975), 182–85; John M. Hart, *Anarchism & The Mexican Working Class, 1860–1931* (Austin: University of Texas Press, 1978), 83–104.

66. Ricardo Flores Magón, "The Chains of The Free," *Regeneración*, October 22, 1910, in *Dreams of Freedom*, ed. Bufe and Verter, 182–85; Antonio Gramsci, *Selections from the Prison Notebooks* (New York: International Publishers, 1971), 5–6; Antonio Gramsci, *The Southern Question* (Toronto: Guernica Editions, 2005), 45.

67. Flores Magón, "The Chains of The Free."

68. Foucault, *Discipline and Punish*, 253. See also Linebaugh, *The London Hanged*, 113–52.

69. Antonio Gramsci, "Some Aspects of the Southern Question," in *The Southern Question*, trans. Pasquale Verdicchio (Toronto: Guernica, 2005), 27–72.

70. On the PLM and its struggle to organize transnational solidarities see Streeby, *Radical Sensations;* Ricardo Flores Magón, "The Repercussions of a Lynching," *Regeneración*, November 12, 1910.

71. Flores Magón, "The Repercussions of a Lynching."

72. Quoted by Harry Weinberger in a letter to *The New Republic*, July 5, 1922, 162.

73. Foucault, *Discipline and Punish*, 13–14.

74. "Address of Enrique Flores Magón in Federal Court, Los Angeles, June 22, 1916," published as "Appendix B" in MacLachlan, *Anarchism and the Mexican Revolution*, 132.

75. Ricardo Flores Magón, letter to Ellen White, November 12, 1922, Ricardo Flores Magón Collection, International Institute for Social History, Amsterdam.

CHAPTER 4. HOW TO MAKE LOVE

Epigraph: Louise Bryant, "Madame Alexandra Kollontai and the Woman's Movement," in *Mirrors of Moscow* (New York: T. Seltzer, 1923), 111. This passage is also partially quoted in Faith Simon's introduction to the reprint of Alexandra Kollontai, *Communism and the Family* (Cleveland: Hera Press, 1982), 1.

1. Daniela Spenser, "Bolsheviks' Encounter with the Mexican Revolution," *Tensões Mundiais* 13, no. 25 (2016): 77–98; William Harrison Richardson, *Mexico through Russian Eyes, 1806–1940* (Pittsburgh: University of Pittsburgh Press, 1988), 142–43; Daniela Spenser, *The Impossible Triangle*, 88; Olcott, "'A Plague of Salaried Marxists'," 980. In her reflections upon leaving Mexico, Kollontai provides a detailed memory about the crowd that awaited her arrival with red flags—"La bandera de la Internacional." The entry from Kollontai's diplomatic diary for June 9, 1927, is titled "La partida" in Spanish translation: Rina Ortiz, ed. and trans., *Alexandra Kollontai en México: Diario y Otros Documentos* (Xalapa: Universidad Veracruzana, 2012), 135.

2. Excerpts from Kollontai's diplomatic diary were also translated into English and published in the Russian journal *International Affairs* in 1989. See Alexandra Kollontai, "Diplomatic Diary: A Record of 23 Years, Part Four, 1926–1927, Mexico," *International Affairs* (February 1989): 122–30. See also Kollontai, "Embajadora en México, 15 de diciembre," in Ortiz, *Alexandra Kollontai en México*, 45.

3. Kollontai, "Embajadora en México, 15 de diciembre," in Ortiz, *Alexandra Kollontai en México*, 45.

4. Manuel Castells, *The City and the Grassroots* (Berkeley: University of California Press, 1983), 48.

5. As described in chapter two, the Mexican Communist Party had been founded not long before in 1919. The report is cited in Margaret Stevens, *Red International and Black Caribbean: Communists in New York City, Mexico, and the West Indies, 1919–1939* (London: Pluto Press, 2017), 77; Carr, *Marxism and Communism in Twentieth-Century Mexico*, 14.

6. Carr, *Marxism and Communism in Twentieth-Century Mexico*, 14.

7. Castells, *The City and the Grassroots*, 40–41.

8. Rodolfo Uranga, "Glosario del Dia," *La Prensa*, December 9, 1926; "No Se Permitio A Mme Kollontay Que Bajara en La Habana," *El Tusconese*, December 9, 1926; Richardson, *Mexico through Russian Eyes*, 142; Kollontai, "Embajadora en México, 15 de diciembre," in Ortiz, *Alexandra Kollontai en México*, 44, 52; also see Kollontai's note to "A.M.M. Litvinov, 16 de diciembre de 1926, Ciudad de México" in Ortiz, *Alexandra Kollontai en México*, 147–48. Publicly downplaying the act to the US press, she explained at the time that her barring had had nothing to do with US attitudes. Rather, she referred to "an article of the Cuban immigration law which prohibits two women traveling alone to land in Cuba" ("Mme. Kollontay Chides U.S. for 'Agitator Bar.'") Some US voices were outraged by the refusal. "We are glad to have Russian business men come here and buy our cotton and locomotives, and plows, and electric machinery, but our fair soil would be polluted if a talented and cultured representative like Madame Kollontay [sic] merely passed over it" ("Is Democracy a Failure," *Aiken Standard Newspaper*, December 10, 1926).

9. Alexandra Kollontai, *The Autobiography of a Sexually Emancipated Communist Woman*, ed. Irving Fetscher, trans. Saltavor Attanasio (New York: Herder and Herder, 1971).

10. Michael Hardt, "Red Love," *The South Atlantic Quarterly* 116, no. 4 (October 2017): 781–96.

11. Richardson, *Mexico through Russian Eyes*, 108; Rina Ortiz Peralta, "La Embajadora Roja: Alexandra Kollontai y México," *Relaciones* 38 (2017): 19.

12. Spenser, *The Impossible Triangle*, 76.

13. Richardson, *Mexico through Russian Eyes*, 108.

14. Spenser, *The Impossible Triangle*, 76; Richardson, *Mexico through Russian Eyes*, 98. According to "Russian Minister Awaited," *Los Angeles Times*, December 7, 1926: "The Russian legation is observing silence on her program, as to whether she will continue the development of the close contact that exists between local Communistic associations and Stanislaus Pestovsky, whom she succeeds as Minister to Mexico."

15. Kollontai, "Embajadora en México, 15 de diciembre," in Ortiz, *Alexandra Kollontai en México*, 45. Rina Ortiz translates Leon's last name as Jaikis. Daniela Spenser cites a letter where it is spelled in Polish as Haykiss; see "Stanislav Pestkovsky: A Soldier of the World Revolution in Mexico," *Journal of Iberian and Latin American Research* 8, no. 1 (2002): 52. His name is anglicized as Gaikis in US papers and publications.

16. Carleton Beals, "The Soviet Wooing of Latin America," *Harpers*, August 1, 1944, 213.

17. Richardson writes that the order not to meet with Kollontai was given by Morones himself (*Mexico through Russian Eyes*, 146). But *The New York Times* quotes an unnamed source: "No members of labor unions were at the station, as the leaders had issued an order forbidding members to take part in any reception on the ground that Mexican and Russian labor had nothing in common" ("Reds of Mexico City Hail Mme Kollontay," December 9, 1926).

18. "En México la situación es compleja y es especialmente fácil cometer errores. Nosotros no estamos interesados en apoyar revueltas presuntamente revolucionarias, azuzadas y pagadas por los Estados Unidos. Los disturbios y rebeliones locales apuntalan la anarquía en México y resultan convenientes para los imperialistas en el país. Usted como representante de la Unión Soviética no debe sucumbir a la falsa idea de la proximidad de una revolución, de la cual México está todavía muy lejos. Su tarea como ministro plenipotenciario consiste en fortalecer las relaciones normales de amistad entre la URSS y México, no dejarse seducir por ninguna aventura revolucionaria" (Kollontai, "Conversación con Stalin," in Ortiz, *Alexandra Kollontai en México*, 33).

19. Peralta, "La Embajadora Roja," 45; Spenser, *The Impossible Triangle*, 108; "Mme. Kollontay Chides U.S. for 'Agitator Bar.'"

20. While a diary may be an imperfect source, Kollontai's biographer, Beatrice Farnsworth, notes that journaling was a consistent source of reflection throughout Kollontai's life, remaining so even when it became precarious for Soviet communists to maintain an open record of their thoughts and disagreements. See Beatrice Farnsworth, "Conversing with Stalin, Surviving the Terror: The Diaries of Aleksandra Kollontai and the Internal Life of Politics," *Slavic Review* 69, no. 4 (Winter 2010): 946. In her foreword to Kollontai's memoir, Germaine Greer notes that the manuscript, like much of Kollontai's writing, has many lines crossed out in blue pencil,

demonstrating either the careful editing choices of a writer or preemptive censorship of a fearful subject. While an imperfect record of the internal subjective life of Kollontai, through the diary and substantiated by other sources, one gains a sense of an overlooked episode in the history of making internationalism. See Greer, foreword to Kollontai, *The Autobiography of a Sexually Emancipated Communist Woman,* xi–xii.

21. Kollontai, "Embajadora en México, 15 de diciembre," in Ortiz, *Alexandra Kollontai en México,* 47.

22. This word "pretext" is repeated cautiously throughout Kollontai's diplomatic diary and correspondence. See Ortiz, *Alexandra Kollontai en México.*

23. Section 30 of Article 123 considered cheap and safe housing an issue of public utility. See Wood, *Revolution in the Street,* 29; John Lear, *Workers, Neighbors, and Citizens: The Revolution in Mexico City* (Lincoln: University of Nebraska Press, 2001), 356; Knight, "The Working Class and the Mexican Revolution, c. 1900–1920."

24. Ann S. Blum, *Domestic Economies: Family, Work, and Welfare in Mexico City, 1884–1943* (Lincoln: University of Nebraska Press, 2009), 183–250; Holly E. Garza, "Caught in the Crossfire: Children during the Mexican Revolution, 1910–1920" (PhD diss., University of Texas at El Paso, 1995), 13–51; Elena Albarrán, *Seen and Heard in Mexico: Children and Revolutionary Cultural Nationalism* (Lincoln: University of Nebraska, 2014), 23–28; Wendy Z. Goldman, *Women, the State, and Revolution: Soviet Family Policy and Social Life, 1917–1936* (Cambridge, MA: Harvard University Press, 1993), 59–100.

25. Heather Fowler-Salamini, "Gender, Work, Trade Unionism, and Working Class Women's Culture in Post-Revolutionary Veracruz," in *Sex in Revolution: Gender, Politics, and Power in Modern Mexico,* eds. Jocelyn Olcott, Mary Kay Vaughan, and Gabriela Cano (Durham, NC: Duke University Press, 2006), 162–80; Stephanie Mitchell, Introduction to *The Women's Revolution in Mexico, 1910–1953,* ed. Stephanie E. Michell and Patience A. Schell (Lanham, MD: Rowman and Littlefield, 2006), 8–13; Tabea Alexa Linhard, *Fearless Women in the Mexican Revolution and the Spanish Civil War* (Columbia: University of Missouri Press, 2005).

26. Gabriela Cano, "Unconcealable Realities of Desire: Amelio Robles's (Transgender) Masculinity in the Mexican Revolution," in *Sex in Revolution: Gender, Politics, and Power in Modern Mexico,* eds. Jocelyn Olcott, Mary Kay Vaughan, and Gabriela Cano (Durham, NC: Duke University Press, 2006); Fowler-Salamini, "Gender, Work, Trade Unionism," 162–80.

27. Bethel, ed. *Mexico Since Independence;* Alan Knight, "Popular Culture and the Revolutionary State in Mexico, 1910–1940," *Hispanic American Historical Review* 74, no. 3 (1994): 411.

28. Mary Kay Vaughan, *Cultural Politics in Revolution: Teachers, Peasants, and Schools in Mexico, 1930–1940* (Tucson: University of Arizona Press, 1997), 25–46; Jocelyn Olcott, *Revolutionary Women in Postrevolutionary Mexico* (Durham, NC: Duke University Press, 2005), 93–122.

29. Jocelyn Olcott, "'Take Off That Streetwalker's Dress': Concha Michel and the Cultural Politics of Gender in Postrevolutionary Mexico," *Journal of Women's*

History 21, no. 3 (2009): 43. On Michel's participation in the Cultural Missions program, see Olcott, *Revolutionary Women in Postrevolutionary Mexico,* 93–94.

30. Vaughan, *Cultural Politics in Revolution,* 30–31.

31. Jean A. Meyer, *The Cristero Rebellion: The Mexican People between Church and State, 1926–1929* (Cambridge, UK: Cambridge University Press, 1976), 13–15; Vaughan, *Cultural Politics in Revolution,* 29–34.

32. Olcott, "'Take Off That Streetwalker's Dress,'" 46.

33. Vaughan, *Cultural Politics in Revolution,* 25–46.

34. Mary Kay Vaughan, "Pancho Villa, the Daughters of Mary, and the Modern Woman: Gender in the Long Mexican Revolution," in *Sex in Revolution: Gender, Politics, and Power in Modern Mexico,* ed. Jocelyn Olcott, Mary Kay Vaughan, and Gabriela Cano (Durham, NC: Duke University Press, 2006), 25.

35. William Suarez-Potts, "The Railroad Strike of 1927: Labor and Law after the Mexican Revolution," *Labor History* 52, no. 4 (2011): 399–416; Spenser, "Bolsheviks' Encounter with the Mexican Revolution," 87–88; Carr, *Marxism and Communism in Twentieth-Century Mexico,* 31.

36. Kollontai, "27 de diciembre," in Ortiz, *Alexandra Kollontai en México,* 57–58; Hamilton, *Limits of State Autonomy,* 73, 106; Cockcroft, *Mexico's Hope,* 111; Grandin, *Empire's Workshop,* 35; James J. Horn, "U.S. Diplomacy and 'The Specter of Bolshevism' in Mexico (1924–1927)," *The Americas* 32, no. 1 (July 1975): 39–40.

37. "La Ministra del Soviet llegó hoy a México," *La Prensa,* December 9, 1926; Spenser, "Bolsheviks' Encounter with the Mexican Revolution," 92.

38. Kollontai, "La partida," in Ortiz, *Alexandra Kollontai en México,* 135.

39. Alan MacDonald, "Russia's Enigma Heads for Mexico," *Cincinnati Commercial Tribune,* November 14, 1926.

40. "Mme. Kollontay Chides U.S. for 'Agitator Bar,'" *New York Herald Tribune,* December 9, 1926.

41. "Mme. Kollontay, Envoy, Lands at Vera Cruz To-day," *New York Herald Tribune,* December 7, 1926; "Mme. Kollontay Chides U.S. for 'Agitator Bar'"; "Woman Envoy's Books Far Outnumber Gowns; Mme. Kollantay Brings Library in Half a Dozen Languages to Mexico City Post," *New York Times,* December 10, 1926.

42. Barbara Evans Clements, *Bolshevik Feminist: The Life of Aleksandra Kollontai* (Bloomington: Indiana University Press, 1979); Barbara Evans Clements, "Emancipation Through Communism: The Ideology of A.M. Kollontai," *Slavic Review* 32, no. 2 (June 1973): 324. Daniela Spenser writes that Kollontai was one of many prominent Bolsheviks "sent abroad after they failed to follow the general line at home" ("Stanislav Pestkovsky," 37).

43. Alexandra Kollontai, "The Third International," *The American Socialist,* October 1915, 2; Clements, *Bolshevik Feminist,* 93; R. Craig Nation, *War on War: Lenin, the Zimmerwald Left, and the Origins of Communist Internationalism* (Durham, NC: Duke University Press, 1989), 55.

44. Kollontai, "The Third International."

45. Alexandra Kollontai, "Till de socialista kvinnorna I alla länder," *Storm-klockan,* November 15, 1914, 2, quoted in Clements, *Bolshevik Feminist,* 85.

46. Clara Zetkin, "Wives of Workers, Women Workers!" in *Clara Zetkin: Selected Writings,* ed. Philip S. Foner (Chicago: Haymarket, 2015), 130–32.

47. Eugène Pottier, "L'Internationale," quoted in Nation, *War on War,* 1.

48. Alexandra Kollontai, "Who Needs War?," in *Selected Writings of Alexandra Kollontai,* trans. and ed. Alix Holt (New York: W. W. Norton, 1977), 88.

49. Clements, *Bolshevik Feminist,* 82–88; Nation, *War on War,* 129–97; Prabhat Patnaik, "Lenin, Imperialism, and the First World War," *Social Scientist* 42, no. 7/8 (July–August 2014): 29–46; Vladimir Ilyich Lenin and G. Y. Zinoviev, "Socialism and War: The Attitude of the Russian Social-Democratic Labour Party Towards the War," in *Lenin Collected Works* (Peking: Foreign Languages Press, 1970), 21: 295–338.

50. Beatrice Farnsworth uses Kollontai's phrase "magnificent illusions" to describe her own romanticism of the immediate postrevolutionary period (*Aleksandra Kollontai: Socialism, Feminism, and the Bolshevik Revolution* [Stanford, CA: Stanford University Press, 1980], 108). For an overview of her disappearance from Soviet literature and "rediscovery" by Western feminists in the 1970s, see Greer, foreword to *The Autobiography of a Sexually Emancipated Communist Woman;* Gustava Zhuravskaya, "Love as an Ideology: The Reflections on 'Sexual Crisis' in Aleksandra Kollontai's Writing" (PhD diss., Central European University, Budapest, 1998); Michele Masucci, "Alexandra Kollontai's Many Lives," in *Red Love: A Reader on Alexandra Kollontai,* ed. Maria Lind, Michele Masucci, et al. (Stockholm: Sternberg Press, 2020), 26–44.

51. Kollontai, "Make Way for Winged Eros: A Letter to Working Youth," in *Selected Writings of Alexandra Kollontai,* 284.

52. Hardt, "Red Love."

53. Kollontai, "Make Way for Winged Eros," 288.

54. Kollontai, "Make Way for Winged Eros," 290; Jodi Dean, *Comrade: An Essay on Political Belonging* (New York: Verso, 2019), 61–67.

55. Alexandra Kollontai, "Who Needs War?," in *Selected Writings of Alexandra Kollontai,* 75.

56. These views can be traced to a number of her writings, most prominently, "Sexual Relations and the Class Struggle," "Communism and the Family" and "Make Way for Winged Eros: A Letter to Working Youth," all republished in *Selected Writings of Alexandra Kollontai,* 237–92. For an excellent primer on the specific evolution of these relations within the context of colonial slavery, see Hall, "Gendering Property, Racing Capital."

57. Kollontai, "Make Way for Winged Eros," 285.

58. Kollontai, "Make Way for Winged Eros," 285.

59. Alexandra Kollontai, "From the Commissariat of Social Welfare, Document no. 1247, 31 January 1918," in *Selected Writings of Alexandra Kollontai,* 140–41.

60. Alexandra Kollontai, *Communism and the Family* (Cleveland: Hera Press, 1982), 18.

61. Bryant, *Mirrors of Moscow,* 122–23.

62. For an overview of Kollontai's efforts and the debates around the women's section of the party, see Goldman, *Women, the State, and Revolution,* 59–100; Farnsworth, *Aleksandra Kollontai,* 127–211.

63. Aaron Schuster, "The Sexual Life of Communists: Reflections on Alexandra Kollontai," in *Red Love,* 303–5; Farnsworth, *Aleksandra Kollontai,* 103, 148–53; Clements, *Bolshevik Feminist,* 129–30.

64. Clements, *Bolshevik Feminist,* 129–33. Clements describes the repurposing of the orphanage. The republication of Kollontai's memoir describes the original building as an elite girls' school (*The Autobiography of a Sexually Emancipated Communist Woman,* 38).

65. Carr, *Marxism and Communism in Twentieth-Century Mexico,* 18.

66. Carr, *Marxism and Communism in Twentieth-Century Mexico,* 18.

67. Carr, *Marxism and Communism in Twentieth-Century Mexico,* 14.

68. Spenser, "Bolsheviks' Encounter with the Mexican Revolution," 92.

69. Kollontai, "El trabajo cotidiano, 28 de diciembre," in Ortiz, *Alexandra Kollontai en México,* 58.

70. Kollontai, "El trabajo cotidiano, 29 de diciembre," in Ortiz, *Alexandra Kollontai en México,* 59.

71. John Lear, *Picturing the Proletariat: Artists and Labor in Revolutionary Mexico, 1908–1940* (Austin: University of Texas Press, 2017), 69–111; Spenser, "Stanislav Pestkovsky," 42–43; Stephanie J. Smith, *The Power and Politics of Art in Postrevolutionary Mexico* (Chapel Hill: University of North Carolina Press, 2017), 22–51.

72. Mauricio Tenorio Trillo, "The Cosmopolitan Mexican Summer, 1920–1949," *Latin American Research Review* 32, no. 3 (1997): 224–42; David Craven, *Art and Revolution in Latin America 1910–1990* (New Haven, CT: Yale University Press, 2002), 9; Leonard Folgarait, *Mural Painting and Social Revolution in Mexico, 1920–1940* (Cambridge, UK: Cambridge University Press, 1998).

73. Spenser, "Stanislav Pestkovsky," 40; Spenser, *Stumbling Its Way Through Mexico,* 57; Yamanouchi Akito, "The Early Comintern in Amsterdam, New York and Mexico City," *Shien* (March 2010): 99–139. There have been many studies of radicals in Mexico City in the 1920s into the 1930s, most famously Helen Delpar, *The Enormous Vogue of Things Mexican: Cultural Relations between the United States and Mexico, 1920–1935* (Birmingham: University of Alabama Press, 1995), and Paco Ignacio Taibo II, *Los Bolsheviquis: Historia Narrativa de los Orígenes del Comunismo en México, 1919–1925* (Mexico City: J. Mortiz, 1986). See also Olcott, "'Take Off That Streetwalker's Dress,'"46.

74. Richardson, *Mexico through Russian Eyes,* 127–40; Letizia Argenteri, *Tina Modotti: Between Art and Revolution* (New Haven, CT: Yale University Press, 2003), 105–13.

75. Quoted in Akito Yamanouchi, "The Letters and Manuscripts of Sen Katayama in Mexico, 1921," *Monthly Journal of Ohara Institute for Social Research* 506 (January 2001): 4.

76. Spenser, "Stanislav Pestkovsky," 38–42.

77. This event is reconstructed in Elena Poniatowska, *Tinisima* (New York: Farrar, Strauss, & Giroux, 1996), 109.

78. Ortiz, *Alexandra Kollontai en México*, 57–92.

79. Kollontai, "El trabajo cotidiano, 28 de diciembre," in Ortiz, *Alexandra Kollontai en México*, 58; Kollontai, "Apuntes del, por así decirlo, agregado comercial (yo misma)," (undated, approximately mid-Feburary, 1927), in Ortiz, *Alexandra Kollontai en México*, 92.

80. Kollontai, "El trabajo cotidiano, 29 de diciembre," in Ortiz, *Alexandra Kollontai en México*, 59–60.

81. Esperanza Tuñón Pablos, *Mujeres que se organizan el frente único pro derechos de la mujer, 1935–1938* (Mexico City: Universidad Nacional Autónoma de México, 1992), 28.

82. Alexandra Kollontai, "On the History of the Movement of Women Workers in Russia [1905–1917]," in *Alexandra Kollontai: Selected Articles and Speeches* (New York, International Publishers, 1984), 142–52; Richard Stites, *The Women's Liberation Movement in Russia: Feminism, Nihilism, and Bolshevism, 1860–1930* (Princeton, NJ : Princeton University Press, 1991), 249–51.

83. Helen Stuhr-Rommereim and Mari Jarris, "Nikolai Chernyshevsky's *What Is to Be Done?* and the Prehistory of International Marxist Feminism," *Feminist German Studies* 36, no. 1 (Spring-Summer 2020): 166–92; Bryant, *Mirrors of Moscow*, 116–17; Kenneth D. Ackerman, *Trotsky in New York, 1917: A Radical on the Eve of Revolution* (Berkeley, CA: Counterpoint, 2016), 53–54.

84. Kollontai, "15 de enero," in Ortiz, *Alexandra Kollontai en México*, 61.

85. Kollontai, "14 de marzo," in Ortiz, *Alexandra Kollontai en México*, 94.

86. Kollontai, "17 de marzo (de una carta a Zoya Shadurskaya)," in Ortiz, *Alexandra Kollontai en México*, 95.

87. *Child welfare extension service: Hearing[s] before the Committee on Interstate and Foreign Commerce, House of Representatives, Seventieth Congress, Second Session, on H.R. 14070, to provide a child welfare extension service and for other purposes*, January 24 and 25, 1929 (Washington, DC: U.S. Government Printing Office, 1929), 269.

88. *Child welfare extension service: Hearing[s]*, 270.

89. "Bolshevik Propaganda—Wednesday, March 5, 1919—U.S. Senate, Subcommittee of the Committee on the Judiciary—Chaired by Senator Overman—Testimony of Bessie Beatty, editor of McCall's Magazine" (Washington, DC: United States Government Printing Office, 1919), 709.

90. Erica Ryan, *Red War on the Family: Sex, Gender, and Americanism in the First Red Scare* (Philadelphia: Temple University Press, 2015), 5, 184; Julian B. Carter, *The Heart of Whiteness: Normal Sexuality and Race in America, 1880–1940* (Durham, NC: Duke University Press, 2007), 75–117.

91. Ortiz, *Alexandra Kollontai en México*, 96–135.

92. Spenser, "Bolsheviks' Encounter with the Mexican Revolution," 92; Ortiz, *Alexandra Kollontai en México*, 96–140.

93. Kollontai, "Conclusiones," in Ortiz, *Alexandra Kollontai en México,* 130. Translation in source.

94. Kollontai, "10 de augusto de 1927 (de una carta a Zoya Shadurskya)," in Ortiz, *Alexandra Kollontai en México,* 143.

CHAPTER 5. HOW TO MAKE A LIVING

1. Dorothy Healey, oral history interview, "Tradition's Chains Have Bound Us" (1982), Dorothy Healey Collections, Special Collections, California State University, Long Beach, 102; Dorothy Healey, interview in *The Internationale,* dir. Peter Miller (Icarus Films, 2000); Michael Denning, "Representing Global Labor," *Social Text* 25, no. 3 (Fall 2007): 21–45.

2. Richard Walker, *The Conquest of Bread: 150 Years of Agribusiness in California* (New York: New Press, 2004), 285.

3. Kevin Starr, *Endangered Dreams: The Great Depression in California* (New York: Oxford University Press, 1996), 63; Kathryn S. Olmsted, *Right Out of California: The 1930s and the Big Business Roots of Modern Conservatism* (New York: New Press, 2015), 3.

4. Miriam Ching Yoon Louie, *Sweatshop Warriors: Immigrant Women Workers Take on the Global Factory* (Cambridge, MA: South End Press, 2001), 196–99; David M. Struthers, *The World in a City: Multiethnic Radicalism in Early Twentieth-Century Los Angeles* (Urbana: Illinois University Press, 2019), 66–80; Francisco E. Balderrama and Raymond Rodríguez, *Decade of Betrayal: Mexican Repatriation in the 1930s* (Albuquerque: University of New Mexico Press, 2006), 68.

5. Balderrama and Rodríguez, *Decade of Betrayal,* 285; Carey McWilliams, *California: The Great Exception* (Berkeley: University of California Press, 1999), 156, 158.

6. As Linda C. Majka and Theo J. Majka describe, "During the rise of farm worker unionism, government at all levels used law enforcement, injunctions, troops, braceros, immigration quotas, discriminatory laws, and relief regulations, with infrequent intervals of reforms and labor legislation" (*Farm Workers, Agribusiness, and the State* [Philadelphia: Temple University Press, 1982], ix).

7. Carlos Bulosan, *America Is in the Heart* (Seattle: University of Washington Press, 1973), 111.

8. Cletus E. Daniel, *Bitter Harvest: A History of California Farmworkers, 1870–1941* (Berkeley: University of California Press, 1981), 223–24.

9. As Zaragosa Vargas notes, "Low wages and small incomes made it harder for Mexican agricultural workers to pay union dues and to hold out through a strike" (*Labor Rights Are Civil Rights: Mexican American Workers in Twentieth-Century America* [Princeton, NJ: Princeton University Press, 2008], 115).

10. As Mike Davis notes, "Vigilantes have been to the American West what the Ku Klux Klan has been to the South: vicious and cowardly bigotry organized as a self-righteous mob" (*In Praise of Barbarians: Essays against Empire* [Chicago: Haymarket Books, 2007], 177).

11. Rosemary Feurer, "The Nutpickers' Union, 1933–34: Crossing the Boundaries of Community and Workplace," in *"We Are All Leaders": The Alternative Unionism of the Early 1930s,* ed. Staughton Lynd (Urbana: University of Illinois Press, 1996), 27–50.

12. David R. Roediger and Elizabeth D. Esch, *The Production of Difference: Race and the Management of Labor in U.S. History* (New York: Oxford University Press, 2014), 193–204; Mike Davis, "Sunshine and the Open Shop: Ford and Darwin in 1920s Los Angeles," *Antipode* 29, no. 4 (October 1997): 358.

13. "The Forty-Year War for a Free City: A History of the Open Shop in Los Angeles," *Los Angeles Times,* October 1, 1929, 2; McWilliams, *California,* 144.

14. Davis, "Sunshine and the Open Shop," 356–82.

15. Communist Party Los Angeles County (CPLAC), "Two Decades of Progress: Communist Party LA County 1919–1939," September 1939, 13; Gilmore, *Golden Gulag,* 133; Dorothy Healey, "Tradition's Chains," 84; Edward J. Escobar, *Race, Police, and the Making of a Political Identity: Mexican Americans and the Los Angeles Police Department, 1900–1945* (Berkeley: University of California Press, 1999), 83–84; Frank Donner, *Protectors of Privilege: Red Squads and Police Repression in Urban America* (Berkeley: University of California Press, 1990), 59–60.

16. John Steinbeck, *Their Blood Is Strong: A Factual Story of the Migratory Agricultural Workers in California* (San Francisco: Simon J. Lubin Foundation, 1938), 26.

17. Camille Guerin-Gonzales, *Mexican Workers and American Dreams: Immigration, Repatriation, and California Farm Labor, 1900–1939* (New Brunswick, NJ: Rutgers University Press, 1994), 45–47; Steinbeck, *Their Blood Is Strong,* 26; Laura Pulido, "Rethinking Environmental Racism: White Privilege and Urban Development in Southern California," *Annals of the Association of American Geographers* 90, no. 1 (2000): 12–40; Almaguer, *Racial Fault Lines,* 51–57.

18. U.S. Congress, *Immigration from Countries of the Western Hemisphere: Hearings,* 2nd Session (Washington, DC: U.S. Government Printing Office, 1921), 425–26.

19. Don Mitchell, *The Lie of the Land: Migrant Workers and the California Landscape* (Minneapolis: University of Minnesota Press, 1996), 17–35; McWilliams, *Factories in the Field,* 233; "California: Gentlemen Farmers," *Time,* December 16, 1940; Clarke A. Chambers, *California Farm Organizations: A Historical Study of the Grange, the Farm Bureau, and the Associated Farmers, 1929–1941* (Berkeley: University of California Press, 1952), 45.

20. Devra Weber, *Dark Sweat, White Gold: California Farm Workers, Cotton, and the New Deal* (Berkeley: University of California Press, 1996), 121; Kelly Lytle Hernández, *Migra! A History of the U.S. Border Patrol* (Berkeley: University of California Press, 2010), 26, 44, 56.

21. C.H. Garrigues, "The Spotlight," *Daily Journal,* 1934; Healey, "Tradition's Chains," 100; Mike Davis, "'What is a Vigilante Man?' White Violence in California History," in *No One Is Illegal: Fighting Violence and State Repression on the U.S.-Mexico Border,* ed. Justin Akers Chacón and Mike Davis (Chicago: Haymarket Books, 2006), 18; Peace Officers Association of the State of California, *A Peace Officer's Manual for Combating Subversive Activities,* January 20, 1935, 21–22;

American League Against War and Fascism, Los Angeles Committee, *California's Brown Book,* October 1934, 3; Isobel Walker Soule, *The Vigilantes Hide Behind the Flag* (New York: International Labor Defense, 1937).

22. Committee on Education and Labor (CEL), Violations of Free Speech and Rights of Labor, *Hearings before a Subcommittee of the Committee on Education and Labor, United Stated Senate, Seventy-Sixth Congress* (Washington, DC: United States Government Printing Office, 1940), 19527; Jess Walsh, "Laboring at the Margins: Welfare and the Regulation of Mexican Workers in Southern California," *Antipode* 31, no. 4 (1999): 398–420; Roediger and Esch, *Production of Difference,* 196; McWilliams, *Factories in the Fields,* 322; "Reveal Jobless Suffering in San Jose and 'Frisco," *Western Worker,* January 1, 1932.

23. Quoted in "Reveal Jobless Suffering in San Jose and 'Frisco."

24. Benny J. Andrés, *Power and Control in the Imperial Valley: Nature, Agribusiness, and Workers on the California Borderland, 1900-1940* (College Station: Texas A&M University Press, 2014), 127–158; González, *Mexican Consuls,* 159–196.

25. Cybelle Fox, "The Boundaries of Social Citizenship: Race, Immigration, and the American Welfare State, 1900–1950" (PhD diss., Harvard University, 2007), 142; "Mexican Workers Get Only 70 Pct. of What Others Do," *Western Worker,* November 6, 1933; McWilliams, *Factories in the Field,* 322.

26. George J. Sánchez, *Becoming Mexican American: Ethnicity, Culture, and Identity in Chicano Los Angeles, 1900–1945* (New York: Oxford University Press, 1993), 211; Ricardo Romo, *East Los Angeles: History of a Barrio* (Austin: University of Texas Press, 1992), 164; "Jail Worker for Begging Food," *Western Worker,* January 1, 1932; Louis B. Perry and Richard S. Perry, *A History of the Los Angeles Labor Movement, 1911–1941* (Berkeley: University of California Press, 1963), 238.

27. Guerin-Gonzales, *Mexican Workers and American Dreams,* 81; Cybelle Fox, "Three Worlds of Relief: Race, Immigration, and Public and Private Social Welfare Spending in American Cities, 1929," *American Journal of Sociology* 116, no. 2 (September 2010): 466–68; Abraham Hoffman, "Stimulus to Repatriation: The 1931 Federal Deportation Drive and the Los Angeles Mexican Community," *Pacific Historical Review* 42, no. 2 (May 1973): 219; Balderrama and Rodríguez, *Decade of Betrayal.*

28. "Jail Worker for Begging Food," *Western Worker,* January 1, 1932; Douglas Monroy, *Rebirth: Mexican Los Angeles from the Great Migration to the Great Depression* (Berkeley: University of California Press, 1999), 210.

29. Donald L. Zelman, "Mexican Migrants and Relief in Depression California: Grower Reaction to Public Relief Policies as They Affected Mexican Migration," *Journal of Mexican American History* 5 (1975): 1–23; Weber, *Dark Sweat, White Gold,* 127; Raymond P. Barry, ed., *A Documentary History of Migratory Farm Labor in California* (Oakland, CA: Federal Writers Project, 1938), 43–44.

30. Hamilton, *Limits of State Autonomy,* 73, 106; Cockcroft, *Mexico's Hope,* 111; Grandin, *Empire's Workshop,* 35; Jessica Kim, "Oilmen and Cactus Rustlers: Los Angeles, Mexico, and the Building of a Regional Empire, 1890–1941" (PhD diss., University of Southern California, 2012), 8.

31. Ashby, *Organized Labor and the Mexican Revolution,* 23–24.

32. Adolfo Gilly, "Chiapas and the Rebellion of the Enchanted World," in *Rural Revolt in Mexico: U.S. Intervention and the Domain of Subaltern Politics,* ed. Daniel Nugent (Durham, NC: Duke University Press, 1998), 261–333; Ashby, *Organized Labor and the Mexican Revolution,* 24–26.

33. Ed Royce, "A Scene from the Cotton Strike," *Western Worker,* October 30, 1933.

34. Healey, "Tradition's Chains," 96.

35. Weber, *Dark Sweat, White Gold,* 87–88, 94.

36. Joe Evans, "Only Communists Lead, Cotton Pickers Learn," *Western Worker,* November 20, 1933.

37. Paul S. Taylor and Clark Kerr, "Documentary History of the Strike of the Cotton Pickers in California 1933," in CEL, *Hearings,* 19994.

38. "Welfare Letter in L.A. Exposes Scabherding Role," *Western Worker,* November 20, 1933; "Cut 20,000 Mexicans Off Relief, Supplies Cotton Field Scabs," *Western Worker,* November 13, 1933; McWilliams, *Factories in the Field,* 286.

39. CEL, *Hearings,* 19530; Taylor and Kerr, "Documentary History," in *Hearings,* 19994.

40. "'Tells Why Mexican Workers Join the Hunger March," *Western Worker,* October 2, 1933.

41. Ira Katznelson, *When Affirmative Action Was White: An Untold History of Racial Inequality in Twentieth-Century America* (New York: W. W. Norton, 2005), 22; Fox, "Boundaries of Social Citizenship,"17; Daniel, *Bitter Harvest,* 261; Bruce Minton, "The Battle of Sacramento," *New Republic,* February 20, 1935, 38–40; Ed Royce, "A Scene from the Cotton Strike," *Western Worker,* October 30, 1933; Sánchez, *Becoming Mexican American,* 224; McWilliams, *Factories in the Field,* 286.

42. Anne Loftis, *Witness to the Struggle: Imagining the 1930s California Labor Movement* (Reno: University of Nevada Press, 1998), 109; Errol Wayne Stevens, *Radical LA: From Coxey's Army to the Watts Riots, 1894–1965* (Norman: University of Oklahoma Press, 2009), 189, 192, 193; Louis Bloch, *Abstract of Hearings on Unemployment Before the California State Unemployment Commission* (April and May 1932), Dorothy Healey Collections, Special Collections, California State University, Long Beach; "Pigeons Urged to Feed the Poor," *Los Angeles Times,* December 22, 1932.

43. Frances Fox Piven and Richard A. Cloward, *Poor People's Movements: Why They Succeed, How They Fail* (New York: Vintage, 1979), 42; Irving Bernstein, *The Lean Years: A History of the American Worker, 1920–1933* (Baltimore: Penguin, 1966), 240, 287; Katznelson, *When Affirmative Action Was White,* 38; Theodore Draper, "Notes on Unemployment," unpublished, Theodore Draper research files, 1919–70, Box 17, Folder 16, Manuscript, Archives, and Rare Book Library, Emory University.

44. Karl Marx and Friedrich Engels, *Collected Works* (New York: International Publishers, 1975), 3:284.

45. Bloch, *Abstract of Hearings,* 3; Meridel Le Sueur, "Women on the Breadlines," in Albert Fried, ed., *Communism in America: A History in Documents* (New York: Columbia University Press, 1997), 196; Moritz Hallgren, "Mobilizing the Poor," in Fried, *Communism in America,* 132.

46. Piven and Cloward, *Poor People's Movements*, 76.

47. Wild, *Street Meeting*, 183; "L.A. Jobless to Fight Relief Cut with Hunger March Oct 2," *Western Worker*, September 11, 1933; "Evicted Family Put Back in the House by Jobless," *Western Worker*, September 18, 1933; "Relief Union in Fight on Eviction of Negro Families," *Western Worker*, September 25, 1933; "All Out for LA County Hunger March Oct. 2," *Western Worker*, October 2, 1933; "LA Jobless Battle Cops at Welfare Office," *Western Worker*, October 23, 1933; Jennie Grey, "12,000 in Militant March Force 10% L.A. Relief Raise," *Western Worker*, November 20, 1933; "Public Works Mean Full Time Work for 45c Per Hr," *Western Worker*, November 27, 1933.

48. "All Out for LA County Hunger March Oct. 2"; Mike Davis, "The Necessary Eloquence of Protest," *The Nation*, March 17, 2009; Harvey Klehr, *The Heyday of American Communism: The Depression Decade* (New York: Basic Books, 1984), 49–68; Healey, "Tradition's Chains," 86; Sadie Amter, "Episodes at Cumberland: Reflections by Sadie Amter," *Daily Worker*, March 23, 1958; Len De Caux, *Labor Radical: From the Wobblies to CIO, A Personal History* (Boston: Beacon, 1970), 162–63.

49. Vivian McGurkin Raineri, *The Red Angel: The Life and Times of Elaine Black Yoneda, 1906–1988* (New York: International Publishers, 1991), 23; Scott Allen McClellan, "Policing the Red Scare: The Los Angeles Police Department's Red Squad and the Repression of Labor Activism in Los Angeles" (PhD diss., University of California, Irvine, 2011), 173; Davis, "The Necessary Eloquence of Protest," 58; Grace M. Burnham, *Unemployment* (New York: International Publishers, 1932), 34.

50. Raineri, *The Red Angel*, 23; Escobar, *Race, Police, and the Making of a Political Identity*, 81; Wild, *Street Meeting*, 191; "Brains Wanted," *Los Angeles Record*, February 28, 1930.

51. Healey, "Tradition's Chains," 48, 73, 72; Wild, *Street Meeting*, 181; Daniel J. Leab, "'United We Eat': The Creation and Organization of the Unemployed Councils in 1930," *Labor History* 8, no. 3 (1967): 300–15; Bloch, *Abstract of Hearings*, 71.

52. Wild, *Street Meeting*, 193; Karl Yoneda, *Ganbatte: Sixty-Year Struggle of a Kibei Worker* (Los Angeles: Asian American Studies Center UCLA, 1983), 21; Dennis McLellan, "Dorothy Healey," 91; "Lifelong Communist Fought for Workers," *Los Angeles Times*, August 8, 2006; Healey, "Tradition's Chains," 48–49; Bernstein, *The Lean Years*, 434.

53. Healey, "Tradition's Chains," 49.

54. Len Meyers and Chris Knox, "Organizing the Unemployed in the Great Depression: Fighting for Unity," *Workers Vanguard* 73, no. 18 (July 1975): 6–7; Shana Bernstein, *Bridges of Reform: Interracial Civil Rights Activism in Twentieth-Century Los Angeles* (New York: Oxford University Press, 2011), 43; Douglas Monroy, "Anarquismo y Comunismo: Mexican Radicalism and the Communist Party in Los Angeles During the 1930s," *Labor History* 24 (Winter 1983): 42.

55. Zaragosa Vargas, "Tejana Radical: Emma Tenayuca and the San Antonio Labor Movement during the Great Depression," *Pacific Historical Review* 66, no. 4 (Nov. 1997): 553–80; Irving Kreitzberg, "For a Decisive Turn in Our Mexican Work

and the Creation of a Mexican Department to Concentrate on the South-West," *Western Worker,* July 1, 1932; George H. Shoaf, "Jose Arispe—Story of Worker's Broken Home," *Western Worker,* May 15, 1932; "Red Suspect Under Arrest," *Los Angeles Times,* November 17, 1929.

56. Marx, *Capital,* 786, 789–90; William A. Sundstrom, "Last Hired, First Fired? Unemployment and Urban Black Workers during the Great Depression," *Journal of Economic History* 52, no. 2 (June 1992): 415–29; Bernstein, *The Lean Years,* 287; Theodore Draper, "Notes on Unemployment," 15.

57. Robin D. G. Kelley, *Hammer and Hoe: Alabama Communists during the Great Depression* (Chapel Hill: University of North Carolina Press, 1990).

58. Scott Kurashige, *The Shifting Grounds of Race: Black and Japanese Americans in the Making of Multiethnic Los Angeles* (Princeton, NJ: Princeton University Press, 2008), 81–82; Josh Sides, *LA City Limits: African American Los Angeles from the Great Depression to the Present* (Berkeley: University of California Press, 2003), 32; Wild, *Street Meeting,* 194; Pettis Perry, *White Chauvinism and the Struggle for Peace* (New York: New Century Publishers, 1952), 18.

59. "Discrimination Against Negroes on LA Jobs," *Western Worker,* December 11, 1933; "Scottsboro Mother, Moore and Carter Tour So. Ca," *Western Worker,* September 25, 1933; Kurashige, *Shifting Grounds of Race,* 78; Fowler, *Japanese and Chinese Immigrant Activists,* 67; Bernstein, *Bridges of Reform,* 40; Fried, *Communism in America,* 98.

60. Miscellaneous clippings, Box 1, Folder 2, Karl Yoneda Papers, Collection 1592, Special Collections, University of California, Los Angeles.

61. Otto Huiswoud, "The Effects of Unemployment on the Negro Masses in the USA," *Inspector,* April 2, 1931, 359.

62. George Padmore, "The Fight for Bread," *Negro Worker* 3, nos. 6–7 (June–July 1933): 3–4.

63. Angelo Herndon, *Let Me Live* (Ann Arbor: University of Michigan Press, 2007), 316.

CHAPTER 6. HOW TO MAKE A DRESS

1. Diana Briggs, "Glamour Is Keynote of Artists, Models Ball," *Chicago Defender,* November 1, 1941, 8.

2. "Models Ball Theme To Be Pan-America," *Chicago Defender,* September 6, 1941, 7; "Beauty Reigns at Artists and Models 1941 Ball," *Chicago Defender,* November 1, 1941, 12; Briggs, "Glamour Is Keynote," 8.

3. Lillian Ross, "Playwright," *New Yorker,* May 9, 1959; Oral history interview with Elizabeth Catlett by Dr. Clifton Johnson, 1983, Amistad Research Center, Tulane University, Tape 2, Side 1 (hereafter Catlett, Amistad). "Howling mobs" comes from Hansberry's description of the violent racists who encircled her home in Chicago, throwing "missiles" at her eight-year-old head, as her father fought against racist covenants in Washington. See Lorraine Hansberry, *To Be Young,*

Gifted and Black, adapted by Robert Nemiroff (New York: Vintage, 1996), 20–21. For a discussion of Carl Hansberry's hope for safety in Mexico and his later participation in the 1945 Inter-American Conference on Problems of War and Peace in Mexico, see Ortiz, *An African American and Latinx History of the United States,* 143–49.

4. James Oles, *South of the Border: Mexico in the American Imagination: 1914–1947* (Washington, DC: Smithsonian Institution Press, 1993), 48–59; Delpar, *The Enormous Vogue of Things Mexican,* 205.

5. Bill Mullen, *Popular Fronts: Chicago and African-American Cultural Politics, 1935–46* (Chicago: University of Illinois Press, 1999), 91–93; Catlett, Amistad, Tape 2, Side 1.

6. Priscilla Peña Ovalle describes the Portuguese-Brazilian Carmen Miranda's arrival in the United States in the 1940s as the "Good Neighbor policy's premier import" (*Dance and the Hollywood Latina: Race, Sex, and Stardom* [New Brunswick, NJ: Rutgers University Press, 2010], 20, 50–55). Catlett, Amistad, Tape 2, Side 1; Briggs, "Glamour Is Keynote"; Tom Nolan, *Three Chords for Beauty's Sake: The Life of Artie Shaw* (New York: W. W. Norton, 2010), 140.

7. Briggs, "Glamour is Keynote"; Catlett, Amistad, Tape 2, Side 1.

8. As Jodi Byrd has described, US imperialism has consistently found cultural cover through idealized representations of Indigeneity. Empire, in her words, has been "transited" across contexts through such representations. Depicting countries and subjects under potential imperial rule as "Indian" symbolically reasserts the foundational US settler mythology and replicates cultural justifications for its rule. Just as the Philippines before, and Haiti under US occupation, so too had Mexico long been represented by these transits in the US spatial imaginary (Byrd, *Transit of Empire,* 1–38).

9. Briggs, "Glamour is Keynote."

10. Uwe Lübken, "'Americans All': The United States, the Nazi Menace, and the Construction of a Pan-American Identity," *Amerikastudien/American Studies* 48, no. 3 (2003): 389–409; Oles, *South of the Border,* 79; Deborah Poole, "An Image of 'Our Indian': Type Photographs and Racial Sentiments in Oaxaca, 1920–1940," *Hispanic American Historical Review* 84, no. 1 (2004): 65. The Pan-American Union became the headquarters of the Organization of the American States (OAS). For a discussion of the Cold War use of culture in the production of Pan-American culture, see Claire F. Fox, *Making Art Panamerican: Cultural Policy and the Cold War* (Minneapolis: University of Minnesota Press, 2013). The unevenly subversive, exploitative, and reflective consumption of Latin American cultures by US "consumer citizens," particularly in Black communities, is explored in depth in Micol Seigel, *Uneven Encounters: Making Race and Nation in Brazil and the United States* (Durham, NC: Duke University Press, 2009).

11. Gigi Peterson names this alliance the "Grassroots Good Neighbor Policy." See "Grassroots Good Neighbors: Connections between Mexican and United States Labor and Civil Rights Activists, 1936–1945" (PhD diss., University of Washington, 1998).

12. Catlett was reticent in her public performance, perhaps an enactment of what Darlene Clark Hine described as "dissemblance," the appearance of openness that shields Black women, particularly in public life, from scrutiny (*Hine Sight: Black Women and the Reconstruction of American History* [Brooklyn: Carlson Publishing, 1994], 37). Mary Helen Washington's *The Other Blacklist: The African American Literary and Cultural Left of the 1950s* (New York: Columbia University Press, 2014) devotes most of the epilogue to unanswered questions about Elizabeth Catlett's politics.

13. Melanie Anne Herzog, "Elizabeth Catlett (1915–2012)," *American Art* 26, no. 3 (Fall 2012): 105–9; Diana Anhalt, *A Gathering of Fugitives: American Political Expatriates in Mexico 1948–1965* (Santa Maria, CA: Archer Books, 2001). The phrase "Cold War Exiles" comes from Rebecca Schreiber, *Cold War Exiles in Mexico: US Dissidents and the Culture of Critical Resistance* (Minneapolis: University of Minnesota Press, 2008).

14. Harry Haywood, *Black Bolshevik: Autobiography of an Afro-American Communist* (Chicago: Liberator Press, 1978), 624. Catlett and her son, David Mora, spoke about Harry Haywood's visits with me at Catlett's home in Cuernavaca, Mexico, on September 30, 2011. Haywood's relationship to her is mentioned in Komozi Woodard, "Citizen Malcolm X Blueprint for Black Liberation: Coming of Age with Rod Bush on Race, Class and Citizenship in the Bandung Era," in *Rod Bush: Lessons from a Radical Black Scholar on Liberation, Love, and Justice,* ed. Melanie E. L. Bush, et al. (Belmont, MA: Ahead, 2019), 172.

15. Schreiber, *Cold War Exiles,* 35–44, offers a thorough overview of Catlett's time in Mexico and poses questions about gaps in her life in the historiography. Marvin X is mentioned in Horne, *Black and Brown,* 190. Quote is from Raquel Tibol, "The Work of Elizabeth Catlett," *Los Universitarios, Magazine of National University of Mexico,* November 1975.

16. Elizabeth Catlett Mora is listed as "a prominent American communist who lived in Mexico City in the early 1960s" according to John R. Tunheim, "Final Report of the Kennedy Assassination Records Review Board" (Washington, DC: U.S. Government Printing Office, 1998), 111.

17. Washington's *The Other Blacklist* briefly discusses Catlett in relation to White but concludes the book with a bold discussion of the need to rebuff the Cold War's silencing of history and restore Catlett's connections to the Left. In my interview with Dr. Gwendolyn Midlo Hall, Harry Haywood's former wife, she confirmed Catlett's quite central presence in Left circles, especially in coordinating communities of political exiles like Haywood who were escaping Cold War state repression in the United States alongside political exiles from other countries, notably those fleeing Spanish fascism. Phone interview with Dr. Gwendolyn Midlo Hall, Guanajuato, Mexico, December 16, 2017.

18. Tiffany Ruby Patterson-Myers, "Forging Freedoms: Internationalization of African American History," The Future of the African American Past conference, sponsored by the American Historical Association, the National Museum of African American History, and the National Endowment for the Humanities, Washington, DC, May 19–21, 2016.

19. José Clemente Orozco, *José Clemente Orozco: An Autobiography* (Mineola, NY: Dover Publications, 1962), 20, 21, 28.

20. Carlos Cortez, ed., *Viva Posada!* (Chicago: Charles Kerr, 2002), passim.

21. Susan Valerie Richards, "Imagining the Political: El Taller de Gráfica Popular in Mexico, 1937–1949" (PhD dis. University of New Mexico, 2001), 4.

22. Orozco, *José Clemente Orozco,* 8.

23. Quoted in Rick A. López, "The Noche Mexicana and the Exhibition of Popular Arts: Two Ways of Exalting Indianness," in *The Eagle and the Virgin: Nation and Cultural Revolution in Mexico, 1920–1940,* ed. Mary Kay Vaughn and Steven E. Lewis (Durham, NC: Duke University Press, 2006), 44.

24. Diego Rivera, "The Revolutionary Spirit in Modern Art," *The Modern Quarterly* 4, no. 3 (Autumn 1932): 51–57.

25. David Craven, *Art and Revolution in Latin America 1910–1990* (New Haven, CT: Yale University Press, 2002), 9; Leonard Folgarait, *Mural Painting and Social Revolution in Mexico, 1920–1940* (Cambridge, UK: Cambridge University Press, 1998).

26. Lizzetta LeFalle-Collins and Shifra M. Goldman, *In the Spirit of Resistance: African-American Modernists and the Mexican Muralist School* (New York: American Federation of Arts, 1996), 9; Shifra M. Goldman, "Six Women Artists of Mexico," *Women's Art Journal* 3, no. 2 (Autumn 1982–Winter 1983): 2.

27. Shifra Goldman, "Resistance and Identity: Street Murals of Occupied Aztlan," *Latin American Literary Review* 5, no. 10 (1977): 124.

28. Charles White, "Path of a Negro Artist," *Masses and Mainstream* 8 (1955): 38.

29. Anthony W. Lee, *Painting on the Left: Diego Rivera, Radical Politics, and San Francisco's Public Murals* (Berkeley: University of California Press, 1999); Peter Linebaugh, *The Magna Carta Manifesto: Liberties and Commons for All* (Berkeley: University of California Press, 2008), 256–57.

30. John Franklin White, ed., *Art in Action: American Art Centers and the New Deal* (Metuchen, NJ: Scarecrow Press, 1987), 160.

31. Stacy I. Morgan, *Rethinking Social Realism: African American Art and Literature, 1930–1953* (Athens: University of Georgia Press, 2004), 51; Andrea D. Barnwell, *Charles White* (San Francisco: Pomegranate, 2002), 26; White, "Path of a Negro Artist," 38; David and Cecile Shapiro, "The Artists' Union in America," in *The Other America: Art and the Labour Movement in the United States,* ed. Philip S. Foner and Reinhard Schultz (London: Journeyman Press, 1985), 93–96.

32. Shifra M. Goldman, *Dimensions of the Americas: Art and Social Change in Latin America and the United States* (Chicago: University of Chicago Press, 1995), 286.

33. Thalia Gouma-Peterson, "Elizabeth Catlett: The Power of Human Feeling and of Art," *Woman's Art Journal* 4, no. 1 (Spring-Summer 1983): 49.

34. Melanie Ann Herzog, *Elizabeth Catlett: An American Artist in Mexico* (Seattle: University of Washington Press, 2000), 53.

35. Catlett, Amistad, Tape 1, Side 1; Oral history interview with Elizabeth Catlett conducted by Camille O. Cosby, 2002, National Visionary Leadership

Project, American Folklife Center, Library of Congress (hereafter, Catlett, National Visionary).]

36. Samella Lewis, *The Art of Elizabeth Catlett* (Los Angeles: Museum of African American Art and Handcraft Studios, 1984), 10.

37. Catlett, Amistad, Tape 1, Side 1; Catlett, National Visionary; Lisa E. Farrington, *Creating Their Own Image: The History of African-American Women Artists* (New York: Oxford University Press, 2005), 119.

38. Catlett, Amistad, Tape 1, Side 1; Lewis, *The Art of Elizabeth Catlett,* 10; Cynthia Taylor, *A. Philip Randolph: The Religious Journey of an African American Labor Leader* (New York: New York University Press, 2006), 160.

39. Quoted in Walter B. Weare, *Black Business in the New South: A Social History of the NC Mutual Life Insurance Company* (Durham, NC: Duke University Press, 1993), 4. Also see pp. 262–64 for discussion of syndicate behavior during the Depression.

40. Catlett, Amistad, Tape 1, side 1; Lewis, *The Art of Elizabeth Catlett,* 12–15.

41. Catlett, Amistad, Tape 2, Side 1; Farrington, *Creating Their Own Image,* 120.

42. Catlett, Amistad, Tape 2, Side 1.

43. Joe Bacon, "Catlett: Just This Side of Formidable," *New Orleans,* February 1984, 42–43.

44. Catlett, Amistad, Tape 2, Side 1; Tape 2, Side 2.

45. Farrington, *Creating Their Own Image,* 120; Catlett Oral History, Tape 2, Side 2.

46. Lewis, *The Art of Elizabeth Catlett;* Catlett, Amistad, Tape 2, Side 2.

47. Lewis, *The Art of Elizabeth Catlett;* Catlett, Amistad, Tape 2, Side 2.

48. Oral history interview with Willie Birch, by author over phone, New Orleans, LA, February 19, 2020.

49. Quote from Michelle Bentley, *Weapons of Mass Destruction and US Foreign Policy: The Strategic Use of a Concept* (New York: Routledge, 2014), 30. A replica of *Guernica* still hangs in the chamber of the UN Security Council. In 2003, when Colin Powell presented the authorization for the war on terror, falsely arguing that Iraq had weapons of mass destruction, the *Guernica* replica was covered with a blue tarp. This move, a UN spokesman said, was meant to "avert a diplomatic incident." Magie Farley, "'Guernica' Cover-Up Raises Suspicions," *Los Angeles Times,* February 6, 2003.

50. Quoted in Herzog, *Elizabeth Catlett,* 163.

51. Herzog, *Elizabeth Catlett,* 163; Mullen, *Popular Fronts,* 85–90; quote from 86.

52. Randi Storch, *Red Chicago: American Communism at Its Grassroots, 1928–35* (Chicago: University of Illinois Press, 2008), 50–52; Morgan, *Rethinking Social Realism,* 17; Erik S. McDuffie, *Sojourning for Freedom: Black Women, American Communism, and the Making of Black Left Feminism* (Durham, NC: Duke University Press, 2011), 202; Elizabeth R. Schroeder, "The Chicago Black Renaissance: Exercises in Aesthetic Ideology and Cultural Geography in Bronzeville, 1932–1945" (PhD diss., Saint Louis University, 2008), 138.

53. Lizzetta LeFalle-Collins, "The Mexican Connection: The New Negro and Border Crossings," *American Visions* 11, no. 6 (December-January 1996): 20; LeFalle-Collins and Goldman, *In the Spirit of Resistance,* 9.

54. Mullen, *Popular Fronts,* 84–93; Haywood, *Black Bolshevik,* 496.

55. Margaret Goss Burroughs, "Chicago's South Side Community Art Center: A Personal Recollection," in *Art in Action: American Art Centers and the New Deal,* ed. John Franklin White (Metuchen, NJ: Scarecrow Press, 1987), 132; White, "Path of a Negro Artist," 37; Robert Bone and Richard A. Courage, *The Muse in Bronzeville: African American Creative Expression in Chicago, 1932–1950* (New Brunswick, NJ: Rutgers University Press, 2011), 148–49; Schroeder, "The Chicago Black Renaissance," 120; Mullen, *Popular Fronts,* 77–82.

56. Mullen, *Popular Fronts,* 86.

57. Burroughs, "Chicago's South Side Community Art Center," 132.

58. White, "Path of a Negro Artist," 36–37.

59. Barnwell, *Charles White,* 16; Mullen, *Popular Fronts,* 79.

60. White, "Path of a Negro Artist," 38.

61. Lewis, *The Art of Elizabeth Catlett,* 159.

62. Quoted in Loa Maie Foushee, "North Carolina's Community Art Centers," in White, *Art in America,* 160.

63. Rita Coburn Whack, *Curators of Culture* (Chicago: WYCC-TV, 2005).

64. Herzog, *Elizabeth Catlett,* 28.

65. LeFalle-Collins, "The Mexican Connection," 20.

66. Melanie Herzog, "The Education of Sculptress Elizabeth Catlett," *The Journal of Blacks in Higher Education* 25 (Autumn, 1999): 77; Lynn Norment, "Elizabeth Catlett: Legendary Artist is Still Creating and Living Life on Her Own Terms," *Ebony,* March 2006, 100–104; Herzog, *Elizabeth Catlett,* 24; Mullen, *Popular Fronts,* 93.

67. Quoted in Mullen, *Popular Fronts,* 86.

68. Catlett, Amistad, Tape 1, Side 2.

69. Catlett, Amistad, Tape 2, Side 2; Barnwell, *Charles White,* 30.

70. Morgan, *Rethinking Social Realism,* 23; McDuffie, *Sojourning for Freedom,* 77, 150; Gerald Horne, *Race Woman: The Lives of Shirley Graham Du Bois* (New York: New York University Press, 2002), 110.

71. Schreiber, *Cold War Exiles in Mexico,* 36; Farrington, *Creating Their Own Image,* 103–4; Oral history with Charles Alston, September 28, 1965, Archives of American Art, Smithsonian Institution.

72. Washington, *The Other Blacklist,* 85; Dayo F. Gore, *Radicalism at the Crossroads: African American Women Activists in the Cold War* (New York: New York University Press, 2012), 137; Paul C. Mishler, *Raising Reds: The Young Pioneers, Radical Summer Camps, and Communist Political Culture in the United States* (New York: Columbia University Press, 1999); Catlett, Amistad, Tape 2, Side 2.

73. National Negro Congress to W. E. B. Du Bois, May 16, 1946; W. E. B. Du Bois to National Negro Congress, May 20, 1946; National Negro Congress to W. E. B. Du Bois, May 25, 1946; W. E. B. Du Bois to National Negro Congress, May

27, 1946. All in W. E. B. Du Bois Papers, Special Collections and University Archives, University of Massachusetts Amherst Libraries (hereafter Du Bois papers).

74. Elizabeth Catlett, "Negro Artists," *New Masses* 59 (April 30, 1946): 27–28.

75. Marvin E. Gettleman, "Defending Left Pedagogy: U.S. Communist Schools Fight Back against the SACB (Subversive Activities Control Board) . . . and Lose (1953–1957)," *Convergence* 41, no. 2–3 (2008): 194.

76. Denning, *The Cultural Front*, 69.

77. Marvin E. Gettleman, "'No Varsity Teams': New York's Jefferson School of Social Science, 1943–1956," *Science and Society* 66, no. 3 (2002): 340.

78. Ramona Lowe, "Harlem's Carver School Draws Capacity Classrooms," *Chicago Defender,* February 5, 1944, 18.

79. Gary Kremer, *George Washington Carver: In His Own Words* (Columbia: University of Missouri Press, 1991), 102–26.

80. Allan Bérubé, "No Race-Baiting, Red-Baiting, or Queer-Baiting! The Marine Cooks and Stewards Union from the Depression to the Cold War," in *My Desire for History: Essays in Gay, Community, and Labor History,* ed. John D'Emilio and Estelle B. Freedman (Durham, NC: University of North Carolina Press, 2011), 294–320.

81. Gouma-Peterson, "Elizabeth Catlett," 50; M. Moran Weston, "Labor Forum," *New York Amsterdam News,* February 10, 1945; Constance Curtis, "George Washington Carver School Has Classes from Sewing to High Science," *New York Amsterdam News,* June 1, 1946.

82. Erik S. Gellman, *Death Blow to Jim Crow: The National Negro Congress and the Rise of Militant Civil Rights* (Chapel Hill: University of North Carolina Press, 2012), 167.

83. Gore, *Radicalism at the Crossroads,* 34–38; Brian Dollinar, *The Black Cultural Front: Black Writers and Artists of the Depression Generation* (Jackson: University Press of Mississippi, 2012); McDuffie, *Sojourning for Freedom;* Keith Gilyard, *Louise Thompson Patterson: A Life of Struggle for Justice* (Durham, NC: Duke University Press, 2017); Cheryl Higashida, *Black Internationalist Feminism: Women Writers of the Black Left, 1945–1995* (Urbana: University of Illinois, 2011).

84. Gore, *Radicalism at the Crossroads,* 5. The concept of intersectionality was most famously articulated by the Combahee River Collective. See Combahee River Collective, "Combahee River Collective Statement" (1977) in Keeanga-Yamahtta Taylor, ed., *How We Get Free: Black Feminism and the Combahee River Collective* (Chicago: Haymarket Books, 2017).

85. Van Gosse, "Locating the Black Intellectual: An Interview with Harold Cruse," *Radical History Review* 71 (1998): 107.

86. See Ellen Schrecker, *No Ivory Tower: McCarthyism and the Universities* (New York: Oxford University Press, 1986), 42–50.

87. Quoted in Mark Starr, "Call for the Organization of Citizens Committee to Defend Free Public Education," TAM19 Mark Starr, Box 13, Intellectual Freedom.

88. Lowe, "Harlem's Carver School Draws Capacity Classrooms."

89. Gouma-Peterson, "Elizabeth Catlett," 50; Weston, "Labor Forum."

90. Earl Conrad, "A Lady Laughs at Fate," *Chicago Defender,* January 5, 1946.

91. Gouma-Peterson, "Elizabeth Catlett," 50; Weston, "Labor Forum"; Constance Curtis, "George Washington Carver School Has Classes."

92. Catlett, Amistad, Tape 2, Side 2.

93. Gouma-Peterson, "Elizabeth Catlett," 50.

94. M. T. Anderson, *Symphony for the City of the Dead: Dmitri Shostakovich and the Siege of Leningrad* (Somerville, MA: Candlewick Press, 2015), 335.

95. Gouma-Peterson, "Elizabeth Catlett," 50.

96. Gouma-Peterson, "Elizabeth Catlett."

97. Joan Brunskill, "Sculptor Emphasizes Dignity," *Sun News* (Myrtle Beach, SC), March 25, 1996.

98. Valerie Gladstone, "Strong Enough to Keep on Till She Got Her Due," *New York Times,* April 7, 2002.

99. Curtia James, "Elizabeth Catlett: Pulling Against the Grain," *American Visions* (February-March 1994): 29–35.

100. Kendra Story, "Elizabeth Catlett: A Legend of Her Craft," *Upscale,* December/January 1999, 84.

101. "Elizabeth Catlett, Sculptor and Printmaker," *Current Biography* 59, no. 5 (May 1998): 7.

102. Lowe, "Harlem's Carver School Draws Capacity Classrooms."

103. Lewis, *Elizabeth Catlett,* 37.

104. James Smethurst, "Remembering Nat Turner: Black Artists, Radical History, and Radical Historiography, 1930–55," in *Lineages of the Literary Left: Essays in Honor of Alan M. Wald,* ed. Howard Brick, Robbie Lieberman, and Paula Rabinowitz (Ann Arbor: Michigan Publishing, University of Michigan Library, 2015).

105. Claudia Jones, "An End to the Neglect of the Problems of the Negro Woman!" in *Words of Fire: An Anthology of African-American Feminist Thought,* ed. Beverly Guy-Sheftall (New York: New Press, 1995), 108–123; Gore, *Radicalism at the Crossroads,* 101.

106. Marvel Cooke and Ella Baker, "The Bronx Slave Market," *The Crisis,* November 1935.

107. Interview with Barbara Winslow, by phone, Brooklyn, NY, May 22, 2020.

108. Herzog, *Elizabeth Catlett.* 39; Catlett, Amistad, Tape 2, Side 1.

109. Cooke and Baker, "The Bronx Slave Market."

110. Herzog, *Elizabeth Catlett,* 39.

111. Peter Stallybrass, "Marx's Coat," in *Border Fetishisms: Material Objects in Unstable Spaces,* ed. Patricia Spyer (New York: Routledge, 1998), 183–207, see 193.

112. Esther Cooper Jackson, "The Negro Woman Domestic Worker in Relation to Trade Unionism," MA thesis, Fisk University, 1940.

113. W. E. B. Du Bois, *Darkwater* (Mineola, NY: Dover Publications, 1999), 115.

114. Anna Indych-López, *Muralism without Walls: Rivera, Orozco, and Siquei-ros in the United States, 1927–1940* (Pittsburgh: University of Pittsburgh Press, 2009), 6–7.

115. Oles, *South of the Border,* 137.

116. Desmond Rochfort, *Mexican Muralists: Orozco, Rivera, Siqueiros* (San Francisco: Chronicle Books, 1993), 145.

117. Schrieber, *Cold War Exiles in Mexico,* 34.

118. Renato González Mello and Diane Miliotes, *José Clemente Orozco in the United States, 1927–1934* (New York: W. W. Norton, 2002), 85–87.

119. Helen Langa, *Radical Art: Printmaking and the Left in 1930s New York* (Berkeley: University of California Press, 2004), 151–60; Helen Langa, "Two Anti-lynching Art Exhibitions: Politicized Viewpoints, Racial Perspectives, Gendered Constraints," *Journal of Contemporary African Art* (Fall 2006): 96–115; Margaret Rose Vendryes, "Hanging on Their Walls: An Art Commentary on Lynching, the Forgotten 1935 Art Exhibition," in *Race Consciousness: African-American Studies for the New Century,* ed. Judith Jackson Fossett and Jeffrey A. Tucker (New York: New York University Press, 1997): 153–76.

120. James Oles, "Noguchi in Mexico: International Themes for a Working-Class Market," *American Art* 15, no. 2 (2001): 10–33; Martha Kearns, "Elizabeth Catlett: The Spirit of Form," *Sculpture,* March 1999; Schrieber, *Cold War Exiles in Mexico,* 36–37; Morgan, *Rethinking Social Realism,* 88–89; Stephanie Mayer Heydt, *Rising Up: Hale Woodruff's Murals at Talladega College* (Seattle: University of Washington Press, 2012).

121. Mary Theresa Avila, "Chronicles of Revolution and Nation: El Taller de Gráfica Popular's 'Estampas de la Revolución Mexicana' (1947)" (PhD diss., University of New Mexico, 2013), 29.

122. Lowery Stokes Sims, "Elizabeth Catlett: A Life in Art and Politics," *American Visions* 13, no. 2 (April-May 1998): 20.

123. Lewis, *The Art of Elizabeth Catlett,* 21.

124. Herzog, *Elizabeth Catlett,* 59.

125. Sandhya Shukla and Heidi Tinsman, eds., *Imagining Our Americas: Toward a Transnational Frame* (Durham, NC: Duke University Press, 2007), 294.

126. McLynn, *Villa and Zapata,* 2.

127. Gilly, "Chiapas and the Rebellion of the Enchanted World," 277.

128. McLynn, *Villa and Zapata,* 8.

129. See Evelyn Hu-DeHart, *Yaqui Resistance and Survival: The Struggle for Land and Autonomy, 1821–1910* (Madison: University of Wisconsin Pres, 2016).

130. Batalla, *México Profundo,* 41; María Josefina Saldaña-Portillo, *The Revolutionary Imagination in the Americas and the Age of Development* (Durham: Duke University Press, 207), 205–13.

131. Angela Y. Davis, "Lectures on Liberation," in Frederick Douglass, *Frederick Douglass, Narrative of the Life of Frederick Douglass, an American Slave, Written by Himself,* ed. Angela Y. Davis (San Francisco: City Lights, 2009), 1–115.

132. Catlett, *National Visionary*. Zadkine was also a teacher to Manuel Felguérez, a Mexican artist who had studied with him in Paris at the Académie de la Grande Chaumière. See Natalie Kitroeff, "Manuel Felguérez, Mexican Abstract Artist, Is Dead at 91," *New York Times,* June 17, 2020.

133. Valerie Gladstone, "Elizabeth Catlett: Role Modeler," *ARTnews,* January 1998.

CONCLUSION. HOW TO MAKE HISTORY

Epigraphs: "The International," in *IWW Songs to Fan the Flames of Discontent: The Little Red Song Book, International Edition* (Ypsilanti, MI: Industrial Workers of the World, 1995), 2; Ricardo Flores Magón, "The Intervention and the Prisoners of Texas," *Regeneración,* May 31, 1914 (reprinted in *Dreams of Freedom,* 214–19); Du Bois, *Black Reconstruction in America,* 728.

1. There are several accounts of this press. See Herzog, *Elizabeth Catlett;* Helga Prignitz-Poda, *TGP, ein Grafiker-Kollektiv in Mexico von 1937–1977* (Berlin: Verlag Richard Seitz & Co., 1981); Gina Costa, *Para la Gente: Art, Politics and Cultural Identity of the Taller de Gráfica Popular* (Notre Dame, IN: Snite Museum of Art, 2009), 12.

2. G. Courbet, Eugène Pottier, et al., "Manifesto of the Paris Federation of Artists," April 1871, trans. Jeff Skinner, available through *Red Wedge,* accessed on December 23, 2020, http://www.redwedgemagazine.com/online-issue/manifesto-federation-artist-commune.

3. Observation by Benoît Malon, translated, quoted, and published in Kristin Ross, *Communal Luxury: The Political Imaginary of the Paris Commune* (London: Verso, 2015), 33. Thirty thousand is the figure given by David Harvey, *Paris, Capital of Modernity* (New York: Routledge, 2006), 305.

4. Ross, *Communal Luxury.*

5. Denning, "Representing Global Labor"; V. I. Lenin, "Eugène Pottier: The 25th Anniversary of His Death," *Pravda,* January 3, 1913; Kenyon Zimmer, *Immigrants Against the State: Yiddish and Italian Anarchism in America* (Urbana: University of Chicago Press, 2015), 49–87; Glenda Sluga and Patricia Clavin, "Rethinking the History of Internationalism," in *Internationalisms: A Twentieth-Century History,* ed. Glenda Sluga and Patricia Clavin (Cambridge, UK: Cambridge University Press, 2017), 3–13.

6. Melvyn Dubofsky, *We Shall Be All: A History of the Industrial Workers of the World* (Chicago: Quadrangle Books, 1969); Jessica Mitford, *A Fine Old Conflict* (New York: Vintage, 1978); Frantz Fanon, *The Wretched of the Earth,* trans. Richard Philcox (New York: Grove Press, 2004); Joel Gardner, *Tradition's Chains Have Bound Us: Dorothy Healey,* University of California, Los Angeles Oral History Program, 1982.

Healey wanted to title her ultimate memoir *Tradition's Chains Have Bound Us.* "If I were to write a book, I'd make the title of the book . . . a phrase out of the

Communist song 'The International.' . . . The phrase goes, 'No more tradition's chains shall bind us.' Well, I would make the title of the book, 'Tradition's Chains Have Bound Us,' because my argument would be that just as . . . capitalism operates through the false consciousness that it gives the majority of people who aren't able to perceive the reality of their own lives . . . so the same thing happens with Marxists. . . . They, too, substitute a false consciousness for a real consciousness. . . . A real revolutionary party [must] be able to constantly keep alive that challenging, questioning and probing of the real scene around it. . . . Our theory never will quite match the reality, but at least one strives to approximate it, to see what is the substance and not just the form." This interview was excerpted in Dorothy Ray Healey and Maurice Isserman, *California Red: A Life in the American Communist Party* (Urbana: University of Illinois Press, 1993), 13–14.

7. Fanon, *Wretched of the Earth,* 145.

8. Famously, the passage "The tradition of all the dead generations weigh like a nightmare on the brain of the living" comes from Karl Marx, *The Eighteenth Brumaire of Louis Bonaparte* (New York: International Publishers, [1963] 2004), 15. Avery Gordon attributes "the nastiness" to Cedric Robinson in her new introduction to *Ghostly Matters: Haunting and the Sociological Imagination* (Minneapolis: University of Minnesota Press, [1997] 2018), xvii.

9. Du Bois, *Black Reconstruction,* 714.

10. Kaplan, *The Anarchy of Empire,* especially chapter 6, and Moon-Ho Jung, "Black Reconstruction and Empire," *South Atlantic Quarterly* 112, no. 3 (Summer 2013): 465–71.

11. Frederick Douglass, "The Color Line," *The North American Review* CXXXII (June 1881): 567–77, republished in Foner, ed., *Frederick Douglass,* 650.

12. In this, the study shares Jordan T. Camp's goal to "contribute to the evolving skills in the way readers understand the world as they struggle to change it" (*Incarcerating the Crisis: Freedom Struggles and the Rise of the Neoliberal State* [Oakland: University of California Press, 2016], 20).

13. Amilcar Cabral, "Tell No Lies, Claim No Easy Victories," *Revolution in Guinea* (London: Stage 1, 1974). In his 1869 preface to the second edition of *The Eighteenth Brumaire of Louis Bonaparte,* Marx critiques other chroniclers of Napoléon III's coup. Of Prodhoun he writes, "Unnoticeably, however, his historical construction of the *coup d'état* becomes a historical apologia for its hero" (8).

BIBLIOGRAPHY

PRIMARY SOURCES

Collections of Papers

Amherst, Massachusetts
    University of Massachusetts, Amherst
        Special Collections and University Archives
            W. E. B. Du Bois Papers
Amsterdam, Netherlands
    International Institute for Social History
        Ricardo Flores Magón Papers
        World Congress Against the Imperialist War Collection
        The Estelle Sylvia Pankhurst Collection/ The Papers of Sylvia Pankhurst
            1882–1960
Ann Arbor, Michigan
    Bentley Historical Library, University of Michigan
        Gwendolyn Midlo Hall Papers 1939–98, 1968–95
Atlanta, Georgia
    Robert W. Woodruff Library, Emory University
        Theodore Draper Papers
        Harvey Klehr Papers
Berkeley, California
    Bancroft Library, University of California, Berkeley
Cambridge, Massachusetts
    Houghton Library, Harvard University
        John Reed Papers
Dublin, Ireland
    National Library of Ireland
        William O'Brien Papers
Kansas City, Missouri
    National Archives, Central Plains Region

Federal Bureau of Prisons Collection
Long Beach, California
  University Library, California State University, Long Beach
    Dorothy Healey Collection
Los Angeles, California
  Los Angeles Public Library
    Photo Collection
  Charles E. Young Research Library, University of California, Los Angeles
    Karl G. Yoneda Papers
  Doheny Memorial Library, University of Southern California
    Los Angeles: United Front Conference Against Hunger
    Boeckmann Center for Iberian and Latin American Studies
    Los Angeles Times Digital Prints Collection
  Southern California Library for Social Studies and Research
    Leo Gallagher Papers, 1922–1963
Madison, Wisconsin
  Wisconsin Historical Society
    McCormick-International Harvester Collection
Mexico City, DF, Mexico
  Archivo General de la Nación de México (AGN)
    Instituto Nacional de Estudios Históricos de la Revolución Mexicana
    Los Revoltosos
  Casa de El Hijo del Ahuizote/Centro Documental Flores Magón, AC
    Hemerográficos Años 20s
    Hemerográficos/Revolución Mexicana
    Libros de Enrique Flores Magón (Penitenciaría Federal de Leavenworth)
      Manuscritos
      Penitenciaría Federal de Leavenworth
      Periódicos Extranjeros
  Centro de Estudios del Movimiento Obrero y Socialista AC (CEMOS)
    Carlos Sánchez Cárdenas (FCSC)
    El Partido Comunista Mexicano (PCM)
    El Machete, 1921–33
    Frente a Frente
    El Obrero Comunista
New Haven, Connecticut
  Sterling Memorial Library, Yale University
    Harry Weinberger Papers
New Orleans, Louisiana
  Amistad Research Center, Tulane University
    Elizabeth Catlett Papers
New York, New York
  Columbia University, Center for Oral History Archives
    Alexandra Kollontai Project

Tamiment Library and Robert F. Wagner Archives, New York University
  Labor Research Association
  Printed Ephemera Collection on Organizations
  General Photograph Collection
  Daily Worker Collection
  Mark Starr Papers
Northampton, Massachusetts
  Smith College, Special Collections
  Sophia Smith Collection of Women's History
Orlando, Florida
  Special Collections and University Archives, University of Central Florida
  PRISM: Political & Rights Issues & Social Movements
San Marino, California
  Huntington Library
    Albert B. Fall Papers
    Llano del Rio Colony Records
    Loren Miller Papers
    Rare Book Collection
    Southern Pacific de Mexico Collection
    Tasker Lowndes Oddie Papers
St. Augustine, Trinidad and Tobago
  Alma Jordan Library, University of the West Indies
    C. L. R. James Collection
Stanford, California
  Green Library, Stanford University
    Estampas de la Revolución Mexicana, Taller de Gráfica Popular (TGP)
Washington, DC
  Library of Congress
    American Folklife Center, Library of Congress
      Oral History of Elizabeth Catlett
    Department of Justice Investigative Files
      RGASPI, Records of the Communist Party USA
    INCOMKA Project, Communist International Archives
    Prints and Photographs Division
      Ben and Beatrice Goldstein Foundation Collection
        Taller de Gráfica Popular
  National Archives, College Park, Maryland
    Ricardo Flores Magón Files
    Jack Johnson Files
Seattle, Washington
  University of Washington Libraries
    Special Collections
    Industrial Workers of the World Photograph Collection

Oral Histories and Interviews

Gardner, Joel. *Tradition's Chains Have Bound Us: Dorothy Healey.* University of California, Los Angeles Oral History Program, 1982.

Interview with Barbara Winslow by author over phone, Brooklyn, NY, May 22, 2020.

Interview with Barbara Evans Clements by Sonya Baevsky, Alexandra Kollontai Oral History Project, Center for Oral History Archives, Columbia University, 1978.

Interview with Willie Birch by author over phone, New Orleans, LA, February 19, 2020.

Oral history with Elizabeth Catlett by author, Cuernavaca, Mexico, September 30, 2011.

Oral history with Elizabeth Catlett and Francisco Mora by Dr. Clifton Johnson, Amistad Research Center, Tulane University, 1983.

Oral history with Elizabeth Catlett by Camille O. Cosby, National Visionary Leadership Project, American Folklife Center, Library of Congress, 2002.

Oral history with Marvel Cooke, New York University Tamiment Collection, n.d.

Oral history with Dr. Gwendolyn Midlo Hall by author over phone, Guanajuato, Mexico, December 16, 2017.

Oral history with Charles Henry Alston, Archives of American Art, Smithsonian Institution, September 28, 1965.

Oral history with Norman Lewis, Archives of American Art, Smithsonian Institution, July 14, 1968.

Oral history with Charles Wilbert White, Archives of American Art, Smithsonian Institution, March 9, 1965.

Oral history with Hale Woodruff, Archives of American Art, Smithsonian Institution, November 18, 1968.

"The Taller de Gráfica Popular: An Interview with Adolfo Mexiac—video produced as part of a panel discussion related to the Art Institute of Chicago's 2014 exhibition "What May Come—The Taller de Gráfica Popular and the Mexican Political Print."

Newspapers, Organs, Official Journals

Appeal to Reason
Baltimore Sun
Bisbee Daily Review
Boston Daily Globe
Chicago Defender
Chicago Examiner
Chicago Tribune
The Crisis
CROM
Daily Worker

Free Society
Frente a Frente
Gale's Magazine
El Heraldo de México
Hutchinson News
The Independent
Indiana Press
Industrial Worker
Inspector
International Socialist Review
Leavenworth New Era
The Liberator
Los Angeles Record
Los Angeles Times
Louisville Courier-Journal
El Machete
The Masses
Masses and Mainstream
Mexican Labor News
Modern Quarterly
The Nation
Negro Worker
The New Republic
New Masses
New York Amsterdam News
New York Call
New York Herald Tribune
New York Times
Nueva Senda
Open Forum
La Prensa
Political Prisoner
Regeneración
Sacramento Bee
Solidaridad
Solidarity
The Toiler
Western Worker

Films

At the Cross Roads. Detroit: Ford Motor Company, 1919.
Coburn Whack, Rita, dir. *Curators of Culture*. Chicago: WYCC-TV, 2005.
Miller, Peter, dir. *The Internationale*. Brooklyn: Icarus Films, 2000.

Pamphlets

American League Against War and Fascism, Los Angeles Committee. *California's Brown Book*. Los Angeles: American League Against War and Fascism, 1934.

Amter, Israel. *The March Against Hunger*. New York: Workers Library Publishers, 1933.

———. *Why the Workers' Unemployment Insurance Bill? How It Can Be Won*. New York: Workers Library Publishers, 1934.

Aurrecoechea, Juan Manuel. *La revoluciòn Mexicana en el espejo de la caricatura Estadounidense*. Mexico City: Museo de Arte Carrillo Gil, 2011.

Benjamin, Herbert. *How to Organize and Conduct United Action for the Right to Live: A Manual for Hunger Fighters*. New York: Workers Library Publishers, 1933.

———. *Shall It Be Hunger Doles or Unemployment Insurance?* New York: Workers Library Publishers, 1933.

Bluestein, Abe. *Forgotten Men, What Now?* New York: Libertarian Publishers, 1935.

Bryant, Louise. *Mirrors of Moscow*. New York: T. Seltzer, 1923.

Burnham, Grace. *Unemployment*. New York: International Pamphlets, 1932.

———. *Work or Wages*. New York: International Pamphlets, 1930.

Communist Party. *The Communist Position on the Farmer's Movement*. New York: Workers Library Publishers, 1933.

Doyle, Arthur Conan. *Crime of the Congo*. London: Hutchinson & Co., 1909.

Ford, James W. *Hunger and Terror in Harlem*. New York: Harlem Section, Communist Party, 1935.

Haywood, H., and Howard, M. *Lynching: A Weapon of National Oppression*. New York: International Pamphlets, 1932.

Industrial Workers of the World. *An Open Letter to President Harding. From 52 Members of the I.W.W. in Leavenworth Penitentiary Who Refuse to Apply for Individual Clemency*. Chicago: General Defense Committee, 1922.

Manila Merchants' Association. *The Philippines, Treasure House of the Tropics, Manila, Pearl of the Orient*. Manila: n.p., 1911.

National Committee of Unemployed Councils. *Why We March*. New York: Workers Library Publishers, 1932.

National Unemployment Council. *Constitution and Regulations of the National Unemployment Council of the U.S.A.* New York: Workers Library Publishers, 1934.

Official Catalogue of Exhibitors: Division of Exhibits, 1915—Panama-Pacific International Exposition. San Francisco: Wahlgreen Company, 1915.

Peace Officers' Association of the State of California. *A Peace Officer's Manual for Combating Subversive Activities*. N.p.: n.p., January 20, 1935.

Perry, Pettis. *Negro Representation: A Step Toward Negro Freedom*. New York: New Century Publishers, 1952.

———. *White Chauvinism and the Struggle for Peace*. New York: New Century Publishers, 1952.

Saleeby, Murad M. *Abaca (Manila Hemp) in the Philippines.* Manila: Bureau of Printing, 1915.

Soule, Isobel Walker. *The Vigilantes Hide Behind the Flag.* New York: International Labor Defense, 1937.

Steinbeck, John. *Their Blood is Strong: A Factual Story of the Migratory Agricultural Workers in California.* San Francisco: Simon J. Lubin Society of California, 1938.

Upson-Walton Company. *Something About Rope: An Encyclical to Our Customers.* Cleveland: Upson-Walton Company, 1902.

Waterbury Company, *General Catalogue and Price List.* New York: Waterbury Company, 1920.

Yoneda, Karl. *A Brief History of U.S. Asian Labor.* New York: Political Affairs, 1976.

———. *The Heritage of Sen Katayama.* New York: Political Affairs, 1975.

Memoirs

Anhalt, Diana. *A Gathering of Fugitives: American Political Expatriates in Mexico 1948–1965.* Santa Maria, CA: Archer Books, 2001.

Chaplin, Ralph. *Wobbly: The Rough-and-Tumble Story of an American Radical.* Chicago: University of Chicago Press, 1948.

Davis, Benjamin Jefferson. *Communist Councilman from Harlem.* New York: International Publishers, 1969.

De Caux, Len. *Labor Radical: From the Wobblies to CIO, A Personal History.* Boston: Beacon, 1970.

Flynn, Elizabeth Gurley. *The Rebel Girl: An Autobiography, My First Life (1906–1926).* New York: International Publishers, 1973.

Grant, Ulysses S. *Personal Memoirs of Ulysses S. Grant.* New York: Cosimo Classics, 2006.

Haywood, Harry. *Black Bolshevik: Autobiography of an Afro-American Communist.* Chicago: Liberator Press, 1978.

Healey, Dorothy, and Maurice Isserman. *California Red: A Life in the American Communist Party.* Urbana: University of Illinois Press, 1993.

Herndon, Angelo. *Let Me Live.* Ann Arbor: University of Michigan Press, 2007.

Hughes, Langston. *The Big Sea: An Autobiography.* New York: Hill and Wang, 2015.

Kollontai, Alexandra. *The Autobiography of a Sexually Emancipated Communist Woman.* Edited by Irving Fetscher. Translated by Salvator Attansio. New York: Herder and Herder, 1971.

Kōchi, Paul Shinsei. *Imin No Aiwa (An Immigrant's Sorrowful Tale).* Translated by Ben Kobashigawa. Los Angeles: privately printed, 1978.

McKay, Claude. *A Long Way from Home.* New York: L. Furman, Inc., 1937.

Mother Jones. *Autobiography of Mother Jones.* Chicago: Charles H. Kerr, 1977.

Orozco, José Clemente. *José Clemente Orozco: An Autobiography.* Mineola, NY: Dover Publications, 1962.

Roy, M.N. *Memoirs*. Delhi: Ajanta Publications, 1984.

Shipman, Charles. *It Had to Be Revolution: Memoirs of an American Radical*. Ithaca, NY: Cornell University Press, 1993.

Wells, Ida B. *Crusade for Justice: The Autobiography of Ida B. Wells*. Edited by Alfreda M. Duster. Chicago: University of Chicago Press, 2020.

Yoneda, Karl. *Ganbatte: Sixty-Year Struggle of a Kibei Worker*. Los Angeles: Asian American Studies Center, University of California, Los Angeles, 1983.

SECONDARY SOURCES

Books

Abbink, Jon, Mirjam de Bruijn, and Klaas van Walraven, eds. *Rethinking Resistance: Revolt and Violence in African History*. Leiden: Brill, 2003.

Ackerman, Kenneth D. *Trotsky in New York, 1917: A Radical on the Eve of Revolution*. Berkeley, CA: Counterpoint, 2016.

Acuña, Rodolfo F. *Corridors of Migration: The Odyssey of Mexican Laborers, 1600–1933*. Tucson: University of Arizona Press, 2007.

Adamic, Louis. *Dynamite: A Century of Class Violence in America, 1830–1930*. London: Rebel Press, 1984.

Adams, David Wallace. *Education for Extinction: American Indians and the Boarding School Experience, 1875–1928*. Lawrence: University Press of Kansas, 1995.

Adams, John A., Jr. *Conflict and Commerce on the Rio Grande: Laredo, 1755–1955*. College Station: Texas A&M University Press, 2008.

Adhikari, G., ed. *Documents of the History of the Communist Party of India*. Vol. 1, *1917–1922*. New Delhi: People's Publishing House, 1971.

Akamine, Mamoru. *The Ryukyu Kingdom: Cornerstone of East Asia*. Edited by Robert N. Huey. Translated by Lina Terrell. Honolulu: University of Hawai'i Press, 2016.

Albarrán, Elena. *Seen and Heard in Mexico: Children and Revolutionary Cultural Nationalism*. Lincoln: University of Nebraska Press, 2014.

Albro, Ward S. *Always a Rebel: Ricardo Flores Magón and the Mexican Revolution*. Fort Worth: Texas Christian University Press, 2003.

Alexander, Paul. *Peace to War: Shifting Allegiances in the Assemblies of God*. Telford, OR: Cascadia Publishing House, 2009.

Almaguer, Tomás. *Racial Fault Lines: The Historical Origins of White Supremacy in California*. Berkeley: University of California Press, 2009.

Anderson, M.T. *Symphony for the City of the Dead: Dmitri Shostakovich and the Siege of Leningrad*. Somerville, MA: Candlewick Press, 2015.

Andrés, Benny J. *Power and Control in the Imperial Valley: Nature, Agribusiness, and Workers on the California Borderland, 1900–1940*. College Station: Texas A&M University Press, 2014.

Argenteri, Letizia. *Tina Modotti: Between Art and Revolution*. New Haven, CT: Yale University Press, 2003.

Arnold, Channing, and Frederick Frost. *The American Egypt: A Record of Travel in Yucatan.* London: Hutchinson, 1909.

Arrighi, Giovanni. *Adam Smith in Beijing: Lineages of the Twenty-First Century.* London: Verso, 2007.

———. *The Long Twentieth Century: Money, Power, and the Origins of Our Times.* New York: Verso, 2010.

Ashby, Joe C. *Organized Labor and the Mexican Revolution Under Lázaro Cárdenas.* Chapel Hill: University of North Carolina Press, 1967.

Avila, Mary Theresa. "Chronicles of Revolution and Nation: El Taller de Gráfica Popular's 'Estampas de la Revolución Mexicana' (1947)." PhD diss., University of New Mexico, 2013.

Avrich, Paul. *The Haymarket Tragedy.* Princeton, NJ: Princeton University Press, 1984.

Balderrama, Francisco E., and Raymond Rodríguez. *Decade of Betrayal: Mexican Repatriation in the 1930s.* Albuquerque: University of New Mexico Press, 2006.

Baldwin, Kate A. *Beyond the Color Line and the Iron Curtain: Reading Encounters Between Black and Red, 1922–1963.* Durham, NC: Duke University Press, 2002.

Barnwell, Andrea D. *Charles White.* San Francisco: Pomegranate Communications, 2002.

Barrera, Mario. *Race and Class in the Southwest: A Theory of Racial Inequality.* Notre Dame, IN: University of Notre Dame Press, 1979.

Barry, Raymond P., ed. *A Documentary History of Migratory Farm Labor in California.* Oakland, CA: Federal Writers Project, 1938.

Baucom, Ian. *Specters of the Atlantic: Finance Capital, Slavery, and the Philosophy of History.* Durham, NC: Duke University Press, 2005.

Baumgartner, Alice L. *South to Freedom: Runaway Slaves to Mexico and the Road to the Civil War.* New York: Basic Books, 2020.

Beckert, Sven. *Empire of Cotton: A Global History.* New York: Alfred A. Knopf, 2014.

Beezley, William H. *Judas at the Jockey Club and Other Episodes of Porfirian Mexico.* Lincoln: University of Nebraska Press, 2018.

Belohlavek, John M. *Patriots, Prostitutes, and Spies: Women and the Mexican-American War.* Charlottesville: University of Virginia Press, 2017.

Benjamin, Walter. *Illuminations.* Translated by Harry Zohn. New York: Schocken Books, 2007.

Bernstein, Irving. *The Lean Years: A History of the American Worker, 1920–1933.* Baltimore: Penguin, 1966.

Bernstein, Shana. *Bridges of Reform: Interracial Civil Rights Activism in Twentieth-Century Los Angeles.* New York: Oxford University Press, 2011.

Bérubé, Allan. "No Race-Baiting, Red-Baiting, or Queer-Baiting! The Marine Cooks and Stewards Union from the Depression to the Cold War." In *My Desire for History: Essays in Gay, Community, and Labor History,* edited by John D'Emilio and Estelle B. Freedman, 294–320. Chapel Hill: University of North Carolina Press, 2011.

Bone, Robert, and Richard A. Courage. *The Muse in Bronzeville: African American Creative Expression in Chicago, 1932–1950*. New Brunswick, NJ: Rutgers University Press, 2011.

Bonfil Batalla, Guillermo. *México Profundo: Reclaiming a Civilization*. Translated by Philip A. Dennis. Austin: University of Texas Press, 1996.

Bosworth, Mary. *Explaining U.S. Imprisonment*. Los Angeles: Sage, 2010.

Brecher, Jeremy. *Strike!* Cambridge, MA: South End Press, 1997.

Broadberry, Stephen, and Mark Harrison. *The Economics of World War I*. New York: Cambridge University Press, 2005.

Blum, Ann S. *Domestic Economies: Family, Work, and Welfare in Mexico City, 1884–1943*. Lincoln: University of Nebraska Press, 2009.

Brown, David Luis. *Waves of Decolonization: Discourses of Race and Hemispheric Citizenship in Cuba, Mexico, and the United States*. Durham, NC: Duke University Press, 2008.

Bufe, Chaz, and Mitchell Cowen Verter, eds. *Dreams of Freedom: A Ricardo Flores Magón Reader*. Oakland, CA: AK Press, 2005.

Bulosan, Carlos. *America Is in the Heart*. Seattle: University of Washington Press, 1973.

Burr, Aaron. *The Private Journal of Aaron Burr*. Rochester, NY: Post Express Printing Co., 1903.

Burroughs, Margaret Goss. "Chicago's South Side Community Art Center: A Personal Recollection." In *Art in Action: American Art Centers and the New Deal*, edited by John Franklin White. Metuchen, NJ: Scarecrow Press, 1987.

Bush, Robert D. *The Louisiana Purchase: A Global Context*. New York: Routledge, 2013.

Bush, Roderick D. *The End of White World Supremacy: Black Internationalism and the Problem of the Color Line*. Philadelphia: Temple University Press, 2009.

Byrd, Jodi. *Transit of Empire: Indigenous Critiques of Colonialism*. Minneapolis: University of Minnesota Press, 2011.

Caplow, Deborah. *Leopoldo Méndez: Revolutionary Art and the Mexican Print*. Austin: University of Texas Press, 2007.

Carby, Hazel. "'On the Threshold of Woman's Era': Lynching, Empire and Sexuality in Black Feminist Theory." In *Feminist Postcolonial Theory: A Reader,* edited by Reina Lewis and Sara Mills, 222–38. New York: Routledge, 2003.

Carr, Barry. *Marxism and Communism in Twentieth-Century Mexico*. Lincoln: University of Nebraska Press, 1992.

Carrasco, Daniel Kent. "México en las Memorias de M.N. Roy: Nostalgia, Devoción Política e Historia." In *Autobiografías y/o Textos Autorreferenciales,* edited by Alicia Sandoval, 95–118. Puebla: Benemérita UNAM de Puebla, 2019.

Carrigan, William D., and Clive Webb. *Forgotten Dead: Mob Violence against Mexicans in the United States*. Oxford, UK: Oxford University Press, 2013.

Carter, Julian B. *The Heart of Whiteness: Normal Sexuality and Race in America, 1880–1940*. Durham, NC: Duke University Press, 2007.

Castells, Manuel. *The City and the Grassroots: A Cross-Cultural Theory of Urban Social Movements*. Berkeley: University of California Press, 1983.

Caulfield, Norman. *Mexican Workers and the State: From the Porfiriato to NAFTA.* Fort Worth: Texas Christian University Press, 1998.

Césaire, Aimé. *Discourse on Colonialism.* New York: Monthly Review Press, 2000.

Chacón, Justin Akers. *Radicals in the Barrio: Magonistas, Socialists, Wobblies, and Communists in the Mexican American Working Class.* Chicago: Haymarket Books, 2018.

Chambers, Clarke A. *California Farm Organizations: A Historical Study of the Grange, the Farm Bureau, and the Associated Farmers, 1929–1941.* Berkeley: University of California Press, 1952.

Christy, Alan S. "The Making of Imperial Subjects in Okinawa." In *Formations of Colonial Modernity in East Asia,* edited by Tani E. Barlow, 141–70. Durham, NC: Duke University Press, 1997.

Chaplin, Ralph. *Wobbly: The Rough and Tumble Story of an American Radical.* Chicago: University of Chicago Press, 1948.

Chowdhuri, Satyabrata Rai. *Leftism in India, 1917–1947.* New York: Palgrave, 2007.

Clements, Barbara Evans. *Bolshevik Feminist: The Life of Aleksandra Kollontai.* Bloomington: Indiana University Press, 1979.

Cockcroft, James D. *Mexico's Hope: An Encounter with Politics and History.* New York: Monthly Review Press, 1998.

———. *Mexico's Revolution Then and Now.* New York: Monthly Review Press, 2010.

———. *Mexico: Class Formation, Capital Accumulation, and the State.* New York: Monthly Review Press, 1983.

Contreras, Joseph. *In the Shadow of the Giant: The Americanization of Modern Mexico.* New Brunswick, NJ: Rutgers University Press, 2009.

Cooper, Anna Julia. *A Voice from the South: By a Black Woman of the South.* Chapel Hill: University of North Carolina Press, 2017.

Cortez, Carlos, ed. *Viva Posada!* Chicago: Charles H. Kerr, 2002.

Costa, Gina. *Para la Gente: Art, Politics and Cultural Identity of the Taller de Gráfica Popular.* Notre Dame, IN: Snite Museum of Art, 2009.

Cot, Annie L. "Jeremy Bentham's Spanish American Utopia." In *Economic Development and Global Crisis: The Latin American Economy in Historical Perspective,* edited by José Luís Cardoso, et al., 34–47. New York: Routledge, 2004.

Craton, Michael. *Testing the Chains: Resistance to Slavery in the British West Indies.* Ithaca, NY: Cornell University Press, 2009.

Craven, David. *Art and Revolution in Latin America, 1910–1990.* New Haven, CT: Yale University Press, 2002.

Dail, Chrystyna. *Stage for Action: US Social Activist Theatre in the 1940s.* Carbondale: Southern Illinois University Press, 2016.

Daniel, Cletus E. *Bitter Harvest: A History of California Farmworkers, 1870–1941.* Berkeley: University of California Press, 1981.

Dazhina, I. M., M. M. Mukhamedzhanov, and R. Y. Tsivlina, eds. *Alexandra Kollontai: Selected Articles and Speeches.* Translated by Cynthia Carlile. New York: International Publishers, 1984.

Davis, Mike. *In Praise of Barbarians: Essays against Empire.* Chicago: Haymarket Books, 2007.

———. *Late Victorian Holocausts: El Niño Famines and the Making of the Third World*. New York: Verso, 2002.

———. *Planet of Slums*. New York: Verso, 2007.

———. "'What is a Vigilante Man?' White Violence in California History," In *No One Is Illegal: Fighting Violence and State Repression on the U.S.-Mexico Border*, edited by Justin Akers Chacón and Mike Davis, 11–86. Chicago: Haymarket Books, 2006.

de Graaf, Lawrence B., Kevin Mulroy, and Quintard Taylor, eds. *Seeking El Dorado: African Americans in California*. Seattle: University of Washington Press, 2001.

Dean, Jodi. *Comrade: An Essay on Political Belonging*. New York: Verso, 2019.

Delpar, Helen. *The Enormous Vogue of Things Mexican: Cultural Relations Between the United States and Mexico, 1920–1935*. Birmingham: University of Alabama Press, 1995.

Denning, Michael. *The Cultural Front: The Laboring of American Culture in the Twentieth Century*. New York: Verso, 1998.

———. *Noise Uprising: The Audiopolitics of a World Musical Revolution*. New Delhi: LeftWord Books, 2016.

Dicken, Peter. "Global Shift—The Role of United States Transnational Corporations." In *The American Century: Consensus and Coercion in the Projection of American Power*, edited by David Slater and Peter J. Taylor. Malden, MA: Blackwell Publishers, 1999.

Dollinar, Brian. *The Black Cultural Front: Black Writers and Artists of the Depression Generation*. Jackson: University Press of Mississippi, 2012.

Donner, Frank. *Protectors of Privilege: Red Squads and Police Repression in Urban America*. Berkeley: University of California Press, 1990.

Drinnon, Richard. *Facing West: The Metaphysics of Indian-Hating and Empire-Building*. Norman: University of Oklahoma Press, 1997.

Du Bois, W. E. B. *Black Reconstruction in America, 1860–1880*. New York: Free Press, 1962.

———. *Darkwater: Voices from Within the Veil*. Mineola, NY: Dover Publications, 1999.

———. *W. E. B. Du Bois: Writings*. Edited by Nathan Huggins. New York: Library of America, 1986.

———. *Dusk of Dawn: An Essay toward an Autobiography of a Race Concept*. New York: Schocken Books, 1940.

Dubois, Laurent. *Avengers of the New World: The Story of the Haitian Revolution*. Cambridge, MA: Harvard University Press, 2005.

Dubovsky, Melvin. *We Shall Be All: A History of the Industrial Workers of the World*. Urbana: University of Illinois Press, 1988.

Dunbar-Ortiz, Roxanne. *Not "A Nation of Immigrants": Settler Colonialism, White Supremacy, and a History of Erasure and Exclusion*. Boston: Beacon, 2021.

———. *An Indigenous Peoples' History of the United States*. Boston: Beacon, 2015.

———. *Roots of Resistance: A History of Land Tenure in New Mexico*. Norman: University of Oklahoma Press, 2007.

Edwards, Brent Hayes. *The Practice of Diaspora: Literature, Translation, and the Rise of Black Internationalism*. Cambridge, MA: Harvard University Press, 2003.

Enoch, Jessica. *Refiguring Rhetorical Education: Women Teaching African American, Native American, and Chicano/a Students, 1865–1911*. Carbondale: Southern Illinois University, 2008.

Enstad, Nan. *Ladies of Labor, Girls of Adventure: Working Women, Popular Culture, and Labor Politics at the Turn of the Twentieth Century*. New York: Columbia University Press, 1999.

Escobar, Edward J. *Race, Police, and the Making of a Political Identity*. Berkeley: University of California Press, 1999.

Evans, Sterling D. *Bound in Twine: The History and Ecology of the Henequen-Wheat Complex for Mexico and the American and Canadian Plains, 1880–1950*. College Station: Texas A&M University Press, 2013.

Fanon, Frantz. *The Wretched of the Earth*. Translated by Richard Philcox. New York: Grove Press, 2004.

Farnsworth, Beatrice. *Aleksandra Kollontai: Socialism, Feminism, and the Bolshevik Revolution*. Stanford, CA: Stanford University Press, 1980.

Farrington, Lisa E. *Creating Their Own Image: The History of African-American Women Artists*. New York: Oxford University Press, 2005.

Featherstone, David. *Solidarity: Hidden Histories and Geographies of Internationalism*. London: Zed Books, 2012.

Federici, Silvia. *Caliban and the Witch: Women, the Body, and Primitive Accumulation*. Brooklyn: Autonomedia, 2004.

Foley, Barbara. *Spectres of 1919: Class and Nation and the Making of the New Negro*. Urbana: University of Illinois, 2003.

Folgarait, Leonard. *Mural Painting and Social Revolution in Mexico, 1920–1940*. Cambridge, UK: Cambridge University Press, 1998.

Foner, Philip S. *British Labor and the American Civil War*. New York: Holmes & Meier, 1981.

———, ed. *Clara Zetkin: Selected Writings*. Chicago: Haymarket Books, 2015.

———, ed. *Frederick Douglass: Selected Speeches and Writings*. Chicago: Chicago Review Press, 2000.

———. *The Industrial Workers of the World, 1905–1917*. Vol. 4, *History of the Labor Movement in the United States*. New York: International Publishers, 1997.

———, ed. *Life and Writings of Frederick Douglass*. New York: International Publishers, 1950.

Foner, Philip, and Reinhard Schultz, eds. *The Other America: Art and the Labour Movement in the United States*. London: Journeyman Press, 1985.

Fossett, Judith Jackson, and Jeffrey A. Tucker, eds. *Race Consciousness: African-American Studies for the New Century*. New York: New York University Press, 1997.

Foucault, Michel. *Discipline and Punish: The Birth of the Prison*. New York: Vintage, 1995.

Fowler, Josephine. *Japanese and Chinese Immigrant Activists: Organizing in American and International Communist Movements, 1919–1933*. New Brunswick, NJ: Rutgers University Press, 2007.

Fowler-Salamini, Heather. *Working Women, Entrepreneurs, and the Mexican Revolution: The Coffee Culture of Córdoba, Veracruz*. Lincoln: University of Nebraska Press, 2013.

Fox, Claire F. *Making Art Panamerican: Cultural Policy and the Cold War*. Minneapolis: University of Minnesota Press, 2013.

Fox, Cybelle. "The Boundaries of Social Citizenship: Race, Immigration, and the American Welfare State, 1900–1950." PhD diss., Harvard University, 2007.

Frank, Patrick. *Posada's Broadsheets: Mexican Popular Imagery, 1890–1910*. Albuquerque: University of New Mexico Press, 1998.

Fried, Albert, ed. *Communism in America: A History in Documents*. New York: Columbia University Press, 1997.

Fuerer, Rosemary. "The Nutpickers' Union, 1933–34: Crossing the Boundaries of Community and Workplace." In *"We are All Leaders": The Alternative Unionism of the Early 1930s,* edited by Staughton Lynd, 27–50. Urbana: University of Illinois Press, 1996.

Fujita Rony, Dorothy B. *American Workers, Colonial Power: Philippine Seattle and the Transpacific West, 1919–1941*. Berkeley: University of California Press, 2003.

Gaffield, Julia, ed. *The Haitian Declaration of Independence: Creation, Context, and Legacy*. Charlottesville: University of Virginia Press, 2016.

Gall, Olivia. *Trotsky en México y la vida política en el periodo de Lázaro Cárdenas, 1937–1940*. Mexico City: Collección Problemas de México, 1991.

Garza, Holly E. "Caught in the Crossfire: Children during the Mexican Revolution, 1910–1920." PhD diss., University of Texas at El Paso, 1995.

Gatewood, Willard B. *"Smoked Yankees" and the Struggle for Empire: Letters from Negro Soldiers, 1898–1902*. Fayetteville: University of Arkansas Press, 1987.

Gellman, Erik S. *Death Blow to Jim Crow: The National Negro Congress and the Rise of Militant Civil Rights*. Chapel Hill: University of North Carolina Press, 2012.

Giddings, Paula K. *Ida: A Sword Among Lions: Ida B. Wells and the Campaign Against Lynching*. New York: Harper Collins, 2008.

Gill, Mario. *Nuestros Buenos Vecinos*. Mexico City: Editorial Azteca, 1964.

Gilly, Adolfo. "Chiapas and the Rebellion of the Enchanted World." In *Rural Revolt in Mexico: US Intervention and the Domain of Subaltern Politics,* edited by Daniel Nugent, 261–333. Durham, NC: Duke University Press, 1998.

———. *The Mexican Revolution*. New York: New Press, 2005.

Gilmore, Glenda. *Defying Dixie: The Radical Roots of Civil Rights, 1919–1950*. New York: W. W. Norton, 2008.

Gilmore, Ruth Wilson. *Golden Gulag: Prisons, Surplus, Crisis, and Opposition in Globalizing California*. Berkeley: University of California Press, 2007.

Gilpin, Toni. *The Long Deep Grudge: A Story of Big Capital, Radical Labor, and Class War in the American Heartland*. Chicago: Haymarket Books, 2020.

Gilyard, Keith. *Louise Thompson Patterson: A Life of Struggle for Justice*. Durham, NC: Duke University Press, 2017.

Gindin, Sam, and Leo Panitch. *The Making of Global Capitalism: The Political Economy of American Empire*. New York: Verso, 2012.

Giraldez, Arturo. *The Age of Trade: The Manila Galleons and the Dawn of the Global Economy*. Lanham, MD: Rowman and Littlefield, 2015.

Goldman, Shifra M. *Dimensions of the Americas: Art and Social Change in Latin America and the United States*. Chicago: University of Chicago Press, 1995.

Goldman, Wendy Z. *Women, the State, and Revolution: Soviet Family Policy and Social Life, 1917–1936*. Cambridge, UK: Cambridge University Press, 1993.

Gómez, Laura E. *Manifest Destinies: The Making of the Mexican American Race*. New York: New York University Press, 2007.

Gómez-Quiñones, Juan. *Sembradores: Ricardo Flores Magón y el Partido Liberal Mexicano: A Eulogy and a Critique*. Los Angeles: Aztlán Publications, 1973.

González, Gilbert G. *Culture of Empire: American Writers, Mexico, and Mexican Immigrants, 1880–1930*. Austin: University of Texas Press, 2004.

———. *Mexican Consuls and Labor Organizing: Imperial Politics in the American Southwest*. Austin: University of Texas Press, 1999.

Gonzales, Michael R. "Rebellion and Repression in Colorado's Coalfields: The 1927–1928 Wobbly Coal Miners' Strike." PhD diss., University of Wisconsin-Milwaukee, Department of History, in progress.

Gonzales-Day, Ken. *Lynching in the West: 1850–1935*. Durham, NC: Duke University Press, 2006.

Gopal, Priyamvada. *Insurgent Empire: Anticolonial Resistance and British Dissent*. London: Verso, 2019.

Gordon, Avery F. *Ghostly Matters: Haunting and the Sociological Imagination*. Minneapolis: University of Minnesota Press, 1997.

Gore, Dayo F. *Radicalism at the Crossroads: African American Women Activists in the Cold War*. New York: New York University Press, 2012.

Gosse, Van. *Where the Boys Are: Cuba, Cold War America and the Making of a New Left*. London: Verso, 1993.

Gramsci, Antonio. *Selections from the Prison Notebooks*. New York: International Publishers, 1971.

———. *Letters from Prison*. Edited by Frank Rosengarten. Translated by Raymond Rosenthal. New York: Columbia University Press, 1994.

———. *The Southern Question*. Translated by Pasquale Verdicchio. Toronto: Guernica Editions, 2005.

Grandin, Greg. *Empire's Workshop: Latin America, the United States, and the Rise of the New Imperialism*. New York: Metropolitan Books, 2006.

Green, James R. *Death in the Haymarket: A Story of Chicago, the First Labor Movement and the Bombing That Divided Gilded Age America*. Toronto: Anchor Books, 2007.

———. *Grass-Roots Socialism: Radical Movements in the Southwest, 1895–1943*. Baton Rouge: Louisiana State University Press, 1980 [1978].

Greenberg, Amy S. *A Wicked War: Polk, Clay, and the 1846 U.S. Invasion of Mexico.* New York: Vintage, 2012.

Greene, A.C. *Sketches from the Five States of Texas.* College Station: Texas A&M University Press, 1998.

Grenier, John. *The First Way of War: American War Making on the Frontier, 1607–1814.* Cambridge, UK: Cambridge University Press, 2005.

Guardino, Peter. *The Dead March: A History of the Mexican-American War.* Cambridge, MA: Harvard University Press, 2017.

Guerin-Gonzales, Camille. *Mexican Workers and American Dreams: Immigration, Repatriation and California Farm Labor, 1900–1939.* New Brunswick, NJ: Rutgers University Press, 1994.

Guha, Ranajit, ed. *Subaltern Studies I: Writings on South Asian History & Society.* New Delhi: Oxford University Press India, 1982.

Guha, Ranajit. "Historiography of Colonial India." In *Subaltern Studies I: Writings on South Asian History & Society,* edited by Ranajit Guha, 37–44. New Delhi: Oxford University Press India, 1982.

———. *Elementary Aspects of Peasant Insurgency in Colonial India.* Durham, NC: Duke University Press, 1999.

Guidotti-Hernández, Nicole M. *Unspeakable Violence: Remapping U.S. and Mexican National Imaginaries.* Durham, NC: Duke University Press, 2011.

Hall, Stuart. "Race, Articulation, and Societies Structured in Dominance." In *Sociological Theories: Race and Colonialism,* 305–45. Paris: UNESCO, 1980.

Hamilton, Nora. *The Limits of State Autonomy: Post-Revolutionary Mexico.* Princeton, NJ: Princeton University Press, 1982.

Hansberry, Lorraine. *To Be Young, Gifted and Black.* Adapted by Robert Nemiroff. New York: Vintage, 1996.

Hanrahan, Gene Z., ed. *The Bad Yankee/ El Peligro Yankee: American Entrepreneurs and Financiers in Mexico.* Vol. 2. Chapel Hill, NC: Documentary Publications, 1985.

Harootunian, Harry. "Some Reflections on Gramsci: The Southern Question in the Deprovincializing of Marx." In *Gramsci in the World,* edited by Fredric Jameson and Robert M. Dainotto, 140–57. Durham, NC: Duke University Press, 2020.

Harris, LaShawn. *Sex Workers, Psychics, and Numbers Runners: Black Women in New York City's Underground Economy.* Urbana: University of Illinois Press, 2016.

Hart, John Mason. *Anarchism and the Mexican Working Class, 1860–1931.* Austin: University of Texas Press, 1987.

———. *Empire and Revolution: The Americans in Mexico Since the Civil War.* Berkeley: University of California Press, 2002.

———. *Revolutionary Mexico: The Coming and Process of the Mexican Revolution.* Berkeley: University of California Press, 1997.

Hart, Paul. *Bitter Harvest: The Social Transformation of Morelos, Mexico, and the Origins of the Zapatista Revolution, 1840–1910.* Albuquerque: University of New Mexico Press, 2006.

Hart, Richard. *From Occupation to Independence: A Short History of the Peoples of the English-Speaking Caribbean Region.* London: Pluto Press, 1998.

Harvey, David. *A Brief History of Neoliberalism.* New York: Oxford University Press, 2005.

———. *The Limits to Capital.* London: Verso, 2006.

———. *Marx, Capital, and the Madness of Economic Reason.* New York: Oxford University Press, 2017.

———. *Paris, Capital of Modernity.* New York: Routledge, 2006.

———. *Spaces of Capital: Towards a Critical Geography.* New York: Routledge, 2012.

———. *Spaces of Neoliberalization: Towards a Theory of Uneven Geographical Development.* Wiesbaden: Franz Steiner Verlag, 2005.

Haynes, Robert V. *A Night of Violence: The Houston Riot of 1917.* Eunice: Louisiana State University Press, 1976.

Hernández, Kelly Lytle. *Migra! A History of the U.S. Border Patrol.* Berkeley: University of California Press, 2010.

Herndon, Angelo. *Let Me Live.* Ann Arbor: University of Michigan Press, 2007.

Herzog, Melanie Ann. *Elizabeth Catlett: An American Artist in Mexico.* Seattle: University of Washington Press, 2000.

Heydt, Stephanie Mayer. *Rising Up: Hale Woodruff's Murals at Talladega College.* Seattle: University of Washington Press, 2012.

Higashida, Cheryl. *Black Internationalist Feminism: Women Writers of the Black Left, 1945–1995.* Urbana: University of Illinois, 2011.

Hill, Christopher. *The World Turned Upside Down: Radical Ideas during the English Revolution.* New York: Viking Press, 1972.

Hill, Rebecca. *Men, Mobs, and Law: Anti-Lynching and Labor Defense in US Radical History.* Durham, NC: Duke University Press, 2008.

Hine, Darlene Clark. *Hine Sight: Black Women and the Reconstruction of American History.* Brooklyn: Carlson Publishing, 1994.

Hobsbawm, Eric. *The Age of Empire, 1875–1914.* New York: Random House, 1987.

———. *The Age of Extremes: A History of the World, 1914–1991.* New York: Random House, 1994.

Hofstadter, Richard. *The American Political Tradition and the Men Who Made It.* New York: Vintage, 1989.

Holt, Alix, ed. and trans. *Selected Writings of Alexandra Kollontai.* New York: W. W. Norton, 1977.

Horne, Gerald. *Black and Brown: African Americans and the Mexican Revolution, 1910–1920.* New York: New York University Press, 2005.

———. *Race Woman: The Lives of Shirley Graham Du Bois.* New York: New York University Press, 2002.

Horsman, Reginald. *Race and Manifest Destiny: The Origins of American Racial Anglo-Saxonism.* Cambridge, MA: Harvard University Press, 1981.

Hu-DeHart, Evelyn. *Yaqui Resistance and Survival: The Struggle for Land and Autonomy, 1821–1910.* Madison: University of Wisconsin Press, 1984.

Ibsen, Kristine. *Maximilian, Mexico, and the Invention of Empire.* Nashville: Vanderbilt University Press, 2010.

Idrissa, Kimba. "The Kawousan War Reconsidered." In *Rethinking Resistance: Revolt and Violence in African History*, edited by Jon Abbink, Mirjam de Bruijn, and Klaas van Walraven, 191–217. Leiden: Brill, 2003.

Ileto, Reynaldo Clemeña. *Pasyon and Revolution: Popular Movements in the Philippines, 1840–1910*. Quezon City: Ateneo de Manila University Press, 1979.

Indych-López, Anna. *Muralism without Walls: Rivera, Orozco, and Siqueiros in the United States, 1927–1940*. Pittsburgh: University of Pittsburgh Press, 2009.

IWW Songs to Fan the Flames of Discontent: The Little Red Song Book, International Edition. Ypsilanti, MI: Industrial Workers of the World, 1995.

Jackson, Esther Cooper. "The Negro Woman Domestic Worker in Relation to Trade Unionism." MA thesis, Fisk University, 1940.

Jackson, Maurice, and Jacqueline Bacon, eds. *African Americans and the Haitian Revolution: Selected Essays and Historical Documents*. New York: Routledge, 2013.

Jacoby, Karl. *The Strange Career of William Ellis: The Texas Slave Who Became a Mexican Millionaire*. New York: W. W. Norton, 2016.

———. "Between North and South: The Alternative Borderlands of William H. Ellis and the African American Colony of 1895." In *Continental Crossroads: Remapping U.S.-Mexico Borderlands History*, edited by Samuel Truett and Elliott Young, 209–40. Durham, NC: Duke University Press, 2004.

James, C. L. R. *The Black Jacobins: Toussaint L'Ouverture and the San Domingo Revolution*. New York: Vintage, 1989.

———. *Mariners, Renegades, and Castaways: The Story of Herman Melville and the World We Live In*. Hanover, NH: University Press of New England, 1989 [1953].

Jameson, Fredric. "Cognitive Mapping." In *Marxism and the Interpretation of Culture*, edited by Cary Nelson and Lawrence Grossberg, 347–60. Urbana: University of Illinois Press, 1988.

Jenson, Deborah. *Beyond the Slave Narrative: Politics, Sex, and Manuscripts in the Haitian Revolution*. Liverpool: Liverpool University Press, 2011.

Johari, J. C. *M. N. Roy, the Great Radical Humanist: Political Biography and Socio-Political Ideas*. New York: Sterling Publishers, 1988.

Johnson, Walter. *River of Dark Dreams: Slavery and Empire in the Cotton Kingdom*. Cambridge, MA: Harvard University Press, 2013.

Joseph, Gilbert M. *Revolution from Without: Yucatán, Mexico, and the United States, 1880–1924*. Durham, NC: Duke University Press, 1987.

Joseph, Gilbert M., and Daniel Nugent, eds. *Everyday Forms of State Formation: Revolution and the Negotiation of Rule in Modern Mexico*. Durham, NC: Duke University Press, 1994.

Kaneshiro, Edith M. "Communists, Christians, and Japanese Imperial Subjects: Okinawan Immigrants within the Japanese Diaspora, 1899 to 1941." In *Studies in Pacific History: Economics, Politics, and Migration*, edited by Dennis O. Flynn, Arturo Giráldez, and James Sobredo, 170–87. London: Routledge, 2018.

———. "'Our home will be the five continents': Okinawan Migration to Hawaii, California, and the Philippines, 1899–1941." PhD diss., University of California, Berkeley, 1999.

Kaplan, Amy. *The Anarchy of Empire in the Making of U.S. Culture.* Cambridge, MA: Harvard University Press, 2002.

Katayama, Sen. *The Labor Movement in Japan.* Chicago: Charles H. Kerr, 1918.

Katz, Friedrich, ed. *Riot, Rebellion, and Revolution: Rural Social Conflict in Mexico.* Princeton, NJ: Princeton University Press, 1988.

———. *The Secret War in Mexico: Europe, the United States, and the Mexican Revolution.* Chicago: University of Chicago Press, 1981.

Katznelson, Ira. *When Affirmative Action Was White.* New York: W. W. Norton, 2005.

Kauanui, J. Kēhaulani. *Hawaiian Blood: Colonialism and the Politics of Sovereignty and Indigeneity.* Durham, NC: Duke University Press, 2008.

Kelley, Robin D. G. *Hammer and Hoe: Alabama Communists during the Great Depression.* Chapel Hill: University of North Carolina Press, 2015 [1990].

———. *Freedom Dreams: The Black Radical Imagination.* Boston: Beacon, 2002.

———. *Thelonious Monk: The Life and Times of an American Original.* New York: Free Press, 2009.

———. "How the West Was One: On the Uses and Limitations of Diaspora." In *The Black Studies Reader,* edited by Jacqueline Bobo, Cynthia Hudley, and Claudine Michel, 41–46. New York: Routledge, 2004.

Keve, Paul W. *Prisons and the American Conscience: A History of U.S. Federal Corrections.* Carbondale: Southern Illinois University Press, 1991.

Khalili, Laleh. *Time in the Shadows: Confinement in Counterinsurgencies.* Stanford, CA: Stanford University Press, 2012.

Kim, Jessica. *Imperial Metropolis: Los Angeles, Mexico, and the Borderlands of American Empire, 1865–1941.* Chapel Hill: University of North Carolina Press, 2019.

Klehr, Harvey. *The Heyday of American Communism: The Depression Decade.* New York: Basic Books, 1984.

Knight, Alan. *The Mexican Revolution.* Vol. 1, *Porfirians, Liberals, and Peasants.* Cambridge, UK: Cambridge University Press, 1987.

———. *The Mexican Revolution.* Vol. 2, *Counter-revolution and Reconstruction.* Lincoln: University of Nebraska Press, 1990.

———. "The United States and the Mexican Peasantry, circa 1880–1940." In *Rural Revolt in Mexico: U.S. Intervention and the Domain of Subaltern Politics,* edited by Daniel Nugent, 25–63. Durham, NC: Duke University Press, 1998.

Kohn, Stephen M. *American Political Prisoners: Prosecutions under the Espionage and Sedition Acts.* Westport, CT: Praeger, 1994.

Kollontai, Alexandra. *Communism and the Family.* Cleveland, OH: Hera Press, 1982.

Kornweibel, Theodore, Jr. *"Investigate Everything": Federal Efforts to Compel Black Loyalty during World War I.* Bloomington: Indiana University Press, 2002.

———. *"Seeing Red": The Federal Campaign against Black Militancy, 1919–1925.* Bloomington: Indiana University Press, 1998.

Kramer, Carl E. *This Place We Call Home: a History of Clark County, Indiana.* Beverly, MA: Quarry Books, 2007.

Kurashige, Scott. *The Shifting Grounds of Race: Black and Japanese Americans in the Making of Multiethnic Los Angeles.* Princeton, NJ: Princeton University Press, 2008.

LaMaster, Kenneth M. *U.S. Penitentiary Leavenworth*. Charleston, SC: Arcadia Publishing, 2008.

Langa, Helen. *Radical Art: Printmaking and the Left in 1930s New York*. Berkeley: University of California Press, 2004.

Langer, Erick. "Indigenous Independence in Spanish South America." In *New Countries: Capitalism, Revolutions, and Nations in the Americas, 1750–1870*, edited by John Tutino, 350–75. Durham, NC: Duke University Press, 2016.

Lear, John. *Workers, Neighbors, and Citizens: The Revolution in Mexico City*. Lincoln: University of Nebraska Press, 2001.

———. *Picturing the Proletariat: Artists and Labor in Revolutionary Mexico, 1908–1940*. Austin: University of Texas Press, 2017.

Lee, Anthony W. *Painting on the Left: Diego Rivera, Radical Politics, and San Francisco's Public Murals*. Berkeley: University of California Press, 1999.

LeFalle-Collins, Lizzetta, and Shifra M. Goldman. *In the Spirit of Resistance: African-American Modernists and the Mexican Muralist School*. New York: American Federation of Arts, 1996.

LeFebvre, Henri. *The Production of Space*. Translated by Donald Nicholson-Smith. Malden, MA: Blackwell Publishing, 1984.

Lehman, Daniel Wayne. *John Reed and the Writing of Revolution*. Athens: Ohio University Press, 2002.

Lenin, V. I. *Imperialism: The Highest Stage of Capitalism*. New York: International Publishers, 1939.

Lenin, V. I., "Preliminary Draft Theses on the National and Colonial Questions." In *Collected Works*. Vol. 31, *April-December 1920*. Moscow: Progress Publishers, 1966.

Lenin, V. I., and G. Y. Zinoviev. "Socialism and War: The Attitude of the Russian Social-Democratic Labour Party Towards the War." In *Lenin Collected Works* (Peking: Foreign Languages Press, 1970).

Lewis, David Levering, ed. *W. E. B. Du Bois: A Reader*. New York: Henry Holt, 1995.

Lewis, Samella. *The Art of Elizabeth Catlett*. Los Angeles: Museum of African American Art and Handcraft Studios, 1984.

Lind, Maria, and Michele Masucci, et al., eds. *Red Love: A Reader on Alexandra Kollontai*. Stockholm: Sternberg Press, 2020.

Linebaugh, Peter. *The London Hanged: Crime and Civil Society in the Eighteenth Century*. London: Verso, 2006 [2003].

———. *The Magna Carta Manifesto: Liberties and Commons for All*. Berkeley: University of California Press, 2008.

———. *Red Round Globe Hot Burning: A Tale at the Crossroads of Commons and Closure, of Love and Terror, of Race and Class, and of Kate and Ned Despard*. Oakland: University of California Press, 2019.

Linebaugh, Peter, and Marcus Rediker. *The Many-Headed Hydra: The Hidden History of the Revolutionary Atlantic*. London: Verso, 2000.

Linhard, Tabea Alexa. *Fearless Women in the Mexican Revolution and the Spanish Civil War*. Columbia: University of Missouri Press, 2005.

Lippit, Akira Mizuta. *Atomic Light (Shadow Optics)*. Minneapolis: University of Minnesota Press, 2005.

Loftis, Anne. *Witness to the Struggle: Imagining the 1930s California Labor Movement*. Reno: University of Nevada Press, 1998.

López, Rick A. "The Noche Mexicana and the Exhibition of Popular Arts: Two Ways of Exalting Indianness." In *The Eagle and the Virgin: Nation and Cultural Revolution in Mexico, 1920–1940*, edited by Mary Kay Vaughn and Steven E. Lewis, 23–42. Durham, NC: Duke University Press, 2006.

Louie, Miriam Ching Yoon. *Sweatshop Warriors: Immigrant Women Workers Take on the Global Factory*. Cambridge, MA: South End Press, 2001.

Lowe, Lisa. *The Intimacies of Four Continents*. Durham, NC: Duke University Press, 2015.

Lowe, Lisa, and David Lloyd, Introduction to *The Politics of Culture in the Shadow of Capital*, edited by Lisa Lowe and David Lloyd, 1–32. Durham, NC: Duke University Press, 1997.

Löwy, Michael. *The Politics of Combined and Uneven Development: The Theory of Permanent Revolution*. Chicago: Haymarket Books, 2010.

Luxemburg, Rosa. *Accumulation of Capital*. London: Routledge, 2003.

MacLachlan, Colin M. *Anarchism and the Mexican Revolution: The Political Trials of Ricardo Flores Magón in the United States*. Berkeley: University of California Press, 1991.

Makalani, Minkah. *In the Cause of Freedom: Radical Black Internationalism from Harlem to London, 1917–1939*. Chapel Hill: University of North Carolina Press, 2011.

Mamdani, Mahmood. *Neither Settler nor Native: The Making and Unmaking of Permanent Minorities*. Cambridge, MA: Harvard University Press, 2020.

Manela, Erez. *The Wilsonian Moment: Self-Determination and the International Origins of Anticolonial Nationalism*. New York: Oxford University Press, 2007.

Manjapra, Kris. *M. N. Roy: Marxism and Colonial Cosmopolitanism*. London: Routledge, 2010.

Marx, Karl. *Capital: A Critique of Political Economy*. Vol. 1. London: Penguin, 1976.

———. *Critique of Hegel's "Philosophy of Right."* Cambridge, UK: University of Cambridge, 1970.

———. *The Eighteenth Brumaire of Louis Bonaparte*. New York: International Publishers, 2004 [1963].

Marx, Karl, and Friedrich Engels. *Collected Works*. Vol. 3. New York: International Publishers, 1975.

———. *The Communist Manifesto*. New York: Penguin, 2002.

———. *The Civil War in the United States*. New York: International Publishers, 1937.

Majka, Linda C., and Theo J. Majka. *Farm Workers, Agribusiness, and the State*. Philadelphia: Temple University Press, 1982.

Mazower, Mark. *Governing the World: The History of an Idea, 1815 to the Present*. New York: Penguin, 2013.

McBroome, Delores Nason. "Harvests of Gold: African American Boosterism, Agriculture and Investment in Allensworth and Little Liberia." In *Seeking El Dorado:*

African Americans in California, edited by Lawrence B. de Graaf, Kevin Mulroy, and Quintard Taylor, 149–80. Seattle: University of Washington Press, 2001.

McClellan, Scott. "Policing the Red Scare: The Los Angeles Police Department Red Squad and the Repression of Labor Activism in Los Angeles, 1900–1938." PhD diss., University of California, Irvine, 2011.

McClintock, Anne. *Imperial Leather: Race, Gender and Sexuality in the Colonial Context.* New York: Routledge, 1995.

McCormick, Thomas J. *America's Half-Century: United States Foreign Policy in the Cold War and After.* Baltimore: Johns Hopkins University Press, 1995.

McCoy, Alfred. *Policing America's Empire: The United States, the Philippines, and the Rise of the Surveillance State.* Madison: University of Wisconsin Press, 2009.

McCulloch, J. R. *A Dictionary, Practical, Theoretical, and Historical, of Commerce and Commercial Navigation.* Vol. 1. Philadelphia: Carey and Hart, 1849.

McDermott, Kevin, and Jeremy Agnew, eds. *The Comintern: A History of International Communism from Lenin to Stalin.* Basingstoke, UK: Macmillan, 1996.

McDuffie, Erik S. *Sojourning for Freedom: Black Women, American Communism, and the Making of Black Left Feminism.* Durham, NC: Duke University Press, 2011.

McGurkin Raineri, Vivian. *The Red Angel: The Life and Times of Elaine Black Yoneda, 1906–1988.* New York: International Publishers, 1991.

McKenna, Rebecca Tinio. *American Imperial Pastoral: The Architecture of US Colonialism in the Philippines.* Chicago: University of Chicago Press, 2017.

McLynn, Frank. *Villa and Zapata: A Biography of the Mexican Revolution.* London: Jonathan Cape, 2000.

McShane, Marilyn D., and Frank P. Williams III, eds. *Encyclopedia of American Prisons.* New York: Garland, 1996.

McWilliams, Carey. *California: The Great Exception.* Berkeley: University of California Press, 1999.

———. *Factories in the Field: The Story of Migratory Farm Labor in California.* Berkeley: University of California Press, 2000.

Mello, Renato González, and Diane Miliotes. *José Clemente Orozco in the United States, 1927–1934.* New York: W. W. Norton, 2002.

Metscher, Priscilla. *James Connolly and the Reconquest of Ireland.* Minneapolis: University of Minnesota Press, 2002.

Meyer, Jean A. *The Cristero Rebellion: The Mexican People between Church and State, 1926–1929.* Cambridge, UK: Cambridge University Press, 1976.

Mitchell, Don. *The Lie of the Land: Migrant Workers and the California Landscape.* Minneapolis: University of Minnesota Press, 1996.

Mitchell, Stephanie E., and Patience A. Schell, eds. *The Women's Revolution in Mexico, 1910–1953.* Lanham, MD: Rowman and Littlefield, 2006.

Millon, Robert P. *Zapata: The Ideology of a Peasant Revolutionary.* New York: International Publishers, 1969.

Mishler, Paul C. *Raising Reds: The Young Pioneers, Radical Summer Camps, and Communist Political Culture in the United States.* New York: Columbia University Press, 1999.

Monroy, Douglas. *Rebirth: Mexican Los Angeles from the Great Migration to the Great Depression.* Berkeley: University of California Press, 1999.

Montalvo Ortega, Enrique. "Revolts and Peasant Mobilizations in Yucatán: Indians, Peons and Peasants from the Caste War to the Revolution." In *Riot, Rebellion, and Revolution: Rural Social Conflict in Mexico,* edited by Friedrich Katz, 295–317. Princeton, NJ: Princeton University Press, 1988.

Montejano, David. "Mexican Merchants and Teamsters on the Texas Cotton Road, 1862–1865." In *Mexico and Mexicans in the Making of the United States,* edited by John Tutino, 141–70. Austin: University of Texas Press, 2012.

Montgomery, David. *Fall of the House of Labor: The Workplace, the State and American Labor Activism, 1865–1925.* Cambridge, UK: Cambridge University Press, 1987.

Morgan, Stacy I. *Rethinking Social Realism: African American Art and Literature, 1930–1953.* Athens: University of Georgia Press, 2004.

Morton, Adam David. *Revolution and State in Modern Mexico: The Political Economy of Uneven Development.* Lanham, MD: Rowman and Littlefield, 2011.

Muhammad, Khalil Gibran. *The Condemnation of Blackness: Race, Crime, and the Making of Modern Urban America.* Cambridge, MA: Harvard University Press, 2010.

Mukherjee, Tapan K. *Taraknath Das: Life and Letters of a Revolutionary in Exile.* Calcutta: National Council of Education, Bengal, 1998.

Mukherji, S. Ani. "The Anticolonial Imagination: Migrant Intellectuals and the Exilic Productions of American Radicalism in Interwar Moscow, 1919–1939." PhD diss., Brown University, 2011.

Mullen, Bill V. *Popular Fronts: Chicago and African-American Cultural Politics, 1935–46.* Urbana: University of Illinois Press, 1999.

Muñoz Martinez, Monica. *The Injustice Never Leaves You: Anti-Mexican Violence in Texas.* Cambridge, MA: Harvard University Press, 2018.

Nation, R. Craig. *War on War: Lenin, the Zimmerwald Left, and the Origins of Communist Internationalism.* Durham, NC: Duke University Press, 1989.

Nelson, Scott Reynolds. *A Nation of Deadbeats: An Uncommon History of America's Financial Disasters.* New York: Alfred A. Knopf, 2012.

Nemser, Daniel. *Infrastructures of Race: Concentration and Biopolitics in Colonial Mexico.* Austin: University of Texas Press, 2017.

Ngai, Mae M. *Impossible Subjects: Illegal Aliens and the Making of Modern America.* Princeton, NJ: Princeton University Press, 2004.

Nolan, Tom. *Three Chords for Beauty's Sake: The Life of Artie Shaw.* New York: W. W. Norton, 2010.

North, Robert C., and Xenia J. Eudin. *M. N. Roy's Mission to China: The Communist-Kuomintang Split of 1927.* New York: Octagon Books, 1977.

Nugent, Daniel, ed. *Rural Revolt in Mexico: U.S. Intervention and the Domain of Subaltern Politics.* Durham, NC: Duke University Press, 1998.

O'Brien, Thomas. *Making the Americas: The United States and Latin America from the Age of Revolutions to the Era of Globalization.* Albuquerque: University of New Mexico Press, 2007.

Okihiro, Gary Y. *The Columbia Guide to Asian American History.* New York: Columbia University Press, 2001.

Olcott, Jocelyn. *Revolutionary Women in Postrevolutionary Mexico.* Durham, NC: Duke University Press, 2005.

Olcott, Jocelyn, Mary Kay Vaughan, and Gabriela Cano, eds. *Sex in Revolution: Gender, Politics, and Power in Modern Mexico.* Durham, NC: Duke University Press, 2006.

Oles, James. *South of the Border: Mexico in the American Imagination, 1914–1947.* Washington, DC: Smithsonian Institution Press, 1993.

Olmsted, Kathryn S. *Right Out of California: The 1930s and the Big Business Roots of Modern Conservatism.* New York: New Press, 2015.

Orozco, Cynthia E. *No Mexicans, Women, or Dogs Allowed: The Rise of the Mexican American Civil Rights Movement.* Austin: University of Texas Press, 2009.

Ortiz, Paul. *An African American and Latinx History of the United States.* Boston: Beacon, 2018.

Ortiz Peralta, Rina, ed. and trans. *Alexandra Kollontai en México: diario y otros documentos.* Xalapa: Universidad Veracruzana, 2012.

Ota Mishima, María Elena. *Destino México: un estudio de las Migraciones Asiáticas a México, siglos XIX y XX.* Mexico City: Colegio de México, Centro de Estudios de Asia y Africa, 1997.

Ovalle, Priscilla Peña. *Dance and the Hollywood Latina: Race, Sex, and Stardom.* New Brunswick, NJ: Rutgers University Press, 2010.

Owen, Norman G. *Prosperity without Progress: Manila Hemp and Material Life in the Colonial Philippines.* Berkeley: University of California Press, 1984.

Pearlman, Michael, ed. and trans. *The Heroic and Creative Meaning of Socialism: Selected Essays of José Carlos Mariátegui.* Atlantic Highlands, NJ: Humanities Press, 1996.

Pérez, Emma. *The Decolonial Imaginary: Writing Chicanas into History.* Bloomington: Indiana University Press, 1999.

Pérez, Louis A. *Cuba and the United States: Ties of Singular Intimacy.* Athens: University of Georgia Press, 2003.

Perry, Louis B., and Richard S. Perry. *A History of the Los Angeles Labor Movement, 1911–1941.* Berkeley: University of California Press, 1963.

Pfeifer, Michael J. Introduction to *Lynching Beyond Dixie: American Mob Violence Outside the South,* edited by Michael J. Pfeifer, 1–18. Urbana: University of Illinois Press, 2013.

Piven, Frances Fox, and Richard A. Cloward. *Poor People's Movements: Why They Succeed, How They Fail.* New York: Vintage, 1979.

Poniatowska, Elena. *Tinisima.* New York: Farrar, Strauss, and Giroux, 1996.

Prignitz-Poda, Helga. *TGP, ein Grafiker-Kollektiv in Mexico von 1937–1977*. Berlin: Seitz, 1981.

Prucha, Francis Paul, ed. *Documents of United States Indian Policy*. 2nd ed. Lincoln: University of Nebraska Press, 1990.

Raat, W. Dirk. *Revoltosos: Mexico's Rebels in the United States, 1903–1923*. College Station: Texas A&M University Press, 1981.

Ramnath, Maia. *From Haj to Utopia: How the Ghadar Movement Charted Global Radicalism and Attempted to Overthrow the British Empire*. Berkeley: University of California Press, 2011.

Ray, Sibnarayan, ed. *Selected Works of M. N. Roy*. Vol. 1, *1917–1922*. Delhi: Oxford University Press, 2000.

Reed, John. *Adventures of a Young Man*. San Francisco: City Lights, 1975.

———. *Insurgent Mexico*. New York: International Publishers, 1969.

———. *Ten Days That Shook the World*. New York: Penguin, 1977.

Richards, Susan Valerie. "Imagining the Political: El Taller de Gráfica Popular in Mexico, 1937–1949." PhD diss., University of New Mexico, 2001.

Richardson, William Harrison. *Mexico through Russian Eyes, 1806–1940*. Pittsburgh: University of Pittsburgh Press, 1988.

Roberts, Randy. *Papa Jack: Jack Johnson and the Era of White Hopes*. New York: Free Press, 1983.

Robinson, Cedric J. *An Anthropology of Marxism*. Aldershot, UK: Ashgate, 2001.

———. *Black Marxism: The Making of the Black Radical Tradition*. Chapel Hill: University of North Carolina Press, 2000.

———. *Forgeries of Memory and Meaning: Blacks and the Regimes of Race in American Theater and Film Before World War II*. Chapel Hill: University of North Carolina Press, 2007.

Rochfort, Desmond. *Mexican Muralists: Orozco, Rivera, Siqueiros*. San Francisco: Chronicle Books, 1993.

Rodney, Walter. *A History of the Guyanese Working People, 1881–1905*. Baltimore: Johns Hopkins University Press, 1981.

———. *How Europe Underdeveloped Africa*. Washington, DC: Howard University Press, 1972.

Roediger, David R. *How Race Survived US History: From Settlement and Slavery to the Obama Phenomenon*. New York: Verso, 2008.

———. *The Wages of Whiteness: Race and the Making of the American Working Class*. London: Verso, 1991.

Roediger, David R., and Elizabeth D. Esch. *The Production of Difference: Race and the Management of Labor in U.S. History*. New York: Oxford University Press, 2012.

Roediger, David, and Franklin Rosemont, eds. *Haymarket Scrapbook*. Chicago: Charles H. Kerr, 1986.

Romero, Robert Chao. *The Chinese in Mexico, 1882–1940*. Tucson: University of Arizona Press, 2011.

Romo, Ricardo. *East Los Angeles: History of a Barrio*. Austin: University of Texas Press, 1992.

Rosenberg, Emily S. *Financial Missionaries to the World: The Politics and Culture of Dollar Diplomacy, 1900–1930.* Cambridge, MA: Harvard University Press, 1999.

Rosenstone, Robert A. *Romantic Revolutionary: A Biography of John Reed.* New York: Vintage, 1975.

Ross, Kristin. *Communal Luxury: The Political Imaginary of the Paris Commune.* London: Verso, 2015.

Roy, M. N. "Draft Supplementary Theses on the National and Colonial Question, 2nd Congress Communist International." In *Documents of the History of the Communist Party of India.* Vol. 1, *1917–1922*, edited by G. Adhikari. New Delhi: People's Publishing House, 1971.

Roy, Samaren. *The Restless Brahmin: Early Life of M. N. Roy.* Bombay: Allied Publishers, 1970.

Royster, Jacqueline Jones, ed. *Southern Horrors and Other Writings: The Anti-Lynching Campaign of Ida B. Wells, 1892–1900.* Boston: Bedford/St. Martin's, 2016.

Ruíz, Ramón Eduardo. *The Great Rebellion: Mexico, 1905–1924.* New York: W. W. Norton, 1980.

Ruíz, Vicki L. *Cannery Women, Cannery Lives: Mexican Women, Unionization, and the California Food Processing Industry, 1930–1950.* Albuquerque: University of New Mexico Press, 1987.

Runstedtler, Theresa. *Jack Johnson, Rebel Sojourner: Boxing in the Shadow of the Global Color Line.* Berkeley: University of California Press, 2012.

Ryan, Erica J. *Red War on the Family: Sex, Gender, and Americanism in the First Red Scare.* Philadelphia: Temple University Press, 2015.

Said, Edward W. *Culture and Imperialism.* New York: Vintage, 1994.

San Juan, E., Jr. *U.S. Imperialism and Revolution in the Philippines.* New York: Palgrave Macmillan, 2007.

Sánchez, George J. *Becoming Mexican American: Ethnicity, Culture and Identity in Chicano Los Angeles, 1900–1945.* New York: Oxford University Press, 1993.

Sandage, Scott A. *Born Losers: A History of Failure in America.* Cambridge, MA: Harvard University Press, 2005.

Saxton, Alexander. *The Indispensable Enemy: Labor and the Anti-Chinese Movement in California.* Berkeley: University of California Press, 1971.

Schreiber, Rebecca M. *Cold War Exiles in Mexico: U.S. Dissidents and the Culture of Resistance.* Minneapolis: University of Minnesota Press, 2008.

Schroeder, Elizabeth R. "The Chicago Black Renaissance: Exercises in Aesthetic Ideology and Cultural Geography in Bronzeville, 1932–1945." PhD diss., Saint Louis University, 2008.

Schubert, Irene, and Frank N. Schubert. *On the Trail of the Buffalo Soldier II: New and Revised Biographies of African Americans in the U.S. Army, 1866–1917.* Lanham, MD: Scarecrow Press, 2004.

Scott, Julius S. *The Common Wind: Afro-American Currents in the Age of the Haitian Revolution.* New York: Verso, 2020.

Sears, Clare. *Arresting Dress: Cross-Dressing, Law, and Fascination in Nineteenth Century San Francisco*. Durham, NC: Duke University Press, 2014.

Seigel, Micol. *Uneven Encounters: Making Race and Nation in Brazil and the United States*. Durham, NC: Duke University Press, 2009.

Sell, Zach. *Trouble of the World: Slavery and Empire in the Age of Capital*. Chapel Hill: University of North Carolina Press, 2021.

Sexton, Jay. *Debtor Diplomacy: Finance and American Foreign Relations in the Civil War Era, 1837–1873*. New York: Oxford University Press, 2005.

———. *The Monroe Doctrine: Empire and Nation in Nineteenth-Century America*. New York: Hill and Wang, 2011.

Seymour, Richard. *American Insurgents: A Brief History of American Anti-Imperialism*. Chicago: Haymarket Books, 2011.

Shapiro, David, and Cecile Shapiro. "The Artists' Union in America." In *The Other America: Art and the Labor Movement in the United States*, edited by Philip S. Foner and Reinhard Schultz, 93–94. London: Journeyman Press, 1985.

Shuler, Jack. *The Thirteenth Turn: A History of the Noose*. New York: Public Affairs, 2014.

Shukla, Sandhya, and Heidi Tinsman, eds. *Imagining Our Americas: Toward a Transnational Frame*. Durham, NC: Duke University Press, 2007.

Sides, Josh. *LA City Limits: African American Los Angeles from the Great Depression to the Present*. Berkeley: University of California Press, 2003.

Silver, Beverly. "Class Struggle and Kondratieff Waves, 1870 to the Present." In *New Findings in Long-Wave Research,* edited by Alfred Kleinknecht, Ernest Mandel, and Immanuel Wallerstein, 279–96. London: St. Martin's Press, 1992.

Simon, Faith. Introduction to *Communism and the Family,* by Alexandra Kollontai, 1–5. Cleveland: Hera Press, 1982.

Simpson, Audra. *Mohawk Interruptus: Political Life Across the Borders of Settler States*. Durham, NC: Duke University Press, 2014.

Sluga, Glenda. *Internationalism in the Age of Nationalism*. Philadelphia: University of Pennsylvania Press, 2013.

Smallwood, Stephanie E. *Saltwater Slavery: A Middle Passage from Africa to American Diaspora*. Cambridge, MA: Harvard University Press, 2008.

Smethurst, James. "Remembering Nat Turner: Black Artists, Radical History, and Radical Historiography, 1930–55." In *Lineages of the Literary Left: Essays in Honor of Alan M. Wald,* edited by Howard Brick, Robbie Lieberman, and Paula Rabinowitz. Ann Arbor: Michigan Publishing, University of Michigan Library, 2015. http://dx.doi.org/10.3998/maize.13545968.0001.001.

Smith, Stephanie J. *The Power and Politics of Art in Postrevolutionary Mexico*. Chapel Hill: University of North Carolina Press, 2017.

Smith, Neil. *American Empire: Roosevelt's Geographer and the Prelude to Globalization*. Berkeley: University of California Press, 2003.

Sohi, Seema. "Echoes of Mutiny: Race, Empire, and Indian Anticolonialism in North America." PhD diss., University of Washington, Seattle, 2008.

Spenser, Daniela. *The Impossible Triangle: Mexico, Soviet Russia, and the United States in the 1920s.* Durham, NC: Duke University Press, 1999.

———. *Stumbling Its Way Through Mexico: The Early Years of the Communist International.* Translated by Peter Gellert. Tuscaloosa: University of Alabama Press, 2011.

Spenser, Daniela, and Rina Ortiz Peralta, *La Internacional Comunista en México: Los Primeros Tropiezos: Documentos, 1919–1922.* México: INEHRM, 2006.

Spierman, Ole. *International Legal Argument in the Permanent Court of International Justice: The Rise of the International Judiciary.* Cambridge, UK: Cambridge University, 2005.

Stallybrass, Peter. "Marx's Coat." In *Border Fetishisms: Material Objects in Unstable Spaces,* edited by Patricia Spyer, 183–207. New York: Routledge, 1998.

Starr, Kevin. *Endangered Dreams: The Great Depression in California.* New York: Oxford University Press, 1996.

Steel, Edward M., ed. *The Correspondence of Mother Jones.* Pittsburgh: University of Pittsburgh Press, 1985.

Stein, Philip. *Siqueiros: His Life and Works.* New York: International Publishers, 1994.

Stevens, Errol Wayne. *Radical LA: From Coxey's Army to the Watts Riots, 1894–1965.* Norman: University of Oklahoma Press, 2009.

Stevens, Margaret. *Red International and Black Caribbean: Communists in New York City, Mexico, and the West Indies, 1919–1939.* London: Pluto Press, 2017.

Stites, Richard. *The Women's Liberation Movement in Russia: Feminism, Nihilism, and Bolshevism, 1860–1930.* Princeton, NJ : Princeton University Press, 1991.

Storch, Randi. *Red Chicago: American Communism at Its Grassroots, 1928–35.* Urbana: University of Illinois Press, 2008.

Streeby, Shelley. *Radical Sensations: World Movements, Violence, and Visual Culture.* Durham, NC: Duke University Press, 2013.

Struthers, David. *The World in a City: Multiethnic Radicalism in Early Twentieth-Century Los Angeles.* Urbana: University of Illinois Press, 2019.

Taibo, Paco Ignacio, II. *Los Bolshevikis: Historia Narrativa de los Orígenes del Comunismo en México, 1919–1925.* Mexico City: J. Mortiz, 1986.

———. *The Shadow of the Shadow.* Translated by William I. Neuman. El Paso, TX: Cinco Puntos Press, 1991.

Takaki, Ronald. *Iron Cages: Race and Culture in 19th-Century America.* New York: Oxford University Press, 2000.

Taylor, Cynthia. *A. Philip Randolph: The Religious Journey of an African American Labor Leader.* New York: New York University Press, 2006.

Taylor, Peter J. "Locating the American Century: A World-Systems Analysis." In *The American Century: Consensus and Coercion in the Projection of American Power,* edited by David Slater and Peter J. Taylor. Oxford, UK: Blackwell, 1999.

Thompson, E. P. *The Making of the English Working Class.* London: IICA, 1963.

Thornton, Christy. *Revolution in Development: Mexico and the Governance of the Global Economy.* Oakland: University of California Press, 2021.

Townsend, Stephen A. *The Yankee Invasion of Texas.* College Station: Texas A&M University Press, 2006.

Traven, B. *The Cotton Pickers.* New York: Hill and Wang, 1969.

Trotsky, Leon. *My Life.* New York: Pathfinder Press, 1970.

———. *On Literature and Art.* New York: Pathfinder Press, 1970.

Trouillot, Michel-Rolph. *Silencing the Past: Power and the Production of History.* Boston: Beacon, 2012.

Truett, Samuel, and Elliott Young, eds. *Continental Crossroads: Remapping U.S.-Mexico Borderlands History.* Durham, NC: Duke University Press, 2004.

Tsuzuki, Chushichi. "The Changing Image of Britain among Japanese Intellectuals." In *The History of Anglo-Japanese Relations, 1600–2000: Social and Cultural Perspectives,* edited by Gordon Daniels and Chushichi Tsuzuki, 17–40. London: Palgrave Macmillan, 2002.

———. *The Pursuit of Power in Modern Japan, 1825–1995.* Oxford, UK: Oxford University Press, 2000.

Tucker, Spencer C. *The Encyclopedia of North American Indian Wars, 1607–1890: A Political, Social, and Military History.* Santa Barbara, CA: ABC-CLIO, 2011.

Tully, John. *Devil's Milk: A Social History of Rubber.* New York: Monthly Review Press, 2011

Tuñón Pablos, Esperanza. *Mujeres que se Organizan: El Frente Único pro Derechos de la Mujer, 1935–1938.* Mexico City: Universidad Nacional Autónoma de México, 1992.

Turner, Ethel Duffy. *Ricardo Flores Magón y el Partido Liberal Mexicano.* Mexico: Comisión Nacional Editorial del CEN, 1984.

Turner, John Kenneth. *Barbarous Mexico.* Chicago: Charles H. Kerr, 1910.

Tutino, John. "The Americas in the Rise of Industrial Capitalism." In *New Countries: Capitalism, Revolutions, and Nations in the Americas, 1750–1870,* edited by John Tutino, 25–70. Durham, NC: Duke University Press, 2016.

———. *The Mexican Heartland: How Communities Shaped Capitalism, a Nation, and World History, 1500–2000.* Princeton, NJ: Princeton University Press, 2017.

———, ed. *Mexico and Mexicans and the Making of the United States.* Austin: University of Texas Press, 2012.

Vanden, Harry E., and Marc Becker, eds. *José Carlos Mariátegui: An Anthology.* New York: Monthly Review Press, 2011.

Vargas, Zaragosa. *Crucible of Struggle: A History of Mexican Americans from Colonial Times to the Present Era.* New York: Oxford University Press, 2001.

———. *Labor Rights Are Civil Rights: Mexican American Workers in Twentieth-Century America.* Princeton, NJ: Princeton University Press, 2005.

Vaughan, Mary Kay. *Cultural Politics in Revolution: Teachers, Peasants, and Schools in Mexico, 1930–1940.* Tucson: University of Arizona Press, 1997.

———, and Steven E. Lewis, eds. *The Eagle and the Virgin: Nation and Cultural Revolution in Mexico, 1920–1940.* Durham, NC: Duke University Press, 2006.

Veeser, Cyrus. *A World Safe for Capitalism: Dollar Diplomacy and America's Rise to Global Power*. New York: Columbia University Press, 2013.

Vendryes, Margaret Rose. "Hanging on Their Walls: An Art Commentary on Lynching, the Forgotten 1935 Art Exhibition." In *Race Consciousness: African-American Studies for the New Century*, edited by Judith Jackson Fossett and Jeffrey A. Tucker, 153–76. New York: New York University Press, 1997.

Walker, Richard. *The Conquest of Bread: 150 Years of Agribusiness in California*. New York: New Press, 2004.

Ward, Geoffrey C. *Unforgivable Blackness: The Rise and Fall of Jack Johnson*. New York: Vintage, 2006.

Warman, Arturo. "The Political Project of Zapatismo." In *Riot, Rebellion, and Revolution: Rural Social Conflict in Mexico*, edited by Friedrich Katz, 321–37. Princeton, NJ: Princeton University Press, 1988.

Washington, Mary Helen. *The Other Blacklist: The African American Literary and Cultural Left of the 1950s*. New York: Columbia University Press, 2014.

Wasserman, Mark. *Everyday Life and Politics in Nineteenth Century Mexico: Men, Women, and War*. Albuquerque: University of New Mexico Press, 2000.

———. *Persistent Oligarchs: Elites and Politics in Chihuahua, Mexico, 1910–1940*. Durham, NC: Duke University Press, 1993.

Weber, Devra. *Dark Sweat, White Gold: California Farm Workers, Cotton, and the New Deal*. Berkeley: University of California Press, 1996.

———. "Keeping Community, Challenging Boundaries: Indigenous Migrants, Internationalist Workers, and Mexican Revolutionaries, 1900–1920." In *Mexico and Mexicans in the Making of the United States*, edited by John Tutino, 208–35. Austin: University of Texas Press, 2012.

Weare, Walter B. *Black Business in the New South: A Social History of the NC Mutual Life Insurance Company*. Durham, NC: Duke University Press, 1993.

Wells, Allen, and Gilbert M. Joseph. *Summer of Discontent, Seasons of Upheaval: Elite Politics and Rural Insurgency in Yucatán, 1876–1915*. Stanford, CA: Stanford University Press, 1996.

Wells-Barnett, Ida. *Collected Work of Ida B. Wells-Barnett*. Charleston, SC: Bibliobazaar, 2007.

Westad, Odd Arne. *The Global Cold War: Third World Interventions and the Making of Our Times*. Cambridge, UK: Cambridge University Press, 2007.

White, John Franklin, ed. *Art in Action: American Art Centers and the New Deal*. Metuchen, NJ: Scarecrow Press, 1987.

Wild, Mark. *Street Meeting: Multiethnic Neighborhoods in Early Twentieth-Century Los Angeles*. Berkeley: University of California Press, 2008.

Williams, Gwyn. *Proletarian Order: Antonio Gramsci, Factory Councils and the Origins of Italian Communism, 1911–1921*. London: Pluto Press, 1975.

Winder, Gordon M. *The American Reaper: Harvesting Networks and Technology, 1830–1910*. New York: Routledge, 2016.

Womack, John, Jr. *Zapata and the Mexican Revolution*. New York: Vintage, 1969.

Wood, Andrew Grant. *Revolution in the Street: Women, Workers, and Urban Protest in Veracruz, 1870–1927*. Wilmington, DE: Scholarly Resources Books, 2001.

Woodard, Komozi. "Citizen Malcolm X Blueprint for Black Liberation: Coming of Age with Rod Bush on Race, Class and Citizenship in the Bandung Era." In *Rod Bush: Lessons from a Radical Black Scholar on Liberation, Love, and Justice*, edited by Melanie E. L. Bush, et al, 171–83. Belmont, MA: Ahead, 2019.

Zhuravskaya, Gustava. "Love as an Ideology: The Reflections on 'Sexual Crisis' in Aleksandra Kollontai's Writing." PhD diss., Central European University, Budapest, 1998.

Zimmerman, Angela ed. *The Civil War in the United States: Karl Marx and Friedrich Engels*. New York: International Publishers, 2016.

Zinn, Howard. *A People's History of the United States*. New York: Harper Collins, 2010.

Articles

Alexander, Ryan M. "The Fever of War: Epidemic Typhus and Public Health in Revolutionary Mexico City, 1915–1917." *Hispanic American Historical Review* 100, no. 1 (2020): 63–92.

———. "The Spanish Flu and the Sanitary Dictatorship: Mexico's Response to the 1918 Influenza Pandemic." *The Americas* 76, no. 3 (July 2019): 443–65.

Alston, Lee J., Shannan Mattiace, and Tomas Nonnenmacher. "Coercion, Culture, and Contracts: Labor and Debt on Henequen Haciendas in Yucatán, Mexico, 1870–1915." *Journal of Economic History* 69, no. 1 (March 2009): 104–37.

Armitage, David R. "Globalizing Jeremy Bentham." *History of Political Thought* 32, no. 1 (2011): 63–82.

Arrighi, Giovanni, and Beverly J. Silver, "Capitalism and World (Dis)Order," *Review of International Studies* 27 (2001): 257–79.

Bannerji, Himani. "Building from Marx: Reflections on Class and Race," *Social Justice* 32, no. 4 (2005): 144–60.

Blackburn, Robin. "Haiti, Slavery, and the Age of the Democratic Revolution." *The William and Mary Quarterly* 63, no. 4 (October 2006): 643–74.

Carroll, Christina. "Imperial Ideologies in the Second Empire: The Mexican Expedition and the Royaume Arabe." *French Historical Studies* 42, no. 1 (February 2019): 67–100.

Clements, Barbara Evans. "Emancipation Through Communism: The Ideology of A. M. Kollontai." *Slavic Review* 32, no. 2 (1973): 323–38.

Coatsworth, John. "Railroads, Landholding, and Agrarian Protest in Early Porfiriato." *Hispanic American Historical Review* 54 (1974): 48–71.

Colley, Linda. "Empires of Writing: Britain, America and Constitutions, 1776–1848." *Law and History Review* 32, no. 2 (May 2014): 237–66.

Correia, David. "Making Destiny Manifest: United States Territorial Expansion and the Dispossession of Two Mexican Property Claims in New Mexico, 1824–1899." *Journal of Historical Geography* 35 (2009): 87–103.

Cowen, Deborah. "Following the Infrastructures of Empire: Notes on Cities, Settler Colonialism, and Method." *Urban Geography* 41, no. 4 (2020): 469–86.

Cowen, Deborah, and Neil Smith. "After Geopolitics? From the Geopolitical Social to Geoeconomics." *Antipode* 41, no. 1 (2009): 22–48.

Davis, Mike. "The Necessary Eloquence of Protest." *The Nation,* March 17, 2009.

———. "Sunshine and the Open Shop: Ford and Darwin in 1920s Los Angeles." *Antipode* 29, no. 4 (October 1997): 356–82.

Denning, Michael. "Cheap Stories: Notes on Popular Fiction and Working-Class Culture in Nineteenth-Century America." *History Workshop* 22 (Autumn 1986): 1–17.

———. "Impeachment as a Social Form." *New Left Review* 122 (March/April 2020): 65–79.

———. "Representing Global Labor." *Social Text* 92, no. 25, no. 3 (Fall 2007): 21–45.

Dirlik Arif. "Performing the World: Reality and Representation in the Making of World Histor(ies)." *Journal of World History* 16, no. 4 (December 2005): 391–410.

Domosh, Mona. "Geoeconomic Imaginations and Economic Geography in the Early Twentieth Century." *Annals of the Association of American Geographers* 103, no. 4 (July 2013): 944–66.

"Elizabeth Catlett, Sculptor and Printmaker." *Current Biography* 59, no. 5 (May 1998): 6–8.

Emmanuel, Arghiri. "White-Settler Colonialism and the Myth of Investment Imperialism." *New Left Review* 73 (May/June 1972): 35–57.

Enstad, Nan. "The 'Sonorous Summons' of the New History of Capitalism, or, What Are We Talking about When We Talk about Economy?" *Modern American History* 2, no. 1 (2019): 83–95.

Farnsworth, Beatrice. "Conversing with Stalin, Surviving the Terror: The Diaries of Aleksandra Kollontai and the Internal Life of Politics." *Slavic Review* 69, no. 4 (Winter 2010): 944–70.

Ferrer, Ada. "Haiti, Free Soil, and Antislavery in the Revolutionary Atlantic." *The American Historical Review* 117, no. 1 (February 2012): 40–66.

Foran, John. "Reinventing the Mexican Revolution: The Competing Paradigms of Alan Knight and John Mason Hart." *Latin American Perspectives* 23, no. 4 (1996): 115–31.

Fox, Cybelle. "Three Worlds of Relief: Race, Immigration, and Public and Private Social Welfare Spending in American Cities, 1929." *American Journal of Sociology* 116, no. 2 (September 2010): 466–68.

Gall, Olivia. "Identidad, exclusión y racismo: reflexiones teóricas y sobre México." *Revista Mexicana de Sociología* 4, no. 2 (2004): 221–59.

Gallagher, John, and Robin Robinson. "The Imperialism of Free Trade." *Economic History Review* 6, no. 1 (August 1953): 1–15.

Gettleman, Marvin E. "Defending Left Pedagogy: U.S. Communist Schools Fight Back against the SACB (Subversive Activities Control Board) . . . and Lose (1953–1957)." *Convergence* 41, no. 2–3 (2008): 193–209.

————. "'No Varsity Teams': New York's Jefferson School of Social Science, 1943–1956." *Science and Society* 66, no. 3 (2002): 336–59.

Gilmore, Ruth Wilson. "Fatal Couplings of Power and Difference: Notes on Racism and Geography." *The Professional Geographer* 54, no. 1 (2002): 15–24.

————. "Race, Prisons, and War: Scenes from the History of U.S. Violence." *Socialist Register* 45 (2009): 73–87.

Goldman, Shifra M. "Resistance and Identity: Street Murals of Occupied Aztlán." *Latin American Literary Review* 5, no. 10 (1977): 124–8.

————. "Six Women Artists of Mexico." *Women's Art Journal* 3, no. 2 (Autumn, 1982–Winter 1983): 2.

Gómez, Alan Eladio. "'Nuestras Vidas Corren Casi Paralelas': Chicanos, Independentistas, and the Prison Rebellions in Leavenworth, 1969–1972." *Latino Studies* 6 (2008): 64–96.

Gosse, Van. "Locating the Black Intellectual: An Interview with Harold Cruse." *Radical History Review* 71 (1998): 97–120.

Gouma-Peterson, Thalia. "Elizabeth Catlett: 'The Power of Human Feeling and of Art.'" *Woman's Art Journal* 4, no. 1 (Spring-Summer 1983): 48–56.

Green, James R. "The Globalization of a Memory: The Enduring Remembrance of the Haymarket Martyrs around the World." *Labor: Studies in Working-Class History of the Americas* 2, no. 4 (2005): 11–24.

Grocott, Chris, and Jo Grady. "'Naked abroad': The Continuing Imperialism of Free Trade." *Capital & Class* 38, no. 3 (2014): 541–642.

Gwin, Catherine Christensen. "'The Selling of American Girls': Mexico's White Slave Trade in the California Imaginary," *California History* 99, no. 1 (2022): 30–54.

Haley, Sarah. "'Like I Was a Man': Chain Gangs, Gender, and the Domestic Carceral Sphere in Jim Crow Georgia." *Signs: Journal of Women and Culture in Society* 39, no. 1 (Autumn 2013): 53–77.

Hall, Catherine. "Gendering Property, Racing Capital." *History Workshop Journal* 78, no. 1 (2014): 22–38.

Hardt, Michael, "Red Love." *The South Atlantic Quarterly* 116, no. 4 (October 2017): 781–96.

Hayase, Shinzo. "American Colonial Policy and the Japanese Abaca Industry in Davao, 1898–1941." *Philippine Studies* 33, no. 4 (1985): 505–17.

————. "Manila Hemp in World, Regional, National, and Local History." *Journal of Asia-Pacific Studies* 31 (March 2018): 171–88.

Hemingway, Andrew. "American Communists View Mexican Muralism: Critical and Artistic Responses." *Crónicas: El Muralismo, Producto de la Revolución en América* 8–9 (March 2001–02): 13–43.

Herzog, Melanie Anne. "The Education of Sculptress Elizabeth Catlett." *The Journal of Blacks in Higher Education* 25 (Autumn 1999), 7.

————. "Elizabeth Catlett (1915–2012)." *American Art* 26, no. 3 (Fall 2012): 105–9.

Horn, James J. "U.S. Diplomacy and 'The Specter of Bolshevism' in Mexico (1924–1927)." *The Americas* 32, no. 1 (July 1975): 39–40.

Hoffman, Abraham. "Stimulus to Repatriation: The 1931 Federal Deportation Drive and the Los Angeles Mexican Community." *Pacific Historical Review* 42, no. 2 (May 1973): 205–19.

Hudson, Peter James. "The National City Bank of New York and Haiti, 1909–1922." *Radical History Review* 115 (Winter 2013): 91–114.

Imada, Adria L. "'Aloha 'Oe': Settler-Colonial Nostalgia and the Genealogy of a Love Song." *American Indian Culture and Research Journal* 37, no. 2 (June 2013): 35–52.

James, Curtia. "Elizabeth Catlett: Pulling against the Curtain." *American Visions* (Feb/March 1994): 29–35.

Kearns, Martha. "Elizabeth Catlett: The Spirit of Form." *Sculpture* 18 (March 1999): 34.

Kelley, Robin D. G. "A New Look at the Communist Manifesto." *Race Traitor* 13–14 (Summer 2001): 135–39.

Kelley, Sean. "'Mexico in His Head': Slavery and the Texas-Mexico Border, 1810–1860." *Journal of Social History* 37, no. 3 (Spring 2004): 709–23.

Knight, Alan. "Mexican Peonage: What Was It and Why Was It?" *Journal of Latin American Studies* 18, no. 1 (1986): 41–74.

———. "Popular Culture and the Revolutionary State in Mexico, 1910–1940." *Hispanic American Historical Review* 74, no. 3 (August 1994): 393–444.

———. "The Working Class and the Mexican Revolution, c. 1900–1920." *Journal of Latin American Studies* 16, no. 1 (May 1984): 51–79.

Kollontai, Alexandra. "Diplomatic Diary: A Record of 23 Years, Part Four, 1926–1927, Mexico." *International Affairs* (February 1989): 122–30.

La Botz, Dan. "American 'Slackers' in the Mexican Revolution: International Proletarian Politics in the Midst of a National Revolution." *The Americas* 62, no. 4 (2006): 563–90.

Langa, Helen. "Two Antilynching Art Exhibitions: Politicized Viewpoints, Racial Perspectives, Gendered Constraints." *Journal of Contemporary African Art* 20 (Fall 2006): 96–115.

Leab, Daniel J. "'United We Eat': The Creation and Organization of the Unemployed Councils in 1930." *Labor History* 8, no. 3 (1967): 300–315.

Lee, Seung-Ook, et al. "Geopolitical Economy and the Production of Territory: The Case of US–China Geopolitical-Economic Competition in Asia." *Environment and Planning A* 50, no. 2 (2017): 416–36.

LeFalle-Collins, Lizzetta. "The Mexican Connection: The New Negro and Border Crossings." *American Visions* 11, no. 6 (December-January 1996): 20–27.

Linebaugh, Peter. "Karl Marx, the Theft of Wood, and Working-Class Composition: A Contribution to the Current Debate." *Social Justice* 40, no. 1–2 (Spring-Summer 2014): 137–61.

———. "All the Atlantic Mountains Shook." *Labour/Le Travailleur* 10 (Autumn 1982): 87–121.

López, Rick A. "The India Bonita Contest of 1921 and the Ethnicization of Mexican National Culture." *Hispanic American Historical Review* 82, no. 2 (2002): 291–328.

Marcus, Irwin. "Benjamin Fletcher: Black Labor Leader." *Negro History Bulletin* 35 (October 1972): 131–40.

Marez, Curtis. "Pancho Villa Meets Sun Yat-sen: Third World Revolution and the History of Hollywood Cinema." *American Literary History* 17, no. 3 (Fall 2005): 486–505.

Mayer, Robert. "The Origins of the American Banking Empire in Latin America: Frank A. Vanderlip and the National City Bank." *Journal of Interamerican Studies and World Affairs* 15, no. 1 (February 1973): 60–76.

McAdams Sibley, Marilyn. "Charles Stillman: A Case Study of Entrepreneurship on the Rio Grande, 1861–1865." *The Southwestern Historical Quarterly* 77, no. 2 (October 1973): 227–40.

McCaa, Robert. "Missing Millions: The Demographic Costs of the Mexican Revolution," *Mexican Studies/Estudios Mexicanos* 19, no. 2 (2003): 367–400.

Meyers, Len, and Chris Knox, "Organizing the Unemployed in the Great Depression: Fighting for Unity," *Workers Vanguard* 73, no. 18 (July 1975): 6–7.

Monroy, Douglas. "Anarquismo y Comunismo: Mexican Radicalism and the Communist Party in Los Angeles during the 1930s." *Labor History* 24 (Winter 1983): 34–59.

Munro, John. "Empire and Intersectionality. Notes on the Production of Knowledge about US Imperialism." *Globality Studies Journal* 2 (November 2008): 1–29.

Olcott, Jocelyn. "'A Plague of Salaried Marxists': Sexuality and Subsistence in the Revolutionary Imaginary of Concha Michel." *Journal of Contemporary History* 52, no. 4 (October 2017): 980–98.

———. "'Take Off That Streetwalker's Dress': Concha Michel and the Cultural Politics of Gender in Postrevolutionary Mexico." *Journal of Women's History* 21, no. 3 (2009): 36–59.

Oles, James. "Noguchi in Mexico: International Themes for a Working-Class Market." *American Art* 15, no. 2 (2001): 10–33.

Ortiz Peralta, Rina. "La Embajadora Roja: Alexandra Kollontai y México." *Relaciones* 38, no. 149 (2017): 13–38.

Perry, Amanda T. "Becoming Indigenous in Haiti, from Dessalines to La Revue Indigène." *Small Axe* 21, no. 2 (July 2017): 45–61.

Poole, Deborah. "An Image of 'Our Indian': Type Photographs and Racial Sentiments in Oaxaca, 1920–1940." *Hispanic American Historical Review* 84, no. 1 (2004): 37–82.

Pulido, Laura. "Rethinking Environmental Racism: White Privilege and Urban Development in Southern California." *Annals of the Association of American Geographers* 90, no. 1 (2000): 12–40.

Rivera, Diego. "The Revolutionary Spirit in Modern Art." *Modern Quarterly* 6, no. 3 (Autumn 1932): 51–57.

Roberson, James E. "Singing Diaspora: Okinawan Songs of Home, Departure, and Return." *Identities* 17, no. 4 (2010): 430–53.

Rydjord, John. "The French Revolution and Mexico." *Hispanic American Historical Review* 9, no. 1 (February 1929): 60–98.

Siddle, Richard. "Colonialism and Identity in Okinawa before 1945." *Japanese Studies* 18, no. 2 (1998): 117–33.

Sims, Lowery Stokes. "Elizabeth Catlett: A Life in Art and Politics." *American Visions* 13, no. 2 (April-May 1998): 20–24.

Spenser, Daniela. "Bolsheviks' Encounter with the Mexican Revolution." *Tensões Mundiais* 13, no. 25 (2016): 77–98.

———. "Radical Mexico: Limits to the Impact of Soviet Communism." Translated by Richard Stoller. *Latin American Perspectives* 35, no. 2 (March 2008): 57–70.

———. "Stanislav Pestkovsky: A Soldier of the World Revolution in Mexico." *Journal of Iberian and Latin American Research* 8, no. 1 (2002): 35–56.

Stuhr-Rommereim, Helen, and Mari Jarris. "Nikolai Chernyshevsky's *What Is to Be Done?* and the Prehistory of International Marxist Feminism." *Feminist German Studies* 36, no. 1 (Spring-Summer 2020): 166–92.

Suarez-Potts, William. "The Railroad Strike of 1927: Labor and Law after the Mexican Revolution." *Labor History* 52, no. 4 (2011): 399–416.

Sundstrom, William A. "Last Hired, First Fired? Unemployment and Urban Black Workers during the Great Depression." *Journal of Economic History* 52, no. 2 (June 1992): 415–29.

Taylor, Paul S., and Clark Kerr. "Documentary History of the Strike of the Cotton Pickers in California 1933." In *Violations of Free Speech and Rights of Labor, Hearings Before a Subcommittee of the Committee on Education and Labor, United States Senate*, Part 54, Agriculture Labor in California (Washington, DC: United States Government Printing Office, 1940): 19994.

Tenorio Trillo, Mauricio. "The Cosmopolitan Mexican Summer, 1920–1949." *Latin American Research Review* 32, no. 3 (1997): 224–42.

Todd, David. "A French Imperial Meridian, 1814–1870." *Past and Present* 210, no. 1 (February 2011): 155–86.

Topik, Steven C. "When Mexico Had the Blues: A Transatlantic Tale of Bonds, Bankers, and Nationalists, 1862–1910." *American Historical Review* 105, no. 3 (June 2000): 714–38.

Vargas, Zaragosa. "Tejana Radical: Emma Tenayuca and the San Antonio Labor Movement During the Great Depression." *Pacific Historical Review* 66, no. 4 (November 1997): 553–80.

Walsh, Jess. "Laboring at the Margins: Welfare and the Regulation of Mexican Workers in Southern California." *Antipode* 31, no. 4 (1999): 398–420.

Wasserman, Mark. "The Mexican Revolution: Region and Theory, Signifying Nothing?" *Latin American Research Review* 25, no. 1 (1990): 231–42.

Werner, Marion, et al. "Feminist Political Economy in Geography: Why Now, What Is Different, and What For?" *Geoforum* 79 (2017): 1–4.

Wolfe, Patrick. "Settler Colonialism and the Elimination of the Native." *Journal of Genocide Research* 8, no. 4 (2006): 387–409.

Wood, Andrew Grant. "Death of a Political Prisoner: Revisiting the Case of Ricardo Flores Magón." *A Contracorriente* 3, no. 1 (Fall 2005): 38–66.

Yamanouchi, Akito. "The Early Comintern in Amsterdam, New York and Mexico City," *Shien* (March 2010): 99–139.

———. "The Letters and Manuscripts of Sen Katayama in Mexico, 1921." *Monthly Journal of Ohara Institute for Social Research* 506 (January 2001), 31–69.

Yonetani, Julia. "Ambiguous Traces and the Politics of Sameness: Placing Okinawa in Meiji Japan." *Japanese Studies* 20, no. 1 (2000): 15–31.

Zelman, Donald L. "Mexican Migrants and Relief in Depression California: Grower Reaction to Public Relief Policies as They Affected Mexican Migration." *Journal of Mexican American History* 5 (1975): 1–23.

INDEX

abolitionists, 30, 34, 35–39, 41–43, 173, 176, 178. *See also individuals*
Academia de San Carlos, 150, 157
Adams, Henry, 43
adult education, 161–66
AFL (American Federation of Labor), 105, 123, 141–42
African Americans, 1–2, 56–57, 62–64; AFL, 123; California, 63, 137; communism/CP, 57, 142, 143; Espionage Act (1917), 78; farmworkers, 124–25; Germany, 63; Great Depression, 143, 157; Haiti, 39; imperialism, 143; International Day of Struggle Against Unemployment, 139; IWW, 81; KKK, 63; labor, 63, 143; Leavenworth Federal Penitentiary, 80, 81, 85–88, 96; "Mac – American" (Reed), 68–69; Mexico, 62–64, 85–86; NAACP, 169; New Imperialism, 64; North Carolina, 153–54; racism, 62, 63, 178; radicalism, 57; socialism, 81; SSCAC, 145; UNIA, 80; US, 62–64, 86; whiteness, 57, 62, 63–64, 78, 81; WW I, 63. *See also* Black artists; Black domestic workers; Black soldiers; Black women; *individuals*; slavery
"African Roots of War, The" (Du Bois), 10, 11
Age of Revolution, 30–31
agribusiness, 4, 123, 127, 128, 130–32, 134–36
agriculture, 122–36; California, 122–32, 134–36; capitalism, 124, 128, 132, 144;

Carver, George Washington, 162;
CAWIU, 140, 141; immigrants, 50, 52; Indigenous people, 15; labor, 123–32; McCormick Harvesting Machine Company, 4; Mexican immigrants, 127–29; Mexican Revolution, 54; racism, 127–28; relief, 130–31; ropes, 3, 4–5; strikes, 54, 122–26, 133–36; US, 12, 122–23. *See also* farmworkers
Aguirre, Ignacio, 169
Ahlteen, Carl, 80–81
Alien Labor Act (1931), 131
Alston, Charles, 160, 169
Alvarado, Salvador, 59
Amador, Graciela, 114–15
Amaru, Túpac, 38
American Artists' Congress Against War and Fascism, 169
American Federation of Arts, 160
American Federation of Labor, 100
American Gothic (Wood), 154
Amistad, 169
anarchism: anarcho-syndicalism, 54, 113, 140; Bolshevik Revolution, 54; Espionage Act (1917), 75; House of the World Worker (Casa del Obrero Mundial), 59–60; "The Internationale" ("La Internacional"), 122, 176; internationalism, 19; IWW, 60, 177; Leavenworth Federal Penitentiary, 84, 96; "Manifesto to the Anarchists of the Entire World and to the Workers in General" (Flores Magón and Rivera), 74, 215n10; PLM,

anarchism *(continued)*
16; Spain, 54, 80; US, 54; Veracruz port,
98. *See also individuals*
And A Special Fear for My Loved Ones
(Catlett), *fig.* 18, 172–73
Andreychine, George, 80
Anguiano, Raúl, 169
Anhalt, Diana, 148
Arispe, Jose, 140–41
Art and Crafts Guild, 156–58
Art Institute of Chicago, 156–57
artists, 114–15, 150–52, 168–73; American
Artists' Congress Against War and
Fascism, 169; Chicago Artists' Union,
160; class, 165–66; colonialism, 150;
convergence space, 181; *El Dia*, 156;
Fédération Des Artistes, 175–76; George
Washington Carver School, 164; Har-
lem, 159–60; imperialism, 148; interna-
tionalism, 151, 181; labor, 149; lynching,
169; Mexican Revolution, 150, 151,
170–73; Mexico, 115, 150–51, 159; Mexico City, 18, 150; racism, 169; radicalism,
114–15, 152, 156, 159; Spain, 150; TGP,
169–70; unions, 160; US, 151–52. *See
also* Black artists; *individuals*; murals;
individual art works
Artists and Models Ball, 145–47, 157, 158
Ashleigh, Charles, 81, 82
Asian immigrants, 8, 10, 41, 48–53, 69,
210n17. *See also individuals*
Associated Farmers, 128, 130
Atlanta Unemployed Council, 143
Atlantic, 10
Azuara, Vicente Aurelio, 80–81, 82

Bagdad, Mexico, 21–26. *See also* Mexico
Baker, Ella, 166–67
Baltimore, Charles W., 87
Bank of America, 124, 128
Barros, Louis, 131
Beals, Carlton, 60
Bearden, Romare, 160–61
Beattie, Bessie, 118–19
Belafonte, Harry, 159
Benjamin, Herbert, 137
Bennett, Gwendolyn, 162–63
Bentham, Jeremy, 30–33, 34, 35, 37

Bentham, Samuel, 32–33
Bhattacharya, Narendranath. *See* Roy,
M.N.
Big Sea, The (Hughes), 63–64
Birch, Willie, 155
Black, Elaine, 139–40
Black artists, 147–49, 156–57, 158, 159,
160–61, 169. *See also individuals*
Black Arts Theater, 148
Black Bolshevik (Haywood), 148
Black domestic workers, 20, 141, 143–44,
149, 154, 165–68
Black Reconstruction in America, 1860–1880
(Du Bois), 175, 178–80, 181, 196n22
Black soldiers, 76, 86–87
"Black Woman, The" (Catlett), 170–71
Black women, 87, 162–63, 169, 170–71, 174,
235n12. *See also* Black domestic workers;
individuals
Bolívar, Simón, 31, 38
Bolshevik Revolution (1917): anarchism,
54; capitalism, 79, 113; children, 103;
colonialism/imperialism, 113; Gaikis,
Leon, 113; gender, 83; "The Internation-
ale" ("La Internacional"), 176; interna-
tionalism, 53–54, 115; Kōchi and Miya-
sato, 51; Kollontai, Alexandra, 109, 113;
labor, 65, 79–80, 113; Leavenworth
Federal Penitentiary, 82, 83; Mexican
Revolution, 54; Mexico, 98, 113–14;
Reed, John, 64–65, 67; Roy, M.N., 58;
Six Red Months in Russia (Bryant), *fig.*
8, 83; Spain, 54, 80, 113; *Ten Days That
Shook the World* (Reed), 64–65; US, 54
Bolshevism, 98–99, 100, 101, 106, 107–8,
109, 119, 120
Border Patrol, 128–29
Boren, Herman, 137
Boston Globe, 97, 107
Brazil, 50
Bread and Roses strike, 176
Brenner, Anita, 115
Breshkovsky, Katherine, 83
Briggs, Diana, 146
Bright, John, 42–43
Britain: abolitionists, 42–43; Bentham,
Samuel, 32–33; capitalism, 25, 34, 79;
China, 33–34; the Civil War (US),

42–43; colonialism, 37, 80, 182; cotton, 23, 31, 42; Douglass, Frederick, 35–36, 42, 43; Du Bois, W. E. B., 42; finance, 79; geoeconomics, 34; Germany, 35; Ghadar Movement, 80; hangings, 6; hegemony, 25, 181; imperialism, 57, 58, 80; India, 33–34, 55, 57, 58, 80; Ireland, 37, 80; labor, 42–43; Marx, Karl, 42; Mexico, 44, 54; racism, 41; railroads, 43; Roy, M. N., 182, 211n30; shipbuilders, 32–33; ships, 34, 35; slavery, 34, 35, 42; US, 31, 39, 40–42, 79

British Empire, the: Bentham, Jeremy, 31; capitalism, 25, 34; colonialism, 33–34; hegemony, 11–13; India, 33–34; internationalism, 33–35; Mexico, 21, 23; New Imperialism, 12, 197n34; ships, 33–35; slavery, 33, 34; territorialism, 31; US-Mexico War, 27

British Socialist Party, 57

Broms, Allen, 82

"Bronx Slave Market" (Cooke and Baker), 166–67

Brooklyn Museum, 160

Brooks, Gwendolyn, 156

Browder, Earl, 80, 81, 84

Brown, John, 2, 7

Bruce, Edward, 152

Bryant, Louise, *fig.* 8, 83, 97, 99, 111

Buffalo soldiers, 76

Bulosan, Carlos, 124

Burke, Selma Hortense, 160

Burr, Aaron, 31

Burroughs, Margaret (Goss), 146, 156–57, 158–59, 162–63

Cahill, Holger, 152

California, 122–44; African Americans, 63, 137; agriculture, 122–32, 134–36; Alien Labor Act (1931), 131; capitalism, 126, 132, 135, 136, 142, 144; El Congreso, 140; CP, 141–42; farmworkers, 19–20, 122–26, 133, 136; fascism, 136; Great Depression, 136–39; Kōchi, Shinsei "Paul," 51; labor, 126–32, 136–40, 141–42; Los Angeles Unemployed Councils, 138; McWilliams, Carey, 128; Mexican Revolution, 132–36; racism, 144; relief,

124–25, 130, 131, 134–37, 144, 176–77; State Commission on Unemployment, 139; strikes, 122–26, 133–36, 143–44; unions, 141–42; white vigilantes, 129, 136

California State Emergency Relief Administration, 130

Calles, Plutarco Elías, 100, 104, 106

Camp Wo-Chi-Ca, 160

capitalism: agribusiness, 135, 136; agriculture, 124, 128, 132, 144; Asian immigrants, 10, 41, 51–52; Bentham, Jeremy, 31–33; Bolshevik Revolution (1917), 79, 113; Britain, 25, 34, 79; California, 126, 132, 135, 136, 142, 144; class, 10–11, 126; class struggles, 26, 30, 199n44; colonialism, 25, 35, 56, 62; color line, 9–10, 61, 130, 141; *Communist Manifesto* (Marx and Engels), 29, 30; convergence space, 17–18, 52; Cooper, Anna Julia, 203n11; Díaz, Porfirio, 44; Douglass, Frederick, 25, 180, 181; Du Bois, W. E. B., 10–11, 180, 181; education, 93; 1848 pivot, 25–26, 28, 29; farmworkers, 127–28, 130, 132, 144; Flores Magón, Ricardo, 74–75, 92, 93, 95, 181; gender, 14, 120; geoeconomics, 11–13, 31, 67, 70, 74–75, 198n40; geopolitics, 13, 24; Germany, 34–35; Gramsci, Antonio, 93, 94; Healey, Dorothy, 242n6; imperialism, 10–11, 59, 62, 115, 144; internationalism, 14, 17–18, 26, 30, 44, 58, 106, 144, 180–81; IWW, 82; Kōchi, Shinsei "Paul," 48, 51–52; Kollontai, Alexandra, 101, 109, 120; labor, 10, 14, 30, 38, 56, 71, 93–94, 126–28, 135, 141; Latin America, 16; Leavenworth Federal Penitentiary, 75, 79; Lenin, Vladimir, 11; literacy, 104; love, 109–10; "Mac – American" (Reed), 70–71; "Manifesto to the Anarchists of the Entire World and to the Workers in General" (Flores Magón and Rivera), 215n10; Marx, Karl, 25, 40, 141; Mexican Revolution, 12, 16, 54, 74–75, 132; Mexico, 15, 22, 44–45, 46, 47, 67, 98, 132–33; militarism, 109; nationalization, 133; New Imperialism, 47–48, 70–71; Perry, Pettis, 142; Posada, José Guada

capitalism *(continued)*
lupe, 150; racism, 7, 10, 14, 24, 57, 59, 61, 63, 67, 79, 95, 144, 180; radicalism, 53, 75; railroads, 172; relief, 125–26, 130; resistance, 14, 17, 26; revolutions, 52, 56, 60–61, 67; ropes, 4–7; Roy, M.N., 55, 56, 58, 60–61, 62; shadow hegemony, 199n43; slavery, 24; strikes, 144, 211n30; struggles, 16–18; territorialism, 11, 25–26, 128; Unemployed Councils, 141, 144; US, 26, 60, 67, 75, 78–79, 115; US and Mexico, 22, 128, 132–33, 134; whiteness, 7, 10–11, 57; WWI, 108; Zapata, Emiliano, 59

Cárdenas, Lázaro, 173

Carranza, Venustiano, 65

Carver, George Washington, 162. *See also* George Washington Carver School

Catholic Welfare Bureau, 130

Catlett, Elizabeth, 145–74; as artist, 147, 148–49, 152–53, 154, 155–56, 169; artists, 165–66; Artists and Models Ball, 145–47; Bennett, Gwendolyn, 162–63; Black artists, 145, 160–61; Black domestic workers, 20, 149, 154, 165–68; Black women, 169, 170–71, 174; Camp Wo-Chi-Ca, 160; children, 174; class, 149–50, 153–54; colonialism, 153, 162; communism, 149, 153, 158–59, 235n16; Covarrubias, Miguel, 153; culture hunger, 159–61; Dillard College, 154–55; dresses, 145–47, 153, 166–68, 173; Du Bois, W.E.B., 159, 160; fascism, 162; FBI, 149; feminism, 149, 173; gender, 149–50, 162; geopolitics, 158; George Washington Carver School, 161–62, 164–66; Great Depression, 153; Harlem, 159–63; Haywood, Harry, 148, 235n14; housing, 168; "The Internationale" ("La Internacional"), 177; internationalism, 14, 148, 149–50, 156, 170, 173–74; labor, 160; "Leningrad" (Shostakovich), 164–65; lynching, *fig.* 18, 152, 172–73; Marvin X, 148; Marxism, 153, 166; Mexican Revolution, 20, 152, 173; Mexico, 145, 147, 148–49, 168–73; Mexico City, 169; Mora, Francisco "Pancho," 173; murals, 152–53; New York City, 168–69; NNC, 160; oil, *fig.* 20, 173; as organizer, *fig.* 16; pedagogy and protest, 152–56; photograph of, *fig.* 17; racism, 149, 153–55, 160, 161, 173; radicalism, 148–50, 152–53, 156, 158–59, 160, 161–63, 170, 173, 235n17; Rosenwald Fellowship, 168, 169, 170; slavery, 153; SSCAC, 145, 156–59; TGP, 149, 169–71, 173, 177; US, 149; White, Charles, 159–61, 168–70, 235n17; women, 147, 162–63; WPA, 150–52; Zadkine, Ossip, 173–74. *See also individual art works*

CAWIU (Cannery and Agricultural Workers Industrial Union), 140, 141

Chambers, Pat, 133

Chaplin, Ralph, 82

Charlot, Jean, 114–15

Chernyshevsky, Nikolai, 117, 120

Chicago Artists' Union, 160

Chicago Defender, 145, 157, 164, 166

Chicago Renaissance, 156

Chicago Tribune, 1–2

children, 54–55, 103, 104, 111–12, 117–19, 133, 174

Childress, Alice, 166

China, 3–4, 12, 28, 33–34, 50, 55, 143, 179

Chinese immigrants, 8, 10, 48, 50, 51, 53, 142, 210n17. *See also* Asian immigrants

Chinese Socialist Workers Party, 57

Chirino, José Leonardo, 38

CIO (Congress of Industrial Organizations), 140

Citibank, 25

Civil War, the (US), 21, 22–24, 28, 30, 42–43, 178

class: artists, 165–66; Asian immigrants, 51; Black domestic workers, 166–68; capitalism, 10–11, 126; Catlett, Elizabeth, 149–50, 153–54; color line, 95, 180; *The Eighteenth Brumaire of Louis Bonaparte* (Marx), 29–30; Flores Magón, Ricardo, 93, 95; Gramsci, Antonio, 93; internationalism, 51, 126, 142; KKK, 9; labor, 143; lynching, 9; Mexican Revolution, 54; New Imperialism, 10–11; open shop, 127; property love, 110; racism, 7, 20, 95; relief, 125–26; whiteness, 10; white vigilantes, 9 class struggles: abolitionists, 43; Bentham, Jeremy, 31; Black domestic workers, 165–66; capitalism, 26, 30, 199n44; colonialism, 62; color line, 56–57, 62, 78, 141, 142; communism, 62; *Communist Manifesto* (Marx and Engels), 30; convergence space, 17–18; CP, 56, 141, 142; debt finance, 41; farmworkers, 130; fascism, 94–95; Flores Magón, Ricardo, 46, 74–75; Haitian Revolution, 37; India, 58, 61; Italy, 94–95; IWMA, 43; IWW, 71, 78; Japanese immigrants, 143; labor, 71, 78; Leavenworth Federal Penitentiary, 75; Marx, Karl, 43; Mexican Revolution, 12, 15–16, 61; racism, 57, 94, 143, 144; Reed, John, 71; relief, 125–26, 130; ropes, 6, 7; Roy, M.N., 62; Unemployed Councils, 138, 143; WWI, 71, 108

Clements, George, 132

colonialism: abolitionists, 36; artists, 150; Bentham, Jeremy, 30–31, 32; Black artists, 156; Bolshevik Revolution (1917), 113; Britain/the British Empire, 33–34, 37, 80, 182; capitalism, 25, 35, 56, 62; Catlett, Elizabeth, 153, 162; class struggles, 62; convergence space, 17; Council on African Affairs, 162; Díaz, Porfirio, 14; Douglass, Frederick, 27, 37; Du Bois, W.E.B., 10; extractive industries, 17; First International (1864), 176; France, 37, 176, 177; Haiti, 37, 38; imperialism, 26, 55; India, 36, 50; Indigenous people, 37–38; Ireland, 35–36, 57, 80; labor, 33, 55, 56; Lenin, Vladimir, 56; Marxism, 57; Mexico, 38, 58; Meyers, Pauline, 153; murals, 105; Napoléon III, Louis Bonaparte, 28; *The Negro Worker*, 143; New Imperialism, 13, 64; racism, 57; revolutions, 56, 57, 61; Roy, M.N., 55–59, 60, 182; slavery, 34, 36; Spain, 2–3, 37–38; territorialism, 24, 26; US, 50. *See also* settler colonialism

color line, the, 7–11, 39–42; Asian immigrants, 8; capitalism, 9–10, 61, 130, 141; class, 95, 180; class struggles, 56–57, 62, 78, 141, 142; CP, 142; Douglass, Frederick, 8, 181; Du Bois, W.E.B., 8–11, 19,

41, 179–80, 181, 196n22, 197n29; farmworkers, 130; Flores Magón, Ricardo, 95, 96; Hughes, Langston, 64; internationalism, 39–42, 53; IWW, 78; labor, 78, 143; Leavenworth Federal Penitentiary, 75; lynching, 8, 69; Mexican Revolution, 95; racism, 8–10, 57, 180; Reed, John, 71; revolutions, 67; ropes, 6, 7–11; Roy, M.N., 61, 62; slavery, 8, 9; unions, 141; US, 8–9

"Color Line, The" (Douglass), 8

Columbia University, 178–79

Comintern (Communist International), 56–57, 65, 80, 107

communism, 54, 57, 62, 113, 140, 147, 201n52

"Communism and the Family" (Kollontai), 111, 118

Communist League, the, 30

Communist Manifesto (Marx and Engels), 26, 29–30, 83, 108

Communist Party, the. *See* CP (the Communist Party)

communists: Catlett, Elizabeth, 149, 153, 158–59, 182, 235n16; Cruse, Harold, 163; Espionage Act (1917), 75; farmworkers, 133–34; Great Depression, 138; Indigenous people, 98; "The Internationale" ("La Internacional"), 122, 176; internationalism, 19; Kollontai, Alexandra, 116; Leavenworth Federal Penitentiary, 96; Mexican Young Communists, 115; migrant workers, 132; nationalization, 173; Perry, Pettis, 142; Pestkovsky, Stanislav, 100; Rapp-Coudert committee investigation, 163; Reed, John, 182; Roy, M.N., 57–59; Soviet Embassy (Mexico), 115

Community Art Centers Project, 158

Connolly, Roddy and James, 57

conscientious objectors, 85

Contreras, Joseph, 23

convergence space, 16–18; artists, 181; capitalism, 17–18, 52; class struggles, 17–18; colonialism, 17; Flores Magón, Ricardo, 92; geoeconomics, 17, 180–81; geopolitics, 180–81; Indigenous people, 17; internationalism, 17–18, 99, 180–81;

convergence space *(continued)*
  Jim Crow, 17; Kollontai, Alexandra, 101;
  Leavenworth Federal Penitentiary, 75,
  92, 96, 181; Martínez, José, 92; Mexican
  Revolution, 18, 52, 180; Mexico, 18;
  radicalism, 80–87, 99; resistance, 17–18;
  revolutions, 17, 52, 101; Rodney, Walter,
  20; slavery, 17; strikes, 181; struggles,
  16–18; TGP, 149
Cooke, Marvel, 162, 166–67
cotton, 22–24; Britain, 23, 31, 42; Carver,
  George Washington, 162; the Civil War
  (US), 22–24; India, 33; Jim Crow, 5;
  labor, 127; "Mac – American" (Reed),
  69; slavery, 22–24, 39–40, 41; strikes,
  123, 133, 134–35; textile workers, 24
Council on African Affairs, 162
counterrevolution, 64–71, 101, 105, 113,
  119, 176
Covarrubias, Miguel, 153
CP (the Communist Party), 56–57, 141–43;
  adult education, 161; AFL, 141–42;
  Browder, Earl, 80, 81; California, 141–
  42; class struggles, 56, 141, 142; color
  line, 142; Cuba, 115; farmworkers, 124,
  142; Great Depression, 141; Healey,
  Dorothy, 140; imperialism, 61; Italian
  Communist Party, 93; Japanese immigrants, 142–43; John Reed Clubs, 156;
  Kollontai, Alexandra, 109; Los Angeles,
  141–42; lynching, 169; Mexican Revolu-
  tion, 212n33; Mexican workers, 140–41;
  Mexican Young Communists, 115;
  Mitford, Jessica, 177; PCM, 61–62, 114;
  Perry, Pettis, 142; racism, 57, 141; relief,
  124, 140, 141; revolutions, 57; strikes,
  124; Unemployed Councils, 140–41,
  142; whiteness, 57, 142; women, 109, 142.
  See also Comintern (Communist Inter-
  national); Mexican Communist Party
CRC (Civil Rights Congress), 162
Crichlow, Ernest, 160–61
Cristero Rebellion, 104
CROM (Confederación Regional Obrera
  Méxicana), 100, 105
Cruse, Harold, 163
Cuba: Black soldiers, 86; Bolshevik Revolu-
  tion (1917), 53; the Communist Party,

115; Du Bois, W. E. B., 10; henequen
  (rope) plantations, 3–4; imperialism, 10;
  Kōchi and Miyasato, 50; Kollontai,
  Alexandra, 98, 221n8; revolutions, 115;
  Rodríguez, Antonio, 7; the Soviet
  Embassy, 115
Cullen, Countee, 160

Daily Journal, 129
Darkwater (Du Bois), 168
Das, Taraknath, 80, 82–83
Davis, Ben, 162
Dawes Act, 4, 194n11
Death, or Lynched Figure (Noguchi), 169
Debs, Eugene V., 77, 89, 118
debt finance, 3–4, 11, 25, 28, 40–41, 44–45,
  51–52, 54–55
De Caux, Len, 138
Degeyter, Pierre, 176
Delgado Museum of Art, 155
deportation, 123–24, 125, 129, 131–32, 138
Depression, the. *See* Great Depression, the
Díaz, Porfirio, 3, 14–16, 44, 54, 65, 171–72
Dillard College, 154–55
Dodge, William, 29
Douglas, Aaron, 159, 160
Douglass, Frederick, 35–37; as abolitionist,
  35–37; Britain, 35–36, 42, 43; capitalism,
  25, 180, 181; the Civil War (US), 42;
  colonialism, 27, 37; color line, 8, 181;
  1848 pivot, 36; geopolitics, 43; imperial-
  ism, 35–36; internationalism, 14, 43, 181;
  Ireland, 27, 35–36; New Imperialism,
  181; slavery, 8, 27, 36, 37, 42; US and
  Mexico, 35; US-Mexico War, 27
Drake, St. Clair, 155
dresses, 145–47, 153, 166–68, 173
Du Bois, Shirley Graham, 159
Du Bois, W. E. B.: abolitionists, 178; "The
  African Roots of War," 10, 11; Black
  domestic workers, 168; *Black Reconstruction in America, 1860–1880*, 175,
  178–80, 181, 196n22; Britain, 42; capitalism, 10–11, 180, 181; Catlett, Elizabeth, 159, 160; colonialism, 10; color
  line, 8–11, 19, 41, 179–80, 181, 196n22,
  197n29; Columbia University, 178–79;
  Council on African Affairs, 162; Cruse,

Harold, 163; Great Depression, 178; internationalism, 14, 19, 181; Lenin, Vladimir, 11; militarism, 8; New Imperialism, 11, 19, 180, 181; portrait of, *fig.* 3; racism, 9–10, 178–79; slavery, 178; US and Mexico, 9, 10, 179; whiteness, 197n29

Dunham, Katherine, 146, 156

Dunning School, 178–79

du Pont, Henry, 29

Eastman, Max, 66

education, 54, 60, 93–94, 104, 105, 133, 161–66. *See also* George Washington Carver school; Leavenworth Federal Penitentiary

Eighteenth Brumaire of Louis Bonaparte, The (Marx), 28–30, 243nn8,13

El Dia, 155–56

Ellington, Duke, 159

El Machete, 114–15

empire, 5, 13, 30–31, 181, 234n8. *See also* British Empire, the; imperialism

"End to Neglect of the Problem of the Negro Woman, An" (Jones), 166

Engel, George, 5

Engels, Friedrich, 26, 29–30, 83, 108, 117, 163

Espionage Act (1917), 74–75, 77, 78, 80

Estampas de la Revolución Mexicana, 170, 171

extractive industries, 12, 17, 44–45, 47–48, 50, 51–52, 132–33. *See also* oil

Fanon, Frantz, 177

farmworkers, 122–36; AFL, 123; African Americans, 124–25; Border Patrol, 128–29; California, 19–20, 122–26, 133, 136; capitalism, 127–28, 130, 132, 144; CAWIU, 140, 141; class struggles, 130; color line, 130; communists, 133–34; convergence space, 18; CP, 124, 142; deportation, 123–24, 125, 129, 131–32; Healey, Dorothy, 19–20, 122, 124, 129, 134; incarceration, 123–24, 129–30, 131, 132, 135; International Day of Struggle Against Unemployment, 139; "The Internationale" ("La Internacional"),

176–77; internationalism, 130; Japanese immigrants, 143; labor, 123–32; law enforcement, 132, 228n6; the New Deal, 136; racism, 123–24, 130; relief, 123–26, 129–32, 134–36, 228n6; strikes, 18, 122–26, 132, 133–36, 142; unions, 228n6; US and Mexico, 131–32; US–Mexico border, 123–24, 128–29; white vigilantes, 129–30, 132; Yoneda, Karl, 143. *See also* agribusiness; agriculture; migrant workers

fascism: adult education, 161; Black artists, 148, 156; California, 136; Catlett, Elizabeth, 162; class struggles, 94–95; *Guernica* (Picasso), 155; Italy, 94–95; Meyers, Pauline, 153; Mitford, Jessica, 177; Smith, Gerald L.K., 160; women, 156; WWII, 147; Zadkine, Ossip, 174

FBI, 149

Federal Children's Bureau, 118

Federal Emergency Relief Administration, 134

Fédération Des Artistes, 175–76

feminism: Bennett, Gwendolyn, 162–63; Black domestic workers, 166–68; Breshkovsky, Katherine, 83; Bryant, Louise, 83; Catlett, Elizabeth, 149, 173; Childress, Alice, 166; Cooke, Marvel, 162, 166–67; counterrevolution, 119; housing and hunger organizers, 139–40; internationalism, 101, 109; Jackson, Esther Cooper, 162, 168; Jones, Claudia, 162, 166; Kollontai, Alexandra, 14, 19, 83, 98, 99, 100, 101, 107–9, 115, 116–19, 120, 182, 225n50; Luxemburg, Rosa, 108; Mexican organizers, 103–4, 116; NNC, 156, 159, 160, 162; PLM, 83; sex workers, 103; shadow hegemony, 199n43; textile workers, 117; Wells, Ida B., 6–7; *What Is To Be Done?* (Chernyshevsky), 117; Zetkin, Clara, 108–9

Ferrer Guardia, Francisco, 60

Filipinos, 2–3, 86, 124–25, 143

finance: Britain, 79; class struggles, 41; extractive industries/geoeconomics, 50; internationalism, 32; Latin America, 41; Mexico, 15, 25; New Imperialism, 11; racism, 41–42; ropes, 5; Roy, M.N., 55;

finance: Britain *(continued)*
strikes, 123; US, 28, 41–42, 78–79; US
and Mexico, 16, 25, 29, 40–42, 44–45,
46. *See also* capitalism; debt finance
Fine Old Conflict, A (Mitford), 177
First International (1864), 19, 26, 43, 176
Fischer, Adolph, 5
Fletcher, Ben, 81
Fletcher, Henry, 99
Flores Magón, Enrique, 16, 81, 82, 83, 96
Flores Magón, Ricardo, 72–75, 89–96;
anarchism, 73–75, 89, 182; capitalism,
74–75, 92, 93, 95, 181; class, 93, 95; class
struggles, 46, 74–75; color line, 95, 96;
death of, *fig.* 7, 72–73, 89–90, 91; education, 93, 104; Gramsci, Antonio, 92–95;
imperialism, 74–75, 92; internationalism,
14, 19, 74, 95–96, 181; IWW, 182; labor,
46, 72–74, 89, 95, 215n10; Leavenworth
Federal Penitentiary, *fig.* 6, 19, 72–75,
89–92, 96; lynching, 95; Marx, Karl, 46;
Mexican Revolution, 60, 73–74; organization, 182; PLM, 16, 60, 73, 81, 89, 91, 93,
182; racism, 75, 95; radicalism, 73, 75, 96;
railroads, 73; *Regeneración*, 7, 93, 175,
215n8; US, 7, 46, 73–75, 181; whiteness, 96
Flynn, Elizabeth Gurley, 85
Ford, Henry, *fig.* 9, 77, 126
Fort-Whiteman, Lovett, 60
France: colonialism, 37, 176, 177; Díaz,
Porfirio, 14; *The Eighteenth Brumaire of
Louis Bonaparte*, 29; *Fédération Des
Artistes*, 175–76; finance, 41; Haiti/
Haitian Revolution, 31, 36, 39; Mar-
tínez, José, 91–92; Mexico, 21, 28–29, 38,
44, 102, 172, 176; Niger, 80; panopticon,
32; Paris Commune, 175–76; slavery, 37;
US, 39, 41
Frazier, E. Franklin, 164
Freedomways Magazine, 166, 168
French Revolution, 37, 38, 41, 59
"Frenesí" (song), 146
Freundlich, Irwin, 164
Furriers' Union (International Fur Work-
ers Union), 160

Gaikis, Leon, 99–100, 102, 113, 116, 120
Gale, Linn A. E., 60

Gale's Magazine, 60
Garis, Roy L., 128
Garvey, Marcus, 80
gender: Black domestic workers, 166, 167;
Bolshevik Revolution (1917), 83; capitalism, 14, 120; Catlett, Elizabeth, 149–50,
162; *Communist Manifesto* (Marx and
Engels), 30; convergence space, 17;
gendered violence, 68; internationalism,
53, 101; Kollontai, Alexandra, 19, 99,
103–5, 107, 110, 111, 120; labor, 99, 111,
130; Leavenworth Federal Penitentiary,
83, 85; "Mac – American" (Reed),
68–69, 69–71; nationalism, 71, 109;
Perry, Pettis, 142; PLM, 83; property
love, 110; racism, 7; resistance, 14; SEP,
104. *See also* feminism; women
Geneva Conventions, 19
geoeconomics: Britain, 34; capitalism,
11–13, 31, 67, 70, 74–75, 198n40; convergence space, 17, 180–81; debt finance, 25,
50; geopolitics v, 197n32; internationalism, 13–14, 31, 35, 52; Kollontai, Alexandra, 119; Mexican Revolution, 12,
198n35; Mexico, 25; New Imperialism,
11, 47–48; racism, 25, 67; revolutions,
52, 67; territorialism, 26, 32; US, 12–13,
25, 41–42, 78–79; US and Mexico, 23,
24–25
"Geographic Pivot of History, The " (Mackinder), 26
geopolitics: capitalism, 13, 24; Catlett,
Elizabeth, 158; convergence space,
180–81; Douglass, Frederick, 43; 1848
pivot, 25; geoeconomics v, 197n32;
internationalism, 26; Kollontai, Alexandra, 100, 119; Mexico, 25; New Imperialism, 11; racism, 25; revolutions, 52; US,
25, 41–42, 79
George Washington Carver School, 149,
161–66
Germany, 21, 27, 29–30, 34–35, 53, 63, 117,
155. *See also* Marx, Karl
Ghadar Movement, 80, 81, 82
Gladstone, William, 42
Goldman, Emma, 66, 77, 99, 117
Gompers, Samuel, 60
Goss, Bernard, 146, 156, 158

Gramsci, Antonio, 92–95
Grant, Ulysses S., 22, 27–28
Great Britain. *See* Britain
Great Depression, the, 125, 136–39, 141, 143, 153, 157, 178. *See also* New Deal, the
"Great Love, A" (Kollontai), 120
Grito de Dolores, El, 150
Guernica (Picasso), 155–56, 237n49
Guerrero, Práxedis G., 7
Guerrero, Vincente, 39
Guyana, 20, 36

Habsburg, Maximilian von (Emperor of Mexico), 28–29, 102
Haiti, 30, 36–38, 39, 41, 80, 156, 234n8
Haitian Revolution, 31, 36–38, 39, 41
Hall, Gwendolyn Midlo, 148, 149, 235n17
Hanged Negroes (Orozco), 169
hanging, 5, 6, 7. *See also* lynching
Hansberry, Carl and Lorraine, 145, 233n3
Harding, Warren, 82
Harlem, 159–66
Harlem Artists Guild, 160
Harlem Arts Center, 160
Hawai'i, 49
Haymarket Affair, 5
Haywood, Bill, 80–81, 118
Haywood, Harry, 148, 156, 235nn14,17
Healey, Dorothy, 122–44; capitalism, 242n6; as communist organizer, 14, 124, 132, 133–34; CP, 140; farmworkers, 19–20, 122, 124, 129, 134; "The Internationale" ("La Internacional"), 122, 176–77, 242n6; Los Angeles Unemployed Councils, 124, 139–40; Marxism, 242n6; Mexican Revolution, 132–36; migrant workers, 132; open shop, 126–32; strikes, 124; *Tradition's Chains Have Bound Us*, 177, 242n6; on white vigilantes, 129
Hearing on Bolshevik Propaganda, 118
hegemony, 11–14, 16, 25–26, 74, 180, 181. *See also* shadow hegemony
henequen (rope) plantations, 3–4, 5
Hennant, Katherine, 164
Herndon, Angelo, 142, 143
Hessler, Carl, 82
heterosexuality, 110

Hidalgo, Miguel (Miguel Hidalgo y Costilla), 38–39
Hill, Joe, 182
Hillier, Harry R., 77
Ho Chi Minh, 55
Hofer, Joseph and Michael, 85
Homecoming of the Worker of the New Day (Orozco), 168–69
Homer, Dorothy, 164
homophobia, 162
Hong Kong, 33
Hoover, J. Edgar, 81
Hoovervilles, 136–37, 138
House of the World Worker (Casa del Obrero Mundial), 5, 59–60
housing, 54, 103, 111–12, 128, 133, 138, 168. *See also* Hoovervilles
Huasteca Petroleum Company, 133
Huastec Indians, 3, 102
Huerta, Victoriano, 65
Hughes, Langston, 63–64, 153, 159
Huiswoud, Otto, 57, 143
hunger marches, 138–39

IH (International Harvester), 4–5
ILD (International Labor Defense), 162
ILGWU (International Ladies' Garment Workers' Union), 163
Imada, Mary Hatsuko, 139–40
Immigrant's Sorrowful Tale, An (Imin no Aiwa) (Kōchi), 48, 52, 208nn2–3
immigration, 50, 52, 69, 123, 127–29. *See also* Asian immigrants; Chinese immigrants; migrant workers
Immigration Act (1917), 49–50
Immigration and Nationality Act (1952), 149
imperialism: African Americans, 143; Black artists, 148, 156; Bolshevik Revolution (1917), 113; Britain, 57, 58, 80; capitalism, 10–11, 59, 62, 115, 144; colonialism, 26, 55; CP, 61; Cuba, 10; Douglass, Frederick, 35–36; First International (1864), 176; Flores Magón, Ricardo, 74–75, 92; gendered violence, 68; Haiti, 156, 234n8; India, 57, 58; Indigenous people, 234n8; Japan, 142, 143; Kōchi, Shinsei "Paul," 52; Kollontai, Alexandra, 120; labor,

imperialism (continued)
109; Latin America, 45–46, 61; Mexican Revolution, 74; Mexico, 60; militarism, 17; murals, 105; Nicaragua, 156; Philippines, 2–3, 10, 124–25, 234n8; racism, 59, 61; radicalism, 53; ropes, 5; Roy, M. N., 55, 61; strikes, 211n30; territorialism, 26; US, 2–3, 5, 10, 45–46, 60, 67, 86, 115, 198n37, 234n8; US and Mexico, 60, 156; whiteness, 10–11. See also New Imperialism, the

incarceration, 76, 123–24, 129–30, 131, 132, 135, 138, 172. See also Leavenworth Federal Penitentiary

India: Britain, 33–34, 55, 57, 58, 80; class struggles, 58, 61; colonialism, 36, 50; Douglass, Frederick, 35–36; Du Bois, W. E. B., 179; imperialism, 57, 58; Lenin, Vladimir, 56; nationalism, 58; racism, 58; revolutions, 55, 56, 57; Roy, M. N., 58–59; US, 12

Indigenous people: agriculture, 15; baldios, 44; Bentham, Jeremy, 31; colonialism, 37–38; color line, 8–9; communists, 98; convergence space, 17; Dawes Act, 4, 194n11; Díaz, Porfirio, 171–72; dispossession, 4, 8, 15, 22–25, 35, 38, 41, 44, 49, 59, 64, 172; ejido lands, 15, 44; gendered violence, 27, 68, 147; Great Rebellion, 37–38; Guerrero, Vincente, 39; henequen (rope) plantations, 3–4, 5–6; imperialism, 234n8; incarceration, 76, 172; Kōchi, Shinsei "Paul," 51, 52; labor, 3; law enforcement, 15; "Mac – American" (Reed), 68–69, 71; mestizaje, 63; Mexican Revolution, 15, 172; Mexico, 15, 22, 27, 31, 63, 64, 172; murals, 105; murder, 69; nationalism, 71, 172; New Imperialism, 64; Niger, 80; "The Porfirian Dictatorship Demagogically Exalts the Native" (La Dictadura Porfiriata Exalta Demagogicamenta al Indigena) (Zalce), fig. 19, 171–73; racism, 64; la raza cosmica, 172; slavery, 35, 102; Spain, 37–38; territorialism, 4, 8, 15, 17, 22, 24, 25, 27, 31, 35, 44, 171, 194n11; US, 49, 147; US-Mexico War, 27; Veracruz, 98, 102; women, 68, 147; Zapata, Emil-

iano, 15, 53, 59, 65, 66, 104, 171. See also settler colonialism; individual groups of Indigenous people

Indigenous people of the United States, 4, 6, 8–9, 31, 39–40, 41, 76, 194n11

Insurgent Mexico (Reed), 66, 71

International Banking Corporation, 12

International Day of Struggle Against Unemployment, 138–39

"Internationale, The" ("La Internacional"): Germany, 53; Healey, Dorothy, 122, 242n6; internationalism, 176–77, 182; Kollontai, Alexandra, 109; Leavenworth Federal Penitentiary, 84; lyrics of, 109, 175; Marx, Karl, 243n8; photograph of, fig. 15; strikes, 66, 122

internationalism, 17–20, 21–46, 48–53, 72–96, 180–83; abolitionists, 35–39, 42–43; anarchism, 19; artists, 151, 181; Asian immigrants, 48–53; Bagdad, Mexico, 21–26; Bentham, Jeremy, 30–33, 34, 35; Black artists, 147–48, 156; Black domestic workers, 149; Bolshevik Revolution (1917), 53–54, 115; the British Empire, 33–35; capitalism, 14, 17–18, 26, 30, 44, 58, 106, 144, 180–81; Catlett, Elizabeth, 14, 148, 149–50, 156, 170, 173–74; class, 51, 126, 142; color line, 39–42, 53; Communist Manifesto (Marx and Engels), 26, 29, 30; communists, 19; convergence space, 17–18, 99, 180–81; Douglass, Frederick, 14, 43, 181; Du Bois, W. E. B., 14, 19, 181; Fanon, Frantz, 177; farmworkers, 130; Fédération Des Artistes, 175–76; feminism, 101, 109; finance, 32; Flores Magón, Ricardo, 14, 19, 74, 95–96, 181; gender, 53, 101; generations, 177–78, 183; geoeconomics, 13–14, 31, 35, 52; geopolitics, 26; Germany, 34–35; Haiti/Haitian Revolution, 36; Hughes, Langston, 64; humanitarianism, 19; International Working Men's Association, 176; Kōchi, Shinsei "Paul," 48–53; Kollontai, Alexandra, 101, 108, 120, 222n20; labor, 19, 176; Leavenworth Federal Penitentiary, 18, 19, 75–80, 92–96, 181; Lenin, Vladimir, 115; liberalism, 19, 30–33; Marx, Karl, 35;

May Day, 115; Mexican Revolution, 12, 13–14, 16, 26, 54, 95, 180, 210n17; Mexico, 21–26, 44–45, 99, 201n52; migrant workers, 180; New Imperialism, 53, 181; Padmore, George, 143; racism, 53, 92–96, 142, 144; radicalism, 53, 99, 140–44, 149, 156; Reed, John, 64–71; relief, 142, 144; revolutions, 18, 52, 53, 176, 180; Rodríguez, Antonio, 7; slavery, 35–39; socialism, 19, 108; the Soviet Embassy, 114, 115, 181; Soviet Union, 99; strikes, 123, 181; struggles, 183; transnational spaces, 210n16; Unemployed Councils, 143; US, 14, 27–30, 45–46; Veracruz port, 102; writers, 177; WW I, 48, 49. *See also* "Internationale, The" ("La Internacional")

International Labor Defense, 169

International Worker's Day, 5, 83–84

International Working Men's Association, 176

Ireland, 27, 35–36, 37, 56, 57, 80–81

Italian Communist Party, 93

Italy, 94–95

IWMA (International Working Men's Association), 43

IWW (Industrial Workers of the World), 60, 71, 78; anarchism, 60, 176; Black organizers, 81; capitalism, 82; class struggles, 71, 78; color line, 78; Fletcher, Ben, 81; Flores Magón, Ricardo, 182; Haywood, Bill, 80–81; Kollontai, Alexandra, 118; Leavenworth Federal Penitentiary, 80–85; PLM, 60; racism, 81, 82; Reed, John, 65, 71, 182; strikes, 65–66, 176, 182

Jackson, Esther Cooper, 162, 168

Japan, 3–4, 10, 13, 48–49, 50, 55, 142, 143. *See also* Asian immigrants; *individuals*

Japanese immigrants, 124–25, 142–43. *See also individuals*; Okinawa

Jefferson, Thomas, 39, 40

Jim Crow, 1–2, 5, 6, 17, 78, 86, 119, 142

John Reed Clubs, 156

Johnson, Jack, 62–63, 85–86

Johnson, James Weldon, 45

Johnson, Sargent, 160–61

Jones, Claudia, 162, 166

Jones, Mary "Mother," 5

Juárez, Benito, 14, 28–29, 44, 102

Kanaka Maoli, 49

Kansas. *See* Leavenworth Federal Penitentiary

Katayama, Sen, 115

Kellogg, Frank, 98, 117–18

Kerr, Clark, 134–35

KKK (Ku Klux Klan), 1–2, 9, 13, 63, 129, 228n10

Knights of Labor (industrial union), 4–5

Kōchi, Shinsei "Paul," 48–53

Kollontai, Alexandra, 97–121; Bolshevik Revolution (1917), 109, 113; Bolshevism, 98–99, 100, 106, 107–8, 109, 119, 120; Bryant, Louise, 83, 97; capitalism, 101, 109, 120; children, 103, 111–12, 117–19; Comintern, 107; "Communism and the Family," 111, 118; communists, 116; convergence space, 101; counterrevolution, 101, 105, 113; CP, 109; Cuba, 98, 221n8; diary, 98, 101, 106–7, 116, 222n20; "The Earth sheds its skin" (La tierra cambia de piel), 121; feminism, 14, 19, 83, 98, 99, 100, 101, 107–9, 115, 116–19, 120, 182, 225n50; Gaikis, Leon, 116; gender, 19, 99, 103–5, 107, 110, 111, 120; geoeconomics, 119; geopolitics, 100, 119; Germany, 117; housing, 111–12; imperialism, 120; "The Internationale" ("La Internacional"), 176; internationalism, 101, 108, 120, 222n20; labor, 99, 100, 101, 111, 116–17, 120, 222n17; Latin America, 98–99, 100, 119; Lenin, Vladimir, 108, 109; literacy, 104; love-comradeship, 110–11, 117–19, 120; "Make Way for Winged Eros," 110; *McCall's*, 118–19; Mexico, *fig.* 14, 97–107, 108, 120–21, 176; Mexico City, 19, 113–21; militarism, 108–9; nationalization, 120; New Imperialism, 101, 109; as Norway ambassador, 98–99, 108, 116, 118; Palace of Motherhood, 111, 112–13; portrait of, *fig.* 13; radicalism, 99–100; railroads, 102–7; religion, 103–5, 112; revolutions, 106–7, 120; as Soviet ambassador, 14,

Kollontai, Alexandra (*continued*)
97–103, 106–7, 108, 113–21, 182, 201n52;
as Soviet Commissar of Social Welfare,
99, 108, 109, 111; Stalin, Joseph, 100, 108,
182; strikes, 105–6, 119; unions, 106, 120,
222n17; US, 98–99, 101, 106, 107, 117–
20, 221n8; US and Mexico, 100–101,
115–16, 117, 119–20; Veracruz, 97–101;
women, 101, 103–4, 105, 108–13, 116–20;
WW I, 107–9, 110, 112
Korea, 3–4, 55
Kreitzberg, Irving, 140
Kropotkin, Piotr, 60

labor: abolitionists, 42–43; adult education, 161; African Americans, 63, 143;
agriculture, 123–32; artists, 149; Asian
immigrants, 50; Bentham, Jeremy, 31;
Black domestic workers, 166–68; Bolshevik Revolution (1917), 65, 79–80, 113;
Border Patrol, 128–29; Britain, 42–43;
California, 126–32, 136–40, 141–42;
capitalism, 10, 30, 38, 56, 71, 93–94,
126–28, 135, 141; Catlett, Elizabeth, 160;
children, 54–55; Chinese immigrants,
210n17; the Civil War (US), 42–43;
class, 143; class struggles, 71, 78; colonialism, 33, 55, 56; color line, 78, 143;
Communist Manifesto (Marx and
Engels), 26, 29, 30; cotton, 127; deportation, 131–32; education, 93–94; Espionage Act (1917), 78; farmworkers, 123–
32; Flores Magón, Ricardo, 46, 72–74,
89, 95, 215n10; Flynn, Elizabeth Gurley,
85; gender, 99, 111, 130; George Washington Carver School, 162, 164, 165;
Gramsci, Antonio, 93; Great Depression, 137; Haitian Revolution, 37;
henequen (rope) plantations, 3–4;
House of the World Worker (Casa del
Obrero Mundial), 59–60; IH, 4; ILD,
162; imperialism, 109; Indigenous
people, 3; "The Internationale" ("La
Internacional"), 176; internationalism,
19, 176; Jones, Mary "Mother," 5; Kollontai, Alexandra, 99, 100, 101, 111,
116–17, 120, 222n17; LACC, 127, 132,
135, 136; LAPD/Red Squad, 127; law

enforcement, 126, 132; Leavenworth
Federal Penitentiary, 76–77, 80–85;
Lenin, Vladimir, 109; Los Angeles,
126–27; "Manifesto to the Anarchists of
the Entire World and to the Workers in
General" (Flores Magón and Rivera),
74, 215n10; Marx, Karl, 42, 43; McCormick Harvesting Machine Company,
4–5; Mexican Constitution (1917),
54–55, 100; Mexican immigrants, 128;
Mexican Revolution, 15, 54, 60; Mexico,
100, 113, 171, 215n10, 222n17; militarism,
78; Morones, Luis, 100; New Imperialism, 11–12, 47; NNC, 156; open shop,
127; panopticon, 33; racism, 57, 67, 78,
81, 127, 143; radicalism, 79–80, 100;
Reed, John, 65–66, 71; relief, 130–32,
135; revolutions, 56, 67; ropes, 6; Roy,
M. N., 211n30; sex workers, 103; shipbuilders, 32–33; SI, 108; slavery, 42–43;
Soviet Union, 100, 222n17; US, 41, 78,
100, 134–35, 137, 215n10, 222n17; US and
Mexico, 88, 100, 133, 222n17; whiteness,
57, 81; women, 116–17, 118–19, 163; WW
I, 108. *See also* Los Angeles Unemployed
Councils; migrant workers; strikes;
individual labor organizations
LACC (Los Angeles Chamber of Commerce), 124, 127, 132, 135, 136
LA Citizens Committee on Coordination
of Unemployment Relief, 131
land redistribution/reform: Mexican
Constitution (1917), 54, 80, 100, 106,
119–20; Mexican Revolution, 12, 54;
Mexico, 54, 66, 100; nationalization,
100, 106, 119–20, 133; property love,
109–10; SEP, 104; US and Mexico, 100,
106; Villa, Pancho, 15; Zapata, Emiliano, 15, 66. *See also* territorialism
Lang, William, 155
Lao Hsiu-Chao, 57
LAPD (Los Angeles Police Department),
124, 127, 129, 139
Latin America: Artists and Models Ball,
147; Asian immigrants, 50; Bentham,
Jeremy, 31; Bolshevism, 119; capitalism,
16; finance, 41; Haitian/French Revolutions, 38; imperialism, 45–46, 61; Kol-

lontai, Alexandra, 98–99, 100, 119; Mexico, 61, 117; *Regeneración*, 215n8; US, 12, 41, 45–46, 98–99, 147; US and Mexico, 103
Latin American Bureau of the Communist International, 61
Latin American League, 61
law enforcement: farmworkers, 132, 228n6; federal legislation, 77; Indigenous people, 15; labor, 126, 132; Presidential Commission on Law Observance and Enforcement, 139; relief, 125, 137, 228n6; strikes, 135; white vigilantes, 129. *See also* incarceration; LAPD (Los Angeles Police Department); Leavenworth Federal Penitentiary
Lawrence, Jacob, 159, 160–61, 169
League of Nations, 19
Leavenworth Federal Penitentiary, 72–96; anarchism, 84, 96; Black prisoners, 80, 81, 85–88, 96; Bolshevik Revolution (1917), 82, 83; capitalism, 75, 79; class struggles/color line, 75; conscientious objectors, 85; convergence space, 75, 92, 96, 181; dining room, *fig.* 10; Flores Magón, Ricardo, *fig.* 6, 19, 72–75, 89–92, 96; Ford, Henry, 77; gender, 83, 85; history of, 75–77; "The Internationale" ("La Internacional"), *fig.* 15, 84, 176; internationalism, 18, 19, 75–80, 92–96, 181; IWW, 80–85; Johnson, Jack, 85–86; labor, 76–77, 80–85; Lockhart, "Andy," 91; Martínez, José, 87–92; Marxism, 82; Mexican Revolution, 176; militarism, 75, 79; political beliefs, 75, 77, 84–85; racism, 75, 79, 85–87, 92–96; radicalism, 60, 71, 75, 77, 80–87, 92; socialism, 75, 84; strikes, 82, 83–84, 90; Tyler, Roy, 86, 87–88; as university, 82–83, 96; US-Mexico War, 76
Leavenworth New Era, fig. 9, 81–82, 83
Lenin, Vladimir, 11, 56, 60–61, 84, 108, 109, 115, 117
"Leningrad" (Shostakovich) (symphony), 164–65
Leonard, Andrew, 87–88, 90
Le Sueur, Meridel, 137
lettuce pickers. *See* farmworkers

Lewis, Samella, 155
liberal internationalism, 30–35
liberalism, 19, 28, 30–33. *See also* PLM (Partido Liberal Mexicano/Mexican Liberal Party)
Liberator, 81, 83
literacy, 104, 133. *See also* education
Locke, Alain, 160, 164
Lockhart, "Andy," 91
London Times, 155
Los Angeles, 19–20, 73, 126–27, 131, 133, 135, 139, 141–42. *See also* California; LACC (Los Angeles Chamber of Commerce); LAPD (Los Angeles Police Department)
Los Angeles Communist Party, 140
Los Angeles County Outdoor Relief Division, 130
Los Angeles Record, 139
Los Angeles Unemployed Councils, 18, 124, 126, 136–44
Louisiana Purchase, 39–41
L'Ouverture, Toussaint, 36
love-comradeship, 110–11, 117–19, 120
Luce, Henry, 13
Luxemburg, Rosa, 108
lynching: artists, 169; Catlett, Elizabeth, *fig.* 18, 152, 172–73; class, 9; color line, 8, 69; CP, 169; *Death, or Lynched Figure* (Noguchi), 169; El Paso, Texas, 91; Flores Magón, Ricardo, 95; "Mac – American" (Reed), 69–70; Mann Act (1912), 85; racism, 6–7; Rodríguez, Antonio, 6–7; ropes, 1–2, 6–7; US, 119; Wells, Ida B., 6–7, 195n17; white vigilantes, 1–2, 6–7, 9; women, 6. *See also* KKK (Ku Klux Klan)

"Mac – American" (Reed), 68–71, 214n63
MacDonald, Alan, 97
Mackinder, Halford, 26
Madero, Francisco, 16, 65
"Make Way for Winged Eros" (Kollontai), 110
Making of the English Working Class, The (Thompson), 181
Man at the Crossroads (Rivera), 169
"Manifesto of the People" (Zapata), 59

"Manifesto to the Anarchists of the Entire World and to the Workers in General" (Flores Magón and Rivera), 74, 215n10

manila (fiber), 2–3, 5

Mann Act (1912), 85

Mariátegui, José Carlos, 38

Marine Cooks and Stewards Union, 162

Marshall, Thurgood, 159

Martí, José, 45

Martínez, José, 87–92

Martínez, Tomas, 81

Marvin X, 148

Marx, Karl: Britain, 42; capitalism, 25, 40, 141; the Civil War (US), 42; class struggles, 43; the Communist League, 30; Cruse, Harold, 163; debt finance, 40; education, 104; *The Eighteenth Brumaire of Louis Bonaparte*, 28–30, 243nn8,13; Flores Magón, Ricardo, 46; India, 33–34; "The Internationale" ("La Internacional"), 243n8; internationalism, 35; labor, 42, 43; revolutions, 29; Roy, M. N., 55; slavery, 43; territorialism, 35; WW I, 108. *See also Communist Manifesto* (Marx and Engels)

Marxism: Catlett, Elizabeth, 153, 166; colonialism, 57; Healey, Dorothy, 242n6; Leavenworth Federal Penitentiary, 82; Mexican Revolution, 66–67; Mexico, 201n52; Roy, M. N., 58, 62

Masses, The, 68

Maya Indians, 3, 15

Mayakovsky, Vladimir, 115

May Day, 4, 5, 83–84, 115

Mayo Indians, 59

McCall's, 118–19

McCormick Harvesting Machine Company, *fig. 2*, 4–5

McDonald, J. A., 83

McEvoy, Peter, 80–81

McGill, William, 156

McKay, Claude, 57, 160

McWilliams, Carey, 128

Mella, Julio Antonio, 115

Mendez, Innocentio, 130

Mennonites, 85

Mérida, Carlos, 114–15

Messenger, 80, 81, 83

Metropolitan Magazine, 65, 66

Metropolitan Museum of Art, 169

Mexican-American War. *See* US-Mexico War

Mexican Communist Party, 61–62, 98, 115, 182, 221n5. *See also* PCM (Mexican Communist Party)

Mexican Constitution (1917): debt finance, 54–55; education, 54, 104; housing, 54, 103; labor, 54–55, 100; land redistribution/reform, 54, 80, 100, 106, 119–20; nationalization, 54, 80, 173; radicalism, 55; religion, 55, 104; slavery, 39; strikes, 105–6, 133; US and Mexico, 54, 100, 106, 119–20

Mexican immigrants, 127–29. *See also* farmworkers

"Mexican Manifesto" (Flores Magón, R.), 46

"Mexican Question in the Southwest, The" (Tenayuca), 141

Mexican Revolution, 14–16; agriculture, 54; artists, 150, 151, 170–73; Asian immigrants, 52–53, 210n17; Black domestic workers, 20; Bolshevik Revolution (1917), 54; California, 132–36; capitalism, 12, 16, 54, 74–75, 132; Catlett, Elizabeth, 20, 152, 173; class, 54; class struggles, 12, 15–16, 61; colonialism, 15; color line, 95; convergence space, 18, 52, 180; CP, 212n33; demographic costs, 54, 200n48; Díaz, Porfirio, 14–16, 54; education, 60; 1848 pivot, 26; Flores Magón, Ricardo, 60, 73–74; fortune hunters, 52–53, 68–69; Fort-Whiteman, Lovett, 60; geoeconomics, 12, 198n35; Healey, Dorothy, 132–36; hegemony, 16; imperialism, 74; Indigenous people, 15, 172; "The Internationale" ("La Internacional"), 176; internationalism, 12, 13–14, 16, 26, 54, 95, 180, 210n17; Johnson, Jack, 85–86; Kōchi and Miyasato, 51; labor, 15, 54, 60; land redistribution/reform, 12, 54; Leavenworth Federal Penitentiary, 176; Marxism, 66–67; Mayakovsky, Vladimir, 115; "Mexican Kaleidoscope" (Flores Magón, E.), 81–82; nationalism, 173; New Imperialism, 16, 64–71; Orozco, José Clemente, 169; Pestkovsky, Stanislav, 113–14; PLM, 60; racism, 74; radicalism, 53; Reed, John, 65–71, 182; religion, 60, 104; revolutions, 59, 212n38; Roy, M.N., 55, 58–59, 62; as social revolution, 7, 14, 16; strikes, 16, 54, 125, 132–36; territorialism, 12, 59; TGP, 170–71, 173; US, 12, 16, 54, 60, 66–67, 198n35; Villa, Pancho, 15, 212n33; women, 66, 105, 122; Zapata, Emiliano, 15, 53, 212n33

Mexican Union of Technical Workers, Painters, and Sculptors (Sindicato de Obreros Tecnicos, Pintores y Escultores), 114, 151

Mexican workers, 140–41. *See also* labor: Mexico

Mexican Young Communists, 115

Mexico: abolitionists, 38–39; African Americans, 62–64, 85–86; artists, 115, 150–51, 159; Bagdad, 21–26; Black artists, 147–49; Bolshevik Revolution (1917), 98, 113–14; Bolshevism, 106; Britain, 44, 54; the British Empire, 21; capitalism, 15, 22, 44–45, 46, 47, 67, 98, 132–33; Catlett, Elizabeth, 145, 147, 148–49, 168–73; class struggles, 15; colonialism, 38, 58; color line, 8; communism, 113, 201n52; convergence space, 18; CP, 61–62; CROM, 100; debt finance, 15, 25, 44–45; 1848 pivot, 26; France, 21, 28–29, 38, 44, 102, 172, 176; geoeconomics/geopolitics, 25; Germany, 21; Haiti, 38; Hansberry, Carl, 233n3; Hansberry, Lorraine, 145; House of the World Worker (Casa del Obrero Mundial), 5, 59–60; imperialism, 60; Indigenous people, 15, 22, 27, 31, 63, 64, 172; internationalism, 21–26, 44–45, 99, 201n52; Johnson, Jack, 62–63, 85–86; Kōchi, Shinsei "Paul," 48, 50–53; Kollontai, Alexandra, *fig.* 14, 97–107, 108, 120–21, 176; labor, 100, 113, 171, 215n10, 222n17; land redistribution/reform, 54, 66, 100; Latin America, 117; Latin American League, 61; Los Angeles, 133; Marxism, 201n52; May Day, 5; militarism, 8, 25, 27–28, 35, 41, 113; mining, 44–45, 132–33; Miyasato, Seitoku, 50–51; modernization, 15; Napoléon III, Louis Bonaparte, 45; nationalization, 100, 119–20, 133, 173; New Imperialism, 64; oil, 12, 98; Pestkovsky, Stanislav, 99–100; racism, 85–86, 88; radicalism, 53, 148–49; railroads, 105–6; Reed, John, 65–71; *Regeneración*, 215n8; ropes, 3–4; Roy, M.N., 57–62; Russia, 21, 120; slavery, 21, 22–24, 25, 38–39, 63, 102, 172; Soviet Union, 61, 97–101, 106, 113–14, 115, 222n17; Spain, 14, 21–22, 30, 31, 38–39, 63, 102, 150, 172; strikes, 133, 143–44, 152; Ten Tragic Days (La Decena Trágica), 65; territorialism, 25, 44, 54–55, 76, 98; War of Independence, 30, 31, 38–39; Williams, Lorraine, 159. *See also* Soviet Embassy (Mexico); US (United States) and Mexico; US–Mexico border

Mexico City: artists, 18, 150; Black artists, 147–48; Catlett, Elizabeth, 169; Hughes, Langston, 63; Jones, Mary "Mother," 5; Juárez, Benito, 28; KKK, 63; Kollontai, Alexandra, 19, 113–21; New York City, 168; Pestkovsky, Stanislav, 99; Roy, M.N., 60–61; the Soviet Embassy, 18, 113–16; Ten Tragic Days (La Decena Trágica), 65; TGP, 149

Meyers, Pauline, 153

Michel, Concha, 104, 114, 116

migrant workers, 14, 124–25, 131–32, 180

militarism: Bolshevism, 109; capitalism, 109; the Civil War (US), 42; Du Bois, W.E.B., 8; Espionage Act (1917), 74, 78; Haiti, 80; imperialism, 17; Kollontai, Alexandra, 108–9; labor, 78; Leavenworth Federal Penitentiary, 75, 79; Mexico, 8, 25, 27–28, 35, 41, 113; New Imperialism, 11; Stillman, Charles, 22; Ten Tragic Days (La Decena Trágica), 65; territorialism, 22; US, 8, 11, 13, 22, 25, 27–28, 40, 41, 45–46, 78, 79; women, 108–9; WWI, 78

Millman, Edward, 158

mining, 44–45, 50, 132–33

Miranda, Carmen, 146, 147

Miranda, Francisco de, 38

Mirrors of Moscow (Bryant), 97
Miyasato, Seitoku, 48–51
Modern Industry (Rivera), 168–69
Modotti, Tina, 115
Mora, David, 148, 235n14
Mora, Francisco "Pancho," 173
Morado, José Chávez, 169
Morgan, J. P., 4, 29
Morones, Luis, 100, 222n17
Mother and Child (Catlett), 154
Msaroš, Stjepan, 161
murals, 105, 114–15, 145–46, 150–53, 168–69

NAACP (National Association for the Advancement of Colored People), 169
Napoléon I, 28, 29–30, 37, 39
Napoléon III, Louis Bonaparte, 28–30, 45, 243nn8,13
Nation, 89
National City Bank of New York, 25
National Erectors' Association, 76–77
nationalism: communism, 140; Espionage Act (1917), 75; gender, 71, 109; Gramsci, Antonio, 94–95; India, 58; Indigenous people, 71, 172; Italy, 94–95; Lenin, Vladimir, 56; Mexican Revolution, 173; racism, 71; radicalism, 53; relief, 130; Roy, M. N., 58–59; WW I, 108, 109
nationalization: capitalism, 133; children, 118–19; communists, 173; education, 133; Kollontai, Alexandra, 120; land redistribution/reform, 100, 106, 119–20, 133; literacy, 133; Mexican Constitution (1917), 54, 80, 173; Mexico, 100, 119–20, 133, 173; oil, 173; railroads, 133; unions, 173; US and Mexico, 100; women, 101, 118–20
National Railways of Mexico, 105–6
Neal, George, 156–57
"Negro Speaks of Rivers, The" (Hughes), 64
"Negro Woman, The" (Catlett), 170–71
Negro Worker, The, 143
New Deal, the, 124, 130, 134, 136, 138, 151–52
New Imperialism, the, 10–13; African Americans, 64; the British Empire, 12, 197n34; capitalism, 47–48, 70–71; class, 10–11; colonialism, 13, 64; counter-revolution, 64–71; debt finance, 11; Douglass, Frederick, 181; Du Bois, W. E. B., 11, 19, 180, 181; geoeconomics, 11, 47–48; geopolitics, 11; hegemony, 180; Indigenous people, 64; internationalism, 53, 181; Kollontai, Alexandra, 101, 109; labor, 11–12, 47; Mexican Revolution, 16, 64–71; Mexico, 64; militarism, 11; racism, 180; railroads, 47; Reed, John, 19, 68, 70–71; rurality, 67; scholarship, 197n34; ships, 47; territorialism, 11, 67; US, 12, 47; US and Mexico, 70–71, 181; whiteness, 181. *See also* imperialism
New Masses, The, 160
New Orleans Museum of Art, 155
New Republic, 136
New School, the, 168–69
Newton, Huey, 148
New Workers' School, 168–69
New York Art Students League, 169
"New York by Day and Night"/*Nueva York de día y noche* (Tablada), 168
New York Call, 89
New York City, 18, 78, 168–69
New York Herald Tribune, 107
New York Times, 62, 107, 222n17
New York Tribune, 42, 88
Nicaragua, 106, 115, 156
Niger, 80
1917, 49–50, 53–55, 59. *See also* Bolshevik Revolution (1917); Espionage Act (1917); Mexican Constitution (1917)
NNC (National Negro Congress), 156, 159, 160, 162
Noguchi, Isamu, 169
North Carolina Mutual Bank, 153–54

Obregón, Álvaro, 65, 114, 151
oil, 12, *fig.* 20, 47, 98, 117, 132–33, 135, 173
Okinawa, 48–49, 50–51, 52
Olsen, Mildred, 139
O'Neill, Eugene, 160
open shop, the, 126–32, 135, 141–42
opium, 33–34
Ordine Nuovo, 93
Origin of the Family, The (Engels), 117
Orozco, José Clemente, 60, 105, 150–51, 157, 168–69

Otis, Harrison Gray, 126
"Outrageous in Mexico" (Royall), 27
Overman, Lee, 78, 118

Padmore, George, 143
Palace of Motherhood, 111, 112–13
Palmer, A. Mitchell, 72
panopticon, 32–33
Paris Commune, 175–76
Parks, Gordon, 156
Parra, Leroy, 134
Parsons, Albert, 5
Partido Socialista Regional Mexico, El, 61
Patterson, Louise Thompson, 162
Patterson, William, 162
PCM (Mexican Communist Party), 61–62,
   114, 182. See also Mexican Communist
   Party
Pegler, Westbrook, 163
Perry, Pettis, 142
Pestkovsky, Stanislav, 99–100, 106, 113–14,
   115–16, 119, 222n14
Pétion, Alexandre, 38
Philippine-American War of 1899–1902, 2
Philippines: Black soldiers, 76, 86; Du Bois,
   W. E. B., 10; Filipinos, 2–3, 86, 124–25,
   143; imperialism, 2–3, 10, 124–25,
   234n8; migrant workers, 124–25; ropes,
   2–3, 4; Roy, M. N., 55; Spain, 2–3; US,
   2–3, 4, 5, 12, 234n8
Phillips, Charles, 60
Picasso, Pablo, 155–56
Pino Suárez, José, 65
PLM (Partido Liberal Mexicano/Mexican
   Liberal Party): feminism, 83; Flores
   Magón, Enrique, 16, 81; Flores Magón,
   Ricardo, 16, 60, 73, 81, 89, 91, 93, 182;
   gender, 83; IWW, 60; Mexican Revolu-
   tion, 60; strikes, 16, 93; US, 16
Pomeroy, Harold E., 130
"Porfirian Dictatorship Demagogically
   Exalts the Native, The" (La Dictadura
   Porfiriata Exalta Demagogicamenta al
   Indígena) (Zalce), fig. 19, 171–73
Porfiriato, the, 14, 44, 150, 210n17. See also
   Díaz, Porfirio
Posada, José Guadalupe, 150–51
Pottier, Eugène, 175–76, 177

Prairie View College, 154
Presidential Commission on Law Observ-
   ance and Enforcement, 139
prisons, 32, 77–78. See also incarceration;
   Leavenworth Federal Penitentiary
Proal, Hernán, 98
Proclamation to the Inhabitants of South
   America (Miranda), 38
Proletarian Unity (Rivera), 168–69
propaganda of history, 178–79, 182
property love, 109–10
Pueblo, El (newspaper), 58
PWAP (Public Works of Art Project),
   151–52, 152–53

racism: AFL, 123; African Americans, 62,
   63, 178; agriculture, 127–28; artists, 169;
   Bentham, Jeremy, 30–31, 32; Black
   artists, 148, 156, 161; Black domestic
   workers, 166, 167; Britain, 41; California, 144; capitalism, 7, 10, 14, 24, 57, 59,
   61, 63, 67, 79, 95, 144, 180; Catlett,
   Elizabeth, 149, 153–55, 160, 161, 173; class,
   7, 20, 95; class struggles, 57, 94, 143, 144;
   colonialism, 57; color line, 8–10, 57, 180;
   Columbia University, 178–79; CP, 57,
   141; debt finance, 41–42; Du Bois,
   W. E. B., 9–10, 178–79; Espionage Act
   (1917), 78; farmworkers, 123–24, 130;
   Flores Magón, Ricardo, 75, 95; gender, 7;
   geoeconomics, 25, 67; geopolitics, 25;
   Great Depression, 137; Hansberry, Carl
   and Lorraine, 233n3; hegemony, 13;
   imperialism, 59, 61; India, 58; Indigenous
   people, 64; internationalism, 53, 92–96,
   142, 144; Italy, 94–95; IWW, 81, 82;
   labor, 57, 67, 78, 81, 127, 143; Leavenworth Federal Penitentiary, 75, 79,
   85–87, 92–96; Los Angeles Unemployed
   Councils, 138, 144; lynching, 6–7; "Mac
   – American" (Reed), 69–70; Marine
   Cooks and Stewards Union, 162; Martínez, José, 88, 91; Mexican immigrants,
   127–28, 141; Mexican Revolution, 74;
   Mexico, 85–86, 88; Meyers, Pauline, 153;
   murals, 152; nationalism, 71; New
   Imperialism, 180; radicalism, 149; relief,
   130; resistance, 14; revolutions, 67;

racism *(continued)*

  Rodríguez, Antonio, 7; ropes, 6–7; Roy, M. N., 61, 62; shadow hegemony, 71, 199n43; slavery, 8; "The Southern Question" (Gramsci), 94; US, 9, 13, 41–42, 46, 50, 119, 149; US and Mexico, 7, 88; Villa, Pancho, 91; whiteness, 9, 57; women, 156; WW I, 91–92. *See also* KKK (Ku Klux Klan); whiteness

radicalism, 80–87, 145–74, 161–63; adult education, 161–63; African Americans, 57; agribusiness, 132, 134; artists, 114–15, 152, 156, 159; Black artists, 147–48, 158; capitalism, 53, 75; convergence space, 80–87, 99; *Fédération Des Artistes*, 175–76; Great Depression, 143; House of the World Worker (Casa del Obrero Mundial), 60; imperialism, 53; "The Internationale" ("La Internacional"), 176; internationalism, 53, 99, 140–44, 149, 156; labor, 79–80, 100; Leavenworth Federal Penitentiary, 60, 71, 75, 77, 80–87, 92; Marine Cooks and Stewards Union, 162; Mexican Constitution, 55; "The Mexican Question in the Southwest" (Tenayuca), 141; Mexican Revolution, 53; Mexico, 53, 148–49; nationalism, 53; racism, 149; Rapp-Coudert committee investigation, 163; relief, 140–44; socialism, 67, 81; the Soviet Embassy, 114; Soviet Union, 101; Spain, 148; SSCAC, 159; TGP, 149; Unemployed Councils, 143; US, 17, 148, 149, 152; US and Mexico, 133, 148; Veracruz port, 98; women, 163. *See also individual radicals*

railroads: Asian immigrants, 41; Associated Farmers, 128; Britain, 43; capitalism, 172; Díaz, Porfirio, 15; Flores Magón, Ricardo, 73; Kollontai, Alexandra, 102–7; nationalization, 133; National Railways of Mexico, 105–6; New Imperialism, 47; strikes, 105–6, 117, 119, 133, 152; US and Mexico, 44, 105–6; Yaqui Indians, 172

Rapp-Coudert committee investigation, 163

"*Red Love*" (*Amor Rojo*), 120

Red Squad, 127, 139

Reed, John, 19, 56–57, 64–71, 156, 182, 214n63

Regeneración, fig. 4, 7, 73, 93, 175, 215n8

relief, 123–26, 129–32, 134–37; agribusiness, 130–31, 132, 134–36; California, 124–25, 130, 131, 134–37, 144, 176–77; capitalism, 125–26, 130; class struggles, 125–26, 130; CP, 124, 140, 141; deportation, 131–32; farmworkers, 123–26, 129–32, 134–36, 228n6; Federal Emergency Relief Administration, 134; Great Depression, 137, 157; "The Internationale" ("La Internacional"), 176–77; internationalism, 142, 144; labor, 130–32, 135; LA relief organizations, 130, 131; law enforcement, 125, 137, 228n6; Los Angeles Unemployed Councils, 124, 138, 140, 144; nationalism, 130; the New Deal, 134; open shop, 126–32; racism, 130; radicalism, 140–44; strikes, 125, 135; US, 134–35; white vigilantes, 125

Relief Workers' Protective Union, 138

religion, 55, 60, 103–5, 112

resistance, 4–5, 6, 7, 14, 17–18, 26, 43. *See also* strikes

revolutions: capitalism, 52, 56, 60–61, 67; class struggles, 41, 61; colonialism, 56, 57, 61; color line, 67; *Communist Manifesto* (Marx and Engels), 30; convergence space, 17, 52, 101; CP, 57; Cuba, 115; education, 93–94; geoeconomics, 52, 67; geopolitics, 52; India, 55, 56, 57; "The Internationale" ("La Internacional"), 176; internationalism, 18, 52, 53, 176, 180; Kollontai, Alexandra, 106–7, 120; labor, 56, 67; Leavenworth Federal Penitentiary, 82; Lenin, Vladimir, 56; love, 110; Marx, Karl, 29; racism, 67; resistance, 17; Roy, M. N., 58, 61, 62; the Soviet Embassy, 114, 115; strikes, 124–25, 133–34; women, 163. *See also* Bolshevik Revolution (1917); counterrevolution; French Revolution; Mexican Revolution

Reza, José Savás, 90

Rivera, Diego, 105, 114, 151, 152–53, 168–69

Rivera, Librardo, 74, 89, 90

Robeson, Paul and Eslanda, 162

Rockefeller, Nelson, 147
Rockefeller Center, 169
Rodney, Walter, 20
Rodríguez, Antonio, 6–7
Roosevelt, Franklin, 151
ropes, 1–7, *fig.* 1. *See also* lynching
Rosenwald Fellowship, 168, 169, 170
Ross, David, 158
Rowell, Chester, 132
Roy, M.N., *fig.* 5, 19, 55–62, 65, 115, 182, 211n30
Royall, Anne, 27
Russia: Fort-Whiteman, Lovett, 60; Kōchi, Shinsei "Paul," 51; Kollontai, Alexandra, 109; Kropotkin, Piotr, 60; "Leningrad" (Shostakovich), 164–65; Mexico, 21, 120; Reed, John, 65, 71; Roy, M.N., 59, 61–62; *Six Red Months in Russia* (Bryant), *fig.* 8, 83; Slovik, James, 80–81; WW II, 164–65. *See also* Bolshevik Revolution (1917); Soviet Union
Russian Revolution. *See* Bolshevik Revolution (1917)
Russian Union of Textile Workers, 117

Sandino, Augusto, 45
San Francisco Chronicle, 132
San Patricio Battalion, 27
Savage, Augusta, 160, 162
Schwab, Charles, 29
Scottsboro boys, 142, 143, 162
Selsam, Howard, 163
SEP (Secretariat of Public Education/ Secretaría de Educación Pública), 104
Serrano, Juan, 130
settler colonialism, 4, 6, 24–27, 31, 39–40, 49, 50, 64, 68–69, 76, 147
sex workers, 42, 60, 103, 154–55, 158, 167
shadow hegemony, 11–14, 71, 199n43
Shadow of the Shadow, The (Taibo), 13–14
Sheffield, James, 106
shipbuilders, 32–33, 78
ships: Bagdad, Mexico, 21; the British Empire, 33–35; Germany, 35; Haiti, 38, 39; Kōchi, Shinsei "Paul," 52; New Imperialism, 47; slavery, 34, 35, 36; Stillman, Charles, 23
Shostakovich, Dimitri, 164–65

SI (Second International) (1889), 19, 108, 109
Simons, H. Austin, 82
Sindicato Revolucionario de Inquilinos, 103
Siporin, Mitchell, 158
Siqueiros, David Alfaro, 105, 114, 151, 169
Six Red Months in Russia (Bryant), *fig.* 8, 83
slavery: *Amistad*, 169; Bentham, Jeremy, 31, 32; Black soldiers, 76; Bolívar, Simón, 38; Britain/the British Empire, 33, 34, 35, 42; Brown, John, 2; capitalism, 24; Catlett, Elizabeth, 153; Chirino, José Leonardo, 38; the Civil War (US), 30; colonialism, 34, 36; color line, 8, 9; convergence space, 17; cotton, 22–24, 39–40, 41; Douglass, Frederick, 8, 27, 36, 37, 42; Du Bois, W.E.B., 178; France, 37; Haiti, 30, 36–38, 41; IH, 4; Indigenous people, 35, 102; internationalism, 35–39; labor, 42–43; Marx, Karl, 43; Mexican Constitution (1917), 39; Mexico, 21, 22–24, 25, 38–39, 63, 102, 172; racism, 8; ships, 34, 35, 36; Spain, 38, 102; Talladega College Savery Library, 169; US, 9, 31, 35, 36, 41; US and Mexico/US–Mexico border, 39; West India Day, 36. *See also* abolitionists; Haitian Revolution
"Slave Ship, The (Slavers Throwing overboard the Dead and Dying—Typhon coming on)" (Turner) (painting), 34
Slovik, James, 80–81
Smith, Gerald L.K., 160
Smith, Hughie Lee, 160–61
socialism: African Americans, 81; Black domestic workers, 168; Flores Magón, Ricardo, 89; "The Internationale" ("La Internacional"), 122, 176; internationalism, 19, 108; Latin American Union, 61; Leavenworth Federal Penitentiary, 75, 84; Mexican workers, 140; radicalism, 67, 81; Reed, John, 66; SI, 108; US, 54; WW I, 108. *See also individual socialists*
Socialist Party, 61, 67, 78
socio-spatial relations, 7, 9, 15, 18, 26, 81, 83. *See also* convergence space
Sorokin, Pitrim, 118
South America, 38

southern California. *See* California
"Southern Question, The" (Gramsci), 94
Soviet Embassy (Mexico), 18, 99, 101, 113–
16, 181. *See also* Gaikis, Leon; Kollontai,
Alexandra: as Soviet ambassador;
Pestkovsky, Stanislav
Soviet Project, the, 60, 61, 182
Soviet Union: CROM, 100; internationalism, 99; labor, 100, 222n17; Mexico, 61,
97–101, 106, 113–14, 115, 222n17;
National Railways of Mexico, 106;
Pestkovsky, Stanislav, 99–100, 222n14;
radicalism, 101; Reed, John, 65, 71;
religion, 104–5; US, 115–16; US and
Mexico, 103. *See also* Bolshevik Revolution (1917); Kollontai, Alexandra: as
Soviet ambassador
Spain: anarchism, 54, 80; artists, 150;
Bentham, Jeremy, 31; Bolívar, Simón, 38;
Bolshevik Revolution (1917), 54, 80, 113;
colonialism, 2–3, 37–38; fascism, 148,
235n17; Ferrer Guardia, Francisco, 60;
Guernica (Picasso), 155; Haiti, 38; Indigenous people, 37–38; Indigenous people
of the US, 40; Mexico, 14, 21–22, 30, 31,
38–39, 63, 102, 150, 172; Miranda, Francisco de, 38; Philippines, 2–3; radicalism, 148; ropes, 3–4; slavery, 38, 102;
strikes, 143–44
Spanish-American War of 1898, 2, 86
Spanish Civil War, 156, 163. *See also Guernica* (Picasso)
Spencer, Kenneth, 159
Spies, August, 5
SSCAC (South Side Community Arts
Center), 145, 146, 149, 156, 158–59
Stalin, Joseph, 100, 108, 182
Starr, Mark, 163
State Commission on Unemployment
(California), 139
Stillman, Charles, 21–26, 28–29
Stirner, Alfred (aka Edgar Woog), 115
strikes: agribusiness, 132, 134–36; agriculture, 54, 122–26, 133–36; Black domestic
workers, 143–44; Bread and Roses
strike, 176; California, 122–26, 133–36,
143–44; capitalism, 144, 211n30; children, 133; convergence space, 181; cotton,

123, 133, 134–35; CP, 124; farmworkers,
18, 122–26, 132, 133–36, 142; finance, 123;
Healey, Dorothy, 124; housing, 133;
imperialism, 211n30; "The Internationale" ("La Internacional"), 66, 122;
internationalism, 123, 181; IWW, 65–66,
176, 182; Japanese immigrants, 143;
Kollontai, Alexandra, 105–6, 119;
LAPD/Red Squad, 127; law enforcement, 129, 135; Leavenworth Federal
Penitentiary, 82, 83–84, 90; "Manifesto
to the Anarchists of the Entire World
and to the Workers in General" (Flores
Magón and Rivera), 74; McCormick
Harvesting Machine Company, 4–5;
Mexican Constitution (1917), 105–6,
133; Mexican Revolution, 16, 54, 125,
132–36; Mexico, 133, 143–44, 152; PLM,
16, 93; railroads, 105–6, 117, 119, 133, 152;
Reed, John, 65–66, 182; relief, 125, 135;
revolutions, 124–25, 133–34; Roy, M.N.,
211n30; sex workers, 103; shipbuilders,
33, 78; the Soviet Embassy, 115; Spain/
sugarcane, 143–44; TGP, 170; Unemployed Councils, 142; US, 134–35,
143–44; US and Mexico, 105–6, 133,
134; US–Mexico border, 16, 18, 123–24;
women, 103–4, 117, 122
struggles, 16–18, 126, 183. *See also* class
struggles; relief; resistance
sugarcane, 31, 49, 59, 143–44
Sumner, Charles, 42–43
Sun, Yat-sen, 55
Swiss Young Communist International, 115
Syngman Rhee, 55

Tablada, José Juan, 168
Table of Universal Brotherhood (Orozco),
168–69
Taibo, Paco Ignacio, II, 13–14, 201n52
Taino people, 37
Talladega College Savery Library, 169
Taylor, Paul, 134–35
Teague, Charles Collins, 130
Telegraph, Le (Haitian newspaper), 38
Tenayuca, Emma, 141
Ten Days That Shook the World (Reed),
64–65

Ten Tragic Days (La Decena Trágica), 65
territorialism: Bentham, Jeremy, 31–32; the
British Empire, 31; capitalism, 11, 25–26,
128; colonialism, 24, 26; geoeconomics,
26, 32; Germany, 34–35; imperialism,
26; Indigenous people, 4, 8, 15, 17, 22,
24, 25, 27, 31, 35, 44, 171, 194n11; liberal
internationalism, 30–35; Marx, Karl, 35;
Mexican Revolution, 12, 59; Mexico, 25,
44, 54–55, 76, 98; militarism, 22;
Napoléon III, Louis Bonaparte, 28;
New Imperialism, 11, 67; Stillman,
Charles, 22; US, 26, 31, 35, 39–40, 41,
76; US and Mexico, 22, 25, 27–28, 32,
41, 44–45, 54, 76, 88; US-Mexico War,
27–28, 45. See also land redistribution/
reform
TGP (Taller de Gráfica Popular), 149,
169–73, 175, 177
Third International (1919), 19, 109
Thompson, E. P., 181
Thompson, Louise, 159
Tibol, Raquel, 149
Tilman, Raymond, 155
Tongva people, 49
"To Pay for Petroleum" (Catlett), 173
trade, 21, 44, 47, 76
Tradition's Chains Have Bound Us (Hea-
ley), 177, 242n6
Treaty of Guadalupe Hidalgo (1848), 21,
22, 28
tres grandes, los (murals), 105, 151, 158, 169
Truth, Sojourner, 171
Turner, Frederick Jackson, 26
Turner, J. M. W., 34
TUUL (Trade Union Unity League), 141
Tyler, Roy, fig. 11, fig. 12, 86–88, 92

Unemployed Councils, 137–39, 140–43. See
also Los Angeles Unemployed Councils
UNIA (Universal Negro Improvement
Association), 80
unions: adult education, 161; artists, 160;
Black domestic workers, 141, 166, 168;
California, 141–42; Catlett, Elizabeth,
149; color line, 141; farmworkers, 141,
228n6; George Washington Carver
School, 164; Kollontai, Alexandra, 106,

120, 222n17; nationalization, 173; oil,
173; sex workers, 103; Siqueiros, David
Alfaro, 114; TGP, 170; White, Charles,
157–58. See also individual unions
Universal, El, 168
universities, 82–83, 96, 178–79
Upson-Walton Company, 1, fig. 1, 2
US (United States): African Americans,
62–64, 86; agriculture, 12, 122–23;
anarchism, 54; artists, 151–52; Asian
immigrants, 10, 49–52; Bolshevik Revolution (1917), 54; Bolshevism, 101; Britain, 31, 39, 40–42, 79; capitalism, 26, 60,
67, 75, 78–79, 115; Catlett, Elizabeth,
149; China, 12; colonialism, 50; color
line, 8–9; communism, 54, 147; Douglass, Frederick, 35; FBI, 149; finance, 28,
41–42, 78–79; Flores Magón, Ricardo, 7,
46, 73–75, 181; France, 39, 41; geoeconomics, 12–13, 25, 41–42, 78–79; geopolitics, 25, 41–42, 79; Haiti, 39, 41, 80,
156, 234n8; Haywood, Harry, 235n17;
Hearing on Bolshevik Propaganda, 118;
hegemony, 11–14, 16, 25–26, 74, 180, 181;
imperialism, 2–3, 5, 10, 45–46, 60, 67,
86, 115, 198n37, 234n8; India, 12; Indigenous people, 49, 147; internationalism,
14, 27–30, 45–46; IWW, 60; Jim Crow,
119; Kōchi and Miyasato, 49–52; Kollontai, Alexandra, 98–99, 101, 106, 107,
117–20, 221n8; labor, 41, 78, 100, 134–35,
137, 215n10, 222n17; Latin America, 12,
41, 45–46, 98–99, 147; Lenin, Vladimir,
56; "Leningrad" (Shostakovich), 165;
lynching, 119; Martínez, José, 91–92;
Mexican Revolution, 12, 16, 54, 60,
66–67, 198n35; militarism, 8, 11, 13, 22,
25, 27–28, 40, 41, 45–46, 78, 79; New
Imperialism, 12, 47; oil, 12; Philippines,
2–3, 4, 5, 12, 234n8; PLM, 16; Pottier,
Eugène, 176; racism, 9, 13, 41–42, 46, 50,
119, 149; radicalism, 17, 148, 149, 152;
Reed, John, 71; Regeneración, 215n8;
relief, 134–35; Rodríguez, Antonio, 6–7;
ropes, 1–5; Roy, M. N., 60; slavery, 9, 31,
35, 36, 41; socialism, 54; Soviet Union,
115–16; strikes, 134–35, 143–44; territories, 26, 31, 35, 39–40, 41, 76; Tyler, Roy,

US (United States) *(continued)*
92; WW I, 74–75, 77, 78–79. *See also* California; Civil War, the (US); Indigenous people of the United States; Leavenworth Federal Penitentiary
US (United States) and Mexico: Bagdad, Mexico, 21–25; Bentham, Jeremy, 31; Bolshevism, 100, 106; Calles, Plutarco Elías, 100; capitalism, 22, 128, 132–33, 134; Douglass, Frederick, 35; Du Bois, W. E. B., 9, 10, 179; farmworkers, 131–32; finance, 16, 25, 29, 40–42, 44–45, 46; Flores Magón, Ricardo, 46; geoeconomics, 23, 24–25; hegemony, 12; imperialism, 60, 156; imports/exports, 106, 132–33; Katayama, Sen, 115; Kollontai, Alexandra, 100–101, 115–16, 117, 119–20; labor, 88, 100, 133, 222n17; land redistribution/reform, 100, 106; Latin America, 103; "Mac – American" (Reed), 68–71, 214n63; Mexican Constitution (1917), 54, 100, 106, 119–20; "Mexican Kaleidoscope" (Flores Magón, E.), 81–82; nationalization, 100; New Imperialism, 70–71, 181; Pestkovsky, Stanislav, 100; "The Porfirian Dictatorship Demagogically Exalts the Native" (*La Dictadura Porfiriata Exalta Demagogicamenta al Indigena*) (Zalce), 172; racism, 7, 88; radicalism, 133, 148; railroads, 44, 105–6; Reed, John, 67–70, 214n63; Rodríguez, Antonio, 6–7; ropes, 3–4; slavery, 39; Soviet Union, 103; Stillman, Charles, 21–26; strikes, 105–6, 133, 134; territories, 22, 25, 27–28, 32, 41, 44–45, 54, 76, 88; trade route, 76; Veracruz port, 102–3
US–Mexico border, 7, 16, 18, 39, 51–52, 62, 123–24, 128–29
US-Mexico War, 9, 22, 26, 27–29, 45, 76, 102

Vasconcelos, José, 105, 151
Venezuela, 38, 115
Veracruz, 16, 28
Veracruz port, 97–101, 102
Villa, Pancho: Black soldiers, 86; Chihuahua, Mexico, 91; education, 104; John-

son, Jack, 62; land redistribution/reform, 15; Mexican Revolution, 15, 212n33; racism, 91; Reed, John, 65, 66, 68; Ten Tragic Days (La Decena Trágica), 65; TGP, 171; white vigilantes, 91
Visel, Charles P., 131

Wagenknecht, Alfred, 140
war economies, 50
War of Independence (Mexico), 30, 31, 38–39. *See also* Mexican Revolution; Spain: Mexico
War of Reform, 102
Waterbury Company, 2
wealth redistribution, 54, 79
Wells, Ida B., 6–7, 195n17
Western Federation of Miners, 182
West India Day, 36
Weston, Edward, 115
Weydemeyer, Joseph, 29–30
What Is To Be Done? (Chernyshevsky), 117, 120
Wheatley, Phillis, 171
White, Charles, 145–46, 148, 152, 157–58, 159–61, 235n17
White, Walter, 160
whiteness: African Americans, 57, 62, 63–64, 78, 81; *Black Reconstruction in America, 1860–1880* (Du Bois), 197n29; Black soldiers, 87; Border Patrol, 128; Browder, Earl, 81; capitalism, 7, 10–11, 57; class, 10; CP, 57, 142; Du Bois, W. E. B., 197n29; Espionage Act (1917), 78; Flores Magón, Ricardo, 96; Hansberry, Carl, 145; imperialism, 10–11; Johnson, Jack, 85; KKK (Ku Klux Klan), 9; labor, 57, 81; Mann Act (1912), 85; New Imperialism, 181; Perry, Pettis, 142; racism, 9, 57
white vigilantes: California, 129, 136; class, 9; farmworkers, 129–30, 132; KKK, 129, 228n10; LAPD, 129; law enforcement, 129; lynching, 1–2, 6–7, 9; relief, 125; Villa, Pancho, 91
Williams, Lorraine, 159
Wilson, Henry Lane, 65
Wilson, John, 160–61
Wilson, Woodrow, 78

Wobblies. *See* IWW (Industrial Workers of the World)

Wolfe, Bertram, 114, 115

women, 97–121; cotton, 24; CP, 109, 142; fascism, 156; henequen (rope) plantations, 4; Indigenous people, 68, 147; "The Internationale" ("La Internacional"), 176; labor, 116–17, 118–19, 163; lynching, 6; "Mac – American" (Reed), 68–69; Mann Act (1912), 85; Mexican Revolution, 66, 105, 122; militarism, 108–9; nationalization, 101, 118–20; "Outrageous in Mexico" (Royall), 27; property love, 110; racism, 156; radicalism, 163; revolutions, 163; SEP, 104; as soldiers, 105; strikes, 103–4, 117, 122; Unemployed Councils, 139–40; US-Mexico War, 27; WW II, 162. *See also* Black domestic workers; Black women; gender; *individuals*

Wood, Grant, 154

Woodruff, Hale, 160–61, 169

Woog, Edgar (aka Alfred Stirner), 115

workers. *See* labor

WPA (Works Progress Administration), 150–52, 158, 160

Wretched of the Earth, The (Fanon), 177

WW I (World War I): African Americans, 63; capitalism, 108; class struggles, 71, 108; conscientious objectors, 85; federal legislation, 74–75, 77, 78; internationalism, 48, 49; Kollontai, Alexandra, 107–9, 110, 112; labor, 108; Los Angeles Unemployed Councils, 138; Martínez, José, 91–92; militarism, 78; nationalism, 108, 109; peace movement, 78, 79; racism, 91–92; SI, 108; socialism, 108; US, 74–75, 77, 78–79

WW II (World War II), 13, 147, 161, 162, 164–65

Yaqui Indians, 3, 15, 51, 63, 172

Yoneda, Karl, 143

Young, Adele, 139–40

Yucatán, 3–4, 5, 6, 59, 60

Zadkine, Ossip, 173–74, 242n132

Zalce, Alfredo, *fig.* 19, 171–73

Zapata, Emiliano, 15, 53, 59, 65, 66, 104, 171, 212n33

Zetkin, Clara, 108–9

Zjenotdel, 109

Zong, 34

AMERICAN CROSSROADS

*Edited by Earl Lewis, George Lipsitz, George Sánchez, Dana
Takagi, Laura Briggs, and Nikhil Pal Singh*

1. *Border Matters: Remapping American Cultural Studies,* by
   José David Saldívar

2. *The White Scourge: Mexicans, Blacks, and Poor Whites in
   Texas Cotton Culture,* by Neil Foley

3. *Indians in the Making: Ethnic Relations and Indian
   Identities around Puget Sound,* by Alexandra Harmon

4. *Aztlán and Viet Nam: Chicano and Chicana Experiences of
   the War,* edited by George Mariscal

5. *Immigration and the Political Economy of Home: West
   Indian Brooklyn and American Indian Minneapolis,
   1945–1992,* by Rachel Buff

6. *Epic Encounters: Culture, Media, and U.S. Interests in the
   Middle East since 1945,* by Melani McAlister

7. *Contagious Divides: Epidemics and Race in San Francisco's
   Chinatown,* by Nayan Shah

8. *Japanese American Celebration and Conflict: A History of
   Ethnic Identity and Festival, 1934–1990,* by Lon Kurashige

9. *American Sensations: Class, Empire, and the Production of
   Popular Culture,* by Shelley Streeby

10. *Colored White: Transcending the Racial Past,* by David R.
    Roediger

11. *Reproducing Empire: Race, Sex, Science, and U.S.
    Imperialism in Puerto Rico,* by Laura Briggs

12. *meXicana Encounters: The Making of Social Identities on
    the Borderlands,* by Rosa Linda Fregoso

13. *Popular Culture in the Age of White Flight: Fear and
    Fantasy in Suburban Los Angeles,* by Eric Avila

14. *Ties That Bind: The Story of an Afro-Cherokee Family in
    Slavery and Freedom,* by Tiya Miles

15. *Cultural Moves: African Americans and the Politics of
    Representation,* by Herman S. Gray

16. *Emancipation Betrayed: The Hidden History of Black
    Organizing and White Violence in Florida from
    Reconstruction to the Bloody Election of 1920,* by Paul Ortiz

17. *Eugenic Nation: Faults and Frontiers of Better Breeding in Modern America,* by Alexandra Stern

18. *Audiotopia: Music, Race, and America,* by Josh Kun

19. *Black, Brown, Yellow, and Left: Radical Activism in Los Angeles,* by Laura Pulido

20. *Fit to Be Citizens? Public Health and Race in Los Angeles, 1879–1939,* by Natalia Molina

21. *Golden Gulag: Prisons, Surplus, Crisis, and Opposition in Globalizing California,* by Ruth Wilson Gilmore

22. *Proud to Be an Okie: Cultural Politics, Country Music, and Migration to Southern California,* by Peter La Chapelle

23. *Playing America's Game: Baseball, Latinos, and the Color Line,* by Adrian Burgos, Jr.

24. *The Power of the Zoot: Youth Culture and Resistance during World War II,* by Luis Alvarez

25. *Guantánamo: A Working-Class History between Empire and Revolution,* by Jana K. Lipman

26. *Between Arab and White: Race and Ethnicity in the Early Syrian-American Diaspora,* by Sarah M. A. Gualtieri

27. *Mean Streets: Chicago Youths and the Everyday Struggle for Empowerment in the Multiracial City, 1908–1969,* by Andrew J. Diamond

28. *In Sight of America: Photography and the Development of U.S. Immigration Policy,* by Anna Pegler-Gordon

29. *Migra! A History of the U.S. Border Patrol,* by Kelly Lytle Hernández

30. *Racial Propositions: Ballot Initiatives and the Making of Postwar California,* by Daniel Martinez HoSang

31. *Stranger Intimacy: Contesting Race, Sexuality, and the Law in the North American West,* by Nayan Shah

32. *The Nicest Kids in Town:* American Bandstand, *Rock 'n' Roll, and the Struggle for Civil Rights in 1950s Philadelphia,* by Matthew F. Delmont

33. *Jack Johnson, Rebel Sojourner: Boxing in the Shadow of the Global Color Line,* by Theresa Rundstedler

34. *Pacific Connections: The Making of the US-Canadian Borderlands,* by Kornel Chang

35. *States of Delinquency: Race and Science in the Making of California's Juvenile Justice System,* by Miroslava Chávez-García

36. *Spaces of Conflict, Sounds of Solidarity: Music, Race, and Spatial Entitlement in Los Angeles,* by Gaye Theresa Johnson

37. *Covert Capital: Landscapes of Denial and the Making of U.S. Empire in the Suburbs of Northern Virginia,* by Andrew Friedman

38. *How Race Is Made in America: Immigration, Citizenship, and the Historical Power of Racial Scripts,* by Natalia Molina

39. *We Sell Drugs: The Alchemy of US Empire,* by Suzanna Reiss

40. *Abrazando el Espíritu: Bracero Families Confront the US-Mexico Border,* by Ana Elizabeth Rosas

41. *Houston Bound: Culture and Color in a Jim Crow City,* by Tyina L. Steptoe

42. *Why Busing Failed: Race, Media, and the National Resistance to School Desegregation,* by Matthew F. Delmont

43. *Incarcerating the Crisis: Freedom Struggles and the Rise of the Neoliberal State,* by Jordan T. Camp

44. *Lavender and Red: Liberation and Solidarity in the Gay and Lesbian Left,* by Emily K. Hobson

45. *Flavors of Empire: Food and the Making of Thai America,* by Mark Padoongpatt

46. *The Life of Paper: Letters and a Poetics of Living Beyond Captivity,* by Sharon Luk

47. *Strategies of Segregation: Race, Residence, and the Struggle for Educational Equality,* by David G. García

48. *Soldiering through Empire: Race and the Making of the Decolonizing Pacific,* by Simeon Man

49. *An American Language: The History of Spanish in the United States,* by Rosina Lozano

50. *The Color Line and the Assembly Line: Managing Race in the Ford Empire,* by Elizabeth D. Esch

51. *Confessions of a Radical Chicano Doo-Wop Singer,* by Rubén Funkahuatl Guevara

52. *Empire's Tracks: Indigenous Peoples, Racial Aliens, and the Transcontinental Railroad*, by Manu Karuka

53. *Collisions at the Crossroads: How Place and Mobility Make Race*, by Genevieve Carpio

54. *Charros: How Mexican Cowboys are Remapping Race and American Identity*, by Laura R. Barraclough

55. *Louder and Faster: Pain, Joy, and the Body Politic in Asian American Taiko*, by Deborah Wong

56. *Badges without Borders: How Global Counterinsurgency Transformed American Policing*, by Stuart Schrader

57. *Colonial Migrants at the Heart of Empire: Puerto Rican Workers on U.S. Farms*, by Ismael García Colón

58. *Assimilation: An Alternative History*, by Catherine S. Ramírez

59. *Boyle Heights: How a Los Angeles Neighborhood Became the Future of American Democracy*, by George J. Sánchez

60. *Not Yo' Butterfly: My Long Song of Relocation, Race, Love, and Revolution*, by Nobuko Miyamoto

61. *The Deportation Express: A History of America through Mass Removal*, by Ethan Blue

62. *An Archive of Skin, An Archive of Kin: Disability and Life-Making during Medical Incarceration*, by Adria L. Imada

63. *Menace to Empire: Anticolonial Solidarities and the Transpacific Origins of the US Security State*, by Moon-Ho Jung

64. *Suburban Empire: Cold War Militarization in the US Pacific*, by Lauren Hirshberg

65. *Archipelago of Resettlement: Vietnamese Refugee Settlers across Guam and Israel-Palestine*, by Evyn Lê Espiritu Gandhi

66. *Arise! Global Radicalism in the Era of the Mexican Revolution*, by Christina Heatherton

Founded in 1893,
UNIVERSITY OF CALIFORNIA PRESS
publishes bold, progressive books and journals
on topics in the arts, humanities, social sciences,
and natural sciences—with a focus on social
justice issues—that inspire thought and action
among readers worldwide.

The UC PRESS FOUNDATION
raises funds to uphold the press's vital role
as an independent, nonprofit publisher, and
receives philanthropic support from a wide
range of individuals and institutions—and from
committed readers like you. To learn more, visit
ucpress.edu/supportus.

Printed in the USA
CPSIA information can be obtained
at www.ICGtesting.com
JSHW021450010424
60352JS00012B/65/J